John Hookham Frere, Henry Bartle Edward Frere, William Frere

Works

In Prose and Verse. Vol. III

John Hookham Frere, Henry Bartle Edward Frere, William Frere

Works
In Prose and Verse. Vol. III

ISBN/EAN: 9783744688338

Printed in Europe, USA, Canada, Australia, Japan

Cover: Foto ©Thomas Meinert / pixelio.de

More available books at **www.hansebooks.com**

THE WORKS OF THE RIGHT HON.

JOHN HOOKHAM FRERE

VOLUME III.

THE WORKS

OF THE RIGHT HONOURABLE

JOHN HOOKHAM FRERE

IN VERSE AND PROSE

VOLUME III

TRANSLATIONS FROM ARISTOPHANES

AND THEOGNIS

EDITED BY W. E. FRERE

Second Edition with Additions

LONDON

BASIL MONTAGU PICKERING

196 PICCADILLY

1874

CONTENTS.

: ACHARNIANS.

THE ACHARNIANS.

ICÆOPOLIS, whose name may be interpreted as conveying the idea of honest policy, is the principal character in the play. He is represented as a humorous shrewd countryman (a sort of Athenian Sancho), who (in consequence of the war, and the invasion of Attica by the Peloponnesian Army) had been driven from his house and property to take shelter in the City. Here his whole thoughts are occupied with regret for the comforts he has lost, and with wishes for a speedy peace. The soliloquy in which he appears in the first scene, represents him seated alone in the place of assembly, having risen early to secure a good place, his constant practice (he says), in order "to bawl, to abuse and interrupt the speakers," with the exception of those and those only, who are arguing in favour of an immediate peace. But the Magistrates and men of business, not having so much leisure on their hands, as the worthy countryman, are less punctual in their attendance, and he is kept waiting to his great discomfort; their seats are empty, and the Citizens in the market-place are talking and idling, or shifting about to avoid a most notable instrument of democratic coercion, namely a cord coloured with ochre, which the officers stretch across the market-place, in order to drive the loiterers to the place of assembly; those that are overtaken by the rope, being marked by the ochre, besides the damage to their dress, becoming liable to a nominal fine. To avoid the sense of weariness, he is in the habit (as he tells us), upon

such occasions, of giving a forced direction to his thoughts; and he gives a sample of his mode of employing this expedient, in the very first lines: he is tasking himself to recollect and sum up all the things that had occurred of late either to gratify or to annoy him. At length, however, he is relieved from the pursuit of this unsatisfactory pastime. The Magistrates arrive and take their seats—the place of Assembly is filled, and silence is proclaimed—when a new personage enters hastily. Here we have an instance of the peculiar character of invention which belongs to the ancient comedy; in which a bodily form and action is given to those images, which have no existence except in the forms of animated or fanciful language. "If a deity were to come down among the Athenians and propose to conclude a peace for them, they would not listen to him"—This phrase is here exhibited in action; for the personage above mentioned is a demigod (descended immediately from Ceres herself, as he proves by a very rapid and confident recitation of his genealogy), but his offer of his services as a mediator are very ill received, and he very narrowly escapes being taken into custody.

The next persons who present themselves to the Assembly are two Envoys returned from a mission to the Court of Persia, which they have contrived to prolong for several years. They relate all the hardships which they had undergone in luxurious entertainments and in tedious journeys with a splendid equipage: they moreover had been detained by an unforeseen circumstance, on their arrival at the Capital. The state of things was such as Autolycus describes: "The King is not at the Palace, he is gone to purge melancholy and air himself;" but the King of Persia was not gone, like the King of Bohemia, "on board a new ship;" he was gone with a magnificent military retinue to the Golden Mountains, where, according to the Ambassador's report, he continued for eight months in an unremitting course of cathartics. On his return to the Capital, they had the honour of being presented and entertained at a most singular and marvellous banquet; finally they had succeeded in their mission, and had brought with them a confidential servant of the Crown of Persia (a nobleman of high rank though rather of a suspicious name),

Shamartabas, commissioned to declare His Majesty's intention to the people of Athens. Shamartabas holds the distinguished office and title of the King's Eye: of course the mask which is assigned him is distinguished by an Eye of enormous size, the appearance of which and the gravity of gesture suited to such an exalted personage excite the rustic republican spleen of honest Dicæopolis. The communications of the great Persian Courtier, being in his own language and consequently unintelligible, are variously interpreted. Dicæopolis takes upon himself to question him peremptorily, and in the course of the examination discovers a couple of effeminate Athenian fops, disguised as Eunuchs, in his train; this discovery however creates no sensation.—The King's Eye is invited with the usual honours to a Banquet in the Prytaneum; but when Dicæopolis sees these impostors and enemies of his country, upon the point of being rewarded with a good dinner, the indignation which is excited in his independent spirit, decides at once his future destinies and the conduct of all the scenes which follow.—In that tone which a person is apt to employ when he fancies that the zeal of his friends gives him a right to command their services, he calls out very peremptorily for Amphitheus, and without any preamble or prefatory request, directs him to proceed to Sparta without loss of time, and to conclude a separate peace for him (Dicæopolis), his wife and family, advancing to him at the same time the principal sum of eight drachmas for that purpose.

Another Envoy now appears, returned from a Court of a different description. He has not, like the former, any complaints to make, of having been overwhelmed with an excess of ostentation and profusion from the Grand Monarque of those times; he has resided with a sort of cotemporary Czar Peter, the Autocrat of Thrace, having lived (of course according to his own account) in a most jolly barbarous intimacy with that rising potentate, and inspiring him with the sincerest hearty zeal in favour of the polished state of Athens. His son, the heir apparent, had been admitted by the Athenians to the freedom of their City, an honour which in their opinion (as well as in that of Mr. Peter Putty in Foote's farce) any prince ought to be proud of: and the assembly are accordingly informed of the delight and enthusiasm with which the compliment had been accepted. They are presented moreover with a specimen of the auxiliary troops, somewhat singularly equipt, which their new ally is willing to employ in their service, but at a rate of pay which Dicæopolis exclaims against as scandalous. He has soon other causes of complaint; for, attracted by the passion for garlic, which it seems is predominant amongst them, the Odomantians (for that is the name of the tribe to which the new warriors belong) begin their operations by plundering the store which Dicæopolis had provided for his own luncheon; outrageous at this injury, after reproaching the Magistrates with their apathy in suffering it, he takes, what it seems was an effectual mode of dissolving the Assembly, by declaring that a storm was coming on, and affirming that he has felt a drop of rain. This sort of Polish Veto nullifies the proceedings of the Assembly, which is accordingly dissolved.—Dicæopolis is left lamenting over the pillage of his provisions, but his spirits are soon revived by the appearance of Amphitheus, who has returned with samples of Treaties of Peace or Truces. These Treaties or Truces are typified by the wines employed in the libations by which they were ratified; a conceit, which in the language of the original appears less extravagant, the Greeks having only one and the same word by which they expressed the idea of a truce, and that of the libation by which it was rendered valid. Amphitheus is in a hurry, having been (as he says) discovered and pursued by a number of old Rustics of Acharnæ, who since the ruin of the vineyards of their village by the invading army, had become furious against a peace. Dicæopolis tastes and discusses the qualities of the wines, and having fixed upon a sample of thirty years' growth, goes away with a determination to avail himself of the change in his affairs, by keeping the Feast of Bacchus once more in his own village; while Amphitheus runs off to avoid the Acharnians whom he had outrun, but who are still in quest of him.

THE ACHARNIANS.

SCENE. THE PNYX.

Dicæopolis.

OW many things there are to cross and vex me,
My comforts I compute at four precisely,
My griefs and miseries at a hundred thousand.
Let's see what there has happen'd to rejoice me
With any real kind of joyfulness;
Come, in the first place I set down five talents,
Which Cleon vomited up again and refunded;
There I rejoiced; I loved the knights for that;
'Twas nobly done, for the interests of all Greece.
But again I suffer'd cruelly in the theatre
A tragical disappointment.—There was I
Gaping to hear old Æschylus, when the herald
Call'd out, "Theognis,* bring your chorus forward."
Imagine what my feelings must have been!
But then Dexitheus pleased me coming forward
And singing his Bœotian melody:
But next came Chæris with his music truly,
That turn'd me sick, and kill'd me very nearly.
But never in my lifetime, man nor boy,
Was I so vext as at this present moment;
To see the Pnyx, at this time of the morning,
Quite empty, when the Assembly should be full.
There are our Citizens in the market-place
Lounging and talking, shifting up and down

* A bad tragic poet, ridiculed in this play.

To escape the painted twine that ought to sweep
The shoal of them this way; not even the presidents
Arrived—they're always last, crowding and jostling
To get the foremost seat; but as for peace
They never think about it—Oh poor country!
As for myself, I'm always the first man.
Alone in the morning, here I take my place,
Here I contemplate, here I stretch my legs;
I think and think—I don't know what to think.
I draw conclusions and comparisons,
I ponder, I reflect, I pick my nose,
I make a stink—I make a metaphor,
I fidget about, and yawn and scratch myself;
Looking in vain to the prospect of the fields,
Loathing the city, longing for a peace,
To return to my poor village and my farm,
That never used to cry "Come, buy my charcoal!"
Nor "Buy my oil!" nor "Buy my any thing!"
But gave me what I wanted, freely and fairly,
Clear of all cost, with never a word of buying,
Or such buy-words. So here I'm come, resolved
To bawl, to abuse, to interrupt the speakers,
Whenever I hear a word of any kind
Except for an immediate peace. Ah there!
The presidents at last; see, there they come!
All scrambling for their seats—I told you so!
Herald. Move forward there! Move forward all of ye!
Further! within the consecrated ground.
Amphitheus. Has any body spoke?
Her. Is any body
Prepared to speak?
Amp. Yes, I.
Her. Who are you and what?
Amp. Amphitheus the demigod.
Her. Not a man?
Amp. No I'm immortal; for the first Amphitheus
Was born of Ceres and Triptolemus,
His only son was Keleüs, Keleüs married
Phænarete my grandmother, Lykinus
My father, was their son; that's proof enough
Of the immortality in our family.
The Gods moreover have dispatch'd me here

Commission'd specially to arrange a peace
Betwixt this city and Sparta—notwithstanding
I find myself rather in want at present
Of a little ready money for my journey.
The magistrates won't assist me.

Her. Constables!

Amp. O Keleüs and Triptolemus, don't forsake me!

Dic. You presidents, I say! you exceed your powers;
You insult the assembly, dragging off a man
That offer'd to make terms and give us peace.

Her. Keep silence there.

Dic. By Jove, but I won't be silent,
Except I hear a motion about peace.

Her. Ho there! the Ambassadors from the King of Persia.

Dic. What King of Persia? what Ambassadors?
I 'm sick of foreigners and foreign animals,
Peacocks * and Coxcombs and Ambassadors.

Her. Keep silence there.

Dic. What's here? What dress is that?
In the name of Ecbatana? † What does it mean?

Amb. You sent us when Euthymenes was Archon,
Some few years back, ambassadors to Persia,
With an appointment of two drachmas each
For daily maintenance.

Dic. Alas, poor drachmas!

Amb. 'Twas no such easy service, I can tell you,
No trifling inconvenience to be dragg'd
Along those dusty dull Caystrian plains,
Smother'd with cushions in the travelling chariots,
Obliged to lodge at night in our pavilions,
Jaded and hack'd to death.

Dic. My service then
Was an easy one, you think! on guard all night,
In the open air, at the outposts, on a mat.

Amb. . . . At our reception we were forced to drink
Strong luscious wine in cups of gold and crystal . . .

Dic. O rock of Athens! sure thy very stones
Should mutiny at such open mockery!

Amb. (*in continuation*)
. . . with the Barbarians 'tis the test of manhood.
There the great drinkers are the greatest men . . .,

Dic. As debauchees and coxcombs are with us.

* Peacocks had been introduced at the public charge, and were exhibited monthly. It is to be supposed that the exhibition had become rather stale.

† The name of an unknown and extraordinary place is sometimes used to express wonder. In New England a thing is said to be "Jerusalem fine." Flanders in the time of Philip III. served the Spaniards for a phrase of wonder "No hay mas Flandes."

Amb. (*in continuation*)
. . . In the fourth year we reach'd the royal residence,
But found the sovereign absent on a progress,
Gone with his army to the Golden Mountains,
To take his ease, and purge his royal person;
There he remain'd eight months.
Dic. When did he close
His course of medicine?
Amb. With the full of the moon
He rose, and left his seat, returning homeward:
There he admitted us to an audience,
And entertain'd us at a royal banquet
With a service of whole oxen baked in crust.
Dic. Oxen in crust! what lies, what trumpery!
Did ever any mortal hear the like?
Amb. Besides they treated us with a curious bird,
Much bigger than our own Cleonymus.
'Tis call'd the Chousibus.
Dic. Ay, by that same token
We're choused of our two drachmas.
Amb. Finally
We've brought you here a nobleman, Shamartabas
By name, by rank and office the King's Eye.
Dic. God send a crow to peck it out, I say,
And yours the Ambassador's into the bargain!
Her. Let the King's Eye come forward.
Dic. Hercules!
What's here? an eye for the head of a ship![1] what point,

[1] The imaginative spirit of antiquity had transformed the head of a ship into the likeness of a human face; the keel served for a nose, a painted eye being inserted on each side, and a portion of the convex projections of the bow was coloured red, to represent a pair of cheeks, whence the epithet "red cheeked" is applied to ships in Homer.—The face thus produced was appropriated to Medusa by the addition of two snakes *diverging from it*, and running along the gunwale (according to Hipponax's description "as if they were going to bite the head of the steersman)." The whole vessel was thus converted into the form of a protecting amulet.—It appears by what Herodotus (iii. 58) says of the oracle addressed to the Siphnians, that the "red cheeks" must have gone out of fashion in his time; but the "eye" is still universal in the Mediterranean, and the writer of this note has seen the snake in its proper position and direction on the gunwale of small craft in the harbour of Valletta and in the Bay of Cadiz.

What headland is he weathering? what's your course?
What makes you steer so steadily and so slowly?

Amb. Come now, Shamartabas, stand forth; declare
The king's intentions to the Athenian people.

[*Shamartabas here utters some words, which Orientalists have supposed to be the common formula prefixed to the edicts of the Persian Monarch*—Iartaman exarksas apissonai satra.

Amb. You understand it?

Dic. No, by Jove, not I.

Amb. [*to Dicæopolis.*] He says the king intends to send us gold.
[*to Shamartabas.*] Explain about the gold; speak more distinctly.

Shamartabas. Sen gooly Jaönau aphooly chest.

Dic. Well, that's distinct enough!

Her. What does he say?

Dic. That it's a foolish jest for the Ionians
To imagine that the king would send them gold.

Amb. No, no!—He's telling ye of chests full of gold.

Dic. What chests? you're an impostor.—Stand away,
Keep off; and let me alone to question him. [*to Shamartabas.*
You, sir, you Persian! answer me distinctly
And plainly, in presence of this fist of mine;
On pain of a royal purple bloody nose.
Will the king send us gold, or will he not?
[*Shamartabas shakes his head.*
Have our ambassadors bamboozled us? [*Shamartabas nods.*
These fellows nod to us in the Grecian fashion;
They're some of our own people, I'll be bound.
One of those eunuchs there I'm sure I know:
I'm positive it's Cleisthenes the Siburtian.
How durst you, you baboon, with such a beard,
And your designing wicked rump close shaved,
To pass yourself upon us for a eunuch?
And who's this other? Sure enough it's Strato!

Her. Silence there! Keep your seats!
The senate have invited the King's Eye
To feast with them in the Prytaneum.

Dic. There—
Ain't it enough to drive one mad? to drive one
To hang himself? to be kept here in attendance,

Working myself into a strangury;
Whilst every door flies open to these fellows.
But I'll do something desperate and decided.
Where is Amphitheus got to?
Amp. Here am I.
Dic. There—take you these eight drachmas on my part,
And make a separate peace for me with Sparta,
For me, my wife and children and maidservant.
And you—go on with your embassies and fooleries.
Her. Theorus, our ambassador into Thrace,
Return'd from King Sitalces!*
Theor. Here am I.
Dic. More coxcombs call'd for!—Here's another coming.
Theor. We should not have remain'd so long in Thrace...
Dic. If you hadn't been overpaid I know you wouldn't.
Theor....But for the snow, which cover'd all the country,
And buried up the roads, and froze the rivers.
'Twas singular this change of weather happen'd
Just when Theognis here, our frosty poet,
Brought out his tragedy.—We past our time
In drinking with Sitalces. He's your friend,
Your friend and lover, if there ever was one,
And writes the name of Athens on his walls.†
His son, your new-made fellow citizen,
Had wish'd to have been enroll'd in proper form
At the Apaturian festival; and meanwhile,
During his absence, earnestly desires
That the Apaturian sausages may be sent him.
He is urgent with his father to befriend
His newly adopted countrymen; and in fine
Sitalces has been so far work'd upon,
He has sworn at last his solemn Thracian oath,
Standing before the sacrifice, to send
Such an army, he said, that all the Athenian people
Shall think that there's a flight of locusts coming.
Dic. Then hang me if I believe a word about it,
Except their being locusts; that seems likely.
Theor. And now he has sent some warriors from a tribe
The fiercest in all Thrace.
Dic. Well, come—that's fair.
Her. The Thracians that came hither with Theorus!
Let them come forward!

* Theorus noted in the Wasps as a flattering, super-civil parasitical person. See his efforts at reconciliation in the next page.

† The common practice of lovers both in ancient and modern times; but in this instance there is probably an allusion to some public monuments which recorded the king's alliance with the Athenians in terms flattering to their national vanity.

Dic. What the plague are these?
Theor. The Odomantian army.
Dic. The Odomantians?
Thracians? and what has brought them here from Thrace
So strangely equipt, disguised, and circumcised?
Theor. These are a race of fellows, if you'd hire 'em,
Only at a couple of drachmas daily pay;
With their light javelins, and their little bucklers,
They'd worry and skirmish over all Bœotia.
Dic. Two drachmas for those scarecrows! and our seamen,
What would they say to it?—left in arrears,
Poor fellows, that are our support and safeguard.
Out, out upon it! I'm a plunder'd man.
I'm robb'd and ruin'd here with the Odomantians.
They're seizing upon my garlic.
Theor. [*to the Thracians.*] Oh, for shame,
Let the man's garlic alone. You shabby fellow,
You countryman, take care what you're about;
Don't venture near them when they're primed with garlic.
Dic. You Magistrates, have you the face to see it,
With your own eyes—your fellow citizen
Here, in the city itself, robb'd by barbarians?
—But I forbid the assembly. There's a change
In the heaven! I felt a drop of rain! I'm witness!
Her. The Thracians must withdraw, to attend again
The first of the next month. The assembly is closed.
Dic. Lord help me, what a luncheon have I lost!
But there's Amphitheus coming back from Sparta.
Welcome Amphitheus!
Amph. I'm not welcome yet,
There are the Acharnians pursuing me!
Dic. How so?
Amph. I was coming here to bring the Treaties,
But a parcel of old Acharnians smelt me out,
Case-harden'd, old, inveterate, hardhanded
Veterans of Marathon, hearts of oak and iron,
Slingers and smiters. They bawl'd out and bellow'd;
"You dog, you villain! now the vines are ruin'd,
"You're come with Treaties, are you?" Then they stopt,
Huddling up handfuls of great slinging stones
In the lappets of their cloaks, and I ran off,
And they came driving after me pell mell,

Roaring and shouting.—
Dic. Ay, why let them roar!
You've brought the Treaties?
Amph. Ay, three samples of 'em;
This here is a five years' growth, taste it and try.
Dic. Don't like it!
Amph. Eh?
Dic. Don't like it; it won't do;
There's an uncommon ugly twang of pitch,
A touch of naval armament about it.
Amph. Well, here's a ten years' growth, may suit you better.
Dic. No, neither of them. There's a sort of sourness
Here in this last, a taste of acid embassies,
And vapid allies turning to vinegar.
Amph. But here's a truce of thirty years entire
Warranted sound.
Dic. O Bacchus and the Bacchanals!
This is your sort! here's nectar and ambrosia!
Here's nothing about providing three days' rations,
It says, "Do what you please, Go where you will."
I choose it, and adopt it, and embrace it,
For sacrifice and for my private drinking.
In spite of all the Acharnians, I'm determined
To remove out of the reach of wars and mischief,
And keep the feast of Bacchus in my farm.
Amph. And I'll run off to escape from those Acharnians.

Masses of men, when in a state of excitement, whatever may be their collective character or purpose, are apt to separate into two divisions; those of a milder and more reasonable temper taking the one side, and the more ardent and intractable taking the other. This is exemplified in the two Semichoruses. The first are upon the point of abandoning their pursuit, while the second persevere in it with unabated eagerness, indefatigable and (as they afterwards show themselves) implacable. The first, on the contrary, are by degrees pacified and induced to listen to reason.

This difference of feeling finally produces a struggle between them, in which those who are of "milder mood" obtain the advantage; and their opponents are obliged to call for assistance from Lamachus, a romantic enthusiastic military character, and, of course, as decided an advocate for war as Dicæopolis (the Poet's dramatic representative) is for peace. Lamachus appears in his gorgeous armour. Dicæopolis, under the affectation of extreme terror and simplicity, contrives to banter and provoke him. Lamachus proceeds to violence, and is foiled; after which a dispute is carried on for some time between them upon equal terms; and they finally separate with a declaration of their respective determinations; the one looking forward to military achievement, and the other to commercial profit and enjoyment.

It may be necessary to say something of an attempt that has been made in the translation of the following Chorus, to convey to the English reader some notion of the metrical character of the original. The Poet himself has described the metre as bold and manly, expressive of firmness and vehemence, and, as such, suitable to the persons of whom his Chorus is composed. The Cretic metre (for that is its name) consists of a quaver between two crotchets (— ⏑ —), and may be considered as a truncated form of the Trochaic, differing from it only by the subtraction of a short or quaver-syllable; the Trochaic itself consisting of four syllables, a crotchet and quaver alternately (— ⏑ — ⏑). In consequence of this affinity, we find that the two metres frequently pass into each other.

In the instance before us, the Chorus begins with the Trochaic, but after the first four lines passes into the Cretic; the second Cretic line exhibits a variety of frequent occurrence in the Greek, the last crotchet being resolved into two quavers (— ⏑ ⏑ ⏑). Moreover the altercation between Dicæopolis and the Chorus is kept up for some time in Trochaics and Cretics alternately.

CHORUS.

Follow faster! all together! search, inquire of every one.
Speak, inform us, have you seen him? whither is the rascal run?
'Tis a point of public service that the traitor should be caught
In the fact, seized and arrested with the treaties that he brought.

SEMICHORUS I.

He's escaped, he's escaped—
Out upon it! Out upon it!—
Out of sight, out of search.

O the sad wearisome
Load of years!
Well do I remember such a burden as I bore
Running with Phayllus * with a hamper at my back,
Out alack,
Years ago.
But, alas, my sixty winters and my sad rheumatic pain
Break my speed and spoil my running,—and that old unlucky sprain.
He's escaped—

* An eminent conqueror in the foot-race at Olympia. There was probably some story of his having been matched (under certain disadvantages) against an active man who had been used to run under a burthen.

SEMICHORUS II.

But we'll pursue him. Whether we be fast or slow,
He shall learn to dread the peril of an old Acharnian foe.
O supreme Powers above,
Merciful Father Jove,
Oh the vile miscreant wretch;
How did he dare,
How did he presume in his unutterable villany to make a peace,
Peace with the detestable abominable Spartan race.
No, the war must not end—
Never end—till the whole Spartan tribe
Are reduced, trampled down,
Tied and bound, hand and foot.

Chorus. Now we must renew the search, pursuing at a steady pace.
Soon or late we shall secure him, hunted down from place to place.
Look about like eager marksmen, ready with your slings and stones.
How I long to fall upon him, the villain, and to smash his bones!

Enter DICÆOPOLIS, HIS WIFE AND DAUGHTER, A SLAVE, &c.

Dic. Peace, peace.
Silence, silence.

Chorus. Stand aside! Keep out of sight! List to the sacrificial cries!
There he comes, the very fellow, going out to sacrifice.
Wait and watch him for a minute, we shall have him by surprise.

Dic. Silence! move forward, the Canephora;
You Xanthias, follow close behind her there,
In a proper manner, with your pole and emblem.
Wife. Set down the basket, daughter, and begin
The ceremony.
Daughter. Give me the cruet, mother,
And let me pour it upon the holy cake.
Dic. Oh blessed Bacchus, what a joy it is
To go thus unmolested, undisturb'd,
My wife, my children, and my family,
With our accustom'd, joyful ceremony,
To celebrate thy festival in my farm.
—Well, here's success to the truce of thirty years.
Wife. Mind your behaviour, child; carry the basket
In a modest proper manner; look demure
And grave; a happy fellow will he be
That has the rummaging of ye.—Come, move on.
Mind your gold trinkets, they'll be stolen else.
Dic. Follow behind there, Xanthias, with the pole,
And I'll strike up the bacchanalian chaunt.
—Wife, you must be spectator; go within,
And mount to the housetop to behold us pass.
Dic. (*Sings*)
Leader of the revel rout,
Of the drunken roar and shout,
Crazy mirth and saucy jesting,
Frolic and intrigue clandestine!
Half a dozen years are past,*
Here we meet in peace at last.
All my wars and fights are o'er:
Other battles please me more,
With my neighbour's maid, the Thracian,
Found marauding in the wood;
Seizing on the fair occasion,
With a quick retaliation
Making an immediate booty
Of her innocence and beauty.—
If a drunken head should ache,
Bones and heads we never break.
If we quarrel over night;
At a full carousing soak,
In the morning all is right;

* This comedy was produced in 425 B. C., the sixth year of the Peloponnesian war.

And the shield hung out of sight
In the chimney smoke.

Chorus. That's the man. Mind your aim;
Pelt away—Pelt away.

Dic. Heaven and Earth! what's here to do? You'll break the pitcher, have a care!

Chor. We'll break your head,
We'll break your bones,
We'll pummel you to death with stones.

Dic. Tell me, most serene Acharnians, wherefore, upon what pretence?

Chor. Impudence! Insolence!
Infamous traitor, do ye dare to ask?
In despite
Of duty and right,—
Duty to the state,
Duty to the laws,—
You've presumed to separate
Your private cause,
With the villanous abuse
Of a treasonable truce.
And you dare,
Standing there,
Void of shame, void of grace,
To look us in the face.

Dic. But my motive—Once again, let me be heard, and I'll explain.

Chor. No reply. You shall die,
Stoned and buried all at once,
Buried in a heap of stones.

Dic. Have patience, do! forbear a bit!
You've never heard my reasons yet.

Chor. We've forborne, long enough;
Say no more. Trash and stuff!
We detest you worse than Cleon, him that, if he gets his dues,
We shall cut up into thongs to serve the knights for straps and shoes.
We'll not hear ye: your alliance with the worst of enemies,
With the wicked hated Spartans, we'll avenge it and chastise.

Dic. Don't be talking of the Spartans; 'tis another question wholly,
All my guilt or innocence depends upon the treaty solely.

Chor. Don't imagine to cajole us with your arguments and fetches;
You confess you made a peace with those abominable wretches.

Dic. Well, the very Spartans, even,—I've my doubts and scruples whether
They've been totally to blame, in every instance, altogether.

Chor. Not to blame in every instance! Villain, vagabond, how dare ye,
Talking treason to our faces, to suppose that we should spare ye.

Dic. Not so totally to blame; and I would shew that, here and there,
The treatment they received from us has not been absolutely [fair.

Chor. What a scandal! what an insult! what an outrage on the state!
Are ye come to plead before us as the Spartans' advocate?

Dic. I'm prepared to plead the cause, and bring my neck here for a pledge,
Placed upon the chopping block, ready to meet the axe's edge.

Chor. Don't be standing shilly shally, comrades, let the traitor die.
Pummel him with stones to pieces, pound and maul him utterly,
Mash the villain to a jelly, like a vat of purple dye.

Dic. I'm astonish'd at your temper. Won't you give me leave to say
Something in my own defence, my good Acharnians? Hear me, pray!

Chor. We're determined not to hear ye.

Dic. That will be severe indeed.

Chor. We're determined.

Dic. Good Acharnians, give me time and hear me plead.

Chor. Death awaits you, death this instant.

Dic. Then the quick resolve is taken.
Know that I've secured a hostage destined to redeem my bacon.*
He, your homebred kindly kinsman, he with me shall live or perish.

Chor. What's the matter? Is there any child or infant that you cherish,

* The extravagant burlesque which follows turns upon the occupation of the Acharnians as charcoal-burners.

Missing here amongst you, neighbours, whom he keeps confined in durance?
What can else inspire the man with such a confident assurance?
Dic. Strike, destroy me then, while I shall act in turn the assassin's part,
If the native love of charcoal moves not your obdurate heart.
[*Dicæopolis discovers a hamper of charcoal, and stands over it in a menacing theatrical attitude, with a sword drawn.*]
Chor. O forbear! see there!
See the poor natural Acharnian hamper of our own,
Ready to be overthrown.
Spare it, I beseech thee, spare.*
Dic. I'll not hear; the word is past. Poor thing, this instant is its last.
Chor. Spare it as our only joy,
Our solace and employ,
The staff of our declining years.
Dic. You, when I besought a hearing, arm'd your hands and shut your ears.
Chor. Yes, but now we'll permit,
We'll dispense, we'll allow
Your defence.
Our beloved
Darling is at stake.
We submit
Wholly for his sake.
Dic. Before we parley or compound, cast me those pebbles to the ground.
Chor. See there, all's fair.
But keep your word, sheathe the sword.
Dic. Other pebbles may be lurking in the lappets of your jerkin.
Chor. Never fear, never doubt;
See them here shaken out.
There's none behind: only mind,
Keep your word, sheathe the sword.
And here I fling stone and sling,
Sling and stone, both away,
Both in one; both are gone.
Dic. Well now, will you please to have done with your noise and nonsense,

* A burlesque of some scene in a contemporary tragedy in which the actors were "brought to a dead lock."—It should seem as if, in the original here parodied, the assailants had been kept at bay by the counter-menace of destroying some royal infant in a cradle, which suggested the substitute of a hamper of charcoal. In one of the existing tragedies of Euripides there is an instance of a dead lock quite as decided as the one which seems to be parodied here.

And fling them away too both. Fine work you've made,
A pretty business! Look there at your hamper.
What a taking the poor creature has been in,
Voiding its coal dust, like a cuttle fish,
For very fright; nearly destroy'd in short,
Merely from a want of temper and discretion
On the part of its own friends.* 'Tis passing strange,
That human nature should be so possest
With a propensity to pelt and bawl;
When gentle easy Reason might decide
All their debates with order, peace, and law;
When I myself stand here resign'd, and ready
To plead my cause before a chopping block,
To vindicate the Spartans and myself.
Yet, I forsooth, can feel the fear of death,
And hold my life as dear as others do.

* Parody of the rhetorical style of Euripides.

Chor. Bring the block! Bring it here!
Rogue, for I long to hear
Speedily whatever you can have to say.
Speak away.

SEMICHORUS.

'Twas your own choice, your own appointed pledge.
Bring forth the chopping block, and speak away.

Dic. Well, there it is. See, there's the chopping block!
And little I myself am the defendant.
Depend upon it, I'll fight manfully.
I'll never hug myself within my shield;
I'll speak my mind, moreover, about the Spartans.
And yet forsooth a secret anxious fear
Appals me; for I know the turn and temper
Of rustic natures, then delighted most
When from some bold declaimer, right or wrong,
They hear their country's praises and their own;
Delighted, but deluded all the while,
Unconsciously bamboozled and befool'd.
And well I know the minds of aged men,
And the malignant pleasure that they feel
In a harsh verdict or an angry vote.
And well I recollect my sufferings past
From Cleon, for my comedy last year;†
And how he dragg'd me to the senate house,
And trod me down, and bellow'd over me,

† The Babylonians.

And lick'd me with the rough side of his tongue;
And maul'd me, till I scarce escaped alive,
All batter'd and bespatter'd and befoul'd.
Permit me, therefore, first to clothe myself
In a pathetical and heart-rending dress.

Chor. It's no use! mere excuse!
Mere pretence!
Take what you will for your defence,
Any thing you think of use,
Even the invisible huge hobgoblin helmet
Of the learned Hieronymus,* if you chuse.
I care not, I;
You may try
The tricks and turns of Sisyphus in the play;†
We grant free leave for all, but no delay.

Dic. Well, I must try then to keep up my spirits,
And trudge away to find Euripides.
Holloa!

Servant. Who's there?

Dic. Euripides within?

Serv. Within, yet not within. You comprehend me?

Dic. Within and not within! why, what do ye mean?

Serv. I speak correctly, old Sire! his outward man
Is in the garret writing tragedy;
While his essential being is abroad,
Pursuing whimsies in the world of fancy.

Dic. O happy Euripides, with such a servant;
So clever and accomplish'd!—call him out.

Serv. It's quite impossible.

Dic. But it must be done.
Positively and absolutely I must see him;
Or I must stand here, rapping at the door.
Euripides! Euripides! come down,
If ever you came down in all your life!
'Tis I, 'tis Dicæopolis from Chollidæ.‡

Eur. I'm not at leisure to come down.

Dic. Perhaps—
But here's the scene-shifter can wheel you round.

Eur. It cannot be.

Dic. But however, notwithstanding.

Eur. Well, there then, I'm wheel'd round; for I had not time
For coming down.

* A lyrical and tragic poet particularly studious of the terrific.

† This play is lost, but Sisyphus had been represented in old poetic legends as so artful a person, that he had persuaded Proserpine to consent to his release from the infernal regions.

‡ A mark of rusticity. Dicæopolis mentions his demus in addition to his name.

Dic. Euripides, I say!
Eur. What say ye?
Dic. Euripides! Euripides!
Good lawk, you're there! upstairs! you write upstairs,
Instead of the ground floor? always upstairs.
Well, now, that's odd! But, dear Euripides,
If you had but a suit of rags that you could lend me.
You're he that brings out cripples in your tragedies;
A'nt ye? You're the new Poet, he that writes
Those characters of beggars and blind people.
Well, dear Euripides, if you could but lend me
A suit of tatters from a cast-off tragedy.
For mercy's sake, for I'm obliged to make
A speech in my own defence before the chorus,
A long pathetic speech this very day;
And if it fails, the doom of death betides me.
Eur. Say, what do ye seek? is it the woful garb
In which the wretched aged Œneus acted?
Dic. No, 'twas a wretcheder man than Œneus, much.*
Eur. Was it blind Phœnix?
Dic. No, not Phœnix, no,
A fellow a great deal wretcheder than Phœnix.
Eur. I wonder what he wants; is it the rags
Which Philoctetes went a begging with?
Dic. No, 'twas a beggar worse than Philoctetes.
Eur. Say, would you wish to wear those loathly weeds,
The habiliments of lame Bellerophon?
Dic. 'Twas not Bellerophon, but very like him.
A kind of smooth, fine-spoken character;
A beggar into the bargain and a cripple,
With a grand command of words, bothering and begging.
Eur. I know your man; 'tis Telephus the Mysian.
Dic. Ah, Telephus!—Yes, Telephus! do, pray,
Give me the things he wore.
Eur. Go fetch them there.
You'll find 'em next to the tatters of Thyestes,
Just over Ino's. Take them, there, and welcome.
Dic. Oh Jupiter, what an infinite endless mass
Of eternal holes and patches! Here it is,
Here's wherewithal to clothe myself in misery.
Euripides, now, since you've gone so far,
Do give me the other articles besides

* This and the names which follow refer to personages in those dramas of Euripides in which his object had been (what in poetry, as in real life, is the meanest of all), to excite compassion.

Belonging to these rags, that suit with them,
With a little Mysian bonnet for my head.
For I must wear a beggar's garb to-day,
Yet be myself in spite of my disguise;
That the audience all may know me; but the chorus,
Poor creatures, must not have the least suspicion
Whilst I cajole them with my rhetoric.
Eur. I'll give it you; your scheme is excellent,
Deep, subtle, natural, a profound device.
Dic. "May the Heavens reward you; and as to Telephus*
"May they decide his destiny as I wish!"
Why, bless me, I'm quite inspired (I think) with phrases.
I shall want the beggar's staff, though, notwithstanding.
Eur. Here, take it, and depart forth from the palace.
Dic. O my poor heart! much hardship hast thou borne,
And must abide new sorrows even now,
Driven hence in want of various articles.
Subdue thy nature to necessity,
Be supple, smooth, importunate, and bend
Thy temper to the level of thy fortune.—
Yet grant me another boon, Euripides;
A little tiny basket let it be,
One that has held a lamp, all burnt and batter'd.
Eur. Why should you need it?
Dic. 'Tis no need, perhaps,
But strong desire, a longing eager wish.
Eur. You're troublesome. Depart.
Dic. Alas, alas!
Yet may you prosper like your noble mother.†
Eur. Depart, I say.
Dic. Don't say so! Give me first,
First give me a pipkin broken at the brim.
Eur. You're troublesome in the mansion. Take it, go!
Dic. Alas, you know not what I feel, Euripides.
Yet grant me a pitcher, good Euripides;
A pitcher with a spunge plugg'd in its mouth.
Eur. Fellow, you'll plunder me a whole tragedy.
Take it, and go.
Dic. Yes; ay forsooth, I'm going.
But how shall I contrive? There's something more
That makes or mars my fortune utterly;
Yet give them, and bid me go, my dear Euripides;

* In the play which is here burlesqued, Telephus had been speaking in an assumed character, and had appeared with a similar ambiguous form, to be imprecating evil upon himself.

† His mother was of very low condition. See next page.

A little bundle of leaves to line my basket.
Eur. For mercy's sake! . . But take them. There they go!
My tragedies and all! ruin'd and robb'd!
Dic. No more I mean to trouble you; no more.
Yes, I retire; in truth I feel myself
Importunate, intruding on the presence
Of chiefs and princes, odious and unwelcome.
But out, alas, that I should so forget
The very point on which my fortune turns;
I wish I may be hang'd, my dear Euripides,
If ever I trouble you for any thing,
Except one little, little, little boon,
A single lettuce from your mother's stall.
Eur. This stranger taunts us. Close the palace gate.
Dic. O my poor soul, endure it and depart,
And take thy sorrowful leave, without a lettuce.
Yet, know'st thou yet the race which must be run,
Pleading the cause of Sparta: and here you stand
Even at the goal; time urges, arm yourself!
Infuse the spirit of Euripides,
His quirks and quibbles, in thine inmost heart!
'Tis well. Now forward, even to the place
Where thou must pledge thy life, and plead the cause
As may befall thee. Forward, forward yet;
A little more. I'm dreadfully out of spirits.

SEMICHORUS II.*

* See above, p. 14, for the characters of the two Semichoruses.

Speak, or are ye dumb,
Thou rogue in grain,
Iron brain!
Heart of stone!
Villain, are ye come,
Venturing your head alone,
Singly to support a treason of your own.

SEMICHORUS I.

He's resolved,
Confident,
Firm in his intent,
Ready to the day.
—Well, my man!

Since that's your plan,
Speak away!

[*In the following lines there is an intentional imitation of the dry drawling style of Euripides's harangues.*]

Dic. Be not surprised, most excellent spectators,
If I that am a beggar have presumed
To claim an audience upon public matters,
Even in a comedy; for comedy
Is conversant in all the rules of justice,
And can distinguish betwixt right and wrong.
The words I speak are bold, but just and true.
Cleon, at least, cannot accuse me now,
That I defame the city before strangers.
For this is the Lenæan festival,
And here we meet, all by ourselves alone;
No deputies are arrived as yet with tribute,
No strangers or allies; but here sit we
A chosen sample, clean as sifted corn,
With our own denizens as a kind of chaff.
First, I detest the Spartans most extremely;
And wish, that Neptune, the Tænarian deity,
Would bury them in their houses with his earthquakes.
For I've had losses—losses, let me tell ye,
Like other people; vines cut down and injured.
But, among friends, (for only friends are here,)
Why should we blame the Spartans for all this?
For people of ours, some people of our own,
Some people from amongst us here, I mean;
But not the people, (pray remember that;)
I never said the people,—but a pack
Of paltry people, mere pretended citizens,
Base counterfeits, went laying informations,
And making a confiscation of the jerkins
Imported here from Megara; pigs moreover,
Pumpkins, and pecks of salt, and ropes of onions,
Were voted to be merchandize from Megara,
Denounced, and seized, and sold upon the spot.
Well, these might pass, as petty local matters.
But now, behold, some doughty drunken youths
Kidnap, and carry away from Megara,
The courtezan Simætha. Those of Megara,
In hot retaliation, seize a brace

Of equal strumpets, hurried force perforce
From Dame Aspasia's house of recreation.
So this was the beginning of the war,
All over Greece, owing to these three strumpets.
For Pericles, like an Olympian Jove,
With all his thunder and his thunderbolts,
Began to storm and lighten dreadfully,
Alarming all the neighbourhood of Greece;
And made decrees, drawn up like drinking songs,
In which it was enacted and concluded,
That the Megarians should remain excluded
From every place where commerce was transacted,
With all their ware—like "old care"—in the ballad:
And this decree, by land and sea, was valid.*
  Then the Megarians, being all half starved,
Desired the Spartans, to desire of us,
Just to repeal those laws; the laws I mention'd,
Occasion'd by the stealing of those strumpets.
And so they begg'd and pray'd us several times;
And we refused; and so they went to war.
You'll say, "They should not." Why, what should they have done?
Just make it your own case; suppose the Spartans
Had mann'd a boat, and landed on your islands,
And stolen a pug puppy from Seriphos;
Would you then have remain'd at home inglorious?
Not so, by no means; at the first report,
You would have launch'd at once three hundred galleys,
And fill'd the city with the noise of troops;
And crews of ships, crowding and clamouring
About the muster-masters and pay-masters;
With measuring corn out at the magazine,
And all the porch choked with the multitude;
With figures of Minerva, newly furbish'd,
Painted and gilt, parading in the streets;
With wineskins, kegs, and firkins, leeks and onions;
With garlic cramm'd in pouches, nets, and pokes;
With garlands, singing girls, and bloody noses.
Our arsenal would have sounded and resounded
With bangs and thwacks of driving bolts and nails
With shaping oars, and holes to put the oar in;
With hacking, hammering, clattering and boring;

* The rhymes in the text are intentional. The Scholiast tells us that the original contains an allusion to the words of a well-known drinking song.

Words of command, whistles and pipes and fifes.
"Such would have been your conduct. Will you say,
"That Telephus should have acted otherwise?"

2 *Semichor.* Really! is it come to that? You rogue, how dare ye,
A beggar, here to come abusing us,
Slandering us all, inveighing against informers?

1 *Semich.* By Jove, but it's all true; truth, every word;
All true; not aggravated in the least.

2 *Semich.* And if it is, what right has he to say so?
None in the world; and he shall suffer for it.

1 *Semich.* Hands off there! what are ye after? Leave him go!
I'll grapple ye else, and heave ye neck and crop.

2 *Semich.* Lamachus! Lamachus!
Lamachus arise!
Let the gaze,
Of thine eyes,
In a blaze,
Daunt and amaze
Thine enemies.
Bring along
All the throng,
Hardy comrades, bold and strong,
For assault or standing fight;
Hasten and assist the right.

Lamachus. Whence came that noise of battle on mine ears?
Where am I summon'd? whither must I rush?
To the rescue or assault? what angry shout
Rouses the slumbering Gorgon on my shield?

Dic. O Lamachus, with your glorious crests and conquests!

2 *Semich.* O Lamachus! if there an't this fellow here
Abusing us and all the state this long while!

Lam. How dare ye, sirrah, a beggar, to talk thus?

Dic. O mighty Lamachus, have mercy upon me,
If, being a beggar, I prated and spoke amiss.

Lam. What were your words? repeat them, can't ye?

Dic. I can't.
I can't remember; I'm so terrified.

The terror of that crest quite turn'd me dizzy;
Do take the hobgoblin away from me, I beseech you.
Lam. There then.
Dic. Now turn it upside down.
Lam. See there.
Dic. Now give me one of the feathers.
Lam. Here, this plume.
Take it.
Dic. Now clasp your hands across my forehead,
For I feel that I shall strain in vomiting.
Those crests turn'd me so sick.
Lam. What are you doing?
You varlet, would you use my plume for a vomit?
Dic. A plume, do you call it? What does it belong to?
Lam. To a bird—
Dic. To a cock lorrel, does it not?
Lam. Ah, you shall die. [*A scuffle, in which Lamachus is foiled.*
Dic. No, Lamachus, not so fast.
That's rather a point above you, stout as you are.
Lam. Is this the sort of language for a beggar
To use to a commander such as me?
Dic. A beggar am I?
Lam. Why, what else are you?
Dic. I'll tell ye! an honest man; that's what I am.
A citizen that has served his time in the army,
As a footsoldier, fairly; not like you,
Pilfering, and drawing pay, with a pack of foreigners.
Lam. They voted me a command.
Dic. Who voted it?
A parcel of cuckoos! Well, I've made my peace.
In short, I could not abide the thing, not I;
To see grey-headed men serve in the ranks,
And lads like you dispatch'd upon commissions;
Some skulking away to Thrace, with their three drachmas;
Tisamenus's, Chares's, and Geres's,
Cheats, coxcombs, vagabonds, and Phænippus's,
And Theodorus's sent off to Gela,*
And Catana, and Camarina, and the Catamountains.
Lam. It past by a vote.
Dic. But what's the reason, pray,
For you to be sent out with salaries always,

* The Scholiast mentions all these persons as disreputable intriguers. The Athenians were already extending their views to Sicily.

* Names allusive to their occupation as charcoal burners.

† Monthly payments to their club.

And none of these good people? You, Marilades,*
Have you been ever sent on an embassy?
You're old enough. He shakes his head. Not he!
Yet he's a hardworking steady sober man.
And you, Euphorides, Prinides,* and the rest,
Have you ever been out into Chaonia,
Or up to Ecbatana?—no, not one of ye.
But Megacles, and Lamachus, and suchlike,
That, with their debts and payments long since due,†
Have heard their friends insisting and repeating,
"Get off," "Keep out of the way;" like the huswife's warning,
That empties a nuisance into the street at night.

Lam. And must we bear all this,—in the name of democracy?

Dic. Yes, just as long as Lamachus draws his salary.

Lam. No matter! Henceforth I devote myself
Against the Peloponnesians, whilst I live,
To assault and harass them by land and sea.

Dic. And I proclaim for all the Peloponnesians
And Thebans and Megarians, a free market;
Where they may trade with me, but not with Lamachus.

The Parabasis, in which the Chorus was brought forward to speak in praise or defence of the author, was a portion of the primitive *satyrical undramatic comedy. In the times of the* antient *or (as we should call it, from the name of the only author whose remains have reached us) the Aristophanic comedy, it seems to have been regarded as nearly superfluous; and is seldom introduced without some alleged motive, as in the instance before us; sometimes a burlesque one, as in the Peace.*

The present, which is the oldest of the existing plays of Aristophanes, was, as he tells us, the first in which he had introduced a Parabasis. Since his alleged, and probably his real, motive was the circumstance to which he had already alluded when speaking in the assumed character of Dicæopolis, he had reverted to his

"sufferings past,
"From Cleon for my comedy last year." p. 21.

This comedy (the Babylonians) seems, as far as we can judge of it from the few fragments that remain, to have been intended, in the first place, as an exposure of existing malpractices and abuses, and, secondly, as a reductio ad absurdum *of the extravagant schemes of Athenian ambition; assuming them to be realized, and exhibiting the result.*

The progressive aggrandizement of Athens had been marked, from the beginning, by the extortion and oppression practised (with a few honorable exceptions) by her military commanders; Themistocles himself having set the first example. In process of time, as the inferior allied states became gradually subject to the more immediate dominion of Athens, they became exposed to the additional pest of professional informers and venal demagogues, subsisting or enriching themselves by extortion and bribery. This state of things, odious and offensive to the whole Grecian race, disgraceful to the Athenian people, and profitable only to the most worthless and unprincipled among them, was the final unsatisfactory result of their vast efforts and indefatigable activity during two generations, the consummation of the ambitious projects of the most able statesmen of a former age. Meanwhile, at the time when this play (the Babylonians) was produced, the same scandals and abuses continued to be perpetrated in the subject states, under the cover of the Athenian supremacy; while the avidity for further conquest and dominion still remained predominant in the minds of the Athenian people.

The Poet then, in the fervour of youthful patriotism, and the pride of conscious genius; not as he was soon afterwards tempted to become and to constitute himself, a professional play-wright, the poetical serf of the community; but with the option of active life still open before him, comparatively therefore independent of his audience, and confident in his own wit and courage as a defence against the resentment of the most powerful opponents; had ventured an appeal to the Athenian people against their whole system of imperial policy both internal and external, against the grievances which they authorized or overlooked, and against their insatiable avidity for empire, tending, if attainable, in its unavoidable results, to the wider extension and aggravation of a system of abuses disgraceful to the name and character of the Athenian people.*

* These inferences are distinctly deducible from the Parabasis of the Knights.

With this view, therefore, taking for his canvas an imaginary empire, extending to the furthest limits to which the wildest ambition of his countrymen would have aspired, he had transferred to its remote localities the practices of the most notorious Athenian characters, and the most flagrant instances of existing oppression and corruption. The demagogues and informers of Athens (under this supposed unlimited extension of Athenian supremacy) were represented as transacting business on a larger scale, and extending to the richest and most distant regions of the East the practices which had hitherto been limited to the Islands of the Archipelago and the shores of Asia Minor.

The Poet however must have been aware, that he had undertaken a task of extreme difficulty and hazard; one in which, more than in any other theatrical attempt, it was necessary for him, at the first outset, to secure the sympathy of his audience; or, more properly speaking, to excite an antipathy against the objects of his attack, similar to that by which he himself was animated. It seems probable, therefore, that the order of subjects in the comedy must have been the same as that which is observable in the Parabasis which follows, and which may be considered as an apologetical analysis of the preceding play. It had begun then with the least criminal perhaps, but to the feelings of the Athenians the most invidious and irritating topic of accusation; namely, the occasional instances of undue advantages obtained for a subject state, by the hired agency of Athenian statesmen and orators, co-operating with the panegyrical cajolery of its deputies and envoys. A fragment has been preserved, evidently belonging to what was called a "long rhesis," a narrative speech, in which a character of this kind is making a triumphant report to his employers; describing his success in captivating the attention of an Athenian auditory, and giving a ridiculous picture of the effect which his oratory had produced upon them.

> "*Then every soul of them sat openmouth'd,*
> *Like roasted oysters, gaping in a row.*" *

* Ap. Athen. p. 86. Compare this with Knights v. 651, and the whole passage to which it belongs.

But the general plan of the play must have included a picture of the abuses and insolence, under which the subject states were suffering: an exhibition of the processes of extortion and intimidation which were practised upon them; an exposure of the persons most notoriously guilty of such practices, and probably also of some flagrant instances which were known to have occurred, and which might have been represented on the stage with no other disguise than that of a remote fanciful locality assigned to them in the new imaginary universal Empire of the Athenian Commonwealth.

This must have been the service, which, as he says, had excited the grateful feelings of the subject states, and their just admiration of the courage of the man "who had risked the perilous enterprise of pleading in behalf of justice, in presence of an Athenian auditory." It is observable that the Poet, after having, with a just feeling of pride and self-estimation, ventured in this way to assert his own merits, immediately after, as if alarmed at his own boldness (like Rabelais or the jesters in Shakespeare, when they are apprehensive of having touched upon too tender a point), makes a sudden escape from the subject, and hurries off into a strain of transcendental nonsense, about the high consideration with which his character and services to the country were regarded by the Persian monarch, and how the Spartans insisted upon obtaining the island of Ægina, from no other motive, than a wish to deprive the Athenians of the advantage which they might derive from his poetical admonitions.

Parabasis of the Chorus.

Our poet has never as yet
Esteem'd it proper or fit,
To detain you with a long
Encomiastic song,
On his own superior wit.
But being abused and accused,
And attack'd of late,
As a foe to the state,
He makes an appeal in his proper defence
To your voluble humour and temper and sense,
  With the following plea;
  Namely that he
Never attempted or ever meant
  To scandalize
  In any wise
Your mighty imperial government.

Moreover he says,
That in various ways
He presumes to have merited honour and praise,
Exhorting you still to stick to your rights,
And no more to be fool'd with rhetorical flights;
Such as of late each envoy tries
On the behalf of your allies,
That come to plead their cause before ye,
With fulsome phrase, and a foolish story
Of *violet crowns*, and *Athenian glory;*
With *sumptuous Athens* at every word;
Sumptuous Athens is always heard,
Sumptuous ever; a suitable phrase
For a dish of meat or a beast at graze.
He therefore affirms,
In confident terms,
That his active courage and earnest zeal
Have usefully served your common weal:
He has openly shewn
The style and tone
Of your democracy ruling abroad.
He has placed its practices on record;
The tyrannical arts, the knavish tricks,
That poison all your politics.
Therefore we shall see, this year,
The allies with tribute arriving here,
Eager and anxious all to behold
Their steady protector, the bard so bold:
The bard, they say, that has dared to speak,
To attack the strong, to defend the weak.
His fame in foreign climes is heard,
And a singular instance lately occurr'd.
It occurr'd in the case of the Persian king,
Sifting and cross-examining
The Spartan envoys. He demanded
Which of the rival states commanded
The Grecian seas? He ask'd them next,
(Wishing to see them more perplext,)
Which of the two contending powers
Was chiefly abused by this bard of ours?
For he said, "Such a bold, so profound an adviser
By dint of abuse would render them wiser,

More active and able; and briefly that they
Must finally prosper and carry the day."
Now mark the Lacedæmonian guile!
Demanding an insignificant isle!
"Ægina," they say, "for a pledge of peace,
"As a means to make all jealousy cease."
Meanwhile their privy design and plan
Is solely to gain this marvellous man,—
Knowing his influence on your fate,—
By obtaining a hold on his estate
Situate in the isle aforesaid.
Therefore there needs to be no more said.
You know their intention, and know that you know it.
You'll keep to your island, and stick to the poet.
And he for his part
Will practise his art
With a patriot heart,
With the honest views
That he now pursues,
And fair buffoonery and abuse;
Not rashly bespattering, or basely beflattering,
Not pimping, or puffing, or acting the ruffian;
  Not sneaking or fawning;
  But openly scorning
  All menace and warning,
  All bribes and suborning:
  He will do his endeavour on your behalf;
  He will teach you to think, he will teach you to laugh.
  So Cleon again and again may try;
  I value him not, nor fear him, I!
  His rage and rhetoric I defy.
  His impudence, his politics,
  His dirty designs, his rascally tricks
  No stain of abuse on me shall fix.
  Justice and right, in his despite,
  Shall aid and attend me, and do me right:
  With these to friend, I ne'er will bend,
  Nor descend
  To an humble tone,
  (Like his own),
  As a sneaking loon,
  A knavish, slavish, poor poltroon.

STROPHE.

Muse of old
  Manly times,
Strike the bold
  Hearty rhymes,
New revived,
  Firm, energetical
Music of Acharnæ;
  Choleric, fiery, quick,
As the sparkle
From the charcoal,
Of the native evergreen
Knotted oak,
  In the smoke
Shows his active fiery spleen.
  Whilst beside
  Stands the dish
  Full of fish
Ready to be fried:
Every face, in the place,
Overjoy'd, all employ'd,
  Junketing apace.
Muse then, as a friend of all,
Hasten, and attend the call.
Give an ear
  To your old,
  Lusty, bold
Townsmen here.

EPIRREMA.

We, the veterans of the city, briefly must expostulate
At the hard ungrateful usage which we meet with from the state,
Suffering men of years and service at your bar to stand indicted,
Bullied by your beardless speakers, worried and perplex'd and frighted;
Aided only by their staff, the staff on which their steps are stay'd;
Old, and impotent, and empty; deaf, decrepit, and decay'd.

There they stand, and pore, and drivel, with a misty pur-blind gleam,
Scarce discerning the tribunal, in a kind of waking dream.
Then the stripling, their accuser, fresh from training, bold and quick,
Pleads in person, fencing, sparring, using every turn and trick;
Grappling with the feeble culprit, dragging him to dangerous ground,
Into pitfalls of dilemmas, to perplex him and confound.
Then the wretched invalid attempts an answer, and at last
After stammering and mumbling, goes away condemn'd and cast;
Moaning to his friends and neighbours, "All the little store I have,
"All is gone! my purchase money for a coffin and my grave."

ANTISTROPHE.

Scandalous and a shame it is,
Seen or told;
Scandalous and a shame to see,
A warrior old;
Crippled in the war,
Worried at the bar;
Him, the veteran, that of old
Firmly stood,
With a fierce and hardy frown,
In the field of Marathon;
Running down
Sweat and blood.
There and then, we were men;
Valorous assailants; now
Poor and low;
Open and exposed to wrong,
From the young;
Every knave, every ass,
Every rogue like Marpsias.*

* Not known in history, but said by the Scholiast to have been noted by the contemporary comic poets as a troublesome contentious orator.

The Thucydides mentioned in the following lines is not the historian (the son of Olorus); but a much older man, and in his time of much greater personal eminence. In the scanty historical notices which have reached us respecting the period in which he lived, he is distinguished from others of the same name, as the son of Melesias; and it should seem that he must have succeeded to Cimon, as the leader of an unavailing opposition to that system of innovation in domestic and foreign policy which Pericles introduced; and by which he secured for himself, at the expense of posterity, a life annuity of power and popularity.

A very characteristic anecdote is alluded to in the 7th and 8th lines. Thucydides had been asked "which of the two (himself or Pericles) was the best wrestler," (i.e. the best debater). To which he answered: "I am the best wrestler; but when I have flung him, he starts up again and persuades the people that he was not thrown down."

ANTEPIRREMA.

Shame and grief it was to witness poor Thucydides's fate,
Indicted by Cephisodemus,* overwhelm'd with words and prate.
I myself when I beheld him, an old statesman of the city,
Dragg'd and held by Scythian archers,[1] I was moved to tears and pity,
Him that I remember once tremendous, terrible, and loud;
Discomfiting the Scythian host, subduing the revolted crowd;
Undaunted, desperate, and bold, that with his hasty grasp could fling
A dozen, in as many casts, of the best wrestlers in the ring.
Three thousand archers of the guard, he bawl'd and roar'd and bore them down.
No living soul he fear'd or spared, or friends or kinsmen of his own.
Since you then refuse to suffer aged men to rest in peace,
Range your criminals in classes, let the present method cease.

* An orator famous, or rather infamous, as a bold and dangerous accuser.

[1] These were purchased slaves, the property of the state, employed by the magistrates as a police-guard: see Thesm. v. 1001. They were also employed to maintain order in the public assembly, and to force disorderly speakers to descend from the bema. This part of their duties is alluded to elsewhere: see Eccles. v. 143, 258.

Give up elderly delinquents to be mumbled, mouth'd, and wrung
By the toothless old accusers; but protect them from the young.
For the younger class of culprits young accusers will be fair,
Prating prostituted fops, and Clinias's son and heir.
Thus we may proceed in order, all of us, with all our might,
Severally, both youths and elders, to defend and to indict.

DICÆOPOLIS.

Well, there's the boundary of my market place,
Mark'd out, for the Peloponnesians and Bœotians
And the Megarians. All are freely welcome
To traffic and sell with me, but not with Lamachus.
Moreover I've appointed constables,
With lawful and sufficient straps and thongs,
To keep the peace, and to coerce and punish
All spies and vagabonds and informing people.
Come, now for the column, with the terms of peace
Inscribed upon it! I must fetch it out,
And fix it here in the centre of my market. [*Exit.*

A writer in the Quarterly Review for July, 1820 *(not a very different person from the writer of this note) adduces the two scenes immediately following, as instances, amongst others, of that tendency to generalization which, as he contends, was no less predominant in the mind of Aristophanes than in that of Shakespeare.*

In reference to this principle it is observed of the following scenes that " the two country people who are introduced as attending Dicæopolis's market, are not merely a Megarian and a Theban distinguished by a difference of dialect and behaviour; they are the two extremes of rustic character—the one (the Megarian) depressed by indigence into meanness, is shifting and selfish, with habits of coarse fraud and vulgar jocularity. The Theban is the direct opposite—a primitive, hearty, frank, unsuspicious, easy-minded fellow; he comes to market with his followers, in a kind of old-fashioned rustic triumph, with his bag-pipers attending him: Dicæopolis (the Athenian, the medium between the two extremes before described) immediately exhibits his superior refinement, by suppressing their minstrelsy; and the honest Theban, instead of being offended, joins in condemning them. He then displays his wares, and the Athenian, with a burlesque tragical rant, takes one of his best articles (a Copaic eel) and delivers it to his own attendants to be conveyed within doors. The Theban, with great simplicity, asks how he is to be paid for it; and the Athenian, in a tone of grave superiority, but with some awkwardness, informs him that he claims it as a toll due to the market. The Theban does not remonstrate, but after some conversation agrees to dispose of all his wares, and to take other goods in return; but here a difficulty arises, for the same articles which the Athenian proposes in exchange, happen to be equally abundant in Bœotia. The scene here passes into burlesque, but it is a burlesque expressive of the character which is assigned to the Theban; a character of primitive simplicity, utterly unacquainted with all the pests by which existence was poisoned in the corrupt community of Athens. A common sycophant or informer is proposed as an article which the Athenian soil produced in great abundance, but which would be considered as a rarity in Bœotia. The Theban agrees to the exchange, saying, that if he could get such an animal to take home, he thinks he could make a handsome profit by exhibiting him."

The scene which immediately follows (that of the Megarian) has been slightly modified, without detriment, it must be hoped, to the genuine humour of the original; perhaps even with advantage; since the attention of the English reader is not distracted by that strange contrast of ancient and modern manners, which strikes the reader of the original with an impression, wholly disproportionate to the intention of the Author, and destructive of that general harmony and breadth of effect, which he had intended to produce, and which, as far as his cotemporaries were concerned, he had succeeded in producing.

Enter a MEGARIAN *with his two little girls.*

Meg. Ah, there's the Athenian market! Heaven bless it, I say; the welcomest sight to a Megarian.

I've look'd for it, and long'd for it, like a child
For its own mother. You, my daughters dear,
Disastrous offspring of a dismal sire,
List to my words; and let them sink impress'd
Upon your empty stomachs; now's the time
That you must seek a livelihood for yourselves.
Therefore resolve at once, and answer me;
Will you be sold abroad, or starve at home?

Both. Let us be sold, papa!—Let us be sold.

Meg. I say so too; but who do ye think will purchase
Such useless mischievous commodities?
However, I have a notion of my own,
A true Megarian* scheme;—I mean to sell ye
Disguised as pigs, with artificial pettitoes.
Here, take them, and put them on. Remember now,
Show yourselves off; do credit to your breeding,
Like decent pigs; or else, by Mercury,
If I'm obliged to take you back to Megara,
There you shall starve, far worse than heretofore.
—This pair of masks too—fasten 'em on your faces,
And crawl into the sack there on the ground.
Mind ye—Remember—you must squeak and whine,
And racket about like little roasting pigs.
—And I'll call out for Dicæopolis.
Hoh Dicæopolis, Dicæopolis!
I say, would you please to buy some pigs of mine?

Dic. What's there? a Megarian?

Meg. (sneakingly). Yes—we're come to market.

Dic. How goes it with you?

Meg. We're all like to starve.

Dic. Well, liking is everything. If you have your liking,
That's all in all: the likeness is a good one,
A pretty likeness! like to starve, you say.
But what else are you doing?

Meg. What we're doing.
I left our governing people all contriving
To ruin us utterly without loss of time.

Dic. It's the only way: it will keep you out of mischief,
Meddling and getting into scrapes.

Meg. Ay, yes.

Dic. Well, what's your other news? How's corn? What price?

* The Athenians could not claim the invention of comedy, which belonged to the Megarians: they therefore indemnified themselves by decrying the humour of the Megarians, as low and vulgar.

Meg. Corn? it's above all price; we worship it.
Dic. But salt? You've salt, I reckon—
Meg. Salt? how should we?
Have not you seized the salt pans?
Dic. No! nor garlic?
Have not ye garlic?
Meg. What do ye talk of garlic?
As if you had not wasted and destroy'd it,
And grubb'd the very roots out of the ground.
Dic. Well, what have you got then? Tell us! Can't ye!
Meg. (*in the tone of a sturdy resolute lie*). Pigs,—
Pigs truly—pigs forsooth, for sacrifice.
Dic. That's well, let's look at 'em.
Meg. Ay, they're handsome ones;
You may feel how heavy they are, if ye hold 'em up.
Dic. Hey day! What's this? What's here?
Meg. A pig to be sure.
Dic. Do ye say so? Where does it come from?
Meg. Come? from Megara.
What, an't it a pig?
Dic. No truly, it does not seem so.
Meg. Did you ever hear the like? Such an unaccountable
Suspicious fellow! it is not a pig, he says!
But I'll be judged; I'll bet ye a bushel of salt,
It's what we call a natural proper pig.
Dic. Perhaps it may, but it's a human pig.
Meg. Human! I'm human; and they're mine, that's all.
Whose should they be, do ye think? so far they're human.
But come, will you hear 'em squeak?
Dic. Ay, yes, by Jove,
With all my heart.
Meg. Come now, pig! now's the time:
Remember what I told ye—squeak directly!
Squeak, can't ye? Curse ye, what's the matter with ye?
Squeak when I bid you, I say; by Mercury
I'll carry you back to Megara if you don't.
Daught. Wee wée.
Meg. Do ye hear the pig?
Dic. The pig, do ye call it?
It will be a different creature before long.
Meg. It will take after the mother, like enough.
Dic. Ay, but this pig won't do for sacrifice.

Meg. Why not? why won't it do for sacrifice?
Dic. Imperfect! here's no tail!
Meg. Poh, never mind;
It will have a tail in time, like all the rest.
But feel this other, just the fellow to it;
With a little further keeping, it would serve
For a pretty dainty sacrifice to Venus.
Dic. You warrant 'em wean'd? they'll feed without the mother?
Meg. Without the mother or the father either.
Dic. But what do they like to eat?
Meg. Just what ye give 'em;
You may ask 'em if you will.
Dic. Pig, pig!
1 *Daught.* Wee wée.
Dic. Pig, are ye fond of peas?
1 *Daught.* Wee wée wee wée.
Dic. Are ye fond of figs?
1 *Daught.* Wee wée wee wée wee wée.
Dic. You little one, are you fond of figs?
2 *Daught.* Wee wée.
Dic. What a squeak was there! they're ravenous for the figs;
Go somebody, fetch out a parcel of figs
For the little pigs! Heh, what, they'll eat, I warrânt.
Lawk there, look at 'em racketing and bustling!
How they do munch and crunch! in the name of heaven,
Why, sure they can't have eaten 'em already!
Meg. (*sneakingly*). Not all, there's this one here, I took myself.
Dic. Well, faith, they're clever comical animals.
What shall I give you for 'em? What do ye ask?
Meg. I must have a gross of onions for this here;
And the other you may take for a peck of salt.
Dic. I'll keep 'em; wait a moment. [*Exit.*
Meg. Heaven be praised!
O blessed Mercury, if I could but manage
To make such another bargain for my wife,
I'd do it to-morrow, or my mother either.

Enter Informer.

Inf. Fellow, from whence?
Meg. From Megara with my pigs.

Inf. Then I denounce your pigs, and you yourself,
As belonging to the enemy.
Meg. There it is!
* See p. 27, vv. 650-52.
The beginning* of all our troubles over again.
Inf. I'll teach you to come Megarizing here:
Let go of the sack there.
Meg. Dicæopolis!
Hoh Dicæopolis! there's a fellow here
Denouncing me.
Dic. Denouncing is he? Constables,
Why don't you keep the market clear of sycophants?
You fellow, I must inform ye, your informing
Is wholly illegal and informal here.
Inf. What, giving information against the enemy;
Is that prohibited?
Dic. At your peril! Carry
Your informations to some other market.
Meg. What a plague it is at Athens, this informing!
Dic. O never fear, Megarian; take it there,
The payment for your pigs, the salt and onions:
And fare you well.
Meg. That's not the fashion amongst us.
We've not been used to faring well.
Dic. No matter.
If it's offensive, I'll revoke the wish;
And imprecate it on myself instead. [*Exit.*
Meg. There now, my little pigs, you must contrive
To munch your bread with salt, if you can get it. [*Exit.*

The following song consists merely of a satyrical enumeration and description of persons, now, for the most part, entirely forgotten. An attempt has therefore been made to give some interest to it (an interest of curiosity at least) by a close imitation of the metre of the original. The Cratinus here mentioned is not the celebrated comic author, but a contemporary lyrical poet, of whom nothing, I believe, is known. The name of Hyperbolus is upon record, as that of a turbulent public speaker and accuser. Cleonymus is noted in this and other comedies (see p. 10, *v.* 112*), as a great overgrown coward, and a voracious intrusive guest.*

CHORUS.

Our friend's affairs improve apace; his lucky speculation
Is raising him to wealth and place, to name and reputation.
With a revenue neat and clear,
Arising without risque or fear,
No sycophant will venture here
To spoil his occupation.
Not Ctesias, the dirty spy, that lately terrified him;
Nor Prepis, with his infamy, will jostle side be-side him.
Clothed in a neat and airy dress,
He'll move at ease among the press,
Without a fear of nastiness,
Or danger to betide him.
Hyperbolus will never dare to indict him nor arrest him.
Cleonymus will not be there to bother and molest him.
Nor he, the bard of little price,
Cratinus, with the curls so nice,
Cratinus in the new device
In which the barber drest him.
Nor he, the paltry saucy rogue, the poor and undeserving,
Lysistratus, that heads the vogue, in impudence unswerving.
Taunt and offence in all he says;
Ruin'd in all kinds of ways;
In every month of thirty days,
Nine and twenty starving.

Enter a THEBAN *with his attendants, all bearing burthens; followed by a train of bagpipers.*

Theb. Goodtroth, I'm right down shoulder-gall'd; my lads,
Set down your bundles. You, take care o' the herbs.
Gently, be sure don't bruise 'em; and now, you minstrels,
That needs would follow us all the way from Thebes;
Blow wind i' the tail of your bag-pipes, puff away.

Dic. Get out! what wind has brought 'em here, I wonder?
A parcel of hornets buzzing about the door!
You humble-bumble drones—get out! get out!

Theb. As Iolaus shall help me, that's well done,
Friend, and I thank you;—coming out of Thebes,
They blew me away the blossom of all these herbs.
You've sarved 'em right. So now would you please to buy
What likes you best, of all my chaffer here;
All kinds, four-footed things and feather'd fowl.

Dic. (suddenly, with the common trick of condescension, as if he had not observed him before).

My little tight Bœotian! Welcome kindly,
My little pudding-eater! What have you brought?
Theb. In a manner, everything, as a body may say;
All the good cheer of Thebes, and the primest wares,
Mats, trefoil, wicks for lamps, sweet marjoram,
Coots, didappers, and water-hens—what not?
Widgeon and teal.
Dic. Why, you're come here amongst us,
Like a north-wind in winter, with your wild fowl.
Theb. Moreover, I've brought geese, and hares moreover,
And eels from the lake Copais, which is more.
Dic. O thou bestower of the best spitchcocks
That ever yet were given to mortal man,
Permit me to salute those charming eels.
Theb. (addressing the eel, and delivering it to Dicæopolis)
Daughter, come forth, and greet the courteous stranger,
First-born of fifty damsels of the lake!
Dic. O long regretted and recover'd late,
Welcome, thrice welcome to the comic quire;
Welcome to me, to Morychus,* and all.
—(Ye slaves, prepare the chafing dish and stove.)
Children, behold her here, the best of eels,
The loveliest and the best, at length return'd
After six years of absence. I myself
Will furnish you with charcoal for her sake.
Salute her with respect, and wait upon
Her entrance there within, with due conveyance.

* At the close of the play, a splendid supper was given by the choregus to the whole comic quire; authors, actors, and judges.—Morychus was a noted epicure.

[*The eel is here carried off by Dicæopolis's servants.*

Grant me, ye gods! so to possess thee still,
While my life lasts, and at my latest hour,
Fresh even and sweet as now, with . . savory sauce.[1]
Theb. But how am I to be paid for it? Won't you tell me?
Dic. Why, with respect to the eel, in the present instance,
I mean to take it as a perquisite,
As a kind of toll to the market; you understand me.
These other things of course are meant for sale.
Theb. Yes sure. I sell 'em all.

---

[1] See Note 1 in "Review of Mitchell's Aristophanes."

Dic. Well, what do you ask?
Or would you take commodities in exchange?

Theb. Ay; think of something of your country produce,
That's plentiful down here, and scarce up there.

Dic. Well, you shall take our pilchards or our pottery.

Theb. Pilchards and pottery!—Naugh, we've plenty of they.
But think of something, as I said before,
That's plentiful down here, and scarce up there.

Dic. (*after a moment's reflection*).
I have it! A true-bred sycophant and informer.—
I'll give you one, tied neatly and corded up,
Like an oil-jar.

Theb. Ay; that's fair; by the holy twins!
He'd bring in money, I warrant, money enough,
Amongst our folks at home, with showing him,
Like a mischiéf-full kind of a foreign ape.

Dic. Well, there's Nicarchus moving down this way,
Laying his informations. There he comes.

Theb. (*contemplating him with the eye of a purchaser*).
'A seems but a small one to look at.

Dic. Ay, but I promise ye,
He's full of tricks and roguery, every inch of him.

Enter Nicarchus.

Nic. (*in the pert peremptory tone of his profession as an informer*).
Whose goods are these? these articles?

Theb. Mine, sure;
We be come here from Thebes.

Nic. Then I denounce them
As enemies' property.

Theb. (*with an immediate outcry*). Why, what harm have they done,
The birds and creatures?—Why do you quarrel with 'em?

Nic. And I'll denounce you too.

Theb. What, me? What for?

Nic. To satisfy the bystanders, I'll explain.—
You've brought in wicks of lamps from an enemy's country.

Dic. (*ironically*). And so, you bring 'em to *light?*

Nic. I bring to light
A plot!—a plot to burn the arsenal!

Dic. (*ironically*). With the wick of a lamp?

Nic. Undoubtedly.

Dic. In what way?

Nic. (*with great gravity.*) A Bœotian might be capable of fixing it
On the back of a cockroach, who might float with it
Into the arsenal, with a north-east wind;
And if once the fire caught hold of a single vessel,
The whole would be in a blaze.

Dic. (*seizing hold of him*). You dog! you villain!
Would a cockroach burn the ships and the arsenal?

Nic. Bear witness, all of ye.

Dic. There, stop his mouth;
And bring me a band of straw to bind him up;
And send him safely away, for fear of damage,
Gently and steadily, like a potter's jar.

The metre of the following song is given as a tolerably near approach to that of the original; in fact, the nearest which has been found consistent with the necessity of rhyme.

Chor. To preserve him safe and sound,
You must have him fairly bound,
With a cordage nicely wound,
Up and down, and round and round;
Securely pack'd.

Dic. I shall have a special care,
For he's a piece of paltry ware;
And as you strike him, here—or there,—(*striking him*)
The noises he returns declare—(*the informer screaming*)
He's partly crack'd.*

Chor. How then is he fit for use?

Dic. As a store-jar of abuse.
Plots and lies he cooks and brews,
Slander and seditious news,
Or any thing.

Chor. Have you stow'd him safe enough?

Dic. Never fear, he's hearty stuff;
Fit for usage hard and rough,
Fit to beat and fit to cuff,
To toss and fling.
You can hang him up or down,†
By the heels or by the crown.

* The soundness of an earthen vessel is ascertained by striking a smart blow upon it, and attending to the tone which it gives out.

† The informer being by this time fairly corded and packed, is flung about and hung up, in confirmation of Dicæopolis's warranty.

Theb. I'm for harvest business bown.
Chor. Fare ye well, my jolly clown.
We wish ye joy.
You've a purchase tight and neat;
A rogue, a sycophant complete;
Fit to bang about and beat,
Fit to stand the cold and heat,
And all employ.
Dic. I'd a hard job with the rascal, tying him up!
Come, my Bœotian, take away your bargain.
Theb. (*speaking to one of his servants*).
Ismenius, stoop your back, and heave him up.
There—softly and fairly—so—now carry him off.
Dic. He's an unlucky commodity; notwithstanding,
If he earns you a profit, you can have to say,
What few can say, you've been the better for him,
And mended your affairs by the informer.

Enter a Slave.

Slave (*in a loud voice*). Hoh, Dicæopolis!
Dic. Well, what's the matter?
Why need ye bawl so?
Slave. Lamachus sends his orders,
With a drachma for a dish of quails, and three
For that Copaic eel, he bid me give you.
Dic. An eel for Lamachus? Who is Lamachus?
Slave. The fierce and hardy warrior; he that wields
The Gorgon shield, and waves the triple plume.
Dic. And if he'd give me his shield, he should not have it:
Let him wave his plumage over a mess of saltfish.
What's more; if he takes it amiss, and makes a riot,
I'll speak to the clerk of the market, you may tell him.
—But as for me, with this my precious basket,
Hence I depart, while ortolans and quails
Attend my passage and partake the gales. [*Exit.*

CHORUS.

An attempt has been here made to reproduce in English the peculiar metre of the original, in which (after an irregular beginning) each line is made to consist of four cretic measures, of which it is requisite that the three first should be of the form already described in p. 15 (namely, a crotchet *followed by three quavers). The difficulty arising from the great scarcity of short syllables in the English language,* as compared with the Greek, has led to some infractions of this rule, in the unequal length of some of the lines, and the substitution of the common cretic measure, in its usual unresolved form;† not to mention one or two indefensible but unavoidable false quantities, together with certain hiatuses and semihiatuses, which in a less restricted metre it would not have been difficult to avoid.*

* The whole of the English liturgy gives only one instance of five short syllables in succession. In the three first lines of Herodotus we find a succession of six and of five.

† As may be seen in vv. 8, 9, 10 and 11.

EPIRREMA.

O behold, O behold
The serene happy sage,
The profound mighty mind,
Miracle of our age,
Calmly wise, prosperous in enterprise,
Cool, correct, boundless in the compass of his intellect.
Savoury commodities and articles of every kind
Pouring in upon him, and accumulating all around.
Some to be reserved apart, ready for domestic use;
Some again, that require
Quickly to be broil'd or roast, hastily devour'd and smoused,
On the spot, piping hot.
See there, as a sample of his hospitable elegance,
Feathers and a litter of his offal at the door display'd!
War is my aversion; I detest the very thought of him.
Never in my life will I receive him in my house again;
Positively never; he behaved in such a beastly way.
There we were assembled at a dinner of the neighbourhood;
Mirth and unanimity prevail'd till he reversed it all,
Coming in among us of a sudden, in a haughty style.
Civilly we treated him enough, with a polite request,
"Please ye to be seated, and to join us in a fair carouse."
Nothing of the kind! but unaccountably he began to storm,
Brandishing a torch as if he meant to set the house afire,
Swaggering and hectoring, abusing and assaulting us.
First he smash'd the jars, he spoilt and spilt the wines;
Next he burnt the stakes, and ruin'd all the vines.

ANTEPIRREMA.

An endeavour to develop with more effect a pretty fanciful allusion in the original, has led to another infraction of the metrical rule above described. It is to be hoped, however, that the passage in question (from v. 1283 to 1290) will not be found to exhibit any marked departure from the general character which belongs to this peculiar form of the cretic metre. The picture, the work of Zeuxis, was an object well known to all the inhabitants of Athens; for the sake of the modern reader, it was necessary to insert a slight sketch of it.

Wherefore are ye gone away,
Whither are ye gone astray,
Lovely Peace,
Vanishing, eloping, and abandoning unhappy Greece?
—Love is as a painter ever, doting on a fair design.
Zeuxis has illustrated a vision and a wish of mine.
Cupid is pourtray'd
Naked, unarray'd,
With an amaranthine braid
Waving in his hand;
With a lover and a maid
Bounden in a band.
Cupid is uniting both,
Nothing loth.
Think then if I saw ye with a Cupid in a tether, dear,
Binding and uniting us eternally together here.
Think of the delight of it; in harmony to live at last,
Making it a principle to cancel all offences past.
Really I propose it, and I promise ye to do my best,
(Old as you may fancy me,) to sacrifice my peace and rest;
Working in my calling as a father of a family,
Labouring and occupied in articles of husbandry.
You shall have an orchard, with the fig trees in a border round
Planted all in order, and a vineyard and an olive ground.
When the month is ended, we'll repose from toil,
With a bath and banquet, wine and anointing oil.

Herald, or Cryer.

Hear ye! good people! hear ye! a festival—
According to antient custom—this same day—
The feast of the pitchers—with the prize for drinkers,
To drink at the sound of the trumpet. He that wins
To receive a wineskin; Ctesiphon's own skin.[1]

[1] The notion of a person's being flayed, and having his skin con-

Dic. O slaves! ye boys and women! Heard ye not
The summons of the herald? Hasten forth,
With quick despatch, to boil, to roast, to fry;
Hacking and cutting, plucking, gutting, flaying;
Hashing and slashing, mincing, fricasseeing.
And plait the garlands nimbly; and bring me here
Those, the least skewers of all, to truss the quails.

When Aristophanes cannot make use of his chorus to sustain an efficient part, he is apt to indemnify himself for the incumbrance they create, by turning the essential characteristics of a chorus into ridicule. Here then, and at the close of the following scene (that between Dicæopolis and the countryman), they are represented as time-serving and obsequious; in the Lysistrata, as dawdling, useless, and silly (l. 319 *to* 49, *ed. Bekk.); and in the Birds, as exciting the spleen and impatience of the practical active man of business, by their vague speculations and poetical pedantry (l.* 1313 *to* 36, *ed. Bekk.). In the Peace, the absurdity of introducing such a chorus is kept out of sight by the absurd, unmanageable behaviour of the chorus itself (l.* 309, *ed. Bekk.).*

Chor. Your designs and public ends,
First attracted us as friends.
But the present boil'd and roast
Surprises and delights us most.
Dic. Wait awhile, if nothing fails,
You shall see a dish of quails.
Cho. We depend upon your care.
Dic. Rouse the fire and mend it there.
Cho. See with what a gait and air,
What a magisterial look,
Like a cool, determined cook,
He conducts the whole affair.[1]

---

verted into a wine-keg, appears to have been familiar to the imagination of the Athenians, and of frequent recurrence in their low colloquial language. Ctesiphon is only known as having been ridiculed by the comic poets for his extreme corpulence. The conqueror, therefore, would be rewarded with a prize of unusual magnitude.

[1] A dignified and authoritative demeanour is an essential requisite to the perfection of the culinary character. The complete cook (as

Enter a Countryman groaning and lamenting.

Countr. O miserable! wretched! wretched man!
Dic. Fellow, take care with those unlucky words.
Apply them to yourself.
Countr. Ah, dear good friend,
So you've got peace; a peace all to yourself!
And if ye could but spare me a little drop,
Just only a little taste, only five years.
Dic. Why, what's the matter with ye?
Countr. I'm ruinated,
Quite and entirely, losing my poor beasts,
My oxen, I lost 'em, both of 'em.
Dic. In what way?
Countr. The Bœotians! the Bœotians! It was they.
They came down at the back of Phyle there,
And drove away my bullocks, both of 'em. . . .
Dic. But you're in white, I see; you're out of mourning.
Countr. (*in continuation.*)
. . . That indeed were all my comfort and support:
That used to serve for my manure and maintenance
In dung and daily bread;—the poor dear beasts.
Dic. And what is it you want?
Countr. I'm blind well nigh,
With weeping and grief.—Derketes is my name,
In a farm here next to Phyle born and bred:
So if ever you wish to do what's friendly by me,
Do smear my two poor eyes with the balsam of peace.
Dic. Friend, I'm not keeping a dispensary.
Countr. Do, just to get me a sight of my poor oxen.
Dic. Impossible! you must go to the hospital.
Countr. Do, pray, just only give me the least drop.
Dic. Not the least drop—not I—go—get ye gone.
Countr. Oh dear! oh dear! oh dear! my poor dear oxen. [*Exit.*

---

described in that admirable piece of good humoured parody, *L'Homme des Champs à Table*)

"Donne avec dignité des loix dans sa cuisine,
Et dispose du sort d'un coq ou d'un dindon,
Avec l'air d'un sultan qui condamne au cordon:
Son maintien est altier, et sa mine farouche."

Chor. He, the chief, is now possessing
Peace as an exclusive blessing,
Which he will not part withal.

Dic. Mix honey with the savoury dishes!
Be careful with the cuttle.fishes!
Stew me the kidneys with the caul!

Chor. Hear him shout there! Hear him bawl!

Dic. (*louder.*) Season and broil him there—that eel!

Chor. You don't consider what we feel;
We're famish'd here with waiting;
While you choke
Us with your smoke,
And deafen us with prating.

Dic. Those cutlets, brown them nicely—there—do ye mind.

Enter a Bridesman.

Brid. Hoh Dicæopolis!

Dic. Who's there? who's that?

Brid. A bridegroom, that has sent a dish of meat
From his marriage feast.

Dic. Well! come! that's handsome of him;
That's proper, whoever he is; that's as it should be.

Brid. In fact, my friend the bridegroom, he that sent it,
Objects to foreign service just at present;
He begs you'd favour him with the balsam of peace;
A trifling quantity, in the box I've brought.

Dic. No, no! take back the dish; I can't receive it.
Dispose it somewhere else; take it away.
I would not part with a particle of my balsam,
For all the world—not for a thousand drachmas.
But that young woman there, who's she?

Bridesman. The bridesmaid;
With a particular message from the bride;
Wishing to speak a word in private with you.

Dic. Well, what have ye got to say? Let's hear it all!
Come—step this way—No, nearer—in a whisper—
Nearer, I say—Come, there now; tell me about it.
[*After listening with comic attention to a supposed whisper.*
—Oh bless me; what a capital, comical,
Extraordinary string of female reasons
For keeping a young bridegroom safe at home!

—Well, we'll indulge her, since she's only a woman ;
She's not obliged to serve ; bring out the balsam !
Come, where's your little vial ?—but I say—
Do you know the manner of it ?—No, not you.
How should you, a girl like you ! What ! I must tell you ?
Yes—and you'll tell the bride ; she must observe ;
When a ballot is on foot for foreign service ;
At the hour of midnight, when he's fast asleep,
Then she must be particularly careful,
Without disturbing him, to anoint him. There !

[*Giving her back the vial. Exit Bridesmaid.*

Now take the balsam back, and bring me a funnel
To rack my wine off. I must mix my wine.

Chor. See yet another ! posting here, it seems,
With awful tidings, anxious and aghast.

Mess. Ho Lamachus, I say ! Lamachus, hoh !
Here's terror and tribulation, wars and woe !

[*Lamachus appears, probably with some appendage, to mark the interest which he had been taking in the culinary operations supposed to be going on behind the stage.*

Lam. What hasty summons shakes the castle gates ?

Mess. The generals have despatch'd an order to you
To muster your caparisons and garrisons,
And march to the mountain passes ; there to wait
In ambush in the snow : for fresh advices
Have been received, with a credible intimation
[illegible] a suspicion of an expedition
Of a marauding party from Bœotia.

Lam. Generals ! ay, generals ! the more the worse.

Dic. Well, is not it hard that a man can't eat his dinner,
But he's to be disturb'd and call'd from table,
With wars, and Lamachus's, and what not ?

Lam. You mock me, alas !

Dic. Say, would you wish to grapple,
In single combat, with this mailed monster ?

[*Showing a lobster.*

Lam. Alas, that dismal fatal messenger !

Dic. But here's a message too, coming for me.

Mess. 2nd. Hoh Dicæopolis !

Dic. Well, what ?

Mess. 2nd. You're summon'd

To go without a moment's loss of time,
With your whole cookery, to the priest of Bacchus.
The company are arrived; you keep them waiting,
Everything else is ready,—couches, tables,
Cushions, and coverlids for mattresses,
Dancing and singing girls for mistresses,
Plum cake and plain, comfits and caraways,
Confectionery, fruits preserved and fresh,
Relishes of all sorts, hot things and bitter,
Savouries and sweets, broil'd biscuits, and what not;
Flowers and perfumes and garlands, everything.
You must not lose a moment.

Lam. Out alas!
Wretch that I am!

Dic. 'Tis your own fault entirely,
For enlisting in the service of the Gorgons.
There, shut the door, and serve the dishes here.

Lam. My knapsack and camp service; bring it out.

Dic. My dinner service; bring it here, you lout.

Lam. Give me my bunch of leeks, the soldiers' fare.

Dic. I'm partial to veal cutlets; bring them there.

Lam. Let's see the saltfish; it seems like to rot.

Dic. I take fresh fish, and broil it on the spot.

Lam. Bring me the lofty feathers of my crest.

Dic. Bring doves and quails; I scarce know which is best.

Lam. Behold this snowy plume of dazzling white.

Dic. Behold the roasted dove, a savoury sight.

Lam. Don't mock these arms of mine, good fellow, prithee.

Dic. These quails of mine, don't think to take them with ye.

Lam. The case that holds my crest,—bring it in haste.

Dic. And the hare-pie for me,—bring it in paste.

Lam. My crest,—have the moths spoilt it? no, not yet.

Dic. My dinner,—shall I spoil it by a whet?

Lam. Fellow, direct not your discourse to me.

Dic. Ay, but this boy and I, we can't agree;
And we've a kind of wager, which is best,
Locusts or quails, forsooth.

Lam. Sirrah, your jest
Is insolent.

Dic. My wager's gone this bout:
He's all, you see, for locusts, out and out.

Various demonstrations of menace and defiance take place between Lamachus and Dicæopolis. Lamachus has called for his lance in anger; Dicæopolis calls for the spit: both are brought, but neither of them in a state fit for service. Lamachus (after a hostile reconnoitring look), conscious of his present disadvantage, proceeds to unsheathe his rusty weapon; but, in the mean time, Dicæopolis has succeeded in disengaging his spit from the roast-meat, and appears again ready to confront him upon equal terms. Here again are reciprocal looks and gestures of hostility, which terminate in mutual forbearance. Any amusement which this scene might have afforded to the spectators, must have been derived from the humour of the performers; to the mere reader, and more particularly to the modern reader, it must be uninteresting; and might have been passed over, but for a wish (which perhaps has been carried too far) to omit nothing that was admissible.

Lam. Bring here my lance; unsheathe the deadly point.
Dic. Bring here the spit, and show the roasted joint.
Lam. This sheath is rusted. Come, boy, tug and try.
Ah, there it comes.
Dic. (*unspitting his roast meat*).
It comes quite easily.
Lam. Bring forth the props of wood, my shield's support.
Dic. Bring bread, for belly-timber; that's your sort!
Lam. My Gorgon-orbed shield; bring it with speed.
Dic. With this full-orbed pancake I proceed.
Lam. Is not this insolence too much to bear?
Dic. Is not this pancake exquisite and rare?
Lam. Pour oil upon the shield! What do I trace
In the divining mirror—'Tis the face
Of an old coward, petrified with fear,
That sees his trial for desertion near.*
Dic. Pour honey on the pancake! what appears?
A comely personage, advanced in years;
Firmly resolved to laugh at and defy
Both Lamachus and the Gorgon family.
Lam. Bring forth my trusty breastplate for the fight.
Dic. Bring forth the lusty goblet, my delight!

* It was a common practice to anoint the shield before battle. There was likewise a species of divination practised by figures reflected from an oiled surface. These two usages are here alluded to. A similar mode of divination appears from the report of modern travellers to be still employed in Egypt.

Lam. I'll charge with this, accoutred every limb.
Dic. I'll charge with this, a bumper to the brim.
Lam. Boys, strap the shield and bedding in a pack!
I'll bear myself my knapsack on my back.
Dic. Boy, strap the basket with my feasting mess;
While I just step within to change my dress.
Lam. Come, boy, take up my shield, and trudge away.
It snows! Good lack; we've wintry work to-day.
Dic. Boy, take the basket. Jolly work, I say.
[*Exeunt severally.*

CHORUS.

Go your ways in sundry wise,
Each upon his enterprise.
One determined to carouse,
With a garland on his brows,
And a comely lass beside him.
His opponent forth hath hied him,
Resolute to pass the night,
In a military plight,
  Undelighted and alone;
    Starving, wheezing,
    Sneezing, freezing,
  With his head upon a stone.

The action of the stage, and even all allusion to it, are suspended during the following songs, which serve to afford an interval of dramatic time during which Dicæopolis may be supposed to have returned from his feast, and Lamachus from his expedition. The Chorus remain in possession of the stage, and of their primitive privilege of desultory individual satire. The latter is directed against Antimachus, who, it seems, had given offence to the dramatic powers by the scantiness of his entertainments. I do not know whether it would be refining too much, to observe that even this capricious sally harmonizes with what has preceded, as well as with the interval which is supposed to elapse, by the culinary images, in the first part, and by the description of a person returning home late at night, in the second. Some circumstances in the original are omitted in the translation, as they seem intended to account for what does not appear unaccountable to a modern; namely, that a man should walk home at night without a stick.—In the passage which im-

mediately follows, the Chorus commence their remonstrance in a calm, sober tone which they are unable to maintain. This effect is produced in the original, by the quiet, prosaic, methodical form of words by which Antimachus is designated —a nicety of tone which it was impossible to attain, or at least to render obvious in a translation.

CHORUS.

We're determined to discuss
Our difference with Antimachus,
Calmly, simply, candidly;
Praying to the powers above,
And the just, almighty Jove,
To—sink and blast him utterly.
He that sent us all away
T'other evening from the play,
Hungry, thirsty, supperless;
Him we shortly trust to see
Sunk in equal misery,
In the like distress,
With a pennyworth of fish,
And a curious eager wish
To behold it fried;
Let him watch, and wait, and turn,
With a hungry, deep concern,
Standing there beside.
Let an accident befall,
Which shall overturn the stall,
And the fishes frying;
There shall he behold the dish
Topsy turvy, with the fish
In the kennel lying.
As he stoops to pick and wipe it,
Let a greedy greyhound gripe it,
Snatch and eat it flying.

Him let other ills befall,
Walking home beneath the wall,
Late at night, attack'd by ruffians,
Orestes and his ragamuffins;
Unprotected and alone,
Groping round to find a stone,

Let him grasp for his defence
A ponderous sir-reverence;
Furious, eager, in the dark,
Let him fling and miss the mark,
Smiting upon the cheek, but not severely,
Cratinus merely!

Messenger, Servant of Lamachus, LAMACHUS, DICÆOPOLIS *and* CHORUS.

The following speech of the Messenger is a burlesque of the tragic speeches in which the arrival of the wounded hero was announced in the last act of a Tragedy.

Messenger.

Ye slaves that dwell in Lamachus's mansion,
Prepare hot water instantly in the pipkin;*
With embrocations and emollients,
And bandages and plaister for your lord.
His foot is maim'd and crippled with a stake,
Which wounded it, as he leap'd across a trench.
His ankle-bone is out, his head is broken,
The Gorgon on his shield all smash'd and spoil'd.
But when the lofty plume of the cock lorel
That deck'd his helm, fell downward in the dirt,
He groaned, and spake aloud despairingly:
"O glorious light of Heaven.—Farewell, Farewell!
"For the last time; my destined days are done."
Thus moaning and lamenting, down he fell
Direct into the ditch; jump'd up again;
Rush'd out afresh; rallied the runaways;
Made the marauders run; ran after them,
With his spear point smiting their hinder parts.
But here he comes himself; set the door open.

* The "pipkin," in allusion to the scantiness of Lamachus's establishment. See p. 56.

Lamachus is brought in, wounded and disabled; his appearance and attendants are caricatures of the exhibition of the wounded heroes, whom it had become the fashion to introduce. The dialogue is a burlesque of the lyrical agonies and lamentations of the same personages.

Lam. Out, out alas!
I'm rack'd and torn,
With agony scarce to be borne,

From that accursed spear:
But worst of all, I fear,
If Dicæopolis beholds me here,
That he, my foe, will chuckle at my fall.
Dic. My charming lass,
What joy is this!
What ecstasy! do give me a kiss!
There coax me, and hug me close, and sympathize;
I've swigg'd the gallon off; I've won the prize.
Lam. O what a consummation of my woes,
What throbs and throes!
Dic. Eh there! my little Lamachus! How goes?
Lam. I'm in distress.
Dic. I'm in no less.
Lam. Mock not at my misery.
Dic. Accuse me not of mockery.
Lam. 'Twas at the final charge; I'd paid before
A number of the rogues; at least a score.
Dic. It was a most expensive charge you bore:
Poor Lamachus! he was forced to pay the score!
Lam. O mercy, mighty Apollo!
Dic. What, do ye holloh
A'ter Apollo? it an't his feast to-day.
Lam. (*to his bearers*).
Don't press me,
Dear friends!
But place me
Gently and tenderly.
Dic. (*to the women*)
Caress me,
Dear girls!
Embrace me
Gently and tenderly.
Lam. Strip off the incumbrance of this warlike gear,
And take me to my bed....
Dic. Strip off incumbrances, my pretty dear,
And take me to your bed.
Lam. Or bear me to the public hospital
With care.
Dic. Bring me before the judges; one and all
Look there!
I've won the prize;

As this true gallon measure testifies.
I've drunk it off.—"I triumph great and glorious."
Chor. And well you may; triumph away, good fellow; you're victorious.
Dic. To show my manhood furthermore, and spirit in the struggle,
I quaff'd it off within my breath; I gulp'd it in a guggle.*
Chor. Then take the wineskin as your due.
We triumph and rejoice with you.
Dic. Then fill my train,
And join the strain.
Chor. With all my heart;
We'll bear a part.
All. "We're triumphant, great and glorious,
"We're victorious,"
Hurrah!
We've won the day,
Wineskin and all!
Hurrah!

* Drinking without deglutition; still practised in Catalonia,—the Thracian Amystis.

THE KNIGHTS.

THE KNIGHTS.

HE following translation not being calculated for general circulation, it is not likely that it should fall into the hands of any reader whose knowledge of antiquity would not enable him to dispense with the fatigue of perusing a prefatory history. Such prefaces are already before the public, accompanying the translations of Mr. Mitchell and Mr. Walsh, and will be found satisfactory to those who may be desirous of preliminary information.

It may not, however, be altogether superfluous to fix a brief summary of preceding circumstances. We have already seen that the Poet, in his comedy of the Babylonians, had made an attack upon the leading demagogues and peculators of his time. In return for this aggression, Cleon (as described in the Acharnians)

"Had dragg'd him to the Senate House,
"And trodden him down and bellow'd over him,
"And maul'd him till he scarce escaped alive."

The Poet, however, recovered himself, and, in the Parabasis of the same play, had defied and insulted the demagogue in the most unsparing terms. In the course, however, of the following summer, Cleon, by a singular concurrence of circumstances, had been raised to the highest pitch of favour and popularity. A body of 400 Spartans having been cut off, and blockaded in an island of the Bay of Pylos, now Navarino, this disaster, in which many of the first families of Sparta were involved, induced that republic to sue for peace; which Cleon, who considered his power and influence as dependent on the continuance of the war, was determined to oppose. Insisting, therefore, that the blockaded troop could be considered in no other light than as actual prisoners, he finally pledged himself, with a given additional force, to reduce the Spartans to surrender within a limited time; this he had the good fortune and dexterity to effect, and to secure the whole credit of the result for himself; having, in virtue of his appointment, superseded the blockading general, Demosthenes; while, at the same time, he secured the benefit of his experience and ability by retaining him as a colleague. The reader, if he has the work at hand, will do well to refer to Mr. Mitford's History, c. xv., *sec.* x., *for a detailed account of this most singular incident, strikingly illustrative of the distinct character of the two rival republics. It was then, immediately after this event, when his adversary's power and popularity were at their height, that the Poet, undeterred by these apparent disadvantages, produced this memorable and extraordinary drama.*

For those readers to whom any further introduction may be necessary, a list of the Dramatis Personæ, with some accompanying explanations, will perhaps be sufficient.

DRAMATIS PERSONÆ.

Demus.—A personification of the Athenian people, the John Bull of Athens, a testy, selfish, suspicious old man, a tyrant to his slaves, with the exception of one (a new acquisition), the Paphlagonian—Cleon, by whom he is cajoled and governed.

Nicias and *Demosthenes.* } The two most fortunate and able generals of the republic, of very opposite characters; the one cautious and superstitious in the extreme; the other a blunt, hearty, resolute, jolly fellow, a very decided lover of good wine. These two, *the servants of the public*, are naturally introduced as *the slaves of Demus.* After complaining of the ill treatment to which they are subject in consequence of their master's partiality to his newly-purchased slave, the Paphlagonian, they determine to supplant him, which they effect in conformity to the directions of a secret Oracle, in which they find it predicted that the Tanner (*i.e.* Cleon the Paphlagonian) shall be superseded by a person of meaner occupation and lower character.

Cleon.—The Tanner (as he is called from his property consisting in a leather manufactory) or the Paphlagonian (a nickname, applied in ridicule of his mode of speaking, from the word *paphlazo*, to foam,) has been already described. He is represented as a fawning, obsequious slave, insolent and arrogant to all except his master, the terror of his fellow-servants.

A Sausage Seller (whose name, Agoracritus, "so called from the Agora where I got my living," is not declared till towards the conclusion of the play) is the person announced by the Oracle, as ordained by fate, to baffle the Paphlagonian, and to supersede him in the favour of his master. His breeding and education are described as having been similar to that of the younger Mr. Weller, in that admirable and most unvulgar exhibition of vulgar life, the "Pickwick Papers." Finally, after a long struggle, his undaunted vulgarity and superior dexterity are crowned with deserved success. He supplants the Paphlagonian, and is installed in the supreme direction of the old gentleman's affairs.

It appears, that the Poet must have been subjected to some particular disadvantages and embarrassments in the production of this play. We have seen, that in the preceding comedy of the Acharnians, Lamachus, a rising military character, had been personated on the stage, and had been addressed by name, without disguise or equivocation, throughout the whole of that play.—This is no longer the case in the play now before us; Nicias, Demosthenes, and Cleon himself are in no instance addressed by name.—It should seem, therefore, that some enactment must have taken place, restraining the licence of comedy in this particular; and here a distinction is to be observed between the choral parts and the dramatic dialogue; for, in this very play, Cleon is most unsparingly abused by name in the choral songs.—The fact seems to have been that the licentious privilege of the "Sacred Chorus," *consecrated by immemorial usage, and connected with the rites of Bacchus, could not be abridged by mere human authority; while the dramatic dialogue (originally derived, in all probability, from scenes in dumb show, which had been introduced to relieve the monotony of the Chorus) was regarded as mere recent invention destitute of any divine sanction, and liable to be modified and restrained by the power of the State.*

With respect to Nicias and Demosthenes, the Poet could have found no difficulty in evading the new law. The masks worn by the actors, presenting a caricature likeness of each of them, would be sufficient to identify them; and it could not be supposed that either of them would be offended at being brought forward in burlesque, when the poet's intention was evidently friendly towards them both; the whole drift of his comedy being directed against their main antagonist and rival. For the caricature in which they themselves were represented, was in no respect calculated to make them unpopular; on the contrary, the blunt heartiness and good fellowship of the one, and the timid scrupulous piety of the other, were qualities which, in different ways, recommended them respectively to the favour and good will of their fellow-citizens, and which were accordingly exhibited and impressed upon the attention of the audience, through the only medium which was consistent with the essential character of the ancient comedy.

But among the audience themselves there would undoubtedly be some gainsayers, who, if they were not silenced at the first outset, might have interrupted the attention of others.—"This is too bad," they might have said;—"the Poet will get himself into a scrape,—here is a manifest "infraction of the new law."—In order to obviate this, the Poet in the first scene, before the proper subject of his comedy is developed, but at the precise point when his individual characters (Nicias and Demosthenes) were sufficiently marked and identified, submits the question to a theatrical vote, appealing to the audience for their sanction and approbation of the course which he has adopted. This appeal, marked as it is with a character of caution and timidity, is, with a humorous propriety, assigned to the part of Nicias. With Cleon, however, the case was different; and there was a difficulty which it required all the courage and ability of the Poet to surmount—no actor dared to expose himself to the resentment of the Demagogue by personating him upon the stage; and among the artists who worked for the theatre, fearful of being considered as accomplices of the Poet in his evasion of the new law, no one could be found who would venture to produce the representation of his countenance in a theatrical mask. The Poet, therefore, undertook the part himself, and, for want of a mask, disguised his own features, according to the rude method of primitive comedy, by smearing them with the lees of wine. It is worthy of remark that, in his effort to surmount this difficulty, he has contrived to identify the Demagogue from the first moment of his appearance, concentrating his essential character and his known peculiarities in a speech of five lines,—his habitual boisterous oath and a slangish use of the dual.

In order to occupy the vacant space which has been left by the printer, the translator, is tempted for once, *to insert a justificatory comment.—The speech of Nicias in the opening page is extended to three lines; in the original it consists of a line and a half, which might be more accurately and concisely translated thus:—*

"Yes, let him perish in the worst way possible,
With all his lies, for a first-rate Paphlagonian."

But there would be one main defect in this accurate translation, namely, that it would not express the intention of the author, nor the effect produced by the actor in repeating the original; for, if we consider it in this view, we find that, short as it is, it contains three distinct breaks; one at the end of the second word, another at the end of the third, and a third at the end of the line. These momentary pauses are characteristic of timid resentment, expressing itself by fits and starts,—a character which, to the English reader perusing a printed text, could not be rendered obvious, without employing a compass of words much larger than the original.

Again we see, that the courage and anger of Nicias, even with the help of the beating which he has just received, are barely sufficient to enable him to follow the example of Demosthenes; even in wrath and pain he is contented to "say ditto" to what his comrade had said before.—The Poet's intention, in this respect, is made more distinctly palpable to the English reader by the first line of the translated speech.

And thus much may serve for a commentary on a passage of three lines, and as a sample of others; which, if they were not wearisome and egotistical, might be extended to every page of this and the preceding play.

THE KNIGHTS.

(*After a noise of lashes and screams from behind the scenes, Demosthenes comes out, and is followed by Nicias, the supposed victim of flagellation (both in the dress of slaves). Demosthenes breaks out in great wrath, while Nicias remains exhibiting various contortions of pain for the amusement of the audience.*)

Demosthenes.

UT! out alas! what a scandal! what a shame!
May Jove in his utter wrath crush and confound
That rascally new-bought Paphlagonian slave!
For from the very first day that he came—
Brought here for a plague and a mischief amongst us all,
We're beaten and abused continually.

Nic. (*whimpering in a broken voice.*)
I say so too, with all my heart I do,
A rascal, with his slanders and lies!
A rascally Paphlagonian! so he is!

Dem. (*roughly and good humouredly*).
How are you, my poor soul?

Nic. (*pettishly and whining*). Why poorly enough;
And so are you for that matter.

[*Nicias continues writhing and moaning.*

Dem. (*as if speaking to a child that had hurt himself*).
Well, come here then!

Come, and we'll cry together, both of us,
We'll sing it to Olympus's old tune.

Both (Demosthenes accompanies Nicias's involuntary sobs, so as to make a tune of them).

Mo moo momoo—momoo momoo—momoo momoo.[1]

Dem. (suddenly and heartily).

Come, grief's no use—It's folly to keep crying.
Let's look about us a bit what's best to be done.

Nic. (recovering himself).

Ay, tell me; what do you think?

Dem. No; you tell me—
Lest we should disagree.

Nic. That's what I won't!
Do you speak boldly first, and I'll speak next.

Dem. (significantly, as quoting a well-known verse).

"You first might utter, what I wish to tell."[2]

Nic. Ay, but I'm so down-hearted, I've not spirit
To bring about the avowal cleverly,
In Euripides's style, by question and answer.

Dem. Well, then, don't talk of Euripides any more,
Or his mother either; don't stand picking endive:*
But think of something in another style,
To the tune of "Trip and away."

* His mother was said to have been an herb woman. See Ach. p. 24, 25.

Nic. Yes, I'll contrive it:
Say "Let us" first; put the first letter to it,
And then the last, and then put E, R, T.
"Let us Az ert." I say, "Let us Azert."
'Tis now your turn—take the next letter to it.
Put B for A.

Dem. "Let us Bezert" I say—

Nic. 'Tis now my turn—"Let us Cezert," I say;
'Tis now your turn.

---

[1] Our common tune, with a syllable added to it, may be made to suit the trimeter iambic, and may be sung lamentably enough.

"When War's alarms first tore my Willy from { me." / my arms. }

A friend who has accidentally taken up this sheet, tells me that he heard this very chaunt, 'Mo moo," &c., on the coast opposite Corfu, in a house where the family were moaning over the dead.

[2] From the tragedy of Hippolytus (v. 345): Phædra is trying to lead her nurse to mention the name of Hippolytus, while she avoids it herself.

Dem. "Let us Dezert," I say.
Nic. You've said it!—and I agree to it—now repeat it
Once more!
Dem. Let us Dezert! Let us Dezert!
Nic. That's well.
Dem. But somehow it seems unlucky, rather,
An awkward omen to meet with in a morning!
"To meet with our Deserts!"
Nic. That's very true;
Therefore I think, in the present state of things,
The best thing for us both, would be, to go
Directly to the shrine of one of the gods;
And pray for mercy, both of us together.
Dem. Shrines? shrines? Why, sure, you don't believe in the gods.
Nic. I do.
Dem. But what's your argument? Where's your proof?
Nic. Because I feel they persecute me and hate me,
In spite of everything I try to please 'em.
Dem. Well, well. That's true; you're right enough in that.
Nic. Let's settle something.
Dem. Come then,—if you like,—
I'll state our case at once, to the audience here.
Nic. It would not be much amiss; but, first of all,
We must entreat of them, if the scene and action
Have entertain'd them hitherto, to declare it,
And encourage us with a little applause beforehand.
Dem. (*to the audience*).
Well, come now! I'll tell ye about it—Here are we
A couple of servants—with a master at home
Next door to the hustings.—He's a man in years,
A kind of a bean-fed,* husky, testy character,
Coleric and brutal at times, and partly deaf.
It's near about a month now, that he went
And bought a slave out of a tanner's yard,
A Paphlagonian born, and brought him home,
As wicked a slanderous wretch as ever lived.
This fellow, the Paphlagonian, has found out
The blind side of our master's understanding,
With fawning and wheedling in this kind of way:

* In allusio to the beans used in balloting.

"Would not you please go to the bath, Sir? surely
It's not worth while to attend the courts to-day."*—
And, "Would not you please to take a little refreshment?
And there's that nice hot broth—And here's the three-
pence
You left behind you—And would not you order supper?"

* Sacrifices with distribution of meat, and largesses to the people on holidays.

Moreover, when we get things out of compliment
As a present for our master, he contrives
To snatch 'em and serve 'em up before our faces.
I'd made a Spartan cake at Pylos lately,
And mix'd and kneaded it well, and watch'd the baking;
But he stole round before me and served it up:
And he never allows us to come near our master
To speak a word; but stands behind his back
At meal-times, with a monstrous leathern fly-flap,
Slapping and whisking it round and rapping us off.
Sometimes the old man falls into moods and fancies,
Searching the prophecies till he gets bewilder'd;
And then the Paphlagonian plies him up,
Driving him mad with oracles and predictions.
And that's his harvest. Then he slanders us,
And gets us beaten and lash'd, and goes his rounds
Bullying in this way, to squeeze presents from us:
"You saw what a lashing Hylas got just now;
You'd best make friends with me, if you love your lives."
Why then, we give him a trifle, or if we don't,
We pay for it; for the old fellow knocks us down,
And kicks us on the ground, and stamps and rages,
And tramples out the very guts of us.—
(*turning to Nicias*)
So now, my worthy fellow, we must take
A fix'd determination;—now's the time,
Which way to turn ourselves and what to do.

Nic. Our last determination was the best:
That which we settled to A' Be Cè *De-zert.*

Dem. Ay, but we could not escape the Paphlagonian,
He overlooks us all; he keeps one foot
In Pylos, and another in the assembly;
And stands with such a stature, stride, and grasp,
That while his mouth is open in Eatolia,†
One hand is firmly clench'd upon the Lucrians,
And the other stretching forth to the Peribribèans.

† Etolia. Locrians. Perrhebians.

Nic. (*in utter despondency, but with a sort of quiet quakerish composure*).
Let's die then, once for all; that's the best way,
Only we must contrive to manage it,
Nobly and manfully in a proper manner.

Dem. Ay, ay—Let's do things manfully! that's my maxim!

Nic. (*as before*). Well, there's the example of Themistocles—
To drink bull's blood: that seems a manly death.

Dem. Bull's blood! The blood of the grape, I say! good wine!
Who knows? it might inspire some plan, some project,
Some notion or other, a good draught of it!

Nic. Wine truly! wine!—still hankering after liquor!
Can wine do anything for us? Will your drink
Enable you to arrange a plan to save us?
Can wisdom ever arise from wine, do ye think?

Dem. Do ye say so? You're a poor spring-water pitcher!
A silly, chilly soul. I'll tell ye what:
It's a very presumptuous thing to speak of liquor,*
As an obstacle to people's understanding;
It's the only thing for business and despatch.
D'ye observe how individuals thrive and flourish
By dint of drink: they prosper in proportion;
They improve their properties; they get promotion;
Make speeches, and make interest, and make friends.
Come, quick now—bring me a lusty stoup of wine,
To moisten my understanding and inspire me.

Nic. Oh dear! your drink will be the ruin of us!

Dem. It will be the making of ye!—Bring it here.
[*Exit Nicias.*
I'll rest me a bit; but when I've got my fill,
I'll overflow them all, with a flood of rhetoric,
With metaphors and phrases, and what not.
[*Nicias returns in a sneaking way with a pot of wine.*

Nic. (*in a sheepish, silly tone of triumph*).
How lucky for me it was, that I escaped
With the wine that I took!

Dem. (*carelessly and bluntly*). Well, where's the Paphlagonian?

* Though Dem. has not been drinking, his speech has the tone of a drunken man.

Nic. (*as before*). He's fast asleep—within there, on his back,
On a heap of hides—the rascal! with his belly full,
With a hash of confiscations half-digested.

Dem. That's well!—Now fill me a hearty, lusty draught.

Nic. (*formally and precisely*).
Make the libation first, and drink this cup
To the good Genius.

Dem. (*respiring after a long draught*). O most worthy Genius!
Good Genius! 'tis your genius that inspires me!

[*Demosthenes remains in a sort of drunken burlesque ecstasy.*

Nic. Why, what's the matter?

Dem. I'm inspired to tell you,
That you must steal the Paphlagonian's Oracles
Whilst he's asleep.[1]

Nic. Oh dear, then, I'm afraid,
This Genius will turn out my evil Genius. [*Exit Nicias.*

Dem. Come, I must meditate, and consult my pitcher;
And moisten my understanding a little more.

[*The interval of Nicias's absence is occupied by action in dumb show: Demosthenes is enjoying himself and getting drunk in private.*

Nic. (*re-entering with a packet*).
How fast asleep the Paphlagonian was!
Lord bless me, how mortally he snored and farted.
However, I've contrived to carry it off,
The sacred Oracle that he kept so secret—
I've stolen it from him.

Dem. (*very drunk*). That's my clever fellow!
Here, give us hold; I must read 'em. Fill me a bumper—
In the meanwhile—make haste now. Let me see now—
What have we got?—What are they,—these same papers?
Oh! oracles! . . . o — ra — cles!—Fill me a stoup of wine.

[*In this part of the scene a contrast is kept up between the subordinate, nervous eagerness of poor Nicias, and the predominant drunken, phlegmatic indiffer-*

---

[1] A general feature of human nature, nowhere more observable than among boys at school; where the poor timid soul is always despatched upon the most perilous expeditions.—Nicias is the fag—Demosthenes the big boy.

ence of Demosthenes; who is supposed to amuse himself with irritating the impatience of his companion, while he details to him by driblets the contents of his own packet.

Nic. (*fidgeting and impatient after giving him the wine*).
Come! come! what says the Oracle?
Dem. Fill it again!
Nic. Does the Oracle say, that I must fill it again?
Dem. (*after tumbling over the papers with a hiccup*).
O Bakis!*
Nic. What?
Dem. Fill me the stoup this instant.
Nic. (*with a sort of puzzled acquiescence*).
Well, Bakis, I've been told, was given to drink;
He prophesied in his liquor people say.
Dem. (*with the papers in his hand*).
Ay, there it is,—you rascally Paphlagonian!
This was the prophecy that you kept so secret.
Nic. What's there?
Dem. Why there's a thing to ruin him,
With the manner of his destruction, all foretold.
Nic. As how?
Dem. (*very drunk*). Why the Oracle tells you how, distinctly,
And all about it—in a perspicuous manner—
*That a jobber in hemp and flax is first ordain'd
To hold the administration of affairs.
Nic. Well, there's one jobber. Who's the next? Read on!
Dem. *A cattle jobber must succeed to him.
Nic. More jobbers! well—then what becomes of him?
Dem. He too shall prosper, till a viler rascal
Shall be raised up, and shall prevail against him,
In the person of a Paphlagonian tanner,
A loud, rapacious, leather-selling ruffian.
Nic. Is it foretold, then, that the cattle jobber
Must be destroy'd by the seller of leather?
Dem. Yes.
Nic. Oh dear! our sellers and jobbers are at an end.
Dem. Not yet; there's still another to succeed him,
Of a most uncommon notable occupation.
Nic. Who's that? Do tell me!
Dem. Must I?

* Dem.'s articulation of this word is assisted by a hiccup.

* After the death of Pericles, Eucrates and Lysicles had each taken the lead for a short time.

Nic. To be sure—

Dem. A sausage-seller it is, that supersedes him.

Nic. (*in the tone of Dominie Sampson*).
A sausage-seller! marvellous indeed,
Most wonderful! But where can he be found?

Dem. We must seek him out.

[*Demosthenes rises and bustles up, with the action of a person who having been drunk is rousing and recollecting himself for a sudden important occasion. His following speeches are all perfectly sober.*

Nic. But see there, where he comes!
ent hither providentially, as it were!

Dem. O happy man! celestial sausage-seller!
Friend, guardian and protector of us all!
Come forward; save your friends, and save the country.

S. S. Do you call me?

Dem. Yes, we call'd to you, to announce
The high and happy destiny that awaits you.

Nic. Come, now you should set him free from the incumbrance[1]
Of his table and basket; and explain to him
The tenor and the purport of the Oracle,
While I go back to watch the Paphlagonian. [*Exit Nicias.*

Dem. (*to the Sausage-seller gravely*).
Set these poor wares aside; and now,—bow down
To the ground; and adore the powers of earth and heaven.

S. S. Heigh day! Why, what do you mean?

Dem. O happy man!
Unconscious of your glorious destiny,
Now mean and unregarded; but to-morrow,
The mightiest of the mighty, Lord of Athens!

S. S. Come, master, what's the use of making game?
Why can't ye let me wash the guts and tripe,
And sell my sausages in peace and quiet?

Dem. O simple mortal, cast those thoughts aside!

---

[1] This speech is intended to express the sudden impression of reverence with which Nicias is affected in the presence of the predestined supreme Sausage-seller.—He does not presume to address him; but obliquely manifests his respect by pointing out to Demosthenes (in his hearing) the marks of attention to which he is entitled.

Bid guts and tripe farewell !—Look there !—Behold
[*Pointing to the audience.*
The mighty assembled multitude before ye !
S. S. (*with a grumble of indifference*).
I see 'em.
Dem. You shall be their lord and master,
The sovereign and the ruler of them all,
Of the assemblies and tribunals, fleets and armies ;
You shall trample down the senate under foot,
Confound and crush the generals and commanders,
Arrest, imprison, and confine in irons,
And feast and fornicate in the council house.[1]
S. S. What I ?
Dem. Yes, you yourself : there's more to come.
Mount here ; and from the tressels of your stall
Survey the subject islands circling round.
S. S. I see 'em.
Dem. And all their ports and merchant vessels ?
S. S. Yes all.
Dem. Then ain't you a fortunate happy man ?
Ain't you content ?—Come then for a further prospect—
Turn your right eye to Caria, and your left
To Carthage !*—and contemplate both together.
S. S. Will it do me good, d'ye think, to learn to squint ?
Dem. Not so ; but everything you see before you
Must be disposed of at your high discretion,
By sale or otherwise ; for the oracle
Predestines you to sovereign power and greatness.
S. S. Are there any means of making a great man
Of a sausage-selling fellow such as I ?
Dem. The very means you have, must make ye so,
Low breeding, vulgar birth and impudence,
These, these must make ye, what you're meant to be.
S. S. I can't imagine that I'm good for much.
Dem. Alas! But why do ye say so?—What's the meaning
Of these misgivings ? I discern within ye
A promise and an inward consciousness

* "Carthage" must be the true reading, the right eye to "Caria" and the left to "Chalcedon" would not constitute a squint.

[1] The Prytaneum, see "Acharnians," v. 151 : the honour of a seat at the public table was sometimes conferred on persons of extraordinary merit in advanced years. See the Parabasis of this play—See also the Apology of Socrates. Cleon had obtained this privilege for himself, and abused it insolently, as appears elsewhere.

Of greatness. Tell me truly; are ye allied
To the families of gentry?
S. S. Naugh, not I;
I'm come from a common, ordinary kindred,
Of the lower order.
Dem. What a happiness!—
What a footing will it give ye! What a groundwork
For confidence and favour at your outset!
S. S. But bless ye! only consider my education!
I can but barely read . . . in a kind of a way.
Dem. That makes against ye!—The only thing against ye—
The being able to read in any way:
For now no lead nor influence is allow'd
To liberal arts or learned education,
But to the brutal, base, and under-bred.
Embrace then and hold fast the promises
Which the Oracles of the gods announce to you.
S. S. But what does the Oracle say?
Dem. Why thus it says,
In a figurative language, but withal
Most singularly intelligible and distinct,
Neatly express'd i' faith, concisely and tersely.[1]

" Moreover, when the eagle in his pride,
With crooked talons and a leathern hide,
Shall seize the black and blood-devouring snake;
Then shall the woeful tanpits quail and quake;
And mighty Jove shall give command and place
To mortals of the sausage-selling race;
Unless they choose, continuing as before,
To sell their sausages for evermore."
S. S. But how does this concern me? Explain it, will ye?
Dem. The leathern eagle is the Paphlagonian.
S. S. What are his talons?
Dem. That explains itself—
Talons for peculation and rapacity.

---

[1] This is perfectly in character. Demosthenes (as we have seen, p. 73, v. 44) does not profess to believe in the gods; yet we see that upon occasion he can discuss the merit of the "sacred classics;" like other critics, therefore, of the same description, he does it with a sort of patronizing tone.

S. S. But what's the snake?
Dem. The snake is clear and obvious:
The snake is long and black, like a black pudding.
The snake is fill'd with blood, like a black pudding.
Our Oracle foretells then, that the snake
Shall baffle and overpower the leathern eagle.
S. S. These oracles hit my fancy! Notwithstanding . . .
I'm partly doubtful, how I could contrive . . .
To manage an administration altogether . . .
Dem. The easiest thing in nature!—nothing easier!
Stick to your present practice: follow it up
In your new calling. Mangle, mince and mash,
Confound and hack, and jumble things together!
And interlard your rhetoric, with lumps
Of mawkish sweet, and greasy flattery.
Be fulsome, coarse, and bloody!—For the rest,
All qualities combine, all circumstances,
To entitle and equip you for command;
A filthy voice, a villanous countenance,
A vulgar birth, and parentage, and breeding.
Nothing is wanting—absolutely nothing.
And the oracles and responses of the gods,
And prophecies, all conspire in your behalf.—
Place then this chaplet on your brows!—and worship
The anarchic powers; and rouse your spirits up
To encounter him.—
S. S. But who do ye think will help me?
For all our wealthier people are alarm'd
And terrified at him; and the meaner sort
In a manner stupefied, grown dull and dumb.
Dem. Why there's a thousand lusty cavaliers,
Ready to back you, that detest and scorn him;
And every worthy, well-born citizen;
And every candid, critical spectator;
And I myself; and the help of Heaven to boot:—
And never fear; his face will not be seen,
For all the manufacturers of masks,
From cowardice, refused to model it.
It matters not; his person will be known:
Our audience is a shrewd one—they can guess.
Nicias (in alarm from behind the scenes).
Oh dear! oh dear! the Paphlagonian 's coming.

Enter Cleon with a furious look and voice.

Cleon. By heaven and earth! you shall abide it dearly,
With your conspiracies and daily plots
Against the sovereign people!—Hah! what's this?—
What's this Chalcidian goblet doing here?—
Are ye tempting the Chalcidians to revolt?—*
Dogs! villains! every soul of ye shall die.
[*The Sausage-seller runs off in a fright.*

* The Chalcidians did in fact revolt in the following year; their intentions were probably suspected at the time.

Dem. Where are ye going?—Where are ye running?—
Stop!
Stand firm, my noble, valiant, sausage-seller!
Never betray the cause. Your friends are nigh.
(*to the Chorus.*)
Cavaliers and noble captains! now's the time! advance in sight!
March in order—make the movement, and out-flank him on the right!
(*to the Sausage-seller.*)
There I see them bustling, hasting!—only turn and make a stand,
Stop but only for a moment, your allies are hard at hand.

It is necessary to repair an omission which the reader may have already noticed: among the Dramatis Personæ enumerated in pages 66-67 no mention has been made of the Chorus, from which, as usual, the comedy derived its title— THE KNIGHTS. This body composing the middle order of the state were, as it appears, decidedly hostile to Cleon.— In the first lines of the preceding play, the merit of having procured his conviction and punishment on a charge of bribery is ascribed to them; and again in the same play the Chorus express their detestation of the demagogue by threatening to sacrifice him to the vengeance of the Knights,† and we have just seen that Demosthenes encourages the Sausage-seller by promising him the assistance of a thousand of them,—" lusty cavaliers," who " scorn and detest " his antagonist.

† See Ach. p. 18, v. 358.

[*During the last lines the Chorus of cavaliers with their hobby horses have entered and occupied their position in the orchestra. They begin their attack upon Cleon.*

Chorus. Close around him, and confound him, the confounder of us all.
Pelt him, pummel him and mawl him; rummage, ransack, overhaul him,
Overbear him and out-bawl him; bear him down and bring him under.
Bellow like a burst of thunder, robber! harpy! sink of plunder!
Rogue and villain! rogue and cheat! rogue and villain I repeat!
Oftener than I can repeat it, has the rogue and villain cheated.
Close around him left and right; spit upon him; spurn and smite:
Spit upon him as you see; spurn and spit at him like me.—
But beware or he'll evade ye, for he knows the private track,
Where Eucrates * was seen escaping, with the mill dust on his back.

Cleon. Worthy veterans of the jury, you that, either right or wrong,
With my three-penny provision,† I've maintain'd and cherish'd long,
Come to my aid! I'm here waylaid—assassinated and betray'd!

Chorus. Rightly served! we serve you rightly, for your hungry love of pelf,
For your gross and greedy rapine, gormandizing by yourself;
You that ere the figs are gather'd, pilfer with a privy twitch
Fat delinquents and defaulters, pulpy, luscious, plump and rich;
Pinching, fingering and pulling—tampering, selecting, culling,
With a nice survey discerning, which are green and which are turning,
Which are ripe for accusation, forfeiture and confiscation.
Him besides, the wealthy man, retired upon an easy rent,
Hating and avoiding party, noble-minded, indolent,
Fearful of official snares, intrigues and intricate affairs;
Him you mark; you fix and hook him, whilst he's gaping unawares;
At a fling, at once you bring him hither from the Chersonese,‡

* See note to p. 77.—He was also an owner of mills, as appears by the scholiast.

† The Juryman's fee, a means of subsistence to poor old men driven from their homes by the war.

‡ Of Thrace. Many Athenians possessed estates, and resided there for a quiet life.

Down you cast him, roast and baste him, and devour him at your ease.

Cleon. Yes! assault, insult, abuse me! this is the return I find,
For the noble testimony, the memorial I design'd:
Meaning to propose proposals for a monument of stone,
On the which your late achievements * should be carved and neatly done.

* In the expedition to Corinth.

Chorus. Out, away with him! the slave! the pompous, empty, fawning knave!
Does he think with idle speeches to delude and cheat us all?
As he does the doting elders, that attend his daily call.†
Pelt him here, and bang him there; and here and there and every where.

† The veterans of the Jury; see note †, p. 83.

Cleon. Save me, neighbours! Oh, the monsters! O my side, my back, my breast!

Chorus. What you're forced to call for help? You brutal, overbearing pest.

S. S. (*returning to Cleon.*)
I'll astound you with my voice, with my bawling looks and noise.

Chorus. If in bawling you surpass him, you'll achieve a victor's crown;
If again you overmatch him, in impudence, the day's our own.

Cleon. I denounce this traitor here, for sailing on clandestine trips,
With supplies of tripe and stuffing to careen the Spartan ships.

S. S. I denounce then and accuse him for a greater, worse abuse:
That he steers his empty paunch, and anchors at the public board;
Running in without a lading, to return completely stored!

Chorus. Yes! and smuggles out moreover loaves and luncheons not a few,
More than ever Pericles, in all his pride, presumed to do.

Cleon. (*in a thundering tone*). Dogs and villains, you shall die!

S. S. (*in a louder shriller tone*).
Ay! I can scream ten times as high.

Cleon. I'll overbear ye, and out-bawl ye.

S. S. But I'll out-scream ye, and out-squall ye.

Cleon. I'll impeach you, whilst abroad,
Commanding on a foreign station.
S. S. I'll have you sliced, and slash'd, and scored.*
Cleon. Your lion's skin of reputation,
Shall be flay'd off your back and tann'd.
S. S. I'll take those guts of yours in hand.
Cleon. Come, bring your eyes and mine to meet!
And stare at me without a wink!
S. S. Yes! in the market place and street,
I had my birth and breeding too;
And from a boy, to blush or blink,
I scorn the thing as much as you.
Cleon. I'll denounce you if you mutter.
S. S. I'll douce ye the first word you utter.
Cleon. My thefts are open and avow'd;
And I confess them, which you dare not.
S. S. But I can take false oaths aloud,
And in the presence of a crowd:
And if they know the fact I care not.
Cleon. What! do you venture to invade
My proper calling and my trade?
—But I denounce here, on the spot,
The sacrificial tripe you've got;
The tithe it owes was never paid:
It owes a tithe, I say, to Jove;
You've wrong'd and robb'd the powers above.

* The threats of each party are in the terms of their respective trades.

Chorus. *Cretic Metre.*†

† See note to Ach. p. 15.

Dark and unsearchably profound abyss,
Gulf of unfathomable
Baseness and iniquity!
Miracle of immense,
Intense impudence!
Every court, every hall,
Juries and assemblies, all
Are stunn'd to death, deafen'd all,
Whilst you bawl.
The bench and bar Ring and jar.
Each decree Smells of thee,
Land and sea Stink of thee,
Whilst we

Scorn and hate, execrate, abominate,
Thee the brawler and embroiler of the nation and the state.
You that on the rocky seat of our assembly raise a din,
Deafening all our ears with uproar, as you rave and howl and grin;
Watching all the while the vessels with revenue sailing in.
Like the tunny-fishers perch'd aloft, to look about and bawl,
When the shoals are seen arriving, ready to secure a haul.

Cleon. I was aware of this affair, and every stitch of it I know,
Where the plot was cobbled up and patch'd together, long ago.

S. S. Cobbling is your own profession, tripe and sausages are mine:
But the country folks complain, that in a fraudulent design,[1]
You retail'd them skins of treaties, that appear'd like trusty leather,
Of a peace secure and lasting; but the wear-and-tear and weather
Proved it all decay'd and rotten, only fit for sale and show.

Dem. Yes! a pretty trick he served me; there was I dispatch'd to go,
Trudged away to Pergasæ, but found upon arriving there,[1]
That myself and my commission, both were out at heels and bare.

In a review of Mr. Mitchell's Aristophanes, a passage in his translation of one of the choruses is noted with particular commendation. It is said, " Mr. Mitchell has hit upon the " very key-note of Aristophanes, whose choruses are so con- " trived throughout this play, as to afford a relief and " contrast to the vulgar acrimony of the dialogue; not in " their logical and grammatical sense, but in their form and " rhythm, and in the selection of the words, which, if heard " imperfectly, would appear to belong to a grave or tender " or beautiful subject." If the occasion had admitted of it,

---

[1] The allusions in these lines relate to some incidents not recorded in history, some artifice by which Cleon had succeeded in deluding and disappointing the party, the country people in particular (long excluded from the enjoyment of their property), who were anxious for peace.

this observation might have been applied more particularly to the first lines of each chorus; for we may remark instances in which the contrast of grave or graceful lines at the commencement, was intended to give additional force to the vehemence of invective immediately following in the chorus itself. Thus, in the original of the chorus which is given above, an expression of wonder and awe is conveyed to the ear by the mere rhythm of the first line, independent of, and in fact, contradictory to the sense of the words themselves, a kind of contrast which appeared unattainable in the English language.—What could not, therefore, be accomplished by "form and rhythm," has, in this instance, been attempted by "the selection of words." But justificatory criticism has already been renounced as absurd and tiresome. This note had been begun, solely for the purpose of bringing under the notice of the reader, with due modification, the observation, somewhat too largely expressed, in the review above mentioned.*

* O altitudo!!

CHORUS.

Even in your tender years,
And your early disposition,
You betray'd an inward sense
Of the conscious impudence,
Which constitutes a politician.
Hence you squeeze and drain alone the rich milch kine of our allies;
Whilst the son of Hippodamus licks his lips with longing eyes.
But now, with eager rapture we behold
A mighty miscreant of baser mould!
A more consummate ruffian!
An energetic ardent ragamuffin!
Behold him there!—He stands before your eyes,
To bear you down, with a superior frown,
A fiercer stare,
And more incessant and exhaustless lies.

The metre of the lines which follow, namely, the tetrameter-iambic, is so essentially base and vulgar, that no English song afforded a specimen fit to be quoted, and the songs themselves were not proper to be mentioned; at last,

Mr. Cornewall Lewis (whose kind importunities had extorted the publication of the preceding play of the Acharnians) suggested, as a producible specimen, the first line of a sufficiently vulgar, but otherwise inoffensive song,

"A Captain bold of Halifax, who lived in country quarters."

It would not be right that Mr. Lewis's name should be mentioned here, without an acknowledgment of the obligations due to him, for his friendly zeal in forwarding that play through the press, and correcting some inaccuracies incidental to the work of a very unsystematic scholar.

The metre, of which so derogatory a character has been given, is always appropriated in the comedies of Aristophanes, to those scenes of argumentative altercation, in which the ascendancy is given to the more ignoble character; in this respect it stands in decided contrast with the anapæstic measure.

Iambic Tetrameter.

Chorus (to the Sausage-seller).

Now then do you, that boast a birth, from whence you might inherit,
And from your breeding have derived a manhood and a spirit,
Unbroken by the rules of art, untamed by education,
Shew forth the native impudence and vigour of the nation!

S. S. Well; if you like then, I'll describe the nature of him clearly,
The kind of rogue I've known him for.

Cleon. My friend, you're somewhat early.
First give *me* leave to speak.

S. S. I won't, by Jove! Ay, you may bellow!
I'll make you know, before I go, that I'm the baser fellow.

Chorus. Ay! stand to that! Stick to the point; and for a further glory,
Say that your family were base, time out of mind before ye.

Cleon. Let me speak first!

S. S. I won't.

Cleon. You shall, by Jove!

S. S. I won't, by Jove, though!

Cleon. By Jupiter, I shall burst with rage!

S. S. No matter, I'll prevent you.

Chorus. No; don't prevent, for Heaven's sake! Don't hinder him from bursting.

Cleon. What means,—what ground of hope have you? —to dare to speak against me?

S. S. What! I can speak! and I can chop—garlic and lard and logic.

Cleon. Ay! you're a speaker, I suppose! I should enjoy to see you,
Like a pert scullion set to cook—to see your talents fairly
Put to the test, with hot blood-raw disjointed news arriving,*
Obliged to hash and season it—and dish it in an instant.
You're like the rest of 'em—the swarm of paltry weak pretenders.
You've made your pretty speech, perhaps, and gain'd a little lawsuit
Against a merchant foreigner, by dint of water-drinking,
And lying long awake o'nights, composing and repeating,
And studying as you walk'd the streets, and wearing out the patience
Of all your friends and intimates, with practising beforehand:
And now you wonder at yourself, elated and delighted
At your own talent for debate—you silly saucy coxcomb.

* When the character of the debate is suddenly changed, by the receipt of unexpected intelligence.

S. S. What's your own diet? How do you contrive to keep the city
Passive and hush'd?—What kind of drink drives ye to that presumption?

Cleon. Why mention any man besides, that's capable to match me;
That, after a sound hearty meal of tunny fish and cutlets,
Can quaff my gallon; and at once without premeditation,
With slang and jabber overpower the generals at Pylos.†

† See Mitford, ch. xv. sect. 10, p. 293.

S. S. But I can eat my paunch of pork, my liver, and my haslets,
And scoup the sauce with both my hands; and with my dirty fingers
I'll seize old Nicias by the throat, and choke the grand debaters.

Chorus. We like your scheme in some respects; but still that style of feeding,
Keeping the sauce all to yourself, appears a gross proceeding.

Cleon. But I can domineer and dine on mullets at Miletus.

S. S. And I can eat my shins of beef, and farm the mines of silver.

Cleon. I'll burst into the Council House, and storm and blow and bluster.

S. S. I'll blow the wind into your tail, and kick you like a bladder.

Cleon. I'll tie you neck and heels at once, and kick ye to the kennel.

Chorus. Begin with us then! Try your skill!—kicking us all together!

Cleon. I'll have ye pilloried in a trice.
S. S. I'll have you tried for cowardice.
Cleon. I'll tan your hide to cover seats.
S. S. Yours shall be made a purse for cheats.
The luckiest skin* that could be found.
Cleon. Dog, I'll pin you to the ground
With ten thousand tenter hooks.
S. S. I'll equip you for the cooks,
Neatly prepared, with skewers and lard.
Cleon. I'll pluck your eye-brows off, I will.
S S. I'll cut your collops out, I will.

* It is well known that purses made from the skins of different animals are more or less lucky.—Among ourselves the skin of a weasel, or of a *black* cat, is esteemed the most universally lucky.

It is evident, that a scuffle or wrestling match takes place here between the two rivals. It continues during the verses of Demosthenes and those of the Chorus; the last of which mark, that the Sausage-seller has the advantage; and the Sausage-seller's speech of four lines, which follows, implies that he is at the same time exhibiting his adversary in a helpless posture.

It is to be observed, that the palæstra was not a mere school of wrestling or boxing.—The attention of the masters of the palæstra (like the dancing masters of former times in France and England) was directed to form their pupils to a general dignity and elegance of carriage.

Hence all awkward or indecent effort was disallowed in the palæstra of the better educated class.—But, as wrestling was an universal national exercise, it would of course be practised vulgarly among the vulgar; and there would be many tricks and casts retained and practised by the lowest class, which were rejected by the more dignified palæstra. The Sausage-seller was represented as foiling his opponent, by some unbecoming, unsightly effort, which was characteristic of a town blackguard.—Thus, the scuffle between them formed a kind of dumb show, analogous to and illustrative of the dialogue; exhibiting in the triumph of the Sausage-seller, the peculiar advantages reserved for superior impudence and vulgarity both in word and deed.

DEMOSTHENES.

Yes, by Jove! and like a swine,
Dangling at the butcher's door,
Dress him cleanly, neat and fine,
Wash'd and scalded o'er and o'er;
Strutting out in all his pride,
With his carcase open wide,
And a skewer in either side;
While the cook with keen intent,
By the steady rules of art,
Scrutinizes every part,
The tongue, the throat, the maw, the vent.

CHORUS.

Some element may prove more fierce than fire!
Some viler scoundrel may be seen,
Than ever yet has been!
And many a speech hereafter, many a word,
More villanous than ever yet was heard.
We marvel at thy prowess and admire!
Therefore proceed!
In word and deed,
Be firm and bold,
Keep stedfast hold!
Only keep your hold upon him! Persevere as you began;
He'll be daunted and subdued; I know the nature of the man.

S. S. Such as here you now behold him, all his life has he been known.
Till he reap'd a reputation, in a harvest not his own;
Now he shews the sheaves* at home, that he clandestinely convey'd,
Tied and bound and heap'd together, till his bargain can be made.

* The Spartan prisoners taken at Pylos, and kept in the most severe confinement.

Cleon. (*released and recovering himself.*)
I'm at ease, I need not fear ye, with the senate on my side,
And the commons all dejected, humble, poor and stupefied.

CHORUS.

Mark his visage! and behold,
How brazen, unabash'd and bold!
How the colour keeps its place
In his face!

Cleon. Let me be the vilest thing, the mattress that Cratinus* stains;
Or be forced to learn to sing Morsimus's† tragic strains;
If I don't despise and loathe, scorn and execrate ye both.

* The famous comic poet, now grown old, and infirm, as it appears!
† Ridiculed elsewhere as a bad writer of tragedy. See the *Peace* l. 775. Ed. Bekk.

CHORUS.

Active, eager, airy thing!
Ever hovering on the wing,
Ever hovering and discovering
Golden sweet secreted honey,
Nature's mintage and her money.
—May thy maw be purged and scour'd,
From the gobbets it devour'd
By the emetic drench of law!
With the cheerful ancient saw,
Then we shall rejoice and sing,
Chaunting out with hearty glee,
"Fill a bumper merrily,
"For the merry news I bring!"
But he, the shrewd and venerable
Manciple‡ of the public table,
Will chaunt and chuckle and rejoice,
With heart and voice.

‡ The old butler and steward of the Prytaneum who had hitherto been used to well-bred company and civil treatment, would be overjoyed at his deliverance from such a guest as Cleon.

Cleon. May I never eat a slice, at any public sacrifice,
If your effrontery and pretence, shall daunt my stedfast impudence.

S. S. Then, by the memory which I value, of all the bastings in our alley,
When from the dog-butcher's tray I stole the lumps of meat away,—

I trust to match you with a feat, and do credit to my meat,
Credit to my meat and feeding, and my bringing up and breeding.

Cleon. Dog's meat! What a dog art thou!—But I shall dog thee fast enow.

[*Cleon pays no attention to the short dialogue which follows between the Sausage-seller and the Chorus.—The actor's part was in dumb show, exhibiting a mimicry of the Demagogue's usual gesture and deportment, when exciting himself in preparation for a vehement burst of oratory.*

S. S. Then, there were other petty tricks, I practised as a child;
Haunting about the butchers' shops, the weather being mild,
"See boys," says I, "the swallow there!—Why summer's come, I say,"
And when they turn'd to gape and stare, I snatch'd a steak away.

Chorus. A clever lad you must have been, you managed matters rarely,
To steal at such an early day, so seasonable and fairly.

S. S. But if by chance they spied it, I contrived to hide it handily;
Clapping it in between my hams, tight and close and even;
Calling on all the powers above, and all the gods in heaven;
And there I stood, and made it good, with staring and forswearing,
So that a statesman of the time, a speaker shrewd and witty,
Was heard to say, "That boy one day will surely rule the city."

Chorus. 'Twas fairly guess'd, by the true test, by your address and daring,
First in stealing, then concealing, and again in swearing.

Cleon. I'll settle ye! Yes, both of ye! the storm of elocution
Is rising here within my breast, to drive you to confusion,
And with a wild commotion, overwhelm the land and ocean.

S. S. Then I shall hand my sausages, and reef 'em close and tight,
And steer away before the wind, and run you out of sight.

Dem. And I shall go, to the hold below, to see that all is right. [*Exit.*

Cleon. By the holy goddess, I declare
Rogue and robber as you are,
I'll not brook it, or overlook it;
The public treasure that you stole,
I'll force you to refund the whole . . . .

Chorus. (Keep near and by—the gale grows high.)

Cleon. (*in continuation.*)
. . . Ten talents, I could prove it here,
Were sent to you from Potidæa.

S. S. Well, will you take a single one
To stop your bawling and have done?

Chorus. Yes I'll be bound—he'll compound,
And take a share—the wind grows fair.
This hurricane will overblow,
Fill the sails and let her go!

Cleon. I'll indict ye, I'll impeach,
I'll denounce ye in a speech;
With four several accusations,
For your former peculations,
Of a hundred talents each.

S. S. But I'll denounce ye,
And I'll trounce ye,
With accusations half-a-score;
Half a score, for having left
Your rank in the army; and for theft
I'll charge ye with a thousand more.

Cleon. I'll rummage out your pedigree,
And prove that all your ancestry
Were sacrilegious and accurst.*

S. S. I'll prove the same of yours; and first
The foulest treasons and the worst—
Their deep contrivance to conceal
Plots against the common weal;
Which I shall publish and declare,—
Publish, and depose and swear.

Cleon. Plots, conceal'd and hidden!—Where?

* Many of the first families were involved in the guilt of a sacrilegious massacre committed near 200 years before. See Mr. Clinton's *Fasti. Olym.* 40.

S. S. Where? where plots have always tried
To hide themselves—beneath a hide!
Cleon. Go for a paltry vulgar slave.
S. S. Get out for a designing knave.
Chorus. Give him back the cuff you got!
Cleon. Murder! help! a plot! a plot!
I'm assaulted and beset!
Chorus. Strike him harder! harder yet!
Pelt him,—Rap him,
Slash him,—Slap him,
Across the chaps there, with a wipe
Of your entrails and your tripe!*
Keep him down—the day's your own.

O cleverest of human kind! the stoutest and the boldest,
The saviour of the state, and us, the friends that thou beholdest;
No words can speak our gratitude; all praise appears too little.
You've fairly done the rascal up, you've nick'd him to a tittle.

* A slap on the face of this kind is proverbial in Spain, as the most outrageous of all insults.

Cleon. By the holy goddess it's not new to me
This scheme of yours. I've known the job long since,
The measurement and the scantling of it all,
And where it was shaped out and tack'd together.

Chorus. Ay! there it is! You must exert yourself;
Come try to match him again with a carpenter's phrase.†

S. S. Does he think I have not track'd him in his intrigues
At Argos?—his pretence to make a treaty
With the people there?—and all his private parley
With the Spartans?—There he works and blows the coals;
And has plenty of other irons in the fire.

Chorus. Well done, the blacksmith beats the carpenter.†

† In these passages, the poet marks the degradation of public oratory, infected with vulgar jargon and low metaphors.

S. S. (*in continuation.*)
And the envoys that come here, are all in a tale;
All beating time to the same tune.—I tell ye,
It's neither gold nor silver, nor the promises,
Nor the messages you send me by your friends,
That will ever serve your turn; or hinder me
From bringing all these facts before the public.

Cleon. Then I'll set off this instant to the senate;
To inform them of your conspiracies and treasons,
Your secret nightly assemblies and cabals,

Your private treaty with the king of Persia,
Your correspondence with Bœotia,
And the business that you keep there in the cheese-press,
Close pack'd, you think, and ripening out of sight.

S. S. Ah! cheese?—Is cheese any cheaper there, d'ye hear?

Cleon. By Hercules! I'll have ye crucified! [*Exit Cleon.*

Chorus (to the S. S.).

Well, how do you feel your heart and spirits now?
Rouse up your powers! If ever in your youth
You swindled and forswore as you profess;
The time is come to show it. Now this instant
He's hurrying headlong to the senate house;
To tumble amongst them like a thunderbolt;
To accuse us all, to rage, and storm, and rave.

S. S. Well, I'll be off then. But these guts and pudding,
I must put them by the while, and the chopping knife.

Chorus. Here, take this lump of lard, to 'noint your neck with;
The grease will give him the less hold upon you,
With the gripe of his accusations.

S. S. That's well thought of.

Chorus. And here's the garlic. Swallow it down!

S. S. What for?

Chorus. It will prime you up,* and make you fight the better.
—Make haste!

S. S. Why so I do.

Chorus. Remember now—
Show blood and game. Drive at him and denounce him!
Dash at his comb, his coxcomb; cuff it soundly!
Peck, scratch and tear, conculcate, clapperclaw!
Bite both his wattles off, and gobble 'em up!
And then return in glory to your friends. [*Exit S. S.*

* Game cocks are dieted with garlic; see Acharnians, p. 13, Theorus's warning to Dicæopolis, where a similar note should have been given.

CHORUS.

Well may you speed
In word and deed.
May all the powers of the market place
Grant ye protection, and help and grace,
With strength of lungs and front and brain;
With a crown of renown, to return again.

(*Turning to the audience*)

But you that have heard and applauded us here,
In every style and in every way,
Grant us an ear, and attend for a while,
To the usual old anapæstic essay.

The following parabasis has been already noticed (*p.* 31 *of the* Acharnians) *in the long preliminary notice prefixed to the parabasis of that play; but the inference which is there so concisely assumed in the marginal note, will be better and more conveniently estimated, when placed in juxtaposition with the composition itself. It has been said, in brief and strong terms, that the poet had become the* poetical serf of the community. *Our knowledge of antiquity is too scanty to enable us to define precisely the mode and degree of this vassalage, to which he thus voluntarily subjected himself; but it is evident that, by demanding (as the text has it)* a chorus for himself, *he was in effect doing that which is expressed in the translation, namely,* embracing a profession, *from which he could not retreat. The whole tenor of the following parabasis turns upon the decisive and irretrievable step, which the Poet (after long hesitation, and resisting the importunity of his friends) had at length determined to take, undeterred by the discouraging example of his predecessors in the same line, whom he enumerates and describes, devoting himself irrevocably and exclusively to the composition of comedy.*

Yet the Poet was already publicly known as the author of three comedies; the Daitaleis, *in which he had exhibited the contrast of two young men, brothers: the one steady and manly, according to the old fashion instructed in the old music and poetry, addicted to gymnastic exercises, living with his father in the country, a lover of hunting and rural sports; the other a thoroughly depraved town rake—a scamp of that new school of which Alcibiades was the patron and the model—aspiring to distinguish himself by foppery, litigation, and speechifying. That excellent comedy of Gresset's,* Le Méchant, *may be considered as somewhat analogous to this—produced with the same intention, and in a state of society and manners not altogether dissimilar.*

His second play, the Babylonians, *has been already mentioned (see* Ach. *p.* 30*); of this he was avowedly the author,* *and had been held responsible for it, as we have already seen.*

The Acharnians, *his third play, is, generally speaking, a comic pleading in favour of peace ; but it includes a justification of the Poet as the author of the preceding play (distinctly and palpably in the parabasis, and in a burlesque form in other parts) ; for Dicæopolis, in his defence before the Chorus, is the representative of the Poet himself ; and that portion of the Chorus, which continues inveterate and unappeased, bring an accusation against him, which has no reference to anything which has occurred in the preceding scenes of the same play ; but which is distinctly applicable to the main purport and argument of the* Babylonians* *(see* Ach. *p.* 28*)—*

* It is noticed as having contained attacks upon a great number of persons.

"inveighing against informers."

The original, more scrupulously translated, would stand thus " abusing any man that happened to be an informer," *an offence, of which the Dicæopolis of the* Acharnians *(for the informer Nicarchus has not yet appeared) had been, up to this point at least, entirely guiltless. Dicæopolis then, in this instance, is a burlesque representative of the poet himself, put upon his trial for misdemeanours perpetrated in a former play. His adversaries attack him, for having stigmatized individuals as informers. The party who are become favourable to him, justify him, by affirming the truth and correctness of all his imputations.—The reply to this is, that though they might be true, he had no right to give publicity to scandalous and offensive truths, and that he deserves to be punished for it.—There is nothing in this altercation which can in any way be made to bear the slightest reference to anything that had occurred in the preceding scenes of the play itself.*

We have made a wide digression in our way to a very unsatisfactory conclusion.—It may be said : we see very clearly, from what has been already stated, that Aristophanes was already an avowed writer for the comic theatre ; regarded as responsible for his productions, when they were deemed objectionable ; justifying them himself, in person, in the first instance, and afterwards, under a feigned character in a subsequent drama.—What then was the change in his condition and prospects which was produced by " demanding a chorus for himself?" *a term, as it appears, of great import; implying a devotion of himself exclusively to the task of writing for the stage.—What were the emoluments and privileges attached to this profession of a comic author thus authentically assumed?—What, on the other hand, were the disadvantages and disabilities by which those privileges and emoluments were counterbalanced?—This is a question of which the learning and industry of continental scholars may perhaps procure a solution, if they have not already afforded it, to those who are conversant in the language and literature of Germany. But something in the meanwhile may be deduced from the testimony of the Poet himself. It appears from the scene of Euripides in the* Acharnians, *that the author must have been entitled to the dresses of the actors; and his perquisites probably extended to the other properties (as they are called) of the stage, with the exception of those which were permanent and immoveable. We find the Poet thus speaking of himself in the parabasis of the* Peace, *contrasting his own conduct with that of other cotemporary comic authors—he says—*

> "*On former occasions he never made use*
> *Of the credit he gain'd to corrupt and seduce;*
> But pack'd up his alls, *after gaining the day,*
> *Contented and joyous, and so went away.*"

We find, moreover, that the comic poets received a salary from the State; for, in the play of the Frogs, *exhibited almost at the close of the war, at a time of great pecuniary difficulty, it seems that their pay was reduced.—And the Poet introduces his Chorus of happy spirits in the Elysian fields, excommunicating the economists, in company with other reprobates and profane persons who are warned to withdraw from the sacred rites:—they include, in their interdict,*

> "*All* statesmen *retrenching the* fees and the salaries
> *Of* theatrical bards *in revenge for the railleries*
> *And jests and lampoons of this holy solemnity.*"

This appears evidently not to have been serious; or, if serious, would have been very unreasonable; for the retrenchment at that period was universal, extending even to the omnipotent jurymen, who were reduced from a daily pay of three oboli to two. Whatever the retrenchment may have been, it seems, as is suggested above, not to have been one which was seriously complained of; and we may safely infer from the general munificence of the Athenians in all matters of art, and from their peculiar passion for the theatre, that in better and more prosperous times the allowances made to the comic poets must have been sufficiently liberal, at least to the three successful competitors; for there were three dramatic prizes, assigned to the first, second, and third best play; a circumstance which of itself implies a considerable pecuniary recompence; for the third, the least of all, must have been worth having, in a pecuniary view; otherwise, to be ranked as a third-rate poet would have been felt as an unqualified mortification.—Supposing the prizes to have been merely honorary, no third prize could have existed, for it could never have been considered as an honour.

From the question of emoluments, we may turn to that of privileges and immunities: and here, in the absence of positive authority, we may be contented for the present, with general inferences and analogy. According to the notions of heathen antiquity, a professed comic poet would have been considered as a person devoted to the service of Bacchus; a certain character of inviolability must therefore have been attached to him, in common with other persons separated and set apart from the common concerns of the state, and dedicated for life to the service of any other deity.—Though modified no doubt in later times, this principle was essentially inherent in the Grecian mind.—The slaughter of a poet, "a servant of the muses," was condemned as an act of sacrilege; and it was in these terms that the assassin of Archilochus was excommunicated by the oracle, and expelled from the temple which he had presumed to enter. It is not conceivable that these feelings, however modified, could have been altogether extinct in the times of which we are now treating; and it is a singular fact, considering the enormous outrages and attacks upon private character, perpetrated by the comic poets, that (with the exception of the exploded fable of the death of Eupolis) there is no trace to be met with of any personal vengeance directed against any of them. The comic poets have been spoken of above as persons separate and set apart from the ordinary concerns of the state: and so they must have been, either by positive law, or by established and authoritative custom; for it is not to be supposed that, to any man standing, in all other respects, upon an equal footing with his fellow citizens, the privilege should have been allowed of assailing them with unlimited ribaldry and abuse.—Whatever may be thought of such a privilege in modern times, it was certainly not consonant to the spirit of antiquity to allow it to be enjoyed by any individual, unaccompanied with corresponding disabilities. The office of a comic poet, during the reign of the Athenian democracy, has not been unaptly compared to that of the court-jester during the middle ages. They were both of them authorized to take the most extraordinary liberties, in reflections on the sovereign, and the highest persons in the state; but theirs was a situation obviously incompatible with the exercise of any other office or privilege. The parallel may be carried further; for it would appear, from many recorded instances, that of these royal jesters many must have been men, not only of a lively fancy and imagination, but of just feelings and a sound judgment, whose privileged sallies occasionally directed the attention of the sovereign to truths, which could not have been conveyed to him by any other channel. Aristophanes was certainly a most judicious, though ineffectual, adviser to the multitudinous sovereign, whom it was his office to amuse; and Charles of Burgundy might have lived and died in prosperity, if his counsels had been moderated by the sarcasms of his jester.

But to return to our subject: Thus far, in the absence of direct and positive information, an attempt has been made, by conjecture and inference, to define the new position, in which the Poet was placing himself, as a member of the community to which he belonged; whether in this respect he had any reason to repent of his resolution, it would be idle and superfluous to risk any conjecture;—but in regard to his success as an author, the forebodings expressed in the parabasis appear to have been verified.—Up to this time, while unengaged and at liberty, he had been courted by the public, and indulged with applause and success; for the strong feeling excited in the public by his play of the Babylonians, *at first hostile, and gradually (like their representatives, the chorus of* Acharnians*) subsiding into acquiescence and approbation, must have been felt as more than an equivalent to the highest theatrical success. But he was now irrevocably engaged in the service of the public: the first prize, as* *a kind of premium for enlisting, was awarded to the present play, the first which he exhibited as a regular writer for the stage; but from this time he was destined, like his predecessors, to experience the rigours and caprices of theatrical discipline. His next play was the* Clouds, *in which, following up the design of the* Daitaleis, *he had traced to its source that sudden change in morality and manners, of which the outward manifestations had been exhibited in the former play. This play of the* Clouds, *which he affirms (adjuring Bacchus as the patron deity of theatrical poets) to have been the best that ever was written, was rejected. The play of the* Wasps, *in which he thus asserted the merit of the* Clouds, *was acted in the following year, and obtained the first prize. But we find that another mortification had, in the meanwhile, befallen him, in the diminished zeal and ardour of his friends, —he had been, as the phrase is,* "had up" *by Cleon before the senate, and subjected to the infliction of a severe invective; during which time he complains that his friends and partizans who were in attendance, and upon whose countenance he depended, "had shewn themselves indifferent and even amused."—They imagined, no doubt, that being once engaged he must go on. But he tells them, that he does not mean to compromise himself to the same extent in future; and reminds them of the fable of the vine, which, being left unsupported, ceased to produce fruit (l. 1291, Ed. Bekk.):—*

"So (the story says) the stake deserted and betray'd the vine."

Here, then, we trace a turn in the poet's mind; he became less of a public personage; and though his fancy and wit remained the same, and his principles continued unchanged, and though his courage and spirit occasionally broke forth in public emergencies, yet having adopted the stage as his occupation, he approached more nearly to the common standard of theatrical writers; and he might have made the same complaint, which was uttered by Shakespeare:

"So that almost my nature is subdued
To what it works in, like the dyer's hand."

But the text is already too much clogged with this long interpolation of prose. We will not stop, therefore, to lament over the loss of the Daitaleis *and the* Babylonians, *composed at an earlier period, and with an unbroken spirit.*

But the money-loving spirit of our age manifests itself even in our literary researches, and we cannot refrain, even with respect to an ancient poet, who lived 2300 years ago, from the invariable inquiry—What was he worth?—*It may be inferred then, from grounds of presumption too long to be detailed here, that he must have belonged to the class of the knights. Now the knights were rated (according to the modus fixed by Solon) at an amount of 300 bushels of corn. But how rated?—As for the sum total of their income? Or, as being that portion of it, which, in cases of emergency, was exigible for the service of the State?—Those students of antiquity, who are not endowed with the faculty of digesting gross absurdities, are under great obligations to Mr. Boeckh, for having relieved them from the cruel necessity of being constrained to believe, that a man with £75 a year (taking corn at five shillings a bushel) was bound to keep a war-horse, and to serve in the cavalry at his own expense; or that another with an income of £225 (estimated according to the same permanent standard of value) could have been charged with the expenses of a ship of war —a proposition, we conceive, wholly contradictory to the experience of the members of the Yacht Club.—Mr. Boeckh has shown, that these sums were the extreme rates of taxation to which the individuals of these classes were subject; a rate which was not always exacted in full; and which we may suppose, at the utmost, to have been a double tithe or four shillings in the pound, a rate of taxation to which, in difficult times, our own country was contented to submit. —The elucidation of this point is by far the greatest service which Mr. Boeckh has rendered to ancient literature, in the whole of his accurate and learned work. To have dissipated these misapprehensions, which, as long as they were implicitly adopted, diffused an air of utter incredibility and unreality over the whole system of antiquity, is a result far more important than the development of details hitherto unknown and unexamined.*

This discussion, already too long, has been prolonged thus far for the sake of restating Mr. Boeckh's discovery; which has been unaccountably overlooked in a recent publication.

With respect to the poet, we may safely conclude, that he was in tolerably easy circumstances, and we find, accor-

dingly, that he was able to give away some of his plays with their contingent emoluments: among the rest the very play (the Frogs*) in which he complained of the new retrenchment, and denounced an anathema against the economists.*

Parabasis

If a veteran author had wished to engage
Our assistance to-day, for a speech from the stage,
We scarce should have granted so bold a request;
But this author of ours, as the bravest and best,
Deserves an indulgence denied to the rest.
For the courage and vigour, the scorn and the hate,
With which he encounters the pests of the state;
A thorough-bred seaman, intrepid and warm,
Steering outright, in the face of the storm.
  But now for the gentle reproaches he bore
On the part of his friends, for refraining before
To embrace the profession, embarking for life
In theatrical storms and poetical strife;
He begs us to state, that for reasons of weight,
He has linger'd so long, and determined so late.
For he deem'd the achievements of comedy hard,
The boldest attempt of a desperate bard!
The Muse he perceived was capricious and coy,
Though many were courting her, few could enjoy.
And he saw without reason, from season to season,
Your humour would shift, and turn poets adrift,
Requiting old friends with unkindness and treason,
Discarded in scorn as exhausted and worn.
  Seeing Magnes's fate, who was reckon'd of late,
For the conduct of comedy, captain and head;
That so oft on the stage, in the flower of his age,
Had defeated the Chorus his rivals had led;
With his sounds of all sort, that were utter'd in sport,
With whims and vagaries unheard of before,
With feathers and wings, and a thousand gay things,
That in frolicsome fancies his Choruses wore—
—When his humour was spent, did your temper relent,
To requite the delight that he gave you before?
—We beheld him displaced, and expell'd, and disgraced,
When his hair and his wit were grown aged and hoar.

Then he saw, for a sample, the dismal example
Of noble Cratinus so splendid and ample,
Full of spirit and blood, and enlarged like a flood,
Whose copious current tore down, with its torrent,
Oaks, ashes, and yew, with the ground where they grew,
And his rivals to boot, wrench'd up by the root,
And his personal foes, who presumed to oppose,
All drown'd and abolish'd, dispersed and demolish'd,
And drifted headlong, with a deluge of song.
And his airs, and his tunes, and his songs and lampoons,
Were recited and sung, by the old and the young—
At feasts and carousals what poet but he?
And "*The fair Amphibribe*" and "*The Sycophant Tree,*"
"*Masters and masons and builders of verse!*"—
Those were the tunes that all tongues could rehearse;
But since in decay, you have cast him away,
Stript of his stops and his musical strings,
Batter'd and shatter'd, a broken old instrument,
Shoved out of sight, among rubbishy things.
His garlands are faded, and what he deems worst,
His tongue and his palate are parching with thirst;
And now you may meet him alone in the street,
Wearied and worn, tatter'd and torn,
All decay'd and forlorn, in his person and dress;
Whom his former success should exempt from distress,
With subsistence at large, at the general charge,
And a seat with the great, at the table of state,*
There to feast every day, and preside at the play
In splendid apparel, triumphant and gay.
Seeing Crates the next, always teased and perplext,
With your tyrannous temper, tormented and vext;
That with taste and good sense, without waste or expense,
From his snug little hoard, provided your board,
With a delicate treat, economic and neat.
Thus hitting or missing, with crowns or with hissing,
Year after year, he pursued his career,
For better or worse, till he finish'd his course.
These precedents held him in long hesitation;
He replied to his friends, with a just observation,
"That a seaman in regular order is bred
To the oar,—to the helm,—and to look out a-head;
Till diligent practice has fix'd in his mind

* The Prytaneum.

The signs of the weather, and changes of wind.
And when every point of the service is known,
Undertakes the command of a ship of his own."
For reasons like these,
If your judgment agrees,
That he did not embark,
Like an ignorant spark,
Or a troublesome lout,
To puzzle and bother, and blunder about,
Give him a shout,
At his first setting out!
And all pull away
With a hearty huzza
For success to the play!
Send him away,
Smiling and gay,
Shining and florid,
With his bald forehead!

The text contains nearly all that is known of two of the three poets here mentioned, Magnes and Crates; the last is recorded, as having become distinguished in the second year of the 82nd Olymp., thirty-six years before the exhibition of the Knights; Magnes must have been older. Of Cratinus some few fragments are still in existence; he lived to vindicate himself from the offensive commiseration here bestowed upon him, by gaining the first prize in the next year, when the comedy of the Clouds was rejected.

STROPHE.

Neptune, lord of land and deep,
From the lofty Sunian steep,
With delight surveying
The fiery-footed steeds,
Frolicking and neighing
As their humour leads—
—And rapid cars contending
Venturous and forward,
Where splendid youths are spending
The money that they borrow'd.
—Thence downward to the Ocean,
And the calmer show

Of the dolphin's motion
  In the depths below;
And the glittering galleys
  Gallantly that steer,
When the squadron sallies,
  With wages in arrear.
List, O list!
Listen and assist,
  Thy Chorus here!
Mighty Saturn's son!
The support of Phormion,*
  In his victories of late;
  To the fair Athenian State
  More propitious far,
  Than all the gods that are,
  In the present war.

* A most able and successful naval commander.

EPIRREMA.

Let us praise our famous fathers, let their glory be recorded
On Minerva's mighty mantle[1] consecrated and embroider'd.
That with many a naval action and with infantry by land,
Still contending, never ending, strove for empire and command.
When they met the foe, disdaining to compute a poor account
Of the number of their armies, of their muster and amount:
But whene'er at wrestling matches,[2] they were worsted in the fray,
Wiped their shoulders from the dust, denied the fall, and fought away.
  Then the generals* never claimed precedence, or a separate seat,

* Tolmide and Myronides, who commanded in the battles here alluded to.

---

[1] This mantle was an enormous piece of tapestry, adorned with the actions and figures of the native heroes and protecting deities. It was renewed every year, and was carried to the temple, at the Panathenaic procession, suspended and displayed from a tall mast fixed on a moveable carriage. See Mr. Wordsworth's *Attica*, p. 184.

[2] Thirty-two years before this time, the Athenians, after being foiled in a great battle at Tanagra, risked another general action at Oinophuta, in which they were victorious, only sixty-two days after the first!—*Fasti Hellenici*, Ol. 81.

Like the present mighty captains, or the public wine or
meat.
As for us, the sole pretension suited to our birth and years,
Is with resolute intention, as determined volunteers,
To defend our fields and altars, as our fathers did before;
Claiming as a recompense this easy boon, and nothing
more:
When our trials with peace are ended, not to view us with
malignity;
When we're curried, sleek and pamper'd, prancing in our
pride and dignity.

Antistrophe.

It will be seen that there is a want of correspondence and proportion between the strophe and antistrophe; the first has been enlarged to give scope for the development of the poetic imagery, tinged with burlesque, which appears in the original. In atonement for this irregularity, the antistrophe, which offered no such temptation, is given as an exact metrical facsimile *of the original. In this respect, it may at least have some merit as a curiosity. The only variation consists in a triple, instead of a double, rhyme.*

Mighty Minerva! thy command
Rules and upholds this happy land;
Attica, famed in every part,
With a renown for arms and art,
  Noted among the nations.
Victory bring—the bard's delight;
She that in faction or in fight,
  Aids us on all occasions.
Goddess, list to the song!—Bring her away with thee,
Haste and bring her along!—Here to the play with thee.
  Bring fair Victory down for us!
  Bring her here with a crown for us!
  Come with speed, as a friend indeed,
  Now or never at our need!

Antepirrema.

It is observable, that the antepirrema is generally in a lower and less serious tone than its preceding epirrema; as if the poet were, or thought it right to appear, apprehensive of having been over earnest in his first address. In the present instance, as the poetical advocate of his party, he had already stated their claims to public confidence and favour; and, in the concluding lines, had deprecated the jealousy and envy to which they were exposed. He now wishes to give a striking instance of their spirit and alacrity in the service of the country; and it is given accordingly, in the most uninvidious manner, in a tone of extravagant burlesque humour.

Let us sing the mighty deeds of our illustrious noble steeds.
They deserve a celebration for their service heretofore,
Charges and attacks, exploits enacted in the days of yore:
These, however, strike me less, as having been perform'd ashore.
But the wonder was to see them, when they fairly went aboard,
With canteens and bread and onions, victuall'd and completely stored,
Then they fix'd and dipt their oars beginning all to shout and neigh,
Just the same as human creatures, "Pull away, boys! Pull away!"
"Bear a hand there, Roan and Sorrel! Have a care there, Black and Bay!"
Then they leapt ashore at Corinth; and the lustier younger sort
Stroll'd about to pick up litter,* for their solace and disport:
And devour'd the crabs of Corinth, as a substitute for clover.
So that a poetic Crabbe,† exclaim'd in anguish, "All is over!
"What awaits us, mighty Neptune, if we cannot hope to keep
From pursuit and persecution in the land or in the deep?"

* The usual licentious excesses of an invading army.
† The poet Carkinus.

The poet Carkinus (Crab) had produced a tragedy on the subject of the daughter of a king of Corinth, who, merely from bathing in the sea, had become unconsciously pregnant by Neptune. The lines here quoted from it were a com-

plaint of the impossibility of preserving the honour of illustrious families, from the licentious aggressions of the gods.

Chorus (*to the Sausage-seller*).
O best of men! thou tightest, heartiest fellow!
What a terror and alarm had you created,
In the hearts of all your friends, by this delay.
But since at length, in safety, you return,
Say what was the result of your attempt.
S. S. The result is, you may call me Nickoboulus,
For I've nick'd the Boule there, the Senate, capitally.

CHORUS.

Then may we chaunt amain
In an exulting strain,
With ecstasy triumphant, bold, and high,
O Thou!
That not in words alone, or subtle thought,
But more in manly deed,
Hast merited, and to fair achievement brought!
Relate at length and tell
The event as it befell:
So would I gladly pass a weary way;
Nor weary would it seem,
Attending to the theme,
Of all the glories of this happy day.
(*In a familiar tone, as if clapping him on the shoulder.*)
Come, my jolly, worthy fellow, never fear!
*We're all delighted with you—let us hear!
S. S. Ay, ay—it's well worth hearing, I can tell ye:
I follow'd after him to the senate-house;
And there was he, storming, and roaring, driving
His thunderbolts about him, bowling down
His biggest words, to crush the cavaliers,
Like stones from a hill top; calling them traitors,
Conspirators—What not? There sat the senate
With their arms folded, and their eyebrows bent,
And their lips pucker'd, with the grave aspect
Of persons utterly humbugg'd and bamboozled.
Seeing the state of things, I paused awhile,
Praying in secret with an under voice.

* The encouragement which the poet administers, *to himself* in fact, is not out of place; he is preparing to attack the senate, with the most contemptuous ridicule.

" Ye influential impudential powers
Of sauciness and jabber, slang and jaw!
Ye spirits of the market-place and street
Where I was rear'd and bred—befriend me now!
Grant me a voluble utterance, and a vast
Unbounded voice, and stedfast impudence!"
Whilst I thus thought and pray'd, on the right hand,
I heard a sound of wind distinctly broken!
I seized the omen at once; and bouncing up,
I burst among the crowd, and bustled through,
And bolted in at the wicket, and bawl'd out:
"News! news! I've brought you news! the best of news!
Yes, Senators, since first the war began,
There never has been known, till now this morning,
Such a haul of pilchards." Then they smiled and seem'd
All tranquillized and placid at the prospect
Of pilchards being likely to be cheap.
I then proceeded and proposed a vote
To meet the emergence secretly and suddenly:
To seize at once the trays of all the workmen,
And go with them to market to buy pilchards,
Before the price was raised. Immediately
They applauded, and sat gaping altogether,
Attentive and admiring. He perceived it;
And framed a motion, suited, as he thought,
To the temper of the assembly.—" I move," says he,
" That on occasion of this happy news,
We should proclaim a general thanksgiving;
With a festival, moreover, and a sacrifice
Of a hundred head of oxen, to the goddess."
Then seeing he meant to drive me to the wall
With his hundred oxen, I overbid him at once;
And said "two hundred," and proposed a vow,
" For a thousand goats to be offer'd to Diana,
Whenever sprats should fall to forty a penny."
With that the senate smiled upon me again;
And he grew stupefied, and lost, and stammering;
And, attempting to interrupt the current business,
Was call'd to order, and silenced and put down.
Then they were breaking up to buy their pilchards:
But he must needs persist, and beg for a hearing—
" For a single moment—for a messenger—

For a herald that was come from Lacedæmon,
With an offer of peace—for an audience to be given him."
But they broke out in an uproar altogether:
" Peace, truly!—Peace, forsooth!—Yes, now's their time
I warrant 'em; when pilchards are so plenty.
They've heard of it; and now they come for peace!
No! no! no peace! The war must take its course."
Then they call'd out to the presidents to adjourn;
And scrambled over the railing and dispersed;
And I dash'd down to the market-place headlong;
And bought up all the fennel, and bestow'd it,
As donative, for garnish to their pilchards,
Among the poorer class of senators;
And they so thank'd and praised me, that, in short,
For twenty-pence, I've purchased and secured them.

CHORUS.

With fair event your first essay began
Betokening a predestined happy man.
The villain now shall meet
In equal war,
A more accomplish'd cheat,
A viler far;
With turns and tricks more various,
More artful and nefarious.
—But thou!
Bethink thee now;
Rouse up thy spirit to the next endeavour!
—Our hands, and hearts, and will,
Both heretofore and ever,
Are with thee still.

S. S. The Paphlagonian! Here he's coming, foaming
And swelling like a breaker in the surf!
With his hobgoblin countenance and look;
For all the world as if he'd swallow me up.

Enter CLEON.

Cleon. May I perish and rot, but I'll consume and ruin ye;
I'll leave no trick, no scheme untried to do it.

S. S. It makes me laugh, it amuses one, to see him
Bluster and storm!—I whistle and snap my fingers.

Cleon. By the powers of earth and heaven! and as I live!
You villain, I'll annihilate and devour ye.

S. S. Devour me! and as I live, I'll swallow ye;
And gulp ye down at a mouthful, without salt.

Cleon. I swear by the precedence, and the seat
Which I achieved at Pylos, I'll destroy ye.

S. S. Seat, precedence truly! I hope to see you,
The last amongst us in the lowest place.

Cleon. I'll clap you in jail, in the stocks—By Heaven
I will.

S. S. To see it how it takes on! Barking and tearing
What ails the creature? Does it want a sop?

Cleon. I'll claw your guts out with these nails of mine.

S. S. I'll pare those nails of yours, from clawing victuals
At the public table.

Cleon. I'll drag you to the assembly
This instant, and accuse ye, and have you punish'd.

S. S. And I'll bring accusations there against you,
Twenty for one, and worse than yours tenfold.

Cleon. Ay, my poor soul! but they won't mind ye or
hear ye,
Whilst I can manage 'em and make fools of 'em.

S. S. You reckon they belong to ye, I suppose?

Cleon. Why should not they, if I feed and diet 'em?

S. S. Ay, ay; and like the licorish greedy nurses,
You swallow ten for one yourself, at least,
For every morsel the poor creatures get.

Cleon. Moreover, in doing business in the assembly,
I have such a superior influence and command,
That I can make them close and hard, and dry,
Or pass a matter easily, as I please.

S. S. Moreover, in doing business, my backside
Has the same sort of influence and command,
And plays at fast and loose, just as it pleases.

Cleon. You sha'n't insult me as you did before the senate.
Come, come, before the assembly.

S. S. (*coolly and dryly*). Ay, yes; why not?
With all my heart! Let's go there; what should hinder us?

[*The scene is supposed to be in front of Demus's house.*

Cleon. My dear good Demus, do step out a moment!

S. S. My dearest little Demus, do step out!

Dem. Who's there? Keep off! What a racket are you making;
Bawling and catterwauling about the door;
To affront the house, and scandalize the neighbours.
Cleon. Come out, do see yourself, how I'm insulted.
Dem. Oh my poor Paphlagonian! What's the matter?
Who has affronted ye?
Cleon. I'm waylaid and beaten,
By that rogue there, and the rake-helly young fellows,
All for your sake.
Dem. How so?
Cleon. Because I love you,
And court you, and wait on you, to win your favour.
Dem. And you there, sirrah! Tell me, what are you?
S. S. (*very rapidly and eagerly*).
A lover of yours, and a rival of his, this long time;
That have wish'd to oblige ye and serve ye in every way:
And many there are besides, good gentlefolks,
That adore ye, and wish to pay their court to ye;
But he contrives to baffle and drive them off,
In short, you're like the silly spendthrift heirs,
That keep away from civil well-bred company,
To pass their time with grooms and low companions,
Cobblers, and curriers, tanners and such like.
Cleon. And have not I merited that preference,
By my service?
S. S. In what way?
Cleon. By bringing back
The Spartan captives tied and bound from Pylos.
S. S. And would not I bring back from the cook's shop
A mess of meat that belonged to another man?
Cleon. Well Demus, call an assembly then directly,
To decide between us, which is your best friend;
And when you've settled it, fix and keep to him.
[*Exit Cleon.*
S. S. Ah do! pray do decide!—but not in the Pnyx—
Dem. It must be there; it can't be any where else;
It's quite impossible: you must go to the Pnyx.
S. S. Oh dear! I'm lost and ruin'd then! the old fellow
Is sharp and clever enough in his own home;
But planted with his rump upon that rock,
He grows completely stupefied and bother'd.

CHORUS.

Now you must get your words and wit, and all your tackle ready,
To make a dash, but don't be rash, be watchful, bold, and steady.
You've a nimble adversary, shifting, and alert, and wary.

[*The scene changes and discovers the Pnyx with Cleon on the Bema, in an orational attitude.*

[1]Look out! have a care! behold him there!
He's bearing upon you—be ready, prepare.
Out with the Dolphin! Haul it hard!
Away with it up to the peak of the yard!
And out with the pinnace[2] to serve for a guard.

Cleon's exordium appears to be marked in the original by a trait of humour, which it is impossible to translate or to represent by an equivalent. The true version is as follows: "I pray to the goddess Minerva, my own patroness, and the protecting deity of the city; that if I stand as a meritorious statesman, in the next rank to Lysicles, Cynna and Salabaccho,† I may be allowed to continue dining in the Prytaneum," &c. &c.*

It should seem that the three discreditable names are

* A statesman of very low repute, who had come forward after the death of Pericles, but speedily sunk into discredit. See marginal note, p. 77.

† Two notorious prostitutes.

[1] Observe that the change of the scene is accompanied by the idea of naval manœuvre. The ancient theatres being open at top, the machinery was worked from below; so that, with the help of a little imagination, the stage might at such a moment be thought to resemble the deck of a ship. Observe too that as by the change of scene and its transfer to the Pnyx (which had been deprecated by the Sausage-seller) the advantage is supposed to be transferred to the less ignoble character, the metre changes from the tetrameter iambic to the anapæst, as in the scenes of altercation in the other comedies, where the ascendancy of the noble or ignoble personage or argument is marked by a change of the metre; though the scenes which follow may perhaps be considered as an exception; for the Sausage-seller has the better even in the anapæst; but his complete triumph is reserved for the tetrameter.

[2] The image is that of a merchant vessel defending itself against the attack of a ship of war: the pinnace was interposed to break the shock of the enemy's prow; and the dolphin, a huge mass of lead, was raised to a great height, at the end of the yard of the enormous lateen sail, (still to be seen in some large old fashioned craft in the Mediterranean) it was then dropt suddenly at the moment of contact, to sink the enemy's vessel by bursting a hole through it.

substituted for those of Pericles, Cymon and Themistocles, with whom it appears that Cleon was in the habit of comparing himself; for we shall see that in the present scene he is attacked for having presumed to place himself in parallel with Themistocles.

It is natural therefore to conclude that with respect to the two other illustrious, but less extraordinary characters, he must have felt still less scrupulous.

The phrase therefore stands as a contemptuous caricature of Cleon's arrogance. He had spoken of himself as the most meritorious public character

μετὰ Περικλέα καὶ Κίμωνα καὶ Θεμιστοκλέα.

The taunting parody of the Poet says:

μετὰ Λυσικλέα καὶ Κύνναν καὶ Σαλαβάκχω.

We see that the two first names have a similarity in sound to those for which they were substituted: (Pericles, Lysicles—Cymon, Cynna). And we may be sure that an exact mimicry of Cleon's manner, and tone of voice, would not have been wanting, to make the caricature as manifest as possible.

To those who have formed a just estimate of the merits of Aristophanes, this explanation of the passage will not appear unnecessary. It occurs in the most striking part of the play, at the very point to which the attention of the audience had been directed; but surely the most implicit admiration for every thing ancient cannot prevent us from perceiving, that, unexplained as it has been hitherto, it appears vapid and senseless in the extreme. We might safely defy the dullest individual to make a poorer attempt at a joke in his own person.

If, on the contrary, we suppose the passage in question to have contained a verbal burlesque heightened by personal mimicry, the audience would hardly have felt a deficiency of amusement at this particular point of the representation.

Cleon. To Minerva the sovereign goddess I call,
Our guide and defender, the hope of us all;
With a prayer and a vow,—That even as now—
If I'm truly your friend, unto my life's end,
I may dine in the hall, doing nothing at all!

But if I despise you, or ever advise you,
Against what is best, for your comfort and rest;
Or neglect to attend you, defend you, befriend you,
—May I perish and pine; may this carcase of mine
Be wither'd and dried, and curried beside;
And straps for your harness cut out from the hide.

S. S. Then Demus—if I tell a word of a lie,
If any man more can dote or adore,
With so tender a care, I make it my prayer,
My prayer and my wish,—to be stew'd in a dish;
To be sliced and slash'd, minced and hash'd,
And the offal remains that are left by the cook,
Dragg'd out to the grave, with my own flesh-hook.

Cleon. O Demus! has any man shown such a zeal,
Such a passion as I for the general weal?
Racking and screwing offenders to ruin;
With torture and threats extorting your debts;
Exhausting all means for enhancing your fortune,
Terror and force and intreaties importune,
With a popular, pure, patriotical aim;
Unmoved by compassion, or friendship, or shame.

S. S. All this I can do; more handily too;
With ease and dispatch; I can pilfer and snatch,
And supply ye with loaves from another man's batch.

But now, to detect his saucy neglect;
(In spite of the boast of his loyalty, due
Is the boil'd and the roast to your table and you.)
—You; that in combat at Marathon sped,
And hew'd down your enemies hand over head,
The Mede and the Persian, achieving a treasure
Of infinite honour and profit and pleasure,
Rhetorical praises and tragical phrases;
Of rich panegyric a capital stock—
—He leaves you to rest on a seat of the rock,
Naked and bare, without comfort or care.
Whilst I—Look ye there!—have quilted and wadded,
And tufted and padded this cushion so neat
To serve for your seat! Rise now, let me slip
It there under your hip, that on board of the ship,
With the toil of the oar, was blister'd and sore,
Enduring the burthen and heat of the day,
At the battle of Salamis working away.

Dem. Whence was it you came! Oh tell me your name—
Your name and your birth; for your kindness and worth
Bespeak you indeed of a patriot breed;
Of the race of Harmodius* sure you must be,
So popular, gracious and friendly to me.
Cleon. Can he win you with ease, with such trifles as these?
S. S. With easier trifles you manage to please.
Cleon. I vow notwithstanding, that never a man
Has acted since first the republic began,
On a more patriotical popular plan:
And if any man else can as truly be said
The friend of the people, I'll forfeit my head;
I'll make it a wager, and stand to the pledge.
S. S. And what is the token you mean to allege
Of that friendship of yours, or the good it ensures?
—Eight seasons are past that he shelters his head
In a barrack, an outhouse, a hovel, a shed,
In nests of the rock where the vultures are bred,
In tubs, and in huts and the towers of the wall:
His friend and protector you witness it all!
But where is thy pity, thou friend of the city;
To smoke him alive, to plunder his hive?
And when Archeptolemus† came on a mission,
With peace in his hand, with a fair proposition
To drive them before you with kicks on the rump,
Peace, treaties and embassies, all in a lump!
Cleon. I did wisely and well; for the prophecies tell,
That if he perseveres, for a period of years,
He shall sit in Arcadia, judging away
In splendour and honour, at fivepence a day:
—Meantime I can feed and provide for his need;
Maintaining him wholly, fairly and foully,
With jurymen's pay, threepence a day.
S. S. No vision or fancy prophetic have you,
Nor dreams of Arcadian empire in view;
A safer concealment is all that you seek:
In the hubbub of war, in the darkness and reek,
To plunder at large; to keep him confined,
Passive, astounded, humbled, blind,
Pining in penury, looking to thee

* The assassin of Hipparchus, canonized by the democratic fanaticism of the Athenians.

† After the surrender of the Spartans at Pylos.

For his daily provision, a juryman's fee.
—But if he returns to his country concerns,
His grapes and his figs, and his furmity kettle,
You'll find him a man of a different mettle.
When he feels that your fees had debarr'd him from these,
He'll trudge up to town, looking eagerly down,
And pick a choice pebble, and keep it in view,
As a token of spite,[1] for a vote against you.—
—Peace sinks you for ever, you feel it and know,
As your shifts and your tricks and your prophecies show.

Cleon. 'Tis a scandal, a shame! to throw slander and blame
On the friend of the people! a patriot name,
A kinder protector, I venture to say,
Than ever Themistocles was in his day,
Better and kinder in every way.

S. S. Witness, ye deities! witness his blasphemies!
You to compare with Themistocles! you!
That found us exhausted, and fill'd us anew
With a bumper of opulence; carving and sharing
Rich slices of empire; and kindly preparing,
While his guests were at dinner, a capital supper,
With a dainty remove, both under and upper,
The fort and the harbour, and many a dish
Of colonies, islands, and such kind of fish.
But now we are stunted, our spirit is blunted,
With paltry defences, and walls of partition;
With silly pretences of poor superstition;
And yet you can dare with him to compare!
But he lost the command, and was banish'd the land,
While you rule over all, and carouse in the hall!

Cleon. This is horrible quite, and his slanderous spite

---

[1] "As a token of spite:" that is, as a memorandum of anticipated vengeance—it is recorded of some old Frenchman, in the early times of the last century, that having suffered in his fortune by the depreciation of the coinage, he set apart a gold piece of the old stamp; and used to show it to his friends, saying, "that he kept it for the hire of a balcony looking into the Place de Grève, against the time, when the minister should be brought out there for execution."—With a similar feeling the Athenian countryman is described as selecting his pebble for a future vindictive vote against Cleon.

Has no motive in view but my friendship for you,
My zeal—

Dem. There, have done with your slang and your stuff,
You've cheated and choused and cajoled me enough.

S. S. My dear little Demus! you'll find it is true.
He behaves like a wretch and a villain to you.
He haunts your garden and there he plies,
Cropping the sprouts of the young supplies,
Munching and crunching enormous rations
Of public sales and confiscations.

Cleon. Don't exult before your time,
Before you've answer'd for your crime,—
A notable theft, that I mean to prove,
Of a hundred talents and above.

S. S. Why do ye plounce and flounce in vain?
Splashing and dashing and splashing again,
Like a silly recruit, just clapt on board?
Your crimes and acts are on record:
The Mytilenian bribe alone
Was forty minæ proved and shown.

CHORUS.*

* The metre now passes from the anapæst to the tetrameter iambic. See p. 115 note.

O thou, the saviour of the state, with joy and admiration,
We contemplate your happy fate and future exaltation,
Doom'd with the trident in your hand to reign in power and glory,
In full career to domineer, to drive the world before ye;
To raise with ease and calm the seas, and also raise a fortune,
While distant tribes, with gifts and bribes, to thee will be resorting.
Keep your advantage, persevere, attack him, work him, bait him,
You'll over-bawl him, never fear, and out-vociferate him.

Cleon. You'll not advance; you've not a chance, good people, of prevailing;
Recorded facts, my warlike acts, will muzzle you from railing;
As long as there remains a shield, of all the trophy taken
At Pylos, I can keep the field, unterrified, unshaken.

S. S. Stop there a bit, don't triumph yet,—those shields afford a handle

For shrewd surmise ; and it implies a treasonable scandal ;
That there they're placed, all strapt and braced, ready prepared for action ;
A plot it is ! a scheme of his ! a project of the faction !
—Dear Demus, he, most wickedly, with villanous advisement,
Prepares a force, as his resource, against your just chastisement :
—The curriers and the tanners all, with sundry crafts of leather,
Young lusty fellows stout and tall, you see them leagued together ;
And there beside them there abide cheesemongers bold and hearty,
Who with the grocers are allied, to join the tanners' party.
—Then if you turn your oyster eye, with ostracising look,
Those his allies will from the pegs those very shields unhook :
Rushing outright, at dark midnight, with insurrection sudden,
To seize perforce the public stores, with all your meal and pudden.

Dem. Well I declare! the straps are there ! O what a deep, surprising,
Uncommon rascal ! What a plot the wretch has been devising.

Cleon. Hear and attend, my worthy friend, and don't directly credit
A tale for truth, because, forsooth—" The man that told me, said it."
—You'll never see a friend like me that well or ill rewarded,
Has uniformly done his best to keep you safely guarded ;
Watching and working night and day, with infinite detections
Of treasons and conspiracies, and plots in all directions.

S. S. Yes, that's your course, your sole resource, the same device for ever.
As country fellows fishing eels, that in the quiet river,
Or the clear lake, have fail'd to take, begin to poke and muddle,
And rouze and rout it all about and work it to a puddle
To catch their game—you do the same in the hubbub and confusion,

Which you create to blind the state, with unobserved collusion,
Grasping at ease your bribes and fees. But answer! Tell me whether
You, that pretend yourself his friend, with all your wealth in leather,
Ever supplied a single hide, to mend his reverend batter'd
Old buskins?
Dem. No; not he, by Jove! Look at them, burst and tatter'd!
S. S. That shows the man! now spick and span, behold my noble largess!
A lovely pair, bought for your wear, at my own cost and charges.
Dem. I see your mind is well inclined, with views and temper suiting,
To place the state of things and toes upon a proper footing.
Cleon. What an abuse! a pair of shoes to purchase your affection!
Whilst all my worth is blotted forth, razed from your recollection;
That was your guide, so proved and tried, that show'd myself so zealous,
And so severe this very year, and of your honour jealous,
Noting betimes all filthy crimes, without respect or pity.
S. S. He that's inclined to filth, may find enough throughout the city:
—A different view determined you; those infamous offenders
Seem'd in your eyes likely to rise aspirants and pretenders;
In bold debate, and ready prate, undaunted rhetoricians;
In impudence and influence, your rival politicians.
But there now, see! this winter he might pass without his clothing;
The season's cold, he's chilly and old; but still you think of nothing!
Whilst I to show my love, bestow this waistcoat, as a present
Comely and new, with sleeves thereto, of flannel warm and pleasant.
Dem. How strange it is! Themistocles was reckon'd mighty clever!
With all his wit, he could not hit on such a project ever,
Such a device, so warm, so nice; in short, it equals fairly

His famous wall, the port and all, that he contrived so rarely.
Cleon. To what a pass you drive me, alas! to what a vulgar level!
S. S. 'Tis your own plan; 'twas you began.—As topers at a revel,
Press'd on a sudden, rise at once, and seize without regarding
Their neighbour's slippers for the nonce, to turn into the garden.
I stand in short upon your shoes—I copy your behaviour,
And take and use, for my own views, your flattery and palaver.
Cleon.—I shall outvie your flatteries, I!—see here this costly favour!
This mantle! take it for my sake—
Dem. Faugh! what a filthy flavour!
Off with it quick! it makes me sick, it stinks of hides and leather.
S. S. 'Twas by design: If you'll combine and put the facts together,
Like his device of Silphium spice—pretending to bedizen
You with a dress! 'Twas nothing less, than an attempt to poison.
He sunk the price of that same spice, and with the same intention,
—You recollect?
Dem. I recollect the circumstance you mention.
S. S. Then recollect the sad effect!—that instance of the jury
All flush'd and hot, fix'd to the spot, and f . . ting in a fury.
To see them was a scene of woe, in that infectious smother,
Winking and blinking in a row, and poisoning one another.
Cleon. Varlet and knave! thou dirty slave! what trash* have you collected?
S. S. 'Tis your own cue—I copy you.—So the oracle directed.
Cleon. I'll match you still, for I can fill his pint-pot of appointment,
For holidays and working days.†
S. S. But here's a box of ointment—
A salve prescribed for heels when kibed, given with my humble duty.

* A reprimand which in this, and one or two other instances, the translator is tempted to transfer to himself!

† Donatives on festival days, when the Courts were closed and the jurymen's pay suspended.

Cleon. I'll pick your white hairs out of sight, and make you quite a beauty.

S. S. But here's a prize for your dear eyes!—a rabbit-scut! See there now!

Cleon. Wipe 'em, and then wipe it again, dear Demus, on my hair now.

S. S. On mine, I say!
On mine do, pray!

[*Demus bestows, in a careless manner, his dirty preference upon the S. S. He pays no attention to the altercation which follows between the two rivals, but remains in the attitude of a solid old juryman sitting upon a difficult cause and exhibiting a variety of contortions indicative of deep cogitation,—a caricature of the originals which were every day to be seen in the courts of justice. During all this time he is supposed to be concocting the decision which he at last pronounces.*

Cleon (to the S. S.).
I shall fit you with a ship,
To provide for and equip
One that has been long forgotten,
Leaky, worm-eaten and rotten.
On it you shall waste and spend
Time and money without end.
Furthermore, if I prevail,
It shall have a rotten sail.

Chorus. There he's foaming, boiling over:
See the froth above the cover.
This combustion to allay,
We must take some sticks away.

Cleon. I shall bring you down to ruin,
With my summoning and suing
For arrears of taxes due,
And charges and assessments new,
In the census you shall pass
Rated in the richest class.

S. S. I reply with nothing worse
Than this just and righteous curse.
—May you stand beside the stove,*
With the fishes that you love,

* It is to be presumed that Cleon is indulging himself in the Prytaneum.

Fizzling in the tempting pan,
A distracted anxious man;
The Milesian question* pending,
Which you then should be defending,
With a talent for your hire
If you gain what they desire.—
—Then their agent, in a sweat,
Comes to say the assembly's met;
All in haste you snatch and follow,
And in vain attempt to swallow;
Running with your gullet fill'd,
Till we see you choked and kill'd.

Chorus. So be it, mighty Jove! so be it!
And, holy Ceres, may I live to see it!

Dem. (*rousing himself gradually from his meditation*).
. . . In truth, and he seems to me by far the best—
—The worthiest that has been long since—the kindest,
And best disposed to the honest, sober class
Of simple humble three-penny citizens.—
—You Paphlagonian, on the contrary,
Have offended and incensed me.—Therefore now
Give back your seal of office!—You must be
No more my steward!—

Cleon. Take it! and withal
Bear this in mind! That he my successor
—Whoever he may be—will prove a rascal
More artful and nefarious than myself—
A bigger rogue, be sure, and baser far!

Dem. This seal is none of mine, or my eyes deceive me!
The figure's not the same, I'm sure!

S. S. Let's see—
What was the proper emblem upon your seal?

Dem. A sirloin of roast beef—

S. S. It is not that!

Dem. Not the roast beef! What is it?

S. S. A cormorant
Haranguing open-mouth'd upon a rock—†

Dem. Oh mercy!

S. S. What's the matter?

Dem. Away with it!
That was Cleonymus's seal, not mine—‡
But here, take this; act with it as my steward.

* The scholiast affords us no light as to the allusion to the Milesian question.

† The Pnyx, the place of assembly, was called the Rock.

‡ Cleonymus's emblem is a bird, to mar his cowardice.—See *Ach.*, p. 10, line 112.—The bird is also one of voracious habits.

Cleon. Not yet, sir, I beseech you! First permit me
To communicate some oracles I possess.
S. S. And me too, some of mine.—
Cleon. Beware of them!
His oracles are most dangerous and infectious!
They strike ye with the leprosy and the jaundice.
S. S. And his will give you the itch and a scald head;
And the glanders and mad-staggers! take my word for it!
Cleon. My oracles foretell, that you shall rule
Over all Greece, and wear a crown of roses.
S. S. And mine foretell, that you shall wear a robe
With golden spangles, and a crown of gold,
And ride in a golden chariot over Thrace;
In triumph with King Smicythes and his queen.—
*Cleon (to the S. S.)**
Well, go for 'em! and bring 'em! and let him hear 'em!
S. S. Yes, sure; and you too, go fetch yours!
Cleon. Heigh-day!
S. S. Heigh-day! Why should not ye? What should hinder ye? [*Exeunt Cleon and S. S.*

* Cleon affects to give orders, which the S. S. retorts.

The following Chorus has no merit whatever in the translation, and not much in the original. The first 6 *lines are composed on the principle of contrast pointed out in p.* 87.

CHORUS.

Joyful will it be and pleasant
To the future times and present,
The benignant happy day,
Which will shine on us at last,
Announcing with his genial ray,
That Cleon is condemn'd and cast!
—Notwithstanding we have heard
From the seniors of the city,†
Jurymen revered and fear'd,
An opinion deep and pithy,
That the state for household use
Wants a pestle and a mortar;
That Cleon serves to pound and bruise,
Or else our income would run shorter.
—But I was told, the boys at school

† There was a portion of the lower class of citizens, who conceived that the state had an interest in supporting the tyrannical exactions of Cleon.—See p. 117.

Observed it as a kind of rule,
That he never could be made
  By any means to play the lyre,
Till he was well and truly *paid*—
  I mean with lashes for his hire.
At length his master all at once
Expell'd him as an utter dunce;
As by nature ill inclined,
And wanting *gifts* of every kind.

Re-enter Cleon and the Sausage-seller—Cleon with a large packet and the Sausage-seller staggering under a porter's load.

Cleon (to Demus).
Well, there's a bundle, you see, I've brought of 'em;
But that's not all; there's more of them to come—
S. S. I grunt and sweat, you see, with the load of 'em;
But that's not all; there's more of 'em to come.—
Dem. But what are these?—all?
Cleon. Oracles.
Dem. What, all?
Cleon. Ah, you're surprised it seems, at the quantity;
That's nothing; I've a trunk full of 'em at home.—
S. S. And I've a garret and out-house both brim-full.
Dem. Let's give 'em a look—Whose oracles are these?
Cleon. Bakis's, mine are.
Dem. (to the S. S.) Well, and whose are yours?
S. S. Mine are from Glanis, Bakis's elder brother.—
Dem. And what are they all about?
Cleon. About the Athenians,—
About the Island of Pylos,—about myself,—
About yourself,—about all kinds of things.
Dem. And what are yours about?
S. S. About the Athenians,—
About pease-pudding and porridge,—about the Spartans,—
About the war,—about the pilchard fishery,—
About the state of things in general,—
About short weights and measures in the market,—
About all things and persons whatsoever,—
About yourself and me.—Bid him go whistle.
Dem. Come, read them out then! that one in particular,

My favourite one of all, about the eagle ;—
About my being an eagle in the clouds.
Cleon. Listen then ! Give your attention to the oracle !
" Son of Erechtheus, mark and ponder well,
This holy warning from Apollo's cell.
It bids thee cherish him the sacred whelp,
Who for thy sake doth bite and bark and yelp.
Guard and protect him from the chattering jay ;
So shall thy juries all be kept in pay."
Dem. That's quite above me ! Erechtheus and a whelp !
What should Erechtheus do with a whelp or a jay ?
What does it mean ? *
Cleon. The meaning of it is this :
I am presignified as a dog, who barks
And watches for you. Apollo therefore bids you
Cherish the sacred whelp—meaning myself.
S. S. I tell ye, the oracle means no such thing :
This whelp has gnaw'd the corner off ; but here
I've a true perfect copy.
Dem. Read it out, then !
Meanwhile I'll pick a stone up for the nonce,
For fear the dog in the oracle should bite me.
S. S. " Son of Erechtheus, 'ware the gap-tooth'd dog,
The crafty mongrel that purloins thy prog ;
Fawning at meals, and filching scraps away,
The whilst you gape and stare another way ;
He prowls by night, and pilfers many a prize,
Amidst the sculleries and the colonies."
Dem. Well, Glanis has the best of it, I declare.
Cleon. First listen, my good friend, and then decide :
" In sacred Athens shall a woman dwell,
Who shall bring forth a lion fierce and fell ;
This lion shall defeat the gnats and flies,
Which are that noble nation's enemies.
Him you must guard and keep for public good,
With iron bulwarks and a wall of wood."
Dem. (*to the S. S.*)
D'ye understand it ?
S. S. No, not I, by Jove !
Cleon. Apollo admonishes you to guard and keep me ;
am the lion here alluded to.
Dem. A lion ! Why, just now you were a dog

* Discussions on the genuine and corrupt copies of oracles were not unfrequent ; we find an instance in Thucydides. See also the scene of the Soothsayer in the *Birds*.

S. S. Ay, but he stifles the true sense of it
Designedly—That "wooden and iron wall,"
In which Apollo tells ye he should be kept.

Dem. What did the deity mean by it? What d'ye think?

S. S. To have him kept in the pillory and the stocks.

Dem. That prophecy seems likely to be verified.

Cleon. "Heed not their strain; for crows and daws abound,
But love your faithful hawk, victorious found,
Who brought the Spartan magpies tied and bound."

S. S. "The Paphlagonian impudent and rash
Risk'd that adventure in a drunken dash.
—O simple son of Cecrops ill advised!
I see desert in arms unfairly prized:
Men only can secure and kill the game;
A woman's deed it is to cook the same."

Cleon. Do listen at least to the oracle about Pylos;
"Pylos there is behind, and eke before,*
The bloody Pylos."

Dem. Let me hear no more!
Those Pylos's are my torment evermore.

S. S. But here's an oracle which you must attend to;
About the navy—a very particular one.

Dem. Yes, I'll attend—I wish it would tell me how
To pay my seamen their arrears of wages.

S. S. "O son of Ægeus, ponder and beware
Of the dog-fox, so crafty, lean and spare,
Subtle and swift." Do ye understand it?

Dem. Yes!
Of course the dog-fox† means Philostratus.

S. S. That's not the meaning—but the Paphlagonian
Is always urging you to send out ships;
Cruizing about, exacting contributions;
A thing that Apollo positively forbids.

Dem. But why are the ships here call'd dog-foxes?

S. S. Why?
Because the ships are swift, and dogs are swift.

Dem. But what has a fox to do with it? Why dog-foxes?

S. S. The fox is a type of the ship's crew; marauding
And eating up the vineyards.

* There were three places of this name, not very distant from each other.

† The dog was (in a bad sense) the type of impudence—the fox of cunning—Philostratus, the compound of the two, gained his subsistence by a very infamous trade.

Dem. Well, so be it!
But how are my foxes to get paid their wages?
S. S. I'll settle it all, and make provision for them,
Three days' provision, presently. Only now,
This instant, let me remind you of an oracle:
" Beware Cullene."
Dem. What's the meaning of it?
S. S. Cullene, in the sense I understand,
Implies a kind of a *culling* asking hand—
The *coiled* hand of an informing bully,
Culling a bribe from his affrighted *cully*,*
A hand like his.
Cleon. No, no! you're quite mistaken,
It alludes to Diopithes's lame hand.†
But here's a glorious prophecy which sings,
" How you shall rule on earth, and rank with kings,
And soar aloft in air on eagle's wings."
S. S. And some of mine foretell that you shall be
" Sovereign of all the world and the Red Sea;
And sit on juries in Ecbatana,
Munching sweet buns and biscuit all the day."
Cleon. But me Minerva loves, and I can tell
Of a portentous vision that befell—
The goddess in my sleep appear'd to me,
Holding a flagon, as it seem'd to be,
From which she pour'd upon the old man's crown
Wealth, health and peace, like ointment running down."
S. S. And I too dreamt a dream, and it was this:
—Minerva came from the Acropolis,
There came likewise her serpent and her owl;
And in her hand she held a certain bowl;
And pour'd ambrosia on the old man's head,
And salt-fish pickle upon yours instead.
Dem. Well, Glanis is the cleverest after all.
And therefore I'm resolved, from this time forth,
To put myself into your charge and keeping,
To be tended in my old age and taken care of.
Cleon. No, do pray wait a little; and see how regularly
I'll furnish you with a daily dole of barley.
Dem. Don't tell me of barley! I can't bear to hear of it!
I've been cajoled and choused more than enough,
By Thouphanes‡ and yourself this long time past.

* The Scholiast tells us that the common informer at Athens, when accosting and threatening persons for the purpose of extortion, had an established token (the hand hollowed and slipt out beneath the cloak) indicating that they were willing to desist for a piece of money.

† As a soothsayer he ought to have been free from any bodily defect.

‡ An adherent of Cleon.

Cleon. Then I'll provide you delicate wheaten flour.

S. S. And I'll provide you manchets and roast meat,
And messes piping hot that cry, "Come eat me."

Dem. Make haste then, both of ye. Whatever you do—
And whichever of the two befriends me most,
I'll give him up the management of the state.

Cleon. Well, I'll be first then.

S. S. No you sha'n't, 'tis I.

[*Both run off; but the Sausage-seller contrives to get the start.*

CHORUS.

Worthy Demus! your estate
Is a glorious thing, we own—
The haughtiest of the proud and great
Watch and tremble at your frown;
Like a sovereign or a chief,
But so easy of belief,
Every fawning rogue and thief
Finds you ready to his hand,
Flatterers you cannot withstand.
To them your confidence is lent
With opinions always bent
To what your last advisers say,
Your noble mind is gone astray.

DEMUS.

Those brains of yours are weak and green;
My wits are sound whate'er ye say:
'Tis nothing but my froward spleen
That affects this false decay:
'Tis my fancy, 'tis my way,
To drawl and drivel through the day.
But though you see me dote and dream,
Never think me what I seem!—
—For my confidential slave
I prefer a pilfering knave;
And when he's pamper'd and full blown;
I snatch him up and—dash him down!

CHORUS.

We approve of your intent,
If you spoke it as you meant;

If you keep them like the beasts,
Fatten'd for your future feasts,
Pamper'd in the public stall,
Till the next occasion call;
Then a little easy vote
Knocks them down, and cuts their throat;
And you dish and serve them up,
As you want to dine or sup.

DEMUS.

Mark me!—when I seem to doze,
When my wearied eyelids close;
Then they think their tricks are hid:
But beneath the drooping lid,
Still I keep a corner left,
Tracing every secret theft.
I shall match them by-and-by!
All the rogues you think so sly,
All the deep intriguing set,
Are but dancing in a net,[1]
Till I purge their stomachs clean
With the hemlock and the bean.

The Sausage-seller and Cleon re-enter separately.

Cleon. Get out there!

S. S. You get out yourself, you rascal!

Cleon. Oh Demus! here have I been waiting, ready
To attend upon ye and serve ye, a long, long time.

S. S. And I've been waiting a longer, longer time—
Ever so long—a great long while ago.

Dem. And I've been waiting here cursing ye both,
A thousand times, a long, long time ago.

S. S. You know what you're to do?

---

[1] Persons subject to an effectual restraint, of which they were themselves unaware, were said to be *dancing in a net.* The Royalists, in Cromwell's time, found themselves baffled in all their attempts, without at all suspecting the system of secret information by which they were circumvented and restrained. When this came to be known afterwards, it was said that Cromwell had kept them *dancing in a net*, *i.e.* joyous and alert, conspiring and corresponding in imaginary security, wholly unconscious of the restraint in which they had been held.

Dem. Yes, yes, I know;
But you may tell me, however, notwithstanding.
S. S. Make it a race, and let us start to serve you,
And win your favour without loss of time.
Dem. So be it.—Start now—one! two! three!
Cleon. Heigh-day!
Dem. Why don't you start?
Cleon. He's cheated and got before me.
[*Exit.*
Dem. Well, truly, indeed, I shall be feasted rarely;
My courtiers and admirers will quite spoil me.
Cleon. There, I'm the first, you see, to bring ye a chair.
S. S. But a table—Here, I've brought it, first and foremost.
Cleon. See here, this little half-meal cake from Pylos,
Made from the flour of victory and success.
S. S. But here's a cake! See here! which the heavenly goddess
Patted and flatted herself, with her ivory hand,
For your own eating.
Dem. Wonderful mighty goddess!
What an awfully large hand she must have had!
Cleon. See this pease-pudding, which the warlike virgin
Achieved at Pylos, and bestows upon you.
S. S. The goddess upholds your whole establishment,
And holds this mess of porridge over your head.
Dem. I say the establishment could not subsist
For a single hour, unless the goddess upheld
The porridge of our affairs most manifestly.[1]
Cleon. She, the dread virgin who delights in battle,
And storm and battery, sends this batter pudding.

---

[1] This refers to a notion very prevalent among the Athenians, and which is alluded to elsewhere.

"Rash and ever in the wrong, a providence protects us ever,
Guiding all your empty plans, assisting every wild endeavour."
Clouds, l. 578, *ed. Bekk.*

It was founded on an anecdote, dating as far back as the time of the contest between Neptune and Minerva. Neptune, in his chagrin, imprecated upon the territory, of which he was dispossessed, the curse of being always governed by "bad councils." This Minerva could not cancel; but she subjoined that these bad councils, bad as they might be, should be successful.

S. S. This savory stew, with comely sippets deck'd,
Is sent you by the Gorgon-bearing goddess,
Who bids you gorge and gormandize thereon.

Cleon. The daughter of Jove array'd in panoply
Presents you a pancake to create a panic
Amongst your enemies.

S. S. And by me she sends
For your behoof this dainty dish of fritters,
Well fried, to strike your foemen with affright;
—And here's a cup of wine—taste it and try.

Dem. It's capital, faith!

S. S. And it ought to be; for Pallas
Mix'd it herself expressly for your palate.

Cleon. This slice of rich sweet-cake, take it from me.

S. S. This whole great rich sweet-cake, take it from me.

Cleon. (*to the S. S.*) Ah, but hare-pie—where will you get hare-pie?

S. S. (*aside*). Hare-pie! What shall I do!—Come, now's the time:
Now for a nimble, knowing, dashing trick.

Cleon (*to the S. S., showing the dish which he is going to present*).
Look there, you poor rabscallion.

S. S. Pshaw! no matter.
I've people of my own there, in attendance.
They're coming here—I see them.

Cleon. Who? What are they?

S. S. Envoys with bags of money.

[*Cleon sets down his hare-pie, and runs off the stage to intercept the supposed envoys.*

Cleon. Where? Where are they?
Where? Where?

S. S. What's that to you? Can't ye be civil?
Why don't you let the foreigners alone?—
There's a hare-pie, my dear own little Demus,
A nice hare-pie, I've brought ye!—See, look there!

Cleon (*returning*). By Jove, he's stolen it, and served it up.

S. S. Just as you did the prisoners at Pylos.

Demus. Where did ye get it? How did ye steal it? Tell me.

S. S. The scheme and the suggestion were divine,
The theft and the execution simply mine.

Cleon. I took the trouble.

S. S. But I served it up.

Demus. Well, he that brings the thing must get the thanks.

Cleon (aside). Alas, I'm circumvented and undone,
Out-faced and over-impudentified.

S. S. Come, Demus, had not you best decide at once,
Which is your truest friend, and best disposed
To the interest of the state, to your belly and you.

Demus. But how can I decide it cleverly?
Which would the audience think is the cleverest way?

S. S. I'll tell ye; take my chest and search it fairly,
Then search the Paphlagonian's and determine.

Demus. Let's look; what's here?

S. S. It's empty, don't you see?
My dear old man, I've given you everything.

Demus. Well, here's a chest indeed, in strict accordance
With the *judgment* of the public: perfectly *empty!*

S. S. Come, now let's rummage out the Paphlagonian's.
See there!

Demus. Oh, bless me, what a hoard of dainties!
And what a lump of cake the fellow has kept,
Compared with the little tiny slice he gave me.

S. S. That was his common practice; to pretend
To make you presents, giving up a trifle,
To keep the biggest portion for himself.

Demus. Oh villain, how you've wronged and cheated me;
Me that have honour'd ye, and have made ye presents.

Cleon. I stole on principle for the public service.

Demus. Pull off your garland—give it back to me,
For him to wear!

S. S. Come, sirrah, give it back!

Cleon. Not so.—There still remains an oracle,
Which marks the fatal sole antagonist,
Predestined for my final overthrow.

S. S. Yes! And it points to me by name and person!

Cleon. Yet would I fain inquire and question you;
How far the signs and tokens of the prophecy
Combine in your behalf.—Answer me truly!
What was your early school? Where did you learn
The rudiments of letters and of music?

S. S. Where hogs are singed and scalded in the shambles,
There was I pummell'd to a proper tune.
Cleon. Hah, sayst thou so? this prophecy begins
To bite me to the soul with deep forebodings.
—Yet tell me again—What was your course of practice
In feats of strength and skill at the palæstra?
S. S. Stealing and staring, perjuring and swearing—
Cleon. O mighty Apollo, your decree condemns me!
Say, what was your employment afterwards?
S. S. I practised as a Sausage-seller chiefly,
Occasionally as pimp and errand boy.
Cleon. Oh misery! lost and gone! totally lost!
(*After a pause.*)
One single hope remains, a feeble thread,
I grasp it to the last.—Yet answer me.
—What was your place of sale for sausages?
Was it the market or the city gate?
S. S. The city gate! Where salted fish are sold!
Cleon. Out! Out, alas! my destiny is fulfill'd:
Hurry me hence within with quick conveyance,
The wreck and ruin of my former self.
Farewell my name and honours! Thou my garland,
Farewell! my successor must wear you now,
To shine in new pre-eminence a rogue,
Perhaps less perfect, but more prosperous!
S. S. O Jove! Patron of Greece! the praise be thine!
Demosthenes (*in a very civil, submissive tone*).
I wish you joy most heartily; and I hope,
Now you're promoted, you'll remember me,
For helping you to advancement. All I ask
Is Phanus's place, to be under-scrivener to you.
Dem. (*to the S. S.*)—You tell me what's your name?
S. S. Agoracritus;
So call'd from the Agora, where I got my living.
Dem. With you then, Agoracritus, in your hands
I place myself; and furthermore consign
This Paphlagonian here to your disposal.
S. S. Then you shall find me a most affectionate
And faithful guardian, the best minister
That ever served the sovereign of the cockneys.
[*Exeunt omnes.*

The actors being withdrawn, the Chorus remain again in possession of the theatre. Their first song is a parody from Pindar, which is converted into a lampoon upon Lysistratus, who, having reduced himself to poverty, had procured (by the assistance of his friends) a lucrative appointment at Delphi. He is mentioned in the Acharnians, *see the song,* *p.* 45.

To record to future years
The lordly wealthy charioteers,
Steeds, and cars, and crowns victorious,
These are worthy themes and glorious.
  Let the Muse refrain from malice,
Nor molest with idle sallies
Him the poor Lysistratus;
Taunted for his empty purse,
Every penny gone and spent,
Lately with Thaumantis sent
On a Delphic embassy,
With a tear in either eye,
Clinging to the deity
To bemoan his misery.

Epirrema.

An attempt is here made to express what the scholiast points out; namely, that the contrast between the two brothers is a piece of dry irony. In other respects the original is hardly capable of translation.

To revile the vile, has ever been accounted just and right,
The business of the comic bard, his proper office, his delight.
On the villanous and base the lashes of invective fall;
While the virtuous and the good are never touch'd or harm'd at all.
Thus without offence, to mark a profligate and wicked brother,
For the sake of explanation, I proceed to name another:
One is wicked and obscure, the brother unimpeach'd and glorious,
Eminent for taste and art, a person famous and notorious.
Arignotus—when I name him, you discern at once, with ease,
The viler and obscurer name, the person meant—Ariphrades.

If he were a rascal only we should let the wretch alone,
He's a rascal, and he knows it, and desires it to be known.
Still we should not have consented to lampoon him into vogue,
As an ordinary rascal, or a villain, or a rogue;
But the wretch is grown inventive, eager to descend and try
Undiscover'd, unattempted depths of filth and infamy;
With his nastiness and lewdness, going on from bad to worse,
With his verses and his music, and his friend Oionychus.
Jolly friends and mates of mine, when with me you quench your thirst,
Spit before you taste the wine—spit upon the fellow first.

Meditating on my bed,
Strange perplexities are bred
In my weary, restless head.
I contemplate and discuss
The nature of Cleonymus,
All the modes of his existence,
His provision and subsistence,
His necessities and wants,
And the houses that he haunts,
Till the master of the table
Accosts him like the gods in fable,
Manifested and adored,
At Baucis' and Philemon's board—
" Mighty sovereign! Mighty lord!
Leave us in mercy and grace.—Forbear!
Our frugal insufficient fare,
Pardon it! and in mercy spare!"

ANTEPIRREMA.

Our Triremes, I was told, held a conference of late:
One, a bulky dame and old, spoke the first in the debate.
" Ladies, have you heard the news? In the town it pass'd for truth,
That a certain low-bred upstart, one Hyperbolus forsooth,
Asks a hundred of our number, with a further proposition,
That we should sail with him to Carthage* on a secret expedition."

* Carthage in this instance may admit of a doubt. See note to p. 79; but it was by no means beyond the speculations of Athenian ambition at that time.

They all were scandalized and shock'd to hear so wild a project plann'd,
A virgin vessel newly dock'd, but which never had been mann'd,
Answer'd instantly with anger, "If the fates will not afford me
Some more suitable proposal, than that wretch to come aboard me,
I would rather rot and perish, and remain from year to year,
Till the worms have eat my bottom, lingering in the harbour here.
No, thank Heaven! For such a master Nauson's daughter is too good;
And if my name were not Nauphantis, I am made of nails and wood.
I propose then to retire, in sanctuary to remain
Near the temple of the Furies or to Theseus and his fane.
Still the project may proceed; Hyperbolus can never fail,
He may launch the trays of wood, in which his lamps were set to *sale*."

AGORACRITUS (*the Sausage-seller*).

Peace be amongst you! Silence! Peace!
Close the courts; let pleadings cease!
All your customary joys,
Juries, accusers, strife and noise!
Be merry, I say! Let the theatre ring
With a shout of applause for the news that I bring.
Chorus. O, thou the protector and hope of the state,
Of the isles and allies of the city, relate
What happy event do you call us to greet,
With bonfire and sacrifice filling the street?
Ag. Old Demus within has moulted his skin;
I've cook'd him, and stew'd him, to render him stronger,
Many years younger, and shabby no longer.
Chorus. Oh, what a change! How sudden and strange!
But where is he now?
Ag. On the citadel's brow,
In the lofty old town of immortal renown,
With the noble Ionian violet crown.

Chorus. What was his vesture, his figure and gesture?
How did you leave him, and how does he look?
Ag. Joyous and bold, as when feasting of old,
When his battles were ended, triumphant and splendid,
With Miltiades sitting carousing at rest,
Or good Aristides, his favourite guest.
You shall see him here straight; for the citadel gate
Is unbarr'd; and the hinges—you hear how they grate!

(*The Scene changes to a view of the Propylæum.*)

Give a shout for the sight of the rocky old height!
And the worthy old wight that inhabits within!
Chorus. Thou glorious hill! pre-eminent still
For splendour of empire and honour and worth!
Exhibit him here, for the Greeks to revere,
Their patron and master, the monarch of earth!
Ag. There, see him, behold! with the jewels of gold
Entwined in his hair, in the fashion of old;
Not dreaming of verdicts or dirty decrees;
But lordly, majestic, attired at his ease,
Perfuming all Greece with an odour of peace.
Chorus. We salute you, and greet you, and bid you rejoice;
With unanimous heart, with unanimous voice,
Our Sovereign Lord, in glory restored,
Returning amongst us in royal array,
Worthy the trophies of Marathon's day!

[*Demus comes forward in his splendid old-fashioned attire: the features of his mask are changed to those of youth, and his carriage, throughout this scene, is marked with the characteristics of youth, warmth, eagerness, and occasional bashfulness and embarrassment.*

Dem. My dearest Agoracritus, come here—
I'm so obliged to you for your cookery!
I feel an alter'd man, you've quite transform'd me.
Ag. What! I? That's nothing; if you did but know
The state you were in before, you'd worship me.
Dem. What was I doing? How did I behave?
Do tell me—inform against me—let me know.
Ag. Why, first, then: if an orator in the assembly
Began with saying, Demus, I'm your friend,

Your faithful, zealous friend, your only friend,
You used to chuckle, and smirk, and hold your head up.

Dem. No, sure!

Ag. So he gain'd his end, and bilk'd and choused ye.

Dem. But did not I perceive it? Was not I told?

Ag. By Jove, and you wore those ears of yours continually
Wide open or close shut, like an umbrella.

Dem. Is it possible? Was I indeed so mere a driveller
In my old age, so superannuated?

Ag. Moreover, if a couple of orators
Were pleading in your presence, one proposing
To equip a fleet, his rival arguing
To get the same supplies distributed
To the jurymen, the patron of the juries
Carried the day.—But why do you hang your head so?
What makes you shuffle about? Can't ye stand still?

Dem. I feel ashamed of myself and all my follies.

*Ag.** 'Twas not your fault—don't think of it. Your advisers
Were most to blame. But for the future—tell me,
If any rascally villanous orator
Should address a jury with such words as these:
"Remember, if you acquit the prisoner
Your daily food and maintenance are at stake;"
How would you treat such a pleader?—Answer me.

* The tone of the S. S. is that of a considerate indulgent preceptor to a young man who has been misbehaving.

Dem. I should toss him headlong into the public pit,
With a halter round his gullet, and Hyperbolus
Tied fast to the end of it.

Ag. That's a noble answer!
Wise and judicious, just and glorious!
Now tell me, in other respects, how do you mean
To manage your affairs?

Dem. Why, first of all,
I'll have the arrears of seamen's wages paid
To a penny, the instant they return to port.

Ag. There's many a worn-out rump will bless ye and thank ye.

Dem. Moreover, no man that has been enroll'd
Upon the list for military service,
Shall have his name erased for fear or favour.

Ag. That gives a bang to Cleonymus's buckler.
Dem. I'll not permit those fellows without beards
To harangue in our assembly, boys or men.
Ag. Then what's to become of Cleisthenes and Strato?*
Where must they speak?
Dem. I mean those kind of youths,
The little puny would-be politicians,
Sitting conversing in perfumers' shops,
Lisping and prating in this kind of way:
"Phæax is sharp—he made a good come-off,
And saved his life in a famous knowing style.
I reckon him a first-rate; quite capital
For energy and compression; so collected,
And such a choice of language! Then to see him
Battling against a mob—it's quite delightful!
He's never cow'd! He bothers 'em completely!"
Ag. It's your own fault; in part you've help'd to spoil 'em,
But what do you mean to do with 'em for the future?
Dem. I shall send them into the country, all the pack of 'em,
To learn to hunt, and leave off making laws.—
Ag. Then I present you here with a folding chair,
And a stout lad to carry it after you.
Dem. Ah, that reminds one of the good old times.
Ag. But what will you say, if I give you a glorious peace,
A lusty strapping truce of thirty years?
Come forward here, my lass, and show yourself.
Dem. By Jove, what a face and figure! I should like
To ratify and conclude incontinently.
Where did you find her?
Ag. Oh, the Paphlagonian,
Of course, had huddled her out of sight, within there.
But now you've got her, take her back with you
Into the country.
Dem. But the Paphlagonian,
What shall we do to punish him? What d' ye think?
Ag. Oh, no great matter. He shall have my trade,
With an exclusive sausage-selling patent,
To traffic openly at the city gates,
And garble his wares with dogs' and asses' flesh;
With a privilege moreover to get drunk,

* See *Ach.*, p. 11, where both are mentioned.

And bully among the strumpets of the suburbs,
And the ragamuffin waiters at the baths.
Dem. That's well imagined; it precisely suits him;
His natural bent, it seems, his proper element
To squabble with poor trulls and low rabscallions.
As for yourself, I give you an invitation
To dine with me in the hall. You'll fill the seat
Which that unhappy villain held before.
Take this new robe! Wear it and follow me!
And you, the rest of you, conduct that fellow
To his future home and place of occupation,
The gate of the city, where the allies and foreigners,
That he maltreated, may be sure to find him.

[*Exeunt.*

THE BIRDS.

INTENDED TO CONVEY SOME NOTION OF ITS EFFECT AS AN ACTED PLAY, AND TO ILLUSTRATE CERTAIN POINTS OF DRAMATIC HUMOUR AND CHARACTER DISCOVERABLE IN THE ORIGINAL.

"Terentius Menandrum, Plautus et Cæcilius, qui veteres Comicos interpretati sunt, numquid hærent in verbis, ac non decorem potius et elegantiam in translatione conservant?"—HIERON. *Epis. de optimo genere interpretandi.*

"Si patrio Graios carmine adire sales
Possumus: optatis plus jam procedimus ipsis.
Hoc satis est."

VIRGIL.

DRAMATIS PERSONÆ.

*EISTHETAIRUS,* an Athenian citizen, but disgusted with his own country, starts on his travels proposing to seek his fortune in the kingdom of the Birds. He is represented as the essential man of business and ability, the true political adventurer; the man who directs every thing and every body; who is never in the wrong, never at a loss, never satisfied with what has been done by others, uniformly successful in his operations. He maintains a constant ascendancy, or if he loses it for a moment, recovers it immediately.

Euelpides, a simple easy-minded droll companion, his natural follower and adherent; as the Merry Andrew is of the Mountebank. It will be seen that, like the Merry Andrew, he interposes his buffoonish comments on the grand oration delivered by his master.

Epops, King of the Birds; formerly Tereus, King of Thrace, but long ago, according to the records of mythology, transformed into a *Hoopoe.* He appears as the courteous dignified sovereign of a primitive uncivilized race, whom he is desirous to improve: he gives a gracious reception to strangers arriving from a country more advanced in civilization; and adopts the projects of aggrandizement suggested to him by Peisthetairus.

The Chorus of Birds, his subjects, retain, on the contrary, their hereditary hatred and suspicion of the human race; they are ready to break out into open mutiny against their king, and to massacre his foreign (human) advisers upon the spot. It is with the greatest difficulty that they can be prevailed upon to hear reason, and attend to the luminous exposition of Peisthetairus. His harangue has the effect of conciliating and convincing them; his projects are adopted without a dissentient voice. War is not immediately declared against the gods, but a sort of Mexican blockade is established by proclamation.

Prometheus, a malcontent deity, the ancient patron of the human race, still retaining a concealed attachment to the deposed dynasty of Saturn. He comes over secretly with intelligence, which Peisthetairus avails himself of, and which proves ultimately decisive of the subjugation of the gods.

Neptune, *Hercules*, *Triballus*, or the *Triballian*, } joint ambassadors from the gods, commissioned to treat with Peisthetairus. *Neptune* is represented as a formal dignified personage of the old school; *Hercules* as a passionate, wrong-headed, greedy blockhead: he is cajoled and gained over by Peisthetairus; and in his turn intimidates the *Triballian*, an ignorant barbarian deity, who is hardly able to speak intelligibly. They join together, Neptune is out-voted, and Peisthetairus concludes a treaty by which his highest pretensions are realized.

The characters above-mentioned are the only ones who contribute in any way to the progress of the drama; the remainder, a very amusing set of persons, are introduced in detached scenes, exemplifying the various interruptions and annoyances incident to the man of business, distracting his attention and embarrassing him in the exercise of his authoritative functions. There are, however, exceptions,—

Iris, who is brought in, having been captured and detained for an infringement of the blockade.

A Priest who comes to sacrifice at the inauguration of the new city.

Two Messengers arriving from different quarters, with very interesting and satisfactory intelligence.

The rest are a mere series of intruders on the time and attention of the great man.

Poet, a ragged vagabond, who comes begging with an inaugural ode on the foundation of the new city.

A Soothsayer, arriving with oracles relative to the same important event, and a demand of perquisites due to himself by divine authority.

Meton, the Astronomer, proposes to make a plan and survey of the new city.

A Commissioner from Athens, a very authoritative personage.

A Vendor of copies of decrees: he enters, reading them aloud, like a hawker to attract purchasers.

Parricide, a young man who has beaten his father, and proposes to strangle him, offers himself as a desirable acquisition to the new colony.

Cinesias, the dithyrambic poet, applies for a pair of wings.

Informer, a young man whose hereditary trade is that of an informer, and whose practice extends to the Islands, comes with the same application.

THE BIRDS.

SCENE.

A wild desolate country with a bare open prospect on one side, and some upright rocks covered with shrubs and brushwood in the centre of the stage. Peisthetairus and Euelpides appear as a couple of worn-out pedestrian travellers, the one with a Raven and the other with a Jackdaw on his hand: they appear to be seeking for a direction from the motions and signals made to them by the Birds.

Euelpides (speaking to his Jackdaw).

RIGHT on, do ye say? to the tree there in the distance?

Peis. (speaking first to his Raven, and then to his companion.

Plague take ye! Why, this creature calls us back!

Eu. What use can it answer tramping up and down?
We're lost, I tell ye: our journey's come to nothing.

Peis. To think of me travelling a thousand stadia
With a Raven for my adviser!

Eu. Think of me too,
Going at the instigation of a Jackdaw,
To wear my toes and my toe-nails to pieces!

Peis. I don't know even the country, where we've got to.

Eu. And yet you expect to find a country here,
A country for yourself!
Peis. Truly, not I;
Not even Execestides* could do it,
That finds himself a native every where.
Eu. Oh dear! We're come to ruin, utter ruin!
Peis. Then go that way, can't ye?—the "Road to Ruin!"
Eu. He has brought us to a fine pass, that crazy fellow,
Philocrates the poulterer; he pretended
To enable us to find where Tereus lives;
The King that was, the Hoopoe that is now;
Persuading us to buy these creatures of him,
That Raven there for three-pence, and this other,—
This little Tharrelides† of a Jackdaw,—
He charged a penny for: but neither of 'em
Are fit for any thing but to bite and scratch.
(*Speaking to his Jackdaw.*)
Well, what are ye after now? gaping and poking!
You've brought us straight to the rock. Where would you take us?
There's no road here!
Peis. No, none, not even a path.
Eu. Nor don't your Raven tell us any thing?
Peis. She's alter'd somehow—she croaks differently.
Eu. But which way does she point? What does she say?
Peis. Say? Why, she says, she'll bite my fingers off.
Eu. Well, truly it's hard upon us, hard indeed,
To go with our own carcasses to the crows,
And not be able to find 'em after all.
(*Turning to the audience.*)[1]
For our design, most excellent spectators,
(Our passion, our disease, or what you will,)
Is the reverse of that which Sacas‡ feels;

* He is attacked again in this play, as a foreign barbarian arrogating to himself the privileges of a true-born Athenian.

† Tharrelides was nicknamed Jackdaw, and Euelpides in contempt of his Jackdaw calls it a Tharrelides! The Raven and the Jackdaw are characteristic. Peisthetairus is the bearer of the sagacious bird, his companion is equipped with a Jackdaw.

‡ Acestor, a tragic poet, not being a genuine Athenian, was called Sacas from the name of a Thracian tribe.

[1] Peisthetairus, it will be seen, allows his companion to put himself forward, with the newly discovered natives; remaining himself in the background as the person of authority, making use of the other as his harbinger; he allows him also to address the audience, not choosing to compromise himself by unnecessary communications. The full and complete account of their motives and design is moreover much better suited to the careless gossipping character of Euelpides.

We may suppose that Peisthetairus must have accompanied this speech with a grave authoritative gesture, indicative of assent and approbation.

For he, though not a native, strives perforce
To make himself a citizen: whilst we,
Known and acknowledged as Athenians born,
(Not hustled off, nor otherwise compell'd,)
Have deem'd it fitting to betake ourselves
To these our legs, and make our person scarce.
  Not through disgust or hatred or disdain
Of our illustrious birth-place, which we deem
Glorious and free; with equal laws ordain'd
For fine and forfeiture and confiscation;
With taxes universally diffused;
And suits and pleas abounding in the Courts.
  For grasshoppers sit only for a month
Chirping upon the twigs; but our Athenians
Sit chirping and discussing all the year,
Perch'd upon points of evidence and law.
  Therefore we trudge upon our present travels,
With these our sacrificial implements,
To seek some easier unlitigious place,
Meaning to settle there and colonize.
Our present errand is in search of Tereus,
(The Hoopoe that is now) to learn from him
If in his expeditions, flights, and journeys,
He ever chanced to light on such a spot.
  Peis. Holloh!
  Eu. What's that?
  Peis. My raven here points upwards.
—Decidedly!
  Eu. Ay, and here's my Jackdaw, too,
Gaping as if she saw something above.—
Yes, I'll be bound for it; this must be the place:
We'll make a noise, and know the truth of it.
  Peis. Then "kick against the rock."*
  Eu. Knock you your head
Against the rock!—and make it a double knock!
  Peis. Then fling a stone at it!
  Eu. With all my heart,
Holloh, there!
  Peis. What do you mean with your Holloh?
You should cry Hoop for a Hoopoe.
  Eu. Well, then, Hoop!
Hoop and holloh, there!—Hoopoe, Hoopoe, I say!

* To "kick against the rock" was proverbial.

Trochilus. What's here? Who's bawling there? Who wants my master?

[*The door is opened, and both parties start at seeing each other.*

Eu. Oh mercy, mighty Apollo! what a beak!

Tr. Out! out upon it! a brace of bird-catchers!

Eu. No, no; don't be disturb'd; think better of us.

Tr. You'll both be put to death.

Eu. But we're not men.

Tr. Not men! what are ye? what do ye call yourselves?

Eu. The fright has turn'd me into a Yellow-Hammer.

Tr. Poh! Stuff and nonsense!

Eu. I can prove it to ye.
Search!

Tr. But your comrade here, what bird is he?

Peis. I'm changed to a Golden Pheasant just at present.

Eu. Now tell me, in heaven's name, what creature are ye?

Tr. I'm a Slave Bird.

Eu. A slave! how did it happen;
Were you made prisoner by a fighting cock?

Tr. No. When my master made himself a Hoopoe,
He begg'd me to turn bird to attend upon him.

Eu. Do birds, then, want attendance?

Tr. Yes, of course;
In his case, having been a man before,
He longs occasionally for human diet,
His old Athenian fare: pilchards for instance,—
Then I must fetch the pilchards; sometimes porridge;
He calls for porridge, and I mix it for him.

*Eu.** Well, you're a dapper waiter, a Didapper;
But Didapper, I say, do step within there,
And call your master out.

Tr. But just at present
He's taking a little rest after his luncheon,
Some myrtle berries and a dish of worms.

Eu. No matter, call him here; we wish to speak to him.

Tr. (*in the tone of Simple, Master Slender's serving man.*)
He'll not be pleased, I'm sure; but notwithstanding,
Since you desire it, I'll make bold to call him. [*Exit.*

Peis. (*looking after him*). Confound ye, I say, you've frighten'd me to death.

* The Trochilus has been unnecessarily communicative, and shown himself a very simple sort of a Serving-man; Euelpides has tact enough to discover this, and assumes the ascendancy accordingly.

Eu. He has scared away my Jackdaw; it's flown away.
Peis. You let it go yourself, you coward.
Eu. Tell me,
Have not you let your Raven go?
Peis. Not I.
Eu. Where is it then?
Peis. Flown off of its own accord.
Eu. You did not let it go! you're a brave fellow!
The Hoopoe (from within). Open the door, I say; let me go forth.

[*The Royal Hoopoe appears with a tremendous beak and crest.*

Eu. O Hercules, what a creature! What a plumage!
And a triple tier of crests; what can it be!
Hoo. Who call'd? who wanted me?
Eu. May the heavenly powers!—
Confound ye! I say (*aside*).
Hoo. You mock at me, perhaps,
Seeing these plumes.—But, stranger, you must know
That once I was a man.
Eu. We did not laugh
At you, Sir.
Hoo. What, then, were you laughing at?
Eu. Only that beak of yours seem'd rather odd.
Hoo. It was your poet Sophocles* that reduced me
To this condition with his tragedies.
Eu. What are you, Tereus? Are you a bird, or what?
Hoo. A Bird.
Eu. Then where are all your feathers?
Hoo. Gone.
Eu. In consequence of an illness?
Hoo. No; the Birds
At this time of the year leave off their feathers.
But you; what are ye? Tell me.
Eu. Mortal men.
Hoo. What countrymen?
Eu. Of the country of the Triremes.†
Hoo. Jurymen, I suppose?
Eu. Quite the reverse,
We're anti-jurymen.
Hoo. Does that breed still
Continue amongst you?

* In his tragedy of Tereus, Sophocles had represented him as transformed (probably only in the last scenes) with the head and beak of a bird.

† Galleys with three banks of oars. The Athenians were at that time undisputed masters of the sea.

Eu. Some few specimens*
You'll meet with here and there in country places.
Hoo. And what has brought you here? What was your object?
Eu. We wish'd to advise with you.
Hoo. With me! For what?
Eu. Because you were a man, the same as us;
And found yourself in debt, the same as us;
And did not like to pay, the same as us;
And after that, you changed into a bird,
And ever since have flown and wander'd far
Over the lands and seas, and have acquired
All knowledge that a bird or man can learn.
Therefore we come, as suppliants, to beseech
Your favour and advice to point us out
Some comfortable country, close and snug,
A country like a blanket or a rug,
Where we might fairly fold ourselves to rest.
Hoo. Do you wish then for a greater state than Athens?
Eu. Not greater, but more suitable for us.
Hoo. It's clear you're fond of aristocracy.
Eu. What, him, the son of Scellias! Aristocrates?†
I abhor him.
Hoo. Well, what kind of a town would suit ye?
Eu. Why, such a kind of town as this, for instance,
A town where the importunities and troubles
Are of this sort. Suppose a neighbour calls
Betimes in the morning with a sudden summons:
"Now, don't forget," says he, "for heaven's sake,
To come to me to-morrow; bring your friends,
Children, and all, we've wedding cheer at home.
Come early, mind ye, and if you fail me now,
Don't let me see your face when I'm in trouble."
Hoo. So you're resolved to encounter all these hardships!
(*To Peisthetairus.*) And what say you?
Peis. My fancy's much the same.
Hoo. How so?
Peis. To find a place of the same sort;
A kind of place where a good, jolly father
Meets and attacks me thus: "What's come to ye
With my young people? You don't take to 'em.
What, they're not reckon'd ugly! You might treat 'em,

* The love of litigation and the passion for sitting on juries, with the exception of a few who retained their old agricultural habits, had infected the whole Athenian community.

† Little or nothing is known of Aristocrates. He lived to the end of the war, and acted in concert with Thrasybulus against Critias. *Dem. in Theocrinem*, p. 1343, ad fin.

As an old friend, with a little attention, surely,
And take a trifling civil freedom with 'em."
Hoo. Ay! You're in love, I see, with difficulties
And miseries. Well, there's a city, in fact,
Much of this sort; one that I think might suit ye,
Near the Red Sea.
Eu. No, no! not near the sea;*
Lest I should have the Salaminian galley†
Arriving some fine morning with a summons
Sent after me, and a poursuivant to arrest me.
But could not you tell us of some Grecian city?
Hoo. Why, there's in Elis there, the town of Lepreum.
Eu. No, no! No Lepreums; nor no lepers neither.
No leprosies for me. Melanthius‡
Has given me a disgust for leprosies.
Hoo. Then there's Opuntius in the land of Locris.
Eu. Opuntius? Me to be like Opuntius!§
With his one eye! Not for a thousand drachmas.
But tell me, among the birds here, how do ye find it?
What kind of an existence?
Hoo. Pretty fair;
Not much amiss. Time passes smoothly enough;
And money is out of the question. We don't use it.
Eu. You've freed yourselves from a great load of dross.
Hoo. We've our field sports. We spend our idle mornings
With banqueting and collations in the gardens,
With poppy seeds and myrtle.
Eu. So your time
Is pass'd like a perpetual wedding-day.

[*Peisthetairus, who has hitherto felt his way by putting Euelpides forward, and allowing him to take the lead, and who has paid no attention to this trifling, inconclusive conversation, breaks out as from a profound reflective reverie.*

Peis. Hah! What a power is here; what opportunities!
If I could only advise you; I see it all!
The means for an infinite empire and command!
Hoo. And what would you have us do? What's your advice?
Peis. Do! what would I have ye do? Why, first of all
Don't flutter and hurry about all open-mouth'd
In that undignified way. With us for instance,

* A humorous blunder. The Red Sea was, in fact, as inaccessible to ancient European navigation as the Caspian.

† The Salaminian galley had been sent to arrest Alcibiades, then one of the joint commanders in Sicily. This was one of the most fatal acts of that popular insanity which it was the poet's object to mitigate and counteract.

‡ A tragic poet, said to have been leprous, ridiculed elsewhere by the author, and by other comic poets, as Plato and Callias.

§ Nothing is recorded of Opuntius, except that he was reckoned a poltroon, and was blind of one eye.

At home, we should cry out, "What creature's that?"
And Teleas would be the first to answer:
"A mere poor creature, a weak restless animal,
A silly bird, that's neither here nor there."*

Hoo. Yes, Teleas might say so. *It would be like him.*
But tell me, what would you have us do?

Peis. (*emphatically.*) Concentrate;
—Bring all your birds together. Build a city.

Hoo. The Birds! How could we build a city? Where?

Peis. Nonsense. You can't be serious. What a question!
Look down.

Hoo. I do.

Peis. Look up now.

Hoo So I do.

Peis. Now turn your neck round.†

Hoo. I should sprain it though.

Peis. Come, what d'ye see?

Hoo. The clouds and sky;—that's all.

Peis. Well, that we call the pole and the atmosphere;
And would it not serve you birds for a metropole?

Hoo. Pole? Is it call'd a pole?

Peis. Yes, that's the name.
Philosophers of late call it the pole;
Because it wheels and rolls itself about,
As it were, in a kind of a roly-poly way.‡
Well, there then, you may build and fortify,
And call it your metropolis,—your acropolis.
From that position you'll command mankind,
And keep them in utter thorough subjugation:
Just as you do the grasshoppers and locusts.
And if the gods offend you, you'll blockade 'em,
And starve 'em to a surrender.

Hoo. In what way?

Peis. Why thus. Your atmosphere is placed, you see,
In a middle point, just betwixt earth and heaven.
A case of the same kind occurs with us.
Our people in Athens, if they send to Delphi
With deputations, offerings, or what not,
Are forced to obtain a pass from the Bœotians:
Thus when mankind on earth are sacrificing,
If you should find the gods grown mutinous
And insubordinate, you could intercept
All their supplies of sacrificial smoke.

* The lines between inverted commas may be understood either as the words of Teleas, or as a description of him; the ambiguity exists in the original, and is evidently intentional. It is continued in the next line of the Hoopoe's answer.

† See in the "Knights" (p. 79) a similar instance of ridiculous stage effect, where the Sausage-seller is mounted on his stool to survey the Athenian empire.

‡ The comic poets ridiculed the new prevailing passion for astronomical and physical science. See further on the Parabasis and the scene where Meton the astronomer is introduced.

Hoo. By the earth and all its springs! springes and nooses! *
Odds, nets and snares! this is the cleverest notion:
And I could find it in my heart to venture,
If the other Birds agree to the proposal.
Peis. But who must state it to them?
Hoo. You yourself,
They'll understand ye, I found them mere barbarians,
But living here a length of time amongst them,
I have taught them to converse and speak correctly. †
Peis. How will you summon them?
Hoo. That's easy enough;
I'll just step into the thicket here hard by,
And call my Nightingale. She'll summon them.
And when they hear her voice, I promise you
You'll see them all come running here pell mell. ‡
Peis. My dearest, best of Birds! don't lose a moment,
I beg, but go directly into the thicket;
Nay, don't stand here, go call your Nightingale.
[*Exit Hoopoe.*

* The Hoopoe's exclamation and oath are in the original, as they are here represented, exactly in the style of Bob Acres!

† The characteristic impertinence of a predominant people, considering their own language as that which ought to be universally spoken.

‡ A female performer on the flute, a great favorite of the public and with the poet, after a long absence from Athens engaged to perform in this play, which was exhibited with an unusual recklessness of expense.

SONG *from behind the scene, supposed to be sung by the Hoopoe.*

Awake! awake!
Sleep no more my gentle mate!
With your tiny tawny bill,
Wake the tuneful echo shrill,
On vale or hill;
Or in her airy rocky seat,
Let her listen and repeat
The tender ditty that you tell,
The sad lament,
The dire event,
To luckless Itys that befell.
Thence the strain
Shall rise again,
And soar amain,
Up to the lofty palace gate,
Where mighty Apollo sits in state
In Jove's abode, with his ivory lyre,
Hymning aloud to the heavenly quire;

While all the gods shall join with thee
In a celestial symphony.

[*A solo on the flute supposed to be the Nightingale's call.*

Peis. Oh, Jupiter! the dear delicious bird!
With what a lovely tone she swells and falls,
Sweetening the wilderness with delicate air.
Eu. Hist!
Peis. What?
Eu. Be quiet, can't ye!
Peis. What's the matter?
Eu. The Hoopoe is just preparing for a song.
Hoo. Hoop! hoop!
Come in a troop,
Come at a call,
One and all,
Birds of a feather,
All together.
Birds of an humble gentle bill
Smooth and shrill,
Dieted on seeds and grain,
Rioting on the furrow'd plain,
Pecking, hopping,
Picking, popping,
Among the barley newly sown.
Birds of bolder louder tone,
Lodging in the shrubs and bushes,
Mavises and Thrushes.
On the summer berries browsing,
On the garden fruits carousing,
All the grubs and vermin smouzing.

You that in an humbler station,
With an active occupation,
Haunt the lowly watery mead,
Warring against the native breed,
The gnats and flies, your enemies;
In the level marshy plain
Of Marathon pursued and slain.

You that in a squadron driving
From the seas are seen arriving,

With the Cormorants and Mews
Haste to land and hear the news!
  All the feather'd airy nation,
Birds of every size and station,
Are convened in convocation.
  For an envoy queer and shrewd
  Means to address the multitude,
And submit to their decision
A surprising proposition,
For the welfare of the state.
  Come in a flurry,
  With a hurry, scurry,
Hurry to the meeting and attend to the debate.

The first appearance of the Chorus must have been a critical point for the success of a play. The audience had been brought into good humour by their favourite musical performer, by whom all the preceding songs were probably executed; for the dialogue on the stage passes solely between Peisthetairus and Euelpides, and the Hoopoe, who is supposed to sing, does not appear. The Chorus now appears, and in the original, forty lines follow, in which Peisthetairus and Euelpides act as showmen to the exhibition of twenty-four figures, dressed in imitation of the plumage of as many different kinds of birds, which are passed in review with suitable remarks as they successively take their places in the orchestra. This passage is here omitted. Whoever wishes to see how well it can be executed, may be referred to Mr. Cary's translation.*

* See what is said in p. 158 of the profuse expense bestowed on the exhibition of this play.

While the Birds are bustling about in their new coop of the orchestra, Euelpides contemplates them with surprise, which soon changes to alarm.

The language of the Birds consists almost wholly of short syllables, the effect of which it is impossible to imitate in English. Some accents, which are added, may serve to make the attempt, they are added also to two spondaic lines, of which the imitation is more practicable.

Eu. Hów they thícken, hów they muster,
How they clutter, hów théy cluster!
Now they ramble here and thither,
Now they scramble altogether.
What a fidgetting and clattering!

What a twittering and chattering!
Don't they mean to threaten us? What think ye?
Peis. Yes, methinks they do.
Eu. They're gaping with an angry look against us both.
Peis. It's very true.
Eu. Where is He, the Màgistrate that assèmbled us to delìberate?
Hoo. Friends and comrades, here am I, your old associate and ally.
Cho. What have ye to commùnicate for the bènefit of the stàte?
Hoo. A proposal safe and useful, practicable, profitable,
Two projectors are arrived here, politicians shrewd and able.
Cho. Whee! whaw! where! where!
What? what? what? what? what?
Hoo. I repeat it—human envoys are arrived, a steady pair,
To disclose without reserve a most stupendous huge affair.
Cho. Chief, of all that ever were, the worst, the most unhappy one!
Speak, explain!
Hoo. Don't be alarm'd!
Cho. Alas, alas! what have you done?
Hoo. I've received a pair of strangers, who desired to settle here.
Cho. Have you risk'd so rash an act?
Hoo. I've done it, and I persevere.
Cho. But where are they?
Hoo. Near beside you; near as I am; very near.
Cho. Oùt, alàs! oùt, alàs!
We are betrày'd, crùelly betray'd
To a calàmitous end.
Our còmrade and our friènd,
Our compànion in the fièlds and in the pàstures
Is the aùthor of all our mìseries and dìsasters,
Our àncient sàcred làws and sòlemn oàth!
Trànsgrèssing bòth!
Trèasonably delìvering us as a prìze
To our hòrrible immemòrial enemiès.
To a detèstable race
Exècrably base!

For the Bird our Chief, hereafter he must answer to the state;
With respect to these intruders, I propose, without debate,
On the spot to tear and hack them.
Eu. There it is, our death and ruin!
Ah, the fault was all your own, you know it; it was all your doing;
You that brought me here, and why?
Peis. Because I wanted an attendant.
Eu. Here to close my life in tears.
Peis. No, that's a foolish fear, depend on't.
Eu. Why a foolish fear?
Peis. Consider; when you're left without an eye,
It's impossible in nature; how could you contrive to cry?
Cho. Form in rank; form in rank;
Then move forward and outflank.
Let me see them overpower'd,
Hack'd, demolish'd, and devour'd,
Neither earth, nor sea, nor sky,
Nor woody fastnesses on high,
Shall protect them if they fly.
Where's the Captain? what detains him? what prevents us to proceed?
On the right there, call the Captain! let him form his troop and lead.
Eu. There it is; where can I fly?
Peis. Sirrah, be quiet; wait a bit.
Eu. What, to be devour'd amongst them!
Peis. Will your legs or will your wit
Serve to escape them?
Eu. I can't tell.
Peis. But I can tell; do as you're bid;
Fight we must. You see the pot just there before ye; take the lid
And present it for a shield; the spit will serve you for a spear;
With it you may scare them off, or spike them if they venture near.
Eu. What can I find to guard my eyes?
Peis. Why, there's the very thing you wish,
Two vizard helmets ready made, the cullender and skimming dish.

Eu. What a clever, capital, lucky device, sudden and new!
Nicias,* with all his tactics, is a simpleton to you.

Cho. Steady, Birds! present your beaks! in double time, charge and attack!
Pounce upon them, smash the potlid, clapperclaw them, tear and hack.

Hoo. Tell me, most unworthy creatures, scandal of the feather'd race,
Must I see my friends and kinsmen massacred before my face?

Cho. What, do you propose to spare them? Where will your forbearance cease,
Hesitating to destroy destructive creatures such as these?

Hoo. Enemies they might have been; but here they come, with fair design,
With proposals of advice, for your advantage and for mine.

Cho. Enemies time out of mind! they that have spilt our fathers' blood,
How should they be friends of ours, or give us counsel for our good?

Hoo. Friendship is a poor adviser; politicians deep and wise
Many times are forced to learn a lesson from their enemies;
Diligent and wary conduct is the method soon or late
Which an adversary teaches; whilst a friend or intimate
Trains us on to sloth and ease; to ready confidence; to rest
In a careless acquiescence; to believe and hope the best.
Look on earth![1] behold the nations, all in emulation vying,
Active all, with busy science engineering, fortifying;
To defend their hearths and homes, with patriotic industry,
Fencing every city round with massy walls of masonry;
Tactical devices old they modify with new design;
Arms offensive and defensive to perfection they refine;

* Nicias was at this time in the chief command of the Sicilian expedition, Alcibiades having been recalled. See note p. 156.

[1] The vast changes and improvement in the practice and the art of war which took place about this time were a subject of general speculation and remark. The concise allusions in the text are, therefore, somewhat enlarged in the translation.

Galleys are equipt and arm'd, and armies train'd to discipline.
Look to life, in every part; in all they practise, all they know,
Every nation has derived its best instruction from the foe.

Cho. We're agreed to grant a hearing; if an enemy can teach
Anything that's wise or useful, let him prove it in his speech.

Peis. (*aside*). Let's retire a pace or two; you see the change in their behaviour.

Hoo. Simple justice I require, and I request it as a favour.

Cho. Faith and equity require it, and the nation hitherto
Never has refused to take direction and advice from you.

Peis. (*aside.*) They're relenting by degrees;
Recover arms and stand at ease.

*Cho.** Back to the rear! resume your station,
Ground your wrath and indignation,
Sheathe your fury, stand at ease!
While I proceed to question these:
What design has brought them here?
Hoh, there, Hoopoe! can't he hear?

Hoo. What's your question?

Cho. Who are these?

Hoo. Strangers from the land of Greece.

Cho. What design has brought them thence?
What's their errand or pretence?

Hoo. They come here simply with a view
To settle and reside with you;
Here to remain and here to live.

Cho. What is the reason that they give?

Hoo. A project marvellous and strange.

Cho. Will it account for such a change,
Coming here so vast a distance?
Does he look for our assistance
To serve a friend or harm a foe?

Hoo. Mighty plans he has to show
(Hinted and proposed in brief)
For a power beyond belief;
Ocean, earth, he says, and air,

* Thirteen lines (from 387 to 400, ed. Bekk.,) which unaccompanied by the action on the stage would appear tiresome and unmeaning, are are here omitted.

All creation everywhere,
Everything that's here or there,
An empire and supremacy
Over all beneath the sky
Is attainable by you,
Your just dominion and your due.

Cho. Tell us, was he fool or mad?

Hoo. No, believe me, grave and sad.

Cho. Did his reasons and replies
Mark him as discreet and wise?

Hoo. With a force, a depth, a reach
Of judgment; a command of speech;
An invention, a facility,
An address, a volubility,
More than could be thought believable;
'Tis a varlet inconceivable!

Cho. Let us hear him! let us hear him!
Bid him begin! for raised on high
Our airy fancy soars; and I
Am rapt in hope, ready to fly.

The King Hoopoe now gives some orders in a pacific spirit, directing that all warlike weapons be removed and hung up at the back of the chimney as before. He then calls upon Peisthetairus to communicate to the assembled commonalty the propositions which had been before discussed in private conference between themselves. Peisthetairus, however, sees his advantage, and insists upon the previous conclusion of a formal treaty of peace; this is done, and the Chorus swear to it (relapsing for a moment into their real character), "as they hope to win the prize by an unanimous vote." But if they should fail, they imprecate upon themselves the penalty of (gaining the prize notwithstanding, but) "gaining it only by a casting vote." Peace is proclaimed, the armament is dissolved by proclamation, and the Chorus recommence singing.

Hoo. (*to the Chorus*). Here you, take these same arms, in the name of Heaven,
And hang them quietly in the chimney-corner; (*turning to Peisthetairus,*)
And you, communicate your scheme, exhibiting

Your proofs and calculations—the discourse
Which they were call'd to attend to.
Peis. No, not I,
By Jove! unless they agree to an armistice;
Such as the little poor baboon, our neighbour,
The sword cutler, concluded with his wife;
That they shan't bite me, or take unfair advantage
In any way.
Cho. We won't.
Peis. Well, swear it then!
Cho. We swear, by our hope of gaining the first prize
With the general approval and consent
Of the whole audience, and of all the judges—
And if we fail, may the reproach befall us,
Of gaining it only by the casting vote.

*It should seem that the success of this play must have been a subject of more than usual anxiety, both to the Poet himself, and to the Choregus * and his friends: we may conceive it to have been intended as a sedative to the mind of the commonalty, excited, as they were at the time, almost to madness by the suspicion of a conspiracy against the religion and laws of the country; a suspicion originating in a profane outrage secretly perpetrated, to a great extent, in mere insolence and wantonness, by some young men of family. In the opinion, however, of the Athenian people, the offence was viewed in a very serious light, as the result of an extensive secret combination (on the part of persons bound and engaged to each other by their common participation in the guilt of sacrilege), preparatory to other attempts still more criminal and dangerous. In this state of things, and while the popular fury and jealousy upon religious subjects was at its height, the Poet ventured to produce this play, in which it will be seen that the burlesque of the national Mythology is carried higher and continued longer than in any of his other existing plays.—The confident hopes expressed by the Chorus were not realized; the first prize was assigned to a play, the title of which, the* Comastæ *or* Drunken Rioters, *seems to imply that its chief interest must have been derived from direct allusions to the outrage above mentioned, and to the individuals suspected to have been engaged in it.*

* The wealthy citizen charged with the expense and management of a theatrical entertainment.

But we must return to the Herald dismissing the troops.

Her. Hear ye, good people all! the troops are order'd
To take their arms within doors; and consult
On the report and entry to be made
Upon our journal of this day's proceedings.

Cho. Since time began
The race of Man
Has ever been deceitful, faithless ever.
Yet may our fears be vain!
Speak therefore and explain:
If in this realm of ours,
Your clearer intellect searching and clever,
Has noticed means or powers
Unknown and undetected,
In unambitious indolence neglected.
Guide and assist our ignorant endeavour:
You, for your willing aid and ready wit,
Will share with us the common benefit.

Now speak to the business and be not afraid,
The Birds will adhere to the truce that we made.

The long series of Anapæstic lines which follows, holds the place of the debates which occur in other comedies, and which are conducted in Anapæstic verse. Peisthetairus could not properly have been matched with an opponent or antagonist; the uniformity of his speech is however relieved by the interruptions and comments of Euelpides, who acts an under part to him, much in the same style as a Merry Andrew to a Mountebank. Observe that Peisthetairus never vouchsafes an answer or takes any kind of notice of his companion, but proceeds continuously, except once or twice in reply to the Chorus and the Hoopoe.

Peis. I'm fill'd with the subject and long to proceed—
My rhetorical leaven is ready to knead.—
Boy, bring me a crown* and a basin and ewer.
Eu. Why, what does he mean? Are we banqueting, sure?
Peis. A rhetorical banquet I mean; and I wish

* A crown was worn by the public orators when haranguing the people, and also at feasts.

To serve them at first with a sumptuous dish,
To astound and delight them. "The grief and compassion
That oppresses my mind on beholding a nation,
A people of sovereigns"* . . .
Cho. Sovereigns we!
Peis. Of all the creation! of this man and me,
And of Jupiter too; for observe that your birth
Was before the old Titans, and Saturn, and Earth.
Cho. And Earth!
Peis. I repeat it.
Cho. That's wonderful news!
Peis. Your wonder implies a neglect to peruse
And examine old Æsop, from whom you might gather
That the lark was embarrass'd to bury his father
On account of the then non-existence of Earth;
And how to repair so distressing a dearth,
He adopted a method unheard of and new.
Cho. If the story you quote is authentic and true,
No doubt can exist of our clear seniority,
And the gods must acknowledge our right to authority.
Eu. Your beaks will be worn with distinction and pride;
The woodpecker's title will scarce be denied;
And Jove the pretender will surely surrender.
Peis. . . . Moreover, most singular facts are combined
In proof that the birds were adored by mankind:
For instance, the Cock was a sovereign of yore
In the empire of Persia, and ruled it before
Darius's time; and you all may have heard
That his title exists as the "Persian bird." . . .
Eu. And hence you behold him stalk in pride,
Majestic and stout, with a royal stride,
With his turban upright, a privilege known
Reserved to kings and kings alone.
Peis. . . . So wide was his empire, so mighty his sway,
That the people of earth to the present day
Attend to his summons and freely obey:
Tinkers, tanners, cobblers, all,
Are roused from rest at his royal call,
And shuffle their shoes on before it is light
To trudge to the workshop.
Eu. I warrant you're right;

* The inverted commas mark the premeditatedly abrupt exordium of Peisthetairus's harangue.

I know to my cost, by the cloak that I lost,
It was owing to him I was robb'd and beguiled.
For a feast had been made for a neighbour's child,
To give it a name; and I went as a guest,
And sat there carousing away with the rest;
But drinking too deep, I fell soundly asleep;
And he began crowing; and I never knowing,
But thinking it morning, went off at the warning
(With the wine in my pate, to the city gate),
And fell in with a footpad, lying in wait,
Just under the town, and was fairly knock'd down;
Then I tried to call out; but before I could shout,
He stripp'd me at once with a sudden pull,
Of a brand new mantle of Phrygian wool.
Peis. . . . Then the kite was the monarch of Greece heretofore.
Hoo. Of Greece?
Peis. . . . and instructed our fathers of yore,
On beholding a kite to fall down and adore . . .
Eu. Well, a thing that befell me, was comical quite,
I threw myself down on beholding a kite;
But turning my face up to stare at his flight,
With a coin in my mouth,* forgetting my penny,
I swallow'd it down, and went home without any.
Peis. . . . In Sidon and Egypt the Cuckoo was king;
They wait to this hour for the Cuckoo to sing;
And when he begins, be it later or early,
They reckon it lawful to gather their barley . . .
Eu. Ah, thence it comes our harvest cry,
Cuckoo, Cuckoo, to the passers-by.
Peis. . . . At an era, moreover, of modern date,
Menelaus the king, Agamemnon the great,
Had a bird as assessor attending in state,
Perch'd on his sceptre, to watch for a share
Of fees and emoluments, secret or fair.
Eu. Ah, there I perceive I was right in my guess,
For when Priam appear'd in his tragical dress,
The bird on his sceptre, I plainly could see,
Was watching Lysicrates† taking a fee.
Peis. . . . Nay, Jupiter now that usurps the command
Appears with an Eagle, appointed to stand
As his emblem of empire; a striking example

* It was usual with the Greeks to put small pieces of silver coin in their mouths; a custom which the turnpike men of Great Britain continued to retain within the recollection of the writer.

† Of Lysicrates the scholiast only informs us that he was a person in office known to be in the habit of taking bribes, a description which in relation to those times is hardly a distinction.

Of authority once so extended and ample:
And each of the gods had his separate fowl,
Apollo a Hawk, and Minerva an Owl.

* This speech seems more properly to belong to the Hoopoe.

*Eu.** That's matter of fact, and you're right in the main;
But what was the reason I wish you'd explain.
Peis. The reason was this: that the bird should be there
To demand as of right a proportional share
Of the entrails and fat; when an offering was made,
A suitable portion before them was laid:
Moreover you'll find that the race of mankind
Always swore by a bird; and it never was heard
That they swore by the gods at the time that I mention.

† As a substitute for common swearing, some persons (Socrates among the rest) made use of less offensive expletives, swearing "by the dog or by the goose."—Lampon was a soothsayer, and thought it right probably to be scrupulous in using the name of the god. He is mentioned again in this play.

And Lampon† himself, with a subtle intention,
Adheres to the old immemorial use;
He perjures and cheats us, and swears "by the goose."
Thus far forth have I proved and shown
The power and estate that were once your own
Now totally broken and overthrown:
And need I describe your present tribe,
Weak, forlorn, exposed to scorn,
Distress'd, oppress'd, never at rest,
Daily pursued with outrage rude,
With cries and noise of men and boys,
Screaming, hooting, pelting, shooting,
The fowler sets his traps and nets,
Twigs of bird-lime, loops, and snares,
To catch you kidnapp'd unawares,
Even within the temple's pale.
They set you forth to public sale,
Paw'd and handled most severely;
And, not content with roasting merely,
In an insolent device,
Sprinkle you with cheese and spice;
With nothing of respect or favour,
Derogating from your flavour.
Or for a further outrage have ye
Soused in greasy sauce and gravy.

Hoo. Sad and dismal is the story,
Human stranger, which you tell,
Of our fathers' ancient glory
Ere the fated empire fell.

From the depth of degradation
  A benignant happy fate
Sends you to restore the nation,
  To redeem and save the state.

I consign to your protection,
  Able to preserve them best,
All my objects of affection,
  My wife, my children, and my nest.

If the reader should be inclined to pass over the next hundred lines, I should feel no wish to detain him. The subject of them has been pretty nearly anticipated, and the whole play is in fact too long.

Hoo. Explain then the method you mean to pursue
To recover our empire and freedom anew.
For thus to remain in dishonour and scorn,
Our life were a burthen no more to be borne.
Peis. Then I move, that the birds shall in common repair
To a centrical point, and encamp in the air;
And intrench and enclose it, and fortify there;
And build up a rampart impregnably strong,
Enormous in thickness, enormously long,
Bigger than Babylon, solid and tall,
With bricks and bitumen, a wonderful wall.
Eu. Bricks and bitumen! I'm longing to see
What a daub of a building the city will be!
Peis. . . . As soon as the fabric is brought to an end,
A herald or envoy to Jove we shall send,
To require his immediate prompt abdication;
And if he refuses, or shows hesitation,
Or evades the demand, we shall further proceed
With legitimate warfare, avow'd and decreed;
With a warning and notices, formally given,
To Jove, and all others residing in heaven,
Forbidding them ever to venture again
To trespass on our atmospheric domain,
With scandalous journeys, to visit a list
Of Alcmenas and Semeles; if they persist,
We warn them that means will be taken moreover
To stop their gallanting and acting the lover.
Another ambassador also will go
Dispatch'd upon earth to the people below,

To notify briefly the fact of accession,
And enforcing our claims upon taking possession;
With orders in future, that every suitor,
Who applies to the gods with an offering made,
Shall begin with a previous offering paid,
To a suitable Bird, of a kind and degree
That accords with the god, whosoever he be.
In Venus's fane if a victim is slain,
First let a Sparrow be feasted with grain.
When gifts and oblations to Neptune are made,
To the Drake let a tribute of barley be paid.
Let the Cormorant's appetite* first be appeased,
And let Hercules then have an Ox for his feast.
If you offer to Jove, as the sovereign above,
A Ram for his own, let the Golden-crown,
As a sovereign bird, be duly preferr'd,
Feasted and honour'd, in right of his reign,
With a jolly fat pismire offer'd and slain.

Eu. A pismire, how droll! I shall laugh till I burst!
Let Jupiter thunder and threaten his worst!

Hoo. But mankind, will they, think ye, respect and adore,
If they see us all flying, the same as before?
They will reckon us merely as Magpies and Crows.

Peis. Poh! nonsense, I tell ye—no blockhead but knows
That Mercury flies; there is Iris too,
Homer informs us how she flew:
"Smooth as a Dove she went sailing along."
And pinions of gold, both in picture and song,
To Cupid and Victory fairly belong.

Hoo. But Jove's thunder has wings; if he send but a volley,
Mankind for a time may abandon us wholly.

Peis. What then? we shall raise a granivorous troop
To sweep their whole crops with a ravenous swoop:
If Ceres is able, perhaps she may deign
To assist their distress with a largess of grain. . . .

Eu. No, no! she'll be making excuses, I warrant.

Peis. . . . Then the Crows will be sent on a different errand,
To pounce all at once, with a sudden surprise,
On their oxen and sheep, to peck out their eyes,

* With the writers of the old comedy extreme voracity was the characteristic attribute of Hercules.

And leave them stone blind for Apollo to cure:
He'll try it; he'll work for his salary, sure!
Eu. Let the cattle alone; I've two beeves of my own:
Let me part with them first, and then do your worst.
Peis. But, if men shall acknowledge your merit and worth
As equal to Saturn, to Neptune, and Earth,
And to every thing else, we shall freely bestow
All manner of blessings.
Hoo. Explain them and show.
Peis. For instance: if locusts arrive to consume
All their hopes of a crop, when the vines are in bloom,
A squadron of Owls may demolish them all;
The Midges moreover, which canker and gall
The figs and the fruit, if the Thrush is employ'd,
By a single battalion will soon be destroy'd.
Hoo. But wealth is their object; and how can we grant it?
Peis. We can point them out mines: and help will be wanted
To inspect and direct navigation and trade;
Their voyages all will be easily made,
With a saving of time and a saving of cost;
And a seaman in future will never be lost.
Hoo. How so?
Peis. We shall warn them: "Now hasten to sail,
Now keep within harbour; your voyage will fail."
Eu. How readily then will a fortune be made!
I'll purchase a vessel and venture on trade.
*Peis.** . . . And old treasure conceal'd will again be reveal'd;
The Birds as they know it will readily show it.
'Tis a saying of old, "My silver and gold
Are so safely secreted, and closely interr'd,
No creature can know it, excepting a Bird."
Eu. I'll part with my vessel, I'll not go aboard;
I'll purchase a mattock and dig up a hoard.
Hoo. We're clear as to wealth; but the blessing of health
Is the gift of the gods.
Peis. It will make no such odds:
If they're going on well, they'll be healthy still,

* The want of stability and good faith both in the Government and individuals obliged the Greeks to secure their moneyed capital by concealment. Hence the vast collections of ancient coin which appear in the cabinets of antiquarians.
Observe the shallow shatter-brained character of Euelpides.

And none are in health that are going on ill.
Hoo. But then for longevity; that is the gift
Of the gods.
Peis. But the Birds can afford them a lift,
And allow them a century, less or more.
Hoo. How so?
Peis. From their own individual store,
They may reckon it fair, to allot them a share; *
For old proverbs affirm, that the final term
Of a Raven's life exceeds the space
Of five generations of human race.
Hoo.† What need have we then for Jove as a king?
Surely the Birds are a better thing!
Peis. Surely! surely! First and most,
We shall economize the cost
Of marbled domes and gilded gates.
The Birds will live at cheaper rates,
Lodging, without shame or scorn,
In a maple or a thorn;
The most exalted and divine
Will have an olive for his shrine.
We need not run to foreign lands,
Or Ammon's temple in the sands;
But perform our easy vows
Among the neighbouring shrubs and boughs;
Paying our oblations fairly
With a pennyworth of barley.
Cho.[1] O best of all envoys, suspected before,
Now known and approved, and respected the more;
To you we resign the political lead,
Our worthy director in council and deed.

Elated with your bold design,
I swear and vow,
If resolutely you combine
Your views and interest with mine,

* The origin of this notion of life being transferable cannot be accounted for; in the form of a wish, it appears to have been common.

† This speech must belong to the Hoopoe. Aristophanes would not leave the result of the scene to be summed up by such a silly fellow as Euelpides. We see besides that Peisthetairus replies to it. He never replies to Euelpides.

[1] There can be no doubt that this speech belongs to the Chorus, though it may seem difficult to account for what is said of the sceptre, which it should seem ought rather to belong to the king. The Hoopoe in answer alludes to the inveterate vice of all Choruses—dawdling and inefficiency.

In steadfast councils as a trusty friend,
Without deceit, or guile, or fraudful end,
They that rule in haughty state,
The gods, ere long shall abdicate
Their high command,
And yield the sceptre to my rightful hand.

Then reckon on us for a number and force ;
As on you we rely for a ready resource,
In council and policy trusting to you
To direct the design we resolve to pursue.

Hoo. That's well, but we've no time, by Jove! to loiter,
And dawdle and postpone like Nicias.*
We should be doing something. First however
I must invite you to my roosting place,
This nest of mine, with its poor twigs and leaves.
And tell me what your names are?

Peis. Certainly ;
My name is Peisthetairus.†

Hoo. And your friend ?

Eu. Euelpides from Thria.

Hoo. Well, you're welcome—
Both of ye.

Peis. We're obliged.

Hoo. Walk in together.

Peis. Go first then, if you please.

Hoo. No, pray move forward.

Peis. But bless me—stop, pray—just for a single moment—
Let's see—do tell me—explain—how shall we manage
To live with you—with a person wearing wings ?
Being both of us unfledged?

Hoo. Perfectly well!

Peis. Yes, but I must observe, that Æsop's fables
Report a case in point—the fox and eagle :
The fox repented of his fellowship,
And with good cause ; you recollect the story.[1]

* The Athenians were at that time disappointed at Nicias's delay, in not advancing immediately against Syracuse.

† Peisthetairus answers like a man of sense, Euelpides like a simpleton ; and we see the effect of it on the king's mind. There is a momentary pause in the invitation, before they are both included in it.

[1] Peisthetairus has shown that he is not deficient in valour upon compulsion. But a character of extreme subtlety is always prone to suspicion, and the recollection of an example derived from ancient documents in "Æsop's Fables," intimidates him for a moment, and

Hoo. Oh! don't be alarm'd; we'll give you a certain root
That immediately promotes the growth of wings.
Peis. Come, let's go in then; Xanthias, do you mind,
And Manodorus,* follow with the bundles.
Cho. Holloh!
Hoo. What's the matter?
Cho. Go in with your party,
And give them a jolly collation and hearty.
But the Bird to the Muses and Graces so dear,
The lovely, sweet Nightingale, bid her appear,
And leave her amongst us, to sport with us here.
Peis. (*with a hurried, nervous eagerness.*)
O yes, by Jove! indeed, you must indulge them;
Do, do me the favour; call her from the thicket!
For heaven's sake—let me entreat you—bring her here,
And let us have a sight of her ourselves.
Hoo. (*with grave good-breeding, implying a kind of rebuke to the fussy importunity into which Peisthetairus had fallen.*)
Since it is your wish and pleasure, it must be so;
Come here to the strangers, Procne! show yourself!
Peis. O Jupiter! what a graceful, charming bird!
What a beautiful creature it is!
Eu. I'll tell ye what;
I could find in my heart to rumple her feathers.
Peis. And what an attire she wears, all bright with gold!
Eu. Well, I should like to kiss her for my part.
Peis. You blockhead! With that beak she'd run you through.
Eu. By Jove, then, one must treat her like an egg;
Just clear away the shell and kiss her—thus.
Hoo. (*gravely disapproving the liberties which are taken in his presence.*) Let's go.

* These slaves do not appear elsewhere in the play; it might be doubted whether they appear here, and whether Peisthetairus does not call for them in mere nervous absence of mind.

---

makes him distrustful of the frank invitation of the king. He is then very much ashamed of himself, and like Bacchus and Master Slender, begins giving orders to his servants, and is importunate and hurried and absurd. Thus the poet, who wanted some lines of strong importunity to mark the entrance of his favourite Musician, has contrived to give them to his principal personage, and at the same time to mark his character itself more distinctly, by this momentary failure of his habitual self-possession, originating in the apprehension of having lowered himself in the estimation of his host.

Peis. Go first, then, and good luck go with us.
[*Exeunt.*

The Actors having left the stage, the Parabasis ought to follow.—It is here prefaced in a singular way by a complimentary song from the Chorus, addressed to the favourite female Musician.

Cho. O lovely, sweet companion meet,
From morn to night my sole delight,
My little happy, gentle mate,
You come, you come, O lucky fate!
Returning here with new delight,*
To charm the sight, to charm the sight,
And charm the ear.
Come, then, anew combine
Your notes in harmony with mine,
And with a tone beyond compare
Begin your Anapæstic air.

* See what is said p. 158. She had been engaged for this performance, and was newly arrived.

The sudden passion for science among the Athenians, and the ridicule of it among the comic poets, have been already noticed.

Much might be said on the subject of the most splendid passage of the Parabasis, and of the philosophic system of which it presents the traces: but this would lead to considerations very remote from the imitation of actual life and manners and character, which, as constituting the most singular excellence of the author, it has been the object of the translator to illustrate.

Of the Parabasis before us, the merits are well known, and perhaps no passage in Aristophanes has been oftener quoted with admiration. To bring the most sublime subjects within the verge of Comedy, and to treat of them with humour and fancy, without falling into vulgarity or offending the principles of good taste, seems a task which no poet, whom we know of, could have accomplished: Though if we were possessed of the words of Epicharmus, it is possible that we might see other specimens of the same style.

Ye Children of Man! whose life is a span,
Protracted with sorrow from day to day,
Naked and featherless, feeble and querulous,
Sickly calamitous creatures of clay!

Attend to the words of the Sovereign Birds,
(Immortal, illustrious, lords of the air,)
Who survey from on high, with a merciful eye,
Your struggles of misery, labour, and care.
Whence you may learn and clearly discern
Such truths as attract your inquisitive turn;
Which is busied of late with a mighty debate,
A profound speculation about the creation,
And organical life, and chaotical strife,
With various notions of heavenly motions,
And rivers and oceans, and valleys and mountains,
And sources of fountains, and meteors on high,
And stars in the sky . . . We propose by-and-by,
(If you'll listen and hear,) to make it all clear.
And Prodicus henceforth shall pass for a dunce,
When his doubts are explain'd and expounded at once.

Before the creation of Æther and Light,
Chaos and Night together were plight,
In the dungeon of Erebus foully bedight.
Nor Ocean, or Air, or substance was there,
Or solid or rare, or figure or form,
But horrible Tartarus ruled in the storm:
At length, in the dreary chaotical closet
Of Erebus old, was a privy deposit,
By Night the primæval in secrecy laid—
A mystical egg, that in silence and shade
Was brooded and hatch'd, till time came about,
And Love, the delightful, in glory flew out,
In rapture and light exulting and bright,
Sparkling and florid, with stars in his forehead,
His forehead and hair, and a flutter and flare,
As he rose in the air, triumphantly furnish'd
To range his dominions on glittering pinions,
All golden and azure, and blooming and burnish'd:
He soon, in the murky Tartarean recesses,
With a hurricane's might, in his fiery caresses
Impregnated Chaos; and hastily snatch'd
To being and life, begotten and hatch'd,
The primitive Birds: but the Deities all,
The celestial Lights, the terrestrial Ball,
Were later of birth, with the dwellers on earth

More tamely combined, of a temperate kind;
When chaotical mixture approach'd to a fixture.
  Our antiquity proved, it remains to be shown
That Love is our author and master alone;
Like him we can ramble, and gambol and fly
O'er ocean and earth, and aloft to the sky:
And all the world over, we're friends to the lover,
And when other means fail, we are found to prevail,
When a Peacock or Pheasant is sent as a present.
  All lessons of primary daily concern
You have learnt from the Birds, and continue to learn,
Your best benefactors and early instructors;
We give you the warning of seasons returning.
  When the Cranes are arranged, and muster afloat
In the middle air, with a creaking note,
Steering away to the Libyan sands,
Then careful farmers sow their lands;
The crazy vessel is haul'd ashore,
The sail, the ropes, the rudder, and oar
Are all unshipp'd, and housed in store.
  The shepherd is warn'd, by the Kite reappearing,
To muster his flock, and be ready for shearing.
  You quit your old cloak at the Swallow's behest,
In assurance of summer, and purchase a vest.
  For Delphi, for Ammon, Dodona, in fine
For every oracular temple and shrine,
The Birds are a substitute equal and fair,
For on us you depend, and to us you repair
For counsel and aid when a marriage is made,
A purchase, a bargain, a venture in trade:
Unlucky or lucky, whatever has struck ye,
An ox or an ass that may happen to pass,
A voice in the street, or a slave that you meet,
A name or a word by chance overheard,
If you deem it an omen, you call it a *Bird;*
And if birds are your omens, it clearly will follow
That birds are a proper prophetic Apollo.

  Then take us as gods, and you'll soon find the odds,
We'll serve for all uses, as prophets and muses;
We'll give ye fine weather, we'll live here together;
We'll not keep away, scornful and proud, a-top of a cloud,

The series of short lines at the end of a Parabasis was to be repeated with the utmost volubility and rapidity as if in a single breath.' A comic effect is sometimes produced in this way on our own stage.

(In Jupiter's way); but attend every day
To prosper and bless all you possess,
And all your affairs, for yourselves and your heirs.
And as long as you live, we shall give
You wealth and health, and pleasure and treasure,
In ample measure;
And never bilk you of pigeon's milk
Or potable gold; you shall live to grow old,
In laughter and mirth, on the face of the earth,
Laughing, quaffing, carousing, boozing,
  Your only distress shall be the excess
  Of ease and abundance and happiness.

SEMICHORUS.

We see here a comic imitation of the Tragic Choruses of Phrynichus, a poet older than Æschylus, of whom Aristophanes always speaks with respect, as an improver of music and poetry, arts which, in the judgment of the ancients, were deemed inseparable; or, if disjoined, essentially defective and imperfect.

Muse, that in the deep recesses
  Of the forest's dreary shade,
Vocal with our wild addresses,
  Or in the lonely lowly glade
Attending near, art pleased to hear
  Our humble bill, tuneful and shrill:

When to the name of omnipotent Pan
  Our notes we raise, or sing in praise
Of mighty Cybele, from whom we began,
  Mother of nature and every creature,
Wing'd or unwing'd, of birds or man;
  Aid and attend, and chaunt with me
The music of Phrynichus, open and plain,
  The first that attempted a loftier strain,
Ever busy like the bee, with the sweets of harmony.

EPIRREMA.

Is there any person present sitting a spectator here,
Who desires to pass his time freely without restraint or
    fear?

Should he wish to colonize, he never need be check'd or chid
For the trifling indiscretions which the testy laws forbid.
Parricides are in esteem: among the birds we deem it fair,
A combat honourably fought betwixt a game-cock and his heir!
There the branded runagate, branded and mottled in the face,
Will be deem'd a motley bird; a motley mark is no disgrace.
Spintharus, the Phrygian born, will pass a muster there with ease,
Counted as a Phrygian fowl, and even Execestides,*
Once a Carian and a slave, may there be nobly born and free,
Plume himself on his descent, and hatch a proper pedigree.

* Already noted as a foreigner in the first scene of this play.

SEMICHORUS.

This second sample of the style of Phrynichus may serve to give us a more distinct idea of it. It seems to have been one of essential grandeur and harmony, but trespassing occasionally into the regions of nonsense.

Thus the Swans in chorus follow,
On the mighty Thracian stream
Hymning their eternal theme—
Praise to Bacchus and Apollo:
The welkin rings with sounding wings,
With songs and cries and melodies,
Up to the thunderous Æther ascending.

Whilst all that breathe on earth beneath,
The beasts of the wood, the plain, and the flood,
In panic amazement are crouching and bending,
With the awful qualm of a sudden calm
Ocean and air in silence blending.
The ridge of Olympus is sounding on high,
Appalling with wonder the lords of the sky,
And the Muses and Graces,
Enthroned in their places,
Join in the solemn symphony.

ANTEPIRREMA.

Nothing can be more delightful than the having wings to wear!
A spectator sitting here, accommodated with a pair,
Might for instance (if he found a tragic chorus dull and heavy)
Take his flight and dine at home, and if he did not choose to leave ye,
Might return in better humour when the weary drawl was ended.
Introduce then wings in use—believe me, matters will be mended:
Patroclides[1] would not need to sit there and befoul his seat;
Flying off, he might return, eased in a moment, clean and neat.
Trust me, wings are all in all! Diitrephes has mounted quicker
Than the rest of our aspirants, soaring on his wings of wicker;
Basket-work and crates and hampers first enabled him to fly;*
First a captain, then promoted to command the cavalry;
With his fortunes daily rising, office and preferment new,
An illustrious, enterprising, airy, gallant Cockatoo.

* His property consisted in a manufactory of this kind, by which he had grown rich.

The exclusive functions of the Chorus being now at an end, the persons of the Drama appear again upon the stage, Peisthetairus and Euelpides having been both in the meanwhile equipped with a sumptuous pair of wings. They are supposed to have been entertained behind the scenes with a royal collation in the palace of the Hoopoe.—Peisthetairus is accordingly in extreme good humour, and being now in the height of his advancement, recollects that it will be right

[1] The posthumous celebrity of Patroclides is not confined to this single event. He survived the accident many years, and was the author of a very salutary decree upon the principles advocated by the Poet in the epirrema of the "Frogs," but (as in the instance before us) he was again fatally too late.—The decree was not passed till after the destruction of the navy at Ægospotamos.

to behave to his former comrade with the hearty familiarity of an old acquaintance; he accordingly begins, with a ludicrous simile[1] *on his appearance (a species of raillery common among the Athenians, but which was considered as the lowest kind of jocularity). He takes his friend's retort in perfect good humour, and Euelpides is admitted as a third person, to consult, with him and the King, upon some unimportant matters, such as the name of the new city, and the choice of a patron deity, upon all which topics his idle buffoonish humour is not misplaced. But a more delicate point is afterwards brought into discussion (nothing less than the choice of a chief commander for the Citadel) which Euelpides treats with the same silly drollery as before; Peisthetairus is irritated, or pretends to be so, and dismisses him in a tone of authority, which the other resents, and appears on the point of mutinying: upon which Peisthetairus smoothes him down again as briefly as possible, and having accomplished this point, immediately turns away from him to call a servant.*

Peis. Well, there it is! Such a comical set out,
By Jove, I never saw!
Eu. Why, what's the matter?
What are you laughing at?
Peis. At your pen-feathers;
I'll tell ye exactly now the thing you're like;
You're just the perfect image of a Goose,
Drawn with a pen in a writing-master's flourish.
Eu. And you're like a pluck'd Blackbird to a tittle.
Peis. Well, then, according to the line in Æschylus,
"It's our own fault, the feathers are our own." *
Eu. Come, what's to be done?
Hoo. First we must choose a name,
Some grand, sonorous name, for our new city;
Then we must sacrifice.
Eu. I think so too.

* Æschylus alludes to a fable in which an eagle complains of being wounded by an arrow feathered from his own wings.

[1] This is the sort of raillery which Bacchus prohibits in the contest between Euripides and Æschylus, and of which we have a specimen in the "Wasps," 1309, ed. Bekk.—Some modern traveller has told us that abusive similes in alternate extempore verse serve for an amusement, at this day, to the boatmen of the Nile.

Peis. Let's see—let's think of a name—what shall it be?
What say ye to the Lacedæmonian name?
Sparta sounds well—suppose we call it Sparta.

* Sparto still retains its name, and is still used for mattresses and occasionally for cordage.

Eu. Sparta! What, *Sparto?**—Rushes!—no, not I,
I'd not put up with *Sparto* for a mattress,
Much less for a city; we're not come to that.
Peis. Come, then, what name shall it be?
Eu. Something appropriate,
Something that sounds majestic, striking, and grand,
Alluding to the clouds and the upper regions.
Peis. What think ye of Clouds and Cuckoos? Cuckoo-cloudlands
Or Nephelococcugia?
Hoo. That will do;
A truly noble and sonorous name!
Eu. I wonder if that Nephelococcugia
Is the same place I've heard of; people tell me
That all Theagenes's rich possessions
Lie there; and Æschines's whole estate.
Peis. Yes;[1] and a better country it is by far
Than all that land in Thrace, the fabulous plain
Of Phlegra, where those earth-born landed giants
Were bullied and out-vapour'd by the gods.
Eu. It will be a genteelish, smart concern, I reckon,
This city of ours.—Which of the deities
Shall we have for a patron? We must weave our mantle,
Our sacred mantle, of course—the yearly mantle †
To one or other of 'em.

See "Knights," p. 107, note 1.

Peis. Well, Minerva?
Why should not we have Minerva? She's establish'd,
Let her continue; she'll do mighty well.
Eu. No—there I object; for a well order'd city
The example would be scandalous, to see

---

[1] Many Athenians (as Miltiades, Alcibiades, and Thucydides the Historian) were proprietors of large estates in Chersonese and along the coasts of Thrace: Theagenes, it seems, and Æschines, boasting of wealth which they did not possess, chose to talk of their estates in Thrace. In the last century the West Indies was the usual locality assigned to *fabulous* estates.—Thrace was also mythologically *fabulous*, as the field of battle between Jupiter and the Titans.

The goddess, a female born, in complete armour
From head to foot, and Cleisthenes * with a distaff.
  Peis. What warden will ye appoint for the Eagle tower,
Your Citadel, the fort upon the rock?
  Hoo. That charge will rest with a chief of our own choice,
Of Persian race, a chicken of the game,
An eminent warrior.
  Eu. Oh my chick-hiddy—
My little master. I should like to see him
Strutting about and roosting on the rock.
  Peis. Come you now! please to step to the atmosphere,
And give a look to the work, and help the workmen;
And between whiles, fetch bricks and tiles, and such like;
Draw water, stamp the mortar,—do it barefoot;
Climb up the ladders; tumble down again;
Keep constant watch and ward; conceal your watch-lights;
Then go the rounds, and give the countersign,
Till you fall fast asleep. Send heralds off,
—A brace of them—one to the gods above,
And another, down below there, to mankind.
Bid them, when they return, inquire for me.
  Eu. For me! for me! You may be hang'd for me.
  Peis. Come, friend, go where I bid you; never mind;
The business can't go on without you, any how.
It's just a sacrifice to these new deities,
That I must wait for, and the priest that's coming.
Holloh, you boy there! bring the basin and ewer!

* Ridiculed for his effeminacy in various comedies.

In the passage which follows, the author ridicules the rage for vulgar realities (a corruption of the theatric art, essentially destructive of all illusion, as we have witnessed at home, with real *water,* real *horses,* real *elephants). The stage of Athens, it should seem, had been degraded by a* real *sacrifice, the paltriness of such a spectacle is marked by the magnificent exhortation of the Chorus, contrasted with the meanness of the execution which they anticipate.*

  Cho. We urge, we exhort you, and advise,
To ordain a mighty sacrifice;
And before the gods to bring
A stupendous offering;
  —Either a sheep or some such thing!—

To please the critics of the age,
Sacrificed upon the stage.—
Sound amain the Pythian strain!
Let Chæris * be brought here to sing.

Peis. Have done there with your puffing—Heaven and Earth,
What's here? I've seen a many curious things,
But never saw the like of this before,
A Crow with a flute and a mouthpiece. Priest, your office:
Perform it! Sacrifice to the new deities!

Pri. I will—but where's the boy gone with the basket?
Let us pray to the holy flame,
And the holy Hawk that guards the same;
To the sovereign Deities,
All and each, of all degrees,
Female and male!

Cho. Hail thou Hawk of Sunium, hail!

Pri. To the Delian and the Pythian Swan,
And to the Latonian Quail,
All hail!

Cho. To the Bird of awful stature,
Mother of Gods, mother of Man;
Great Cybele! nurse of Nature!
Glorious Ostrich, hear our cry,
Fearful and enormous creature,
Hugest of all things that fly,
O preserve and prosper us
Thou mother of Cleocritus †
Grant the blessings that we seek
For us and for the Chians eke!

Peis. That's right, the Chians—don't forget the Chians!

Pri. To the Heroes, Birds, and Heroes' sons,
We call at once, we call and cry,
To the Woodpecker, the Jay, the Pie,
To the Mallard and the Widgeon,
To the Ringdove and the Pigeon,
To the Petrel and Sea-mew,
To the Dottrel and Curlew,
To the Vultures and the Hawks,
To the Cormorants and Storks,
To the Rail, to the Quail,
To the Peewit, to the Tomtit—

* Chæris, a bad musician (the constant butt of the comic poets) is called for, to complete the shabbiness of the performance. His representative, the Crow, (who is the Chæris among the birds) sounds some discordant notes till Peisthetairus stops him.

† Of Cleocritus nothing is known except that he was unfortunate in his figure, which was thought to resemble that of an ostrich.

Peisthetairus, who can do every thing better than every body else, undertakes to perform the sacrifice. This is sufficiently in character. By making him the chief operator, a greater comic effect is given to the series of interruptions which disturb him; until in despair he determines to transfer the sacrifice elsewhere. In this way the Poet avoids the vulgar reality which he had before ridiculed.

Peis. Have done there! call no more of 'em; are you mad?
Inviting all the Cormorants and Vultures,
For a victim such as this! Why don't you see,
A Kite at a single swoop would carry it off?
Get out of my way there with your Crowns and Fillets!
I'll do it myself. I'll make the sacrifice!
Priest. Then must I commence again,
In a simple humble strain;
And invite the gods anew,
To visit us—but very few—
Or only just a single one,
All alone
In a quiet easy way;
Wishing you may find enough,
If you dine with us to-day;
Our victim is so poor and thin,
Merely bones, in fact, and skin.
Peis. We sacrifice and pray to the winged deities.

Ridicule of the vulgar reality, the poor half-starved sheep being standing on the stage.

Enter a Poet, very ragged and shabby, with a very mellifluous, submissive, mendicatory demeanour. Peisthetairus, the essential man of business and activity, entertaining a supreme contempt for his profession and person, is at no great pains to conceal it; but recollecting, at the same time, that it is advisable to secure the suffrages of the literary world, and that the character of a patron is creditable to a great man, he patronizes him accordingly, not at his own expense, but by bestowing upon him certain articles of apparel put in requisition for that purpose. This first act of confiscation is directed against the property of the church; the scholiast informs us that he begins by stripping the Priest.

Poet. "For the festive, happy day,
Muse, prepare an early lay
To Nephelococcugia."

Peis. What's here to do? What are you? Where do you come from?

Poet. An humble menial of the Muses' train,
As Homer expresses it.

Peis. A menial, are you,
With your long hair?* A menial?

Poet. 'Tis not that,
No!—but professors of the poetical art
Are simply styled, the "Menials of the Muses,"
As Homer expresses it.

Peis. Ay, the Muse has given you
A ragged livery. Well, but friend, I say—
Friend! Poet! What the plague has brought you here?

Poet. I've made an Ode upon your new-built City,
And a charming composition for a Chorus,
And another in Simonides's manner.

Peis. (*in a sharp cross-examining tone*). When were they made?
What time? How long ago?

Poet. From early date, I celebrate in song
The noble Nephelococcugian state.

Peis. That's strange, when I'm just sacrificing here,
For the first time, to give the town a name.

Poet. Intimations swift as air
To the Muses' ear are carried,
Swifter than the speed and force
Of the fiery-footed horse,
Hence, the tidings never tarried;
Father,† patron, mighty lord,
Founder of the rising state,
What thy bounty can afford,
Be it little, be it great,
With a quick resolve incline
To bestow on me and mine.

Peis. This fellow will breed a bustle, and make mischief,
If we don't give him a trifle, and get rid of him.
You there, you've a spare waistcoat; pull it off!
And give it this same clever ingenious poet—
There, take the waistcoat, friend. Ye seem to want it!

* Slaves were forbidden to wear long hair.

† The Scholiast informs us that these lines are in ridicule of certain mendicatory passages in the Odes of Pindar; one in particular, addressed to Hiero on the foundation of a new city.

Poet. Freely, with a thankful heart,
What the bounteous hand bestows,
Is received in friendly part;
But amid the Thracian snows,
Or the chilly Scythian plain,
He the wanderer, cold and lonely,
With an under-waistcoat only,
Must a further wish retain;
Which, the Muse, averse to mention,
To your gentle comprehension
Trusts her enigmatic strain.

Peis. I comprehend it enough; you want a jerkin.
Here, give him yours; one ought to encourage genius.
There, take it, and good-bye to ye!

*Poet.** Well, I'm going;
And, as soon as I get to the town, I'll set to work;
And finish something, in this kind of way.
"Seated on your golden throne,
Muse, prepare a solemn ditty
To the mighty,
To the flighty,
To the cloudy, quivering, shivering,
To the lofty seated city."

* The Poet withdraws gradually, turning round and reciting. Peisthetairus does not appear to take notice, but watches till he is fairly gone.

Peis. Well, I should have thought, that jerkin might have cured him
Of his "quiverings and shiverings." How the plague
Did the fellow find us out? I should not have thought it.
Come, once again, go round with the basin and ewer.
Peace! Silence, silence!

Enter a Soothsayer, with a great air of arrogance and self-importance. He comes on the authority of a book of Oracles (which he pretends to possess, but which he never produces), in virtue of which he lays claim to certain sacrificial perquisites and fees. Peisthetairus encounters him with a different version, composed upon the spot, in virtue of which he dismisses the Soothsayer with a good lashing.

Sooth. Stop the sacrifice!
Peis. What are you?
Sooth. A Soothsayer, that's what I am.
Peis. The worse luck for ye.

See p. 127 in the "Knights," where there is the same allusion to disputes on the authentic copies of oracles.

Sooth. Friend, are you in your senses?
Don't trifle absurdly with religious matters.
Here's a prophecy of Bakis, which expressly
Alludes to Nephelococcugia.

Peis. How came it, then, you never prophesied
Your prophecies, before the town was built?

Sooth. The spirit withheld me.

Peis. And is it allowable now,
To give us a communication of them?

Sooth. Hem!

"Moreover, when the Crows and Daws unite,
To build and settle, in the midway right
Between tall Corinth and fair Sicyon's height,
Then to Pandora let a milk white Goat
Be slain, and offer'd, and a comely coat
Given to the soothsayer, and shoes a pair;
When he to you this oracle shall bear."

Peis. Are the shoes mention'd?

Sooth. (*pretending to feel for his papers.*) Look at the book, and see!

"And let him have the entrails for his share."

Peis. Are the Entrails mention'd?

Sooth. (*as before.*) Look at the book, and see!

"If you, predestined youth, shall do these things,
Then you shall soar aloft, on eagle's wings;
But, if you do not, you shall never be
An Eagle, nor a Hawk, nor bird of high degree."

Peis. Is all this there?

Sooth. (*as before.*) Look at the book, and see!

Peis. This oracle differs most remarkably
From that which I transcribed in Apollo's temple.

"If at the sacrifice . .*. . which you prepare,
An uninvited vagabond . . . . should dare
To interrupt you, and demand a share,
Let cuffs and buffets . . . . be the varlet's lot.
Smite him between the ribs . . . . and spare him not."

Sooth. Nonsense you're talking!

Peis. (*with the same action as the Soothsayer, as if he were feeling for papers.*) Look at the book, and see!

"Thou shalt in no wise heed them, or forbear
To lash and smite those Eagles of the air.

* The breaks in the text . . may serve to indicate what was more distinctly expressed by the actor, viz. that Peisthetairus's oracle is an extempore production.

Neither regard their names, for it is written,
Lampon and Diopeithes shall be smitten."

Sooth. Is all this there?

Peis. (*producing a horsewhip.*) Look at the book, and see!
Get out, with a plague and a vengeance.

Sooth. Oh dear! oh!

Peis. Go soothsay somewhere else, you rascal, run!

[*Exit Soothsayer.*

Meton the Astronomer appears, encumbered with a load of mathematical instruments, which are disposed about his person. He advances with short steps, a straight back, and his chin in the air, modifying, by what he conceives to be a tone of condescending familiarity, a manner of habitual self-importance.

Met. I'm come, you see, to join you.

Peis. (*aside.*) (Another plague!)
For what? What's your design? Your plan, your notion?
Your scheme,—your apparatus,—your equipment,
Your outfit? What's the meaning of it all?

Met. I mean to take a geometrical plan
Of your atmosphere—to allot it, and survey it
In a scientific form.

Peis. In the name of heaven!
Who are ye and what? What name? What manner of man?

Met. Who am I and what? Meton's my name, well known
In Greece, and in the village of Colonos.

Peis. (*going up to him and pulling them about.*) But tell me, pray;—these implements, these articles,
What are they meant for?

Met. These are—*Instruments!*
An atmospherical geometrical scale.
First, you must understand, that the atmosphere
Is form'd,—in a manner,—altogether,—partly,
In the fashion of a furnace, or a funnel;
I take this circular arc, with the moveable arm,
And so, by shifting it round, till it coincides
At the angle—you understand me?

Peis. Not in the least.

Met. (*with animation and action illustrative of the proposed plan.*) . . . . I obtain a true division, with the quadrature
Of the equilateral circle. Here, I trace
Your market place, in the centre, with the streets,—
Converging inwards,—and the roads, diverging—
From the circular wall, without—like solar rays
From the circular circumference of the Sun.

Peis. (*in a pretended soliloquy; then calling to him with a tone of mystery and alarm.*)
Another Thales! absolutely, a Thales!—
Meton!

Met. (*startled.*) Why, what's the matter?

Peis. You're aware
That I've a regard for you. Take my advice;
Don't be seen here—Withdraw yourself; abscond!

Met. Is there any alarm or risk?

Peis. Why, much the same
As it might be in Lacedæmon. There's a bustle
Of expelling aliens; people are dragg'd out
From the inns and lodgings, with a deal of uproar,
And blows and abuse in plenty, to be met with
In the public streets.

Met. A popular tumult—heh?

Peis. (*scandalized at the supposition.*) Oh, fie! no, nothing of that kind.

During this speech Peisthetairus keeps his eye quietly fixed upon the Astronomer.

Met. How do you mean then?

Peis. We're carrying into effect a resolution
Adopted lately; to discard and cudgel—
Coxcombs and Mountebanks—of every kind.

Met. Perhaps—I had best withdraw.

Peis. Why yes, *perhaps*—
But yet, I would not answer for it, neither;
Perhaps, you may be too late; the blows I mention'd
Are coming—close upon you—there they come!

Met. Oh bless me!

Peis. Did not I tell you, and give you warning?
Get out, you coxcomb, find out by your Geometry
The road you came, and measure it back you'd best.

[*Exit Meton.*

A Commissioner from Athens advances with an air of importance and ascendancy; like other consequential persons sent on a foreign mission he wishes it to be understood that he considers it a sort of banishment.

Com. Is nobody here? None of the Proxeni,
To receive and attend upon me?
Peis. What's all this?
Sardanapalus * in person come amongst us!
Com. I come, appointed as Commissioner
To Nephelococcugia.
Peis. A Commissioner!
What brings you here?
Com. A paltry scrap of paper,
A trifling silly decree, that sent me away
Here to this place of yours.
Peis. Well now! suppose,
To make things easy on both sides—could not you
Just take your salary at once; and so return,
Without any further trouble?
Com. Truly yes,
I've other affairs at home: a speech and a motion,
That I meant to have made in the general assembly,
About a business, that I took in hand
On the part of my friend Pharnaces, the satrap.
Peis. Agreed then, and farewell. Here, take your salary.
Com. What's here?

[*Peisthetairus has held out his left hand as if with an offer of money, he grasps the right hand of the Commissioner, and with this advantage proceeds to buffet him.*

Peis. A motion on the part of Pharnaces!
Com. Bear witness here! I'm beaten and abused
In my character of Commissioner! [*Exit Com.*
Peis. Get out!
With your balloting-box and all. It's quite a shame,
Quite scandalous! They send commissioners here,†
Before we've finish'd our first sacrifice.

Enter a Hawker with copies of new laws relating to the colony, which he has brought out with him, for sale. Like

* A name proverbial for pomp and luxury.

† Peisthetairus, in expectation of the Commissioner's return, is working himself into a proper state of wrath in order to be ready for him. Mere gratuitous complaint would not be suitable to his character.

all itinerant vendors of literature, he is trying to attract purchasers by reciting and bawling out select passages from the papers in his hand. The sale of them is his only object; and he is quite unconscious that the specimen which he recites is applicable to an incident which has just occurred. He enters on the opposite side with the monotonous chaunt of the vendor of a last dying speech, confronting Peisthetairus, who is returning after having driven out the Commissioner.

Haw. "Moreover, if a Nephelococcugian
Should assault or smite an Athenian citizen"—
Peis. What's this? What's all this trumpery paper here?
Haw. I've brought you the new laws and ordinances,
And copies of the last decrees to sell.
Peis. (*dryly and bitterly*). Let's hear 'em.
Haw. "It's enacted and ordain'd,
That the Nephelococcugians shall use
Such standard weights and measures"—
Peis. Friend, you'll find
Hard *measure* here, and a heavy *weight*, I promise you,
Upon your shoulders shortly.
Haw. What's the matter?
What's come to you?
Peis. Get out, with your decrees!
I've bloody decrees against you, dire decrees.
[*Drives him off.*
Com. (*returning*). I summon Peisthetairus to his answer,
In an action of assault and battery,
For the first day of the month Munychion.
Peis. Hah! say you so? You're there again! Have at you. [*Drives him off.*
Haw. (*returning*). "And in case of any assault or violence,
Against the person of the Magistrate"—
Peis. Bless me! What you! You're there again.
[*Drives him off.*
Com. (*returning again*). I'll ruin you;
I'll lay my damages at ten thousand drachmas.
Peis. In the mean time, I'll smash your balloting boxes.
Com. Remember, how you effaced the public monument,*
On the pillar, and defiled it late last night.

* The sort of accusations which were current at the time similar to those of the mutilation of the Hermæ. Peisthetairus does not take any notice or bestow a whole line upon his accuser; the last words of the verse are addressed to the Hawker.

Peis. Pah! stuff! There, seize him, somebody. What you're off, too.
Come, let's remove, and get away from hence,
And sacrifice our goat to the Gods within doors.

It is to be feared that without having it pointed out to him, the Reader will hardly be aware, that in some of the following lines an attempt is made to imitate the effect of the spondaic passages in the original.

CHORUS.

Henceforth—Our Worth,
Our Right—Our Might,
Shall be shewn,
Acknowledged, known;
Mankind shall raise
Prayers, vows, praise,
To the Birds alone.
Our employ, is to destroy
The vermin train,
Ravaging amain
Your fruits and grain:
We're the wardens
Of your gardens,
To watch and chase
The wicked race,
And cut them shorter
In hasty slaughter.

The first lines of the Epirrema are descriptive of the cruel madness of the times. See note to page 166. *Diagoras was a Poet, a foreigner resident at Athens. Being suspected of Atheism, and consequently of being an accomplice in the imaginary plot, he was proscribed and a price set upon his head; it seems also that in other instances which are alluded to, assassination was encouraged by public rewards.*

The history of a similar period, the times of Titus Oates's plot, (admirably described by Roger North in his Examen,) may serve to illustrate the lines 13 *and* 14, *the community, in both instances, remaining subject to a reign of terror under obscure wretches, whose sole instrument of dominion was perjury; as it was necessary for those Sovereign Wit-*

nesses to extort respectable subsidiary evidence in support of their main system of perjury, threats and imprisonment were the means employed in both instances, as appears by the narrative of Andocides.

EPIRREMA.

At the present urgent crisis, all your efforts and attention
Are directed to secure Diagoras's apprehension:
Handsome bounties have been offer'd of a talent for his head,
Likewise with respect to Tyrants (Tyrants, that are gone and dead)
Bounties of a talent each, for all that can be kill'd or caught.
With a zealous emulation, we, the Birds, have also thought
Just and proper to proclaim, from this time forth, that we withdraw
From Philocrates, the fowler, the protection of the law:
Furthermore, we fix a price for bringing him alive or dead,
Four, if he's secured alive, a single talent for his head:
He, that Ortolans and Quails to market has presumed to bring,
And the Sparrows, six a penny, tied together in a string,
With a wicked art retaining sundry Doves in his employ,
Fasten'd, with their feet in fetters, forced to serve for a decoy.
Farther, we declare and publish our command to men below,
All the Birds you keep in prison, to release and let them go.
We shall, else, revenge ourselves, and we shall teach the tyrants yet,
How to chirp and dance in fetters, in the tangles of a net.

CHORUS.

Blest are they,
The Birds alway,
With perfect clothing,
Fearing nothing,
Cold or sleet or summer heat.
As it chances,
As he fancies,

Each his own vagary follows,
Dwelling in the dells and hollows;
When, with eager weary strain,
The shrilly grasshoppers complain,
Parch'd upon the sultry plain,
Madden'd with the raging heat;
We secure a cool retreat,
In the shady nooks and coves,
Recesses of the sacred groves,
Many an herb, and many a berry
Serves to feast, and make us merry.

ANTEPIRREMA.

To the judges of the prize, we wish to mention in a word
The return we mean to make, if our performance is preferr'd.
First, then, in your empty coffers you shall see the sterling Owl,*
From the mines of Laurium, familiar as a common fowl;
Roosting among the bags and pouches, each at ease upon his nest;
Undisturb'd rearing and hatching little broods of interest:
If you wish to cheat in office, but are inexpert and raw,
You should have a Kite for agent, capable to gripe and claw;
Cranes and Cormorants shall help you to a stomach and a throat
When you feast abroad. But if you give a vile, unfriendly vote,
Hasten and provide yourselves, each, with a little silver plate,
Like the statues of the gods, for the protection of his pate;
Else, when forth abroad you ramble on a summer holiday,
We shall take a dirty vengeance, and befoul your best array.

* The figure of an owl stamped on the coin of Athens.

In the following scene a foot messenger arrives at full speed from the new city, apparently in a state of great exhaustion. He communicates his important intelligence to Peisthetairus in a single gasp of breath. "Your fortification's finished!" The report, which he makes of the building of a new Babylon, by the nation of the Birds, as it considerably exceeds, even, that licence of assuming impossi-

bilities, which is the privilege of the ancient comedy, may lead us to examine the mode of humorous contrivance by which the author has managed, in some degree, to maintain that balance between truth and falsehood, which I have (in another place) endeavoured to point out, as essential to the character of all dramatic representations whether serious or comic.

The interest which we take in the development of moral truth, and in the illustration of human character, is so much stronger than that which we attach to mere matter-of-fact, that, where the two are combined (that is to say, where a supposed fact is made the foundation of a new and striking illustration of character) our attention is, generally speaking, wholly directed to the latter, and we are inclined to take the fact for granted; as we allow the scrawl, which a mathematician draws, to stand for a circle or square, our whole attention being absorbed in the acquisition of a general and a permanent truth. It is, we believe, an established axiom in the art of lying, that almost anything may be made credible of almost any person, provided that the imaginary facts are accompanied by a just representation of the behaviour of the person, such as it might be supposed to be under the alleged circumstances; and this will be more strikingly the case if some trait of his character, not generally observed, but likely to be immediately recognized, is exhibited for the first time. It has been observed elsewhere of the Aristophanic, or ancient comedy, that it is essentially a grave, humorous, impossible Great Lie, *related with an accurate mimicry of the language and manners of the persons introduced. As the humour of a* Narrative Lie *is more easily comprehended than that of a dramatic one, we may venture to examine the drama, such as it would have appeared if it had been helped out, in some degree, by a narrative comment. If, like the explanatory heroic prologue in Henry the Fifth, the ancient comedy had made use of a buffoonish prologue, explanatory and preparatory to the different scenes, we might suppose Aristophanes or his prolocutor on this occasion to have said—" Gentlemen, the information which I apprehend you will shortly receive of the progress of the new buildings at Nephelococcugia, may perhaps strike you as extraordinary. I should not be surprised if to some amongst you it should appear little short of being absolutely incredible; but I would not have you rely entirely upon your own judgment. There is Peisthetairus, who has every means of information, and of whose abilities you can have no doubt: you will see him as much astonished as any amongst you; and you will see him so for the first and only time. But will he disbelieve the fact? Far from it. Like the judicious amongst yourselves, he will not entertain the least doubt of it. On the contrary, unless I am very much mistaken in his character, you will be able to detect evident symptoms of jealousy and uneasiness at the idea of such an object having been accomplished independently of his direction and superintendence, and, indeed, not without reason; for you will see that both the chorus and the messenger himself appear to abate something of their accustomed respect and deference to him. You will observe, likewise, that the messenger is far from anticipating the slightest incredulity as to the general fact of the completion of the work, of which he himself has been a witness, while he is apparently very anxious in his negative testimony as to the total absence of any extraneous aid or assistance whatever."*

PEISTHETAIRUS.

Well, Friends and Birds, the sacrifice has succeeded;
Our omens have been good ones, good and fair.
But what's the meaning of it? We've no news
From the new building yet! No messenger!
Oh! there at last, I see,—There's somebody
Running at speed, and panting like a racer.

[*Enter a messenger quite out of breath, and speaking in short snatches.*

Mess. Where is he? Where? Where is he? Where?
Where is he?—
The president, Peisthetairus?
Peis. (*coolly*). Here am I.
Mess. (*in a gasp of breath*). Your fortification's finish'd.
Peis. Well! that's well.
Mess. A most amazing, astonishing work it is!
So that Theagenes and Proxenides*
Might flourish, and gasconade, and prance away,
Quite at their ease, both of them four-in-hand,

* Pretenders to great wealth and affecting extraordinary expense and display.—See note 1 to p. 184.

Driving abreast upon the breadth of the wall,
Each in his own new chariot.
Peis. You surprise me.
Mess. And the height (for I made the measurement myself)
Is exactly a hundred fathom.
Peis. Heaven and earth!
How could it be? Such a mass! Who could have built it?
Mess. The Birds; no creature else—no foreigners,
Egyptian bricklayers,* workmen or masons,
But they themselves alone, by their own efforts
(Even to my surprise, as an eye-witness)—
The Birds, I say, completed everything.
There came a body of thirty thousand Cranes
(I won't be positive, there might be more)
With stones from Africa, in their craws and gizzards,
Which the Stone-curlews and Stone-chatterers
Work'd into shape and finish'd. The Sand-Martins,
And Mud-larks, too, were busy in their department,
Mixing the mortar, while the Water-Birds,
As fast as it was wanted, brought the water
To temper, and work it.
Peis. (*in a fidget*). But who served the masons?
Who did you get to carry it?
Mess. To carry it?
Of course, the Carrion Crows and Carrying Pigeons.
Peis. (*in a fuss, which he endeavours to conceal*).
Yes! yes! But after all, to load your hods—
How did you manage that?
Mess. Oh, capitally,
I promise you.—There were the Geese, all barefoot,
Trampling the mortar, and, when all was ready,
They handed it into the hods so cleverly
With their flat feet!
Peis. (*A bad joke, as a vent for irritation. Like Falstaff, when he is annoyed and perplexed, joking perforce*).
They *footed* it, you mean.
Come; it was handily done though, I confess.
Mess. Indeed, I assure you, it was a sight to see them;
And trains of Ducks there were, clambering the ladders,
With their duck legs, like bricklayer's 'prentices,
All dapper and handy, with their little trowels.

* Egyptian labourers are mentioned in the "Frogs."

*Peis.** In fact, then, it's no use engaging foreigners;
Mere folly and waste; we've all within ourselves.
Ah, well now, come! But about the woodwork? Heh!
Who were the carpenters? Answer me that!
Mess. The Woodpeckers, of course: and there they were,
Labouring upon the gates, driving and banging,
With their hard hatchet beaks, and such a din,
Such a clatter as they made, hammering and hacking,
In a perpetual peal, pelting away
Like shipwrights hard at work in the arsenal.
And now their work is finish'd, gates and all,
Staples and bolts, and bars, and everything;
The sentries at their posts; patrols appointed;
The watchmen in the barbican; the beacons
Ready prepared for lighting; all their signals
Arranged—But I'll step out, just for a moment,
To wash my hands.—You'll settle all the rest. [*Exit.*

* Peisthetairus is at a loss, unable to think of a new objection; he maintains his importance by a wise observation. As soon as an objection occurs he states it with great eagerness, but with no better success than before.

[*Peisthetairus, surprised at the rapid conclusion of the work, feeling from the volubility and easy manner of the messenger the blow which his authority has received; seeing that nothing is left for him to superintend, nothing to direct, nothing to suggest, or to find fault with, remains in an attitude of perplexity and astonishment, with his hands clasped across his forehead.*

Chorus (*to Peisthetairus, in a sort of self-satisfied, drawling tone*).

Heighday! Why, what's the matter with ye? Sure!
Ah! well now, I calculate, you're quite astonish'd;
You did not know the nature of our birds:
I guess you thought it an impossible thing
To finish up your fortification job
Within the time so cleverly.
Peis. (*recovering himself and looking round*). Yes, truly.
Yes, I'm surprised, indeed, I must confess—
I could almost imagine to myself—
It was a dream, an illusion altogether—
—But there's the watchman of the town, I see!
In alarm and haste it seems! He's running here—
[*The watchman enters, with a shout of alarm.*

Well, what's the matter?
W. A most dreadful business!
One of the Gods just now—Jupiter's Gods—
Has bolted through the gates and driven on
Right into the atmosphere, in spite of us,
And all the Jackdaws, that were mounting guard.
Peis. (*animated at the prospect of having something to manage*).
What an outrage! What an insult! Which of 'em?
Which of the Gods?
W. We can't pretend to say;
We just could ascertain that he wore wings.
We're clear upon that point.
Peis. But a light party
Ought surely to have been sent in such a case;
A detachment—
W. A detachment has been sent
Already: a squadron of ten thousand Hawks,
Besides a corps of twenty thousand Hobby-hawks,
As a light cavalry, to scour the country:
Vultures and Falcons, Ospreys, Eagles, all
Have sallied forth; the sound of wings is heard,
Rushing and whizzing round on every side
In eager search.—The fugitive divinity
Is not far off, and soon must be discover'd.
Peis. Did nobody think of slingers? Where are they?
Where are the slingers got to? Give me a sling.
Arrows and slings, I say!—Make haste with 'em.

Peisthetairus is exposed to a fresh mortification; the orders which he was ready to give have been anticipated! He contrives, however, to detect an omission, and, upon the strength of it, to assume a tone of authority and command.

Chorus.

The verses which follow belong to a species of songs, which are alluded to in Aristophanes more than once. They may properly be called "Watch-Songs," being sung by the Watchmen and Soldiers on guard, to keep themselves and their comrades awake and alert.

War is at hand,
On air and land,
  Proclaim'd and fix'd.
War and strife,
Eager and rife,
  Are kindled a-twixt

This state of ours,
And the heavenly powers.
Look with care
To the circuit of air;
Watch lest he,
The Deity,
Whatever he be,
Should unaware
Escape and flee.

But, hark! The rushing sound of hasty wings
Approaches us. The deity is at hand.

Peis. Holloh, you! Where are ye flying? Where are ye going?
Hold! Halt! Stop there, I tell ye!—Stop this instant!
What are ye? Where do you come from? Speak, explain.

Iris. Me? From the Gods, to be sure! the Olympian Gods.

Peis. (*pointing to the flaunting appendages of her dress*).*
What are ye, with all your flying trumpery?
A helmet, or a galley? What's your name?

Iris. Iris, the messenger of the Gods.

Peis. A messenger!
Oh, you're a naval messenger, I reckon;
The Salaminian galley, or the Paralian?†
—You're in full sail, I see.

Iris. What's here to do?

Peis. Are there no birds in waiting? Nobody
To take her into custody?

Iris. Me—to custody?
Why, what's all this?

Peis. You'll find to your cost, I promise ye.

Iris. Well, this seems quite unaccountable!

Peis. Which of the gates
Did ye enter at, ye jade? How came you here?

Iris. Gates!—I know nothing about your gates, not I.

Peis. Fine innocent, ignorant airs she gives herself!
You applied to the Pelicans, I suppose?—The captain
Of the Cormorants on guard admitted you?

Iris. Why, what the plague! what's this?

Peis. So you confess!
—You came without permission!

* Iris, the rainbow personified, is of course attired in all the colours of the rainbow, with abundance of lappets and streamers.

† The two sacred galleys of the Athenians.—The most splendidly equipped were despatched upon the most important occasions.—See note †, p. 156.

Iris. Are you mad?

Peis. Did neither the sitting magistrates nor bird-masters
Examine and pass you?

Iris. Examine me, forsooth!

Peis. This is the way then!—without thanks or leave
You ramble and fly, committing trespasses
In an atmosphere belonging to your neighbours!

Iris. And where would you have us fly then? Us, the Gods!

Peis. I neither know nor care.—But I know this—
They sha'n't fly here.—And another thing I know;
I know that, if there ever was an instance
Of an Iris or a rainbow, such as you,
Detected in the fact, fairly condemn'd,
And justly put to death, it would be you.

Iris. But I'm immortal.

Peis. (*coolly and peremptorily*). That would make no difference;
We should be strangely circumstanced indeed,
With the possession of a Sovereign Power,
And you, the Gods, in no subordination,
No kind of order, fairly mutinying,
Infringing and disputing our commands.
—Now then, you'll please to tell me where you're going?
Which way you're steering with those wings of yours?

Iris (*in a great fright, hesitating and hurried, but attempting to assume a tone of authority*).
I?...I'm commission'd from my father Jove
To summon human mortals to perform
Their rites and offerings and oblations, due
To the powers above.

Peis. And who do you mean? what powers?

Iris. What powers? Ourselves, the Olympian Deities!

Peis. So then, you're deities, the rest of ye!

Iris. Yes, to be sure; what others should there be?

Peis. Remember—once for all—that we, the Birds,
Are the only deities from this time forth,
And not your father Jove. By Jove! not he!

Iris. Oh, rash, presumptuous wretch! Incense no more
The wrath of the angry Gods, lest Ruin drive *
Her ploughshare o'er thy mansion; and Destruction,

* A medley from terrific passages in the tragic poets.

With hasty besom, sweep thee to the dust;
Or flaming lightning smite thee with a flash,
Left in an instant smouldering and extinct.

Peis. Do ye hear her?—Quite in tragedy!—quite sublime!
Come, let me try for a bouncer in return.*
Let's see.—Let's recollect.—"Me dost thou deem,
Like a base Lydian or a Phrygian slave,
With hyperbolical bombast to scare?"
I tell ye, and you may tell him—Jupiter,
If he provokes me and pushes things too far,
Will see some eagles of mine, to outnumber his,
With firebrands in their claws, about his house.
And I shall send a flight of my Porphyrions,†
A hundred covey or more, arm'd *cap-à-pie*,
To assault him in his sublime celestial towers:
Perhaps he may remember, in old times
He found enough to do with one Porphyrion.
And for you, Madam Iris, I shall strip
Your rainbow-shanks, if you're impertinent,
Depend upon it, and I, myself, in person,
Will ravish you, myself,—old as I am.

Iris. Curse ye, you wretch, and all your filthy words.

Peis. Come, scuttle away; convey your person elsewhere;
Be brisk, and leave a vacancy. Brush off.

Iris. I shall inform my father. He shall know
Your rudeness and impertinence. He shall—
He'll settle ye and keep ye in order.—You shall see.

Peis. Oh dear! is it come to that? No, you're mistaken,
Young woman, upon that point; I'm not your man;
I'm an old fellow grown; I'm thunder proof;
Proof against flames and darts and female arts:
You'd best look out for a younger customer.

* Peisthetairus at last hits upon a tragic passage which he thinks will serve for a suitable reply.
A vulgar line which disfigures a very fine scene of the Alcestis of Euripides.

† The Greek name for a flamingo, also the name of one of the giants who made war against the gods.

Poor Iris, in her rage, unwittingly makes use of the same sort of phrase with which a young girl at Athens would repel, or affect to repel, improper familiarities. Peisthetairus, taking advantage of this, pretends to consider her indignation as a mere coquettish artifice intended to inveigle and allure him.

The Athenian Father—"*I shall inform my father*"—

may be considered as equivalent to the Irish Brother.—*The menace in one case would imply a duel, in the other a law-suit.*

CHORUS.

Notice is hereby given
To the deities of heaven,
Not to trespass here
Upon our atmosphere.
Take notice—from the present day
No smoke or incense is allow'd
To pass this way.

Peis. Quite strange it is! quite unaccountable!
That herald to mankind that was dispatch'd,
What has become of him? He's not yet return'd.

Enter HERALD.

Herald. Oh, Peisthetairus, happiest, wisest, best,
Cleverest of men! Oh, most illustrious!
Oh, most inordinately fortunate!
Oh, most...Oh, do, for shame, do bid me have done.
Peis. What are you saying?
Her. All the people of Earth
Have join'd in a complimentary vote, decreeing
A crown of gold to you, for your exertions.
Peis. I'm much obliged to the people of Earth. But why?
What was their motive?
Her. Oh, most noble founder
Of this supereminent, celestial city,
You can't conceive the clamour of applause,
The enthusiastic popularity,
That attends upon your name; th' impulse and stir
That moves among mankind, to colonize
And migrate hither. In the time before,
There was a Spartan mania, and people went
Stalking about the streets with Spartan staves,
With their long hair unwash'd and slovenly,
Like so many Socrateses; but of late
Birds are the fashion—Birds are all in all—
Their modes of life are grown to be mere copies

Of the birds' habits ; rising with the Lark ;
Scratching and scrabbling suits and informations ;
Picking and pecking upon points of law ;
Brooding and hatching evidence ;—in short,
It has grown to such a pitch, that names of Birds
Are given to individuals ; Chærophon
Is call'd an Owl, Theagenes a Goose,
Philocles a Cock Sparrow, Midias
A Dunghill Cock.—And all the songs in vogue
Have something about Birds, Swallows or Doves ;
Or about flying, or a wish for wings.
  Such is the state of things, and I must warn you,
That you may expect to see some thousands of them
Arriving here, almost immediately,
With a clamorous demand for wings and claws :
I advise you to provide yourself in time.
  Peis. Come, it won't do then, to stand dawdling here
Go you, fill the hampers and the baskets there
With wings, and bid the loutish porter bring them,
While I stop here, to encounter the new comers.

It has been already observed in reference to the Chorus of the Acharnians (p. 52), *that when his Choruses have ceased to contribute to the progressive action of the Drama, the Poet has sometimes relieved himself from the embarrassment which they created, by turning into ridicule the essential character and attributes of the Chorus itself.*

In that Comedy, as in the present, the hostility of the Chorus had given spirit and animation to some of the earlier scenes, but, from the moment when their hostility ceased, they had remained a mere superfluous appendage ; nothing being left for them to be done, and scarcely anything to be said, they could barely contrive to make their existence manifest from time to time by interposing with the expression of their acquiescence and approbation. The Poet then, having no further use for them, amuses his audience at their expense. The character of Choruses (except when they happen to be in a violent passion) being habitually obsequious and conformable, their obsequiousness is represented as connected with the display of Dicæopolis's good cheer, the sight of which confirms their favourable opinion of his political principles, and induces them to pass over his selfish treatment of the poor countryman with an apologetical observation.

But with respect to the chorus now before us (that of the Birds) *there is another point of the choral character (arising out of the very condition of their existence as a chorus) which must not be overlooked. All Choruses are essentially poetic and imaginative, the votaries of ideal harmony and beauty. Under this point of view, the following passage places them in amusing contrast with the practical active bustling spirit of Peisthetairus. The Chorus begin chaunting their namby pamby anticipations of future splendour and happiness, Peisthetairus, in the first instance, favouring them with a sort of gruff acquiescence. But as they proceed he loses all patience, contriving however to relieve himself, and give a vent to his ill-humour, by scolding the servant. The obsequious character of the Chorus now displays itself; they affect to sympathize with his impatience; expressing their own displeasure in a style suited to their choral character, that is to say, pedantic and formal. Peisthetairus, utterly disgusted with them, evades their sympathy by relapsing into comparative good humour. The Chorus then betake themselves to their usual practice of exhorting and advising.—This is more than he can endure —instead of taking any notice of them, he flies into a pretended rage against his servant; and is running off the stage to beat him, when he is encountered by the first specimen of the new colonists.*

This explanation must not be regarded as fanciful or superfluous. We should in that case be compelled to adopt a conclusion, in which the admirers of Aristophanes would not readily acquiesce, namely, that the Poet had (in a play already of unusual length) inserted a passage of twenty-four lines destitute of poetical merit, without any comic intention and wholly unamusing as a dramatic exhibition.

Peisthetairus says little in the following scene, but is not the less amusing from his restless fidget and ill disguised impatience and disgust.

CHORUS.

Shortly shall the noble town,
Populous and gay,
Shine in honour and renown.

Peis. (*dryly*). Why, perhaps she may.
Chorus. The benignant powers of love,
From their happy sphere,
From the blest abodes above—
Peis. (*venting his ill humour on the servant*).
Curse ye, rascal! can't ye move?
Chorus. —Are descending here,
Where in all this earthly range,
He that wishes for a change,
Can he find a seat,
Joyous and secure as this,
Fill'd with happiness and bliss,
Such a fair retreat?
Here are all the lovely faces,
Gentle Venus and the Graces,
And the little Cupid;
Order, ease and harmony,
Peace and affability.
Peis. The scoundrel is so stupid,
Quicker, sirrah! bring it quicker!
Chorus. Let him bring the woven wicker
With the winged store.
I, myself, in very deed,
With the varlet will proceed,
And smite him more and more;
Like a sluggish ass he seems,
Or even as a man that dreams,
Therefore smite him sore.
Peis. (*determined to cross them, relapses into good humour*).
He's a lazy rogue, it's true.
Chorus. Now range them forth, display'd in order due,
Feathers of every form and size and hue,
With shrewd intent adapting every pinion
To the new residents of your dominion.
Peis. I vow by the Hawks and Eagles, I won't bear it;
I'll beat ye, I will myself, you lazy rascal!

The Chorus in their idealizing and poetical character.

Chorus in their obsequious character, but with a formal pedantic tone.

The Chorus assume their admonitory character; Peisthetairus can bear it no longer; he breaks from them, and runs off the stage, as if to beat the servant.

As a practical comment upon the anticipations of the Chorus, and as a sample of the kind of population likely to resort to a new colony, the first arrival is that of a young reprobate, who wishes his father out of the way; and who conceives that the laws of the Birds will permit him to hasten that desirable conclusion. Peisthetairus receives and attends to him, without being betrayed into any expression of moral indignation, which would be inconsistent with his character, as a perfect politician. He merely states, as a matter of fact, some difficulties arising out of a point of law, professes a wish to serve him, as a hearty partizan well disposed to the cause of the new colony; and finally, in an easy way, recalls to his recollection one of the precepts of his Catechism; and, at the same time, points out to him a mode of life suited to his situation and tastes. The young man, who is more of a wild desperate than a confirmed villain, is struck with the suggestion, expresses a resolution to adopt it, and departs.

Enter a fellow (singing).

"Oh! for an Eagle's force and might,*
Loftily to soar
Over land and sea, to light
On a lonely shore."

* From Chorus of Sophocles; dramatic poetry and music was popular, like opera airs on the continent. See "Knights," p. 105.

Peis. Well, here's a song that's something to the purpose.
Y. Man. Ay, ay, there's nothing like it—wings and flying!
Wings are your only sort. I'm a bird fancier.
In the new fashion quite. I've taken a notion
To settle and live amongst ye. I like your laws.
Peis. (*very gravely and methodically*). What laws do you mean? We've many laws amongst us.
Y. Man. Your laws in general; but particularly
The law that allows of beating one's own father.
Peis. Why truly, Yes! we esteem it a point of valour
In a Chicken, if he clapperclaws the old Cock.
Y. Man. That was my view, feeling a wish in fact
To throttle mine, and seize the property.
Peis. (*with great candour and composure, simply stating a fact*).
Yes, but you'd find some difficulties here;
An obstacle insurmountable, I conceive;
An ancient statute standing unrepeal'd,
Engraved upon our old Ciconian columns.
It says: that when a Stork or a Ciconia
Has brought his lawful progeny of young Storks
To bird's estate, and enabled them to fly,

The sire shall stand entitled to a maintenance,
At the son's cost and charge, in his old age.

Y. Man (*with a start of disappointment, slapping his forehead*).
I've managed finely, it seems, to mend myself!
Forced to maintain my father after all!

Peis. (*in a soothing consolatory tone*). No, no; not quite so bad; since you're come here,
As a well-wisher to the establishment,
Zealous and friendly, we'll contrive to equip you
With a suit of armour, as a soldier's orphan.*
And now, young man, let me suggest some notions,
Things that were taught me when a boy. "Your father?"[1]
"Strike him not!" rather take this pair of wings;
And this cockspur (*giving him a sword*); imagine you've a coxcomb
Upon your head, to serve you for a helmet;
Look out for service, and enlist yourself;
Get into a garrison; live upon your pay;
And let your father live. You're fond of fighting,
And fond of flying—take a flight to Thrace;
There you may please yourself, and fight your fill.

* The sons of citizens slain were publicly presented wit a suit of armour.

Y. Man. By Jove, you're right. The notion 's not a bad one.
I'll follow it up!

Peis. (*very gravely and quietly*).
You'll find it the best way. [*Exit Y. Man.*

Cinesias, a lame dithyrambic poet and musician, arrives in the hopes of being able to provide himself with wings, which will enable him to look after his concerns among the clouds, the great emporium for business with all persons who are embarked in the dithyrambic line. Peisthetairus amuses himself with affronting and laughing at him, but he persists in his purpose, and professes his determination to continue worrying and persevering till it is accomplished.

---

[1] A want of harmony in the original verse appears to indicate the insertion of a formula—but again if we resolve this formula into its two component parts the Question and Answer, with a consequent pause between them, the harmony of the verse is very sensibly improved. The formula was part of a series of moral prohibitions taught to children by Question and Answer.

The reader who refers to the original will perceive that the interruptions with which Peisthetairus breaks in upon Cinesias's recitation or song are omitted in the translation. To the Athenian audience, the original must have been familiar, and probably sufficiently hackneyed, to make them feel amusement at hearing it accompanied with burlesque interruptions. But as only one other fragment of dithyrambic poetry has been preserved to modern times, and neither of them has appeared in our language, it seemed more advisable to present it to the English reader in an unbroken form.*

* It is singular that this other fragment presents the image of flying.

Enter Cinesias, *singing.*

"Fearless, I direct my flight
To the vast Olympian height;
Thence at random I repair,
Wafted in the whirling air,
With an eddy, wild and strong,
Over all the fields of song."

Peis. Ah! well, Cinesias, I'm quite glad to see ye;
But what has brought ye and all your songs and music,
Hobbling along with your old chromatic joints?
Cin. (singing). "Let me live, and let me sing,
Like a bird upon the wing."
Peis. No more of that; but tell us plainly, in prose,
What are ye come for? what's your scheme, your object?
Cin. I was anxious to procure a pair of wings,
To say the truth, wishing to make a tour
Among the clouds, collecting images,
And metaphors, and things of that description.
Peis. How so! do you procure 'em from the clouds?
Cin. Entirely! Our dithyrambic business absolutely
Depends upon them; our most approved commodities,
The dusky, misty, murky articles,
With the suitable wings and feathers, are imported
Exclusively from thence. I'll give you a sample,
A thing of my own composing. You shall judge.
Peis. But, indeed, I'd rather not.
Cin. But, indeed, you must;
It's a summary view of flying, comprehending it
In all its parts, in every point of view.

Cinesias (singing).

"Ye gentle feather'd tribes
Of every plume and hue,
That, in uninhabited air
Are hurrying here and there;
Oh! that I, like you,
Could leave this earthly level,
For a wild aërial revel;
O'er the waste of ocean
To wander and to dally
With the billow's motion;
Or, in an eager sally,
Soaring to the sky,
To range and rove on high
With my plumy sails,
Buffeted and baffled with the gusty gales,
Buffeted and baffled......"

[*While Cinesias is repeating these last lines Peisthetairus comes behind him and gives him a flap with a huge pair of wings.*

Cin. A pretty, civil joke indeed!

Peis. What joke?
I'm only buffeting you with the plumy sails;
I thought it was what you wanted.

Cin. Well, that's fine!
Pretty respect for a master such as me;
A leader of the band that all the tribes
Are ready to fight for, to bespeak him first.

Peis. Well, we've a little unfledged chorus here,
That Leotrophides* hatch'd, poor puny nestlings,
I'll give 'em you for scholars.

Cin. Ah, laugh on!
Laugh on! but take my word for it, here I stay
Till you provide me with a pair of wings,
Proper to circumnavigate the skies. [*Exit Cin.*

* Cinesias was ridiculed for his slight flimsy figure, adapted for flying. Leotrophides, the scholiast tells us, resembled him in this respect.

Peisthetairus is represented in the following scene as a perfect master of his art, amusing himself in angling and playing with a stupid, impudent young scoundrel; sometimes twitching him in with a slight jerk of his hook, and again allowing him to run out to the full length of his line. If any one passage were to be selected from the remains of Aristophanes as particularly illustrative of the manner in which he delights to exhibit character, perhaps it would be this; it is not a serious struggle for ascendancy such as he displays elsewhere; in this instance he shows Peisthetairus, as a consummate practitioner, relinquishing and re-assuming it at pleasure. But this is one of those scenes which, to be thoroughly appreciated, would require to be developed in dramatic action by a superior comedian. The mere printed page, unless we suppose the reader to bestow as much attention on it as an actor would do in studying his part, will be found to convey a very confused and inadequate notion of it.

The song, with which the Sycophant enters, is said, by the scholiast, to be from Alcæus; it should seem more consonant to his character to suppose it to be some modern parody or adaptation from one of the comedies of the time.

Enter SYCOPHANT, *singing.*

"Tell us who the strangers are,
Gentle Swallow! Birds of air,
Party-colour'd, poor and bare,
Tell us who the strangers are;
Gentle Swallow, tell me true."

Peis. Here's a fine plague broke out! See yonder fellow
Sauntering along this way, swaggering and singing.

Syc. Hoh! gentle Swallow! I say, my gentle Swallow,
My gentle Swallow! How often must I call? *

Peis. Why, there it is; the prodigal in the fable
Seeking for Swallows in a ragged coat.

Syc. (*in an arrogant, overbearing tone*).
Who's he that's set to serve out wings? Where is he?

Peis. 'Tis I; but what do you want? You should explain.

Syc. Wings! Wings! You need not have ask'd me. Wings I want.

Peis. Do you mean to fly for flannel to Pellene? †

Syc. (*a little disconcerted at this allusion to his attire*).
No, no! But I'm employ'd... I employ myself
In fact, among the allies and islanders;
I'm in the informing line.

* An expression of impatience in the original has been hitherto mistranslated.

† Pellene was famous for woollen stuff. Pieces of it were given as prizes at their public games.

Peis. (*in a tone of very grave irony, which the Sycophant not perceiving, he proceeds more fluently than before*).

I wish you joy.

Syc. And a mover and manager for prosecutions
In criminal suits and so forth; you understand me;
So I wish to equip myself with a pair of wings
To whisk about and trounce the islanders.

Peis. Would it be doing things in better form
To serve a summons flying, think ye?

Syc. (*not knowing very well what to make of him*). No,
Not that, but just to avoid the risk of pirates,
To return in company with a flight of cranes,
(As they do with the gravel in their gizzards)
With a belly-full of lawsuits for my ballast.

Peis. (*in a grave, primitive, and somewhat twaddling tone, intended to re-animate the impertinence of the Sycophant*).
So this is your employment! A young man
Like you to be an informer! Is it possible?

Syc. Why shouldn't it? I was never bred to labour.

Peis. (*as before*). But sure, there are other lawful occupations,
In which a brisk young fellow, such as you,
Might earn an honest, decent livelihood
In credit and good will, without informing.

Syc. (*thoroughly taken in, and thinking he has to deal with a mere silly, well-meaning old man, becomes emphatically insolent*).
Wings, my good fellow!—wings I want—not words!

Peis. (*dryly*). I'm giving you wings already.

Syc. (*a little puzzled and taken aback*).

What, with words?

Is that your way?

Peis. (*in a tone of very grave banter*).

Yes, for mankind in general
Are wing'd, as it were, and brought to plume themselves
In different ways, by speeches and discourse.

Syc. (*confused and puzzled*). What, all?

Peis. (*as before*). Yes, all. I'll give you a striking instance:
You must have heard yourself elderly people

Sitting conversing in the barber's shop.
And one says—"Well, Diitrephes has talk'd
So much to my young man, he has brought him at last
To plume himself in driving." And another
Says that his son is quite amongst the clouds,
Grown flighty of late with studying tragedy.

Syc. (*with a sort of hesitating laugh*).
So words are wings, you say.

Peis. No doubt of it.
I say it, and I repeat it; human nature
Is marvellously raised and elevated
By words. I was in hopes that I might raise you,
By words of good advice, to another sphere,
To live in an honest calling.

Syc. (*feeling himself bantered and beaten but restive and angry*).
But I won't, though.

Peis. (*coolly*). Why, what will you do?

Syc. (*sulkily at first, but animating as he proceeds*).
Why, I won't disgrace my family:
My father, and my grandfather before him,
Served as informers; and I'll stick to it,
The profession.—So you'll please to hand 'em me out,
A pair of your best wings, Vultures or Hawks,
To fly to the islands, with my summonses,
And home again to record them in the courts,
And out again, to the islands.

Peis. (*in a tone of interest and sympathy, as if he was himself an amateur desirous of displaying his professional knowledge*). Yes, that's well;
I understand ye, I think; your method is,
To be beforehand with 'em? Your defendant,
You get him cast for non-appearance, heh!
Before he can arrive; and finish him
In his absence, heh?

Syc. (*completely taken in, delighted, rubbing his hands*).
By Jove, you're up to it!

Peis. Then, whilst he's sailing here you get the start,
And fly, to pounce upon the property,
To rummage out the chattels.

Syc. That's the trick,
The notion of it!—I see you're up to it.—

A man must whisk about, here and away,
Just like a whipping-top.
Peis. Ay, yes, you're right;
I understand you. The instance is a good one.
A whipping-top, you say. Well, by good luck,
I've here a capital, slashing suit of wings
To serve ye, made of a cow-hide from Corcyra.
Syc. Oh, heaven! what's there? a horsewhip?
Peis. Wings, I tell ye,
To whisk ye about; to flog ye and make ye fly.
Syc. Oh dear! oh dear!
Peis. Scamper away, you scoundrel!
Vanish, you vagabond! whisk yourself off!
I'll pay ye for your practices in the courts—
Your pettifoggicorascalities. [*Exit Syc.*
(*To the attendants*)
Come, bundle up the wings; let's take 'em back. [*Exeunt.*

Fabulous notions respecting the unknown portions of the world seem to have been nearly the same (or at least of the same character) in the time of Aristophanes as in the days of Sir John Mandeville.

The marvels of these regions, known only to the Birds, are naturally expatiated upon by a chorus of Birds when released from the business of the stage and placed in immediate communication with the audience. But it will be seen that, by a strange coincidence, those wonderful and remote objects have an unaccountable analogy to things and persons at Athens, as in the following instance of the enormous tree, which, by the botanists, was considered as belonging to the Sycophantic genus, but which was vulgarly called a Cleonymus, whereas at Athens there happened to be a person precisely of the same name, "Cleonymus," equally distinguished for his size, and having the same peculiarity of being classed among the Sycophants. And what is more singular, as the Athenian Cleonymus had lost his shield in battle, it so happened that his vegetable counterpart was a deciduous tree, with leaves of a scutiform or shieldlike shape, which it was also in the habit of losing.

The antistrophe is a romantic and mysterious description of a junketing public-house which seems to have been in vogue, but from which it was not safe to return to town after dusk. Orestes, an heroic name, was also the name, or the nickname, of a noted robber (see The Acharnians, *p.* 59). *It was reckoned extremely dangerous to meet a demigod after sunset.*

CHORUS. STROPHE.

We have flown and we have run,
Viewing marvels many a one,
In every land beneath the sun.
  But the strangest sight to see
Was a huge exotic tree,
Growing, without heart or pith,
Weak and sappy, like a wyth;
But with leaves and boughs withal,
Comely, flourishing, and tall.
  This the learned all ascribe
To the Sycophantic tribe;
But the natives there, like us,
Call it a Cleonymus.
In the spring's delightful hours
It blossoms with rhetoric flowers;
I saw it standing in the field,
With leaves in figure like a shield;
On the first tempestuous day
I saw it cast those leaves away.

ANTISTROPHE.

There lies a region out of sight,
Far within the realm of night,
Far from torch and candle-light.
There in feasts of meal and wine
Men and demigods may join;
There they banquet and they dine,
Whilst the light of day prevails;
At sunset their assurance fails.
If any mortal then presumes,
Orestes, sallying from the tombs,
Like a fierce heroic sprite,
Assaults and strips the lonely wight.

The scene which follows may be considered as a short abstract of the mode in which clandestine political informa-

tion is received, attended to, and dismissed. The informant presents himself with an extraordinary display of precaution and apprehension; he is received with eagerness and cordiality; attended to with great earnestness, interrupted only by some little ill-humour on the part of the man of business, when in seeking for information he is obliged to betray the want of it; finally he is dismissed with a sort of indifference approaching to derision, after having been thoroughly pumped and drained of his intelligence.

PROMETHEUS, PEISTHETAIRUS, CHORUS.

Pro. (*enters muffled up, peeping about him with a look of anxiety and suspicion*).
Oh, dear! If Jupiter should chance to see me!
Where's Peisthetairus? Where?
Peis. Why, what's all this?
This fellow muffled up?
Pro. Do look behind me;
Is anybody watching? any Gods
Following and spying after me?
Peis. No, none;
None that I see; there's nobody—But you!
What are ye?
Pro. Tell me, what's the time of day?
Peis. Why, noon; past noon; but tell me, who are ye? Speak.
Pro. Much past? How much?
Peis. (*aside*). Confound the fool, I say!
The insufferable blockhead!
Pro. How's the sky?
Open or overcast? Are there any clouds?
Peis. (*aloud and angrily*).
Be hang'd!
Pro. Then I'll disguise myself no longer.
Peis. My dear Prometheus!
Pro. Hold your tongue, I beg;
Don't mention my name! If Jupiter should see me
Or overhear ye, I'm ruin'd and undone.
—But now, to give you a full complete account
Of everything that's passing there in Heaven...
The present state of things...But first, I'll trouble you

To take the umbrella, and hold it overhead,
Lest they should overlook us.
Peis. What a thought!
Just like yourself! A true Promethean thought!
Stand under it, here! Speak boldly; never fear.
Pro. D'ye mind me?
Peis. Yes, I mind ye; speak away.
Pro. (*emphatically*). Jupiter's ruin'd!
Peis. Ruin'd! How? Since when?
Pro. From the first hour you fortified and planted
Your atmospheric settlements. Ever since
There's not a mortal offers anything
In the shape of sacrifice.—No smoke of victims!
No fumes of incense! Absolutely nothing!
We're keeping a strict fast—fasting perforce,
From day to day—the whole community.
And the inland barbarous Gods in the upper country
Are broken out, quite mutinous and savage,
With hunger and anger; threatening to come down
With all their force, if Jupiter refuses
To open the ports and allow them a free traffic
For their entrails and intestines, as before.
Peis. (*a little annoyed at being obliged to ask the question*).
What, are there other barbarous Gods besides
In the upper country?
Pro. Barbarous? To be sure;
They're all of Execestides's kindred.*
Peis. (*as before hesitating, but with a sort of affected ease*).
Well...but...the name now: These same barbarous deities...
What name do you call 'em?
Pro. (*surprised at Peisthetairus's ignorance*).
Call them! The Triballi!
Peis. (*giving vent to his irritation by a forced joke*).
Ah! well, then, that accounts for our old saying—
Confound the *Tribe* of them!
Pro. (*annoyed and drily*). Precisely so.
But now to business. Thus much I can tell ye—
That envoys will arrive immediately
From Jupiter and those upland wild Triballi,
To treat for a peace. But you must not consent
To ratify or conclude, till Jupiter

* Noted elsewhere in this play as having no just claim to the rights of a citizen—See p. 151 and p. 181.

Acknowledges the sovereignty of the Birds,
Surrendering up to you the Sovereign Queen,
Whom you must marry.
Peis. Why, what Queen is that?
Pro. What Queen?—A most delightful, charming girl—
Jove's housekeeper, that manages his matters,
Serves out his thunderbolts, arranges everything;
The constitutional laws and liberties,
Morals and manners, the marine department,
Freedom of speech, and threepence for the juries.
Peis. Why, that seems all in all.
Pro. Yes, everything
I tell ye; in having her, you've everything;
I came down hastily to say thus much;
I'm hearty, ye know; I stick to principle.
Steady to the human interest—always was.[1]
Peis. Yes, we're obliged to you for our roast victuals.
Pro. And I hate these present Gods, you know, most thoroughly:
I need not tell you that.
Peis. (*with a sort of half sneer*). No, no, you need not,*
You're known of old for an enemy to the Gods.
Pro. Yes, yes, like Timon; I'm a perfect Timon;
Just such another. But I must be going;
Give me the umbrella; if Jupiter should see me,
He'll think that I'm attending a procession.
Peis. That's well; but don't forget the folding chair,
For a part of your disguise. Here, take it with you.
[*Exeunt.*

* Peisthetairus, who has learnt all that he wanted to know, does not care to lose his time in listening to professions of zeal and attachment. He contrives, however, to conclude civilly, with a piece of obliging attention

Under the same form of a description of the wonders of the Terra Incognita, we have here again one of those pieces of personal satire peculiar to the ancient comedy. It is directed against Socrates and his school, including by name his friend Chærephon.

The uncleanly habits imputed to them ("Where baths and washing are forbidden") *will have been seen already alluded to in p.* 206 ("Unwash'd and slovenly like so many

---

[1] Prometheus had incurred the wrath of Jupiter by his kindness to mankind in having bestowed on them the gift of fire.

[2] The Canephoroi were followed by a person bearing an umbrella and a folding chair.

Socrateses").—*But it is difficult to conceive what is the imputation conveyed or alluded to by describing them as engaged in the evocation of spirits.*

It is a question which might form a curious subject of enquiry for those who have the means of prosecuting it, and who are better acquainted with the history of the Socratic school.

Pisander seems to have been an object of the Poet's peculiar aversion; in his first political comedy, the Babylonians, *he had been mentioned in company with* two[1] *others, as having given occasion to the origin of the war by their extortion of compulsory presents from the subject states, an accusation which is repeated in the* Lysistrata, *v.* 490; *again in the* Peace, *v.* 389, *ed. Bekk. his military pomp and arrogance are mentioned as objects of extreme disgust and contempt; and it seems that he must have been the Commander described at length in the Epirrema of the same comedy, most splendidly caparisoned and foremost in running away. He had also been stigmatised by Eupolis as having been guilty of cowardly conduct.*

It seems that he is brought in here, by the bye, not as a follower or disciple of Socrates, but in allusion to his want of military courage as a person whose spirit wanted to be raised, *and who therefore naturally resorted to a place where* spirits were raised.

Chærephon was the most zealous admirer of Socrates; he is recorded to have been a person of most singular aspect.

CHORUS.

Beyond the navigable seas,
Amongst the fierce Antipodes,
There lies a lake, obscure and holy,
Lazy, deep and melancholy,
Solitary, secret, hidden,
Where baths and washing are forbidden.
  Socrates, beside the brink,
Summons from the murky sink

[1] "Two"—For, by putting the participle in the dual, and transposing the verb and the proper name, the true metre of the fragment (the long Anapæst) may be restored. See Frag. v. Βαβυλώνιοι, ed. Bekk. vol. ii. p. 266.

Many a disembodied ghost ;
And Pisander reach'd the coast
To raise the spirit that he lost ;
With a victim strange and new,
*A gawky Camel which he slew,
Like Ulysses—Whereupon
The grizzly sprite of Chærephon
Flitted round him, and appear'd
With his eyebrows and his beard,
Like a strange infernal fowl,
Half a Vampyre, half an Owl.

* A simile by juxtaposition indirectly expressed, as when Adam is described "tall and fair beneath"[1] a palm tree, and the gigantic warriors in Homer standing before the "lofty" gates. The indirect simile may be either beautiful or sublime, or, as in the present instance, ludicrous.

It is usual with Aristophanes to omit that explanation which a poet of the new comedy would have put into a soliloquy or into a confidential conversation between the master and his slave. He gives his audience credit for being able to comprehend at once the previous views of the person whom he introduces.

Neptune, the chief of the Embassy, in which Hercules and the barbarous Triballian Deity are joined with him, has settled in his own mind a very satisfactory plan for the management of it. "Hercules is my nephew, and of course looks up to me. He will be easily managed if I can appear to consult and advise exclusively with him. But I must begin by putting the Triballian wholly out of the question as a ragamuffin whom we are both equally ashamed of. Otherwise their understandings are so much upon a par, my poor nephew, I am sorry to say, is such a blockhead, that he and that beast, the Triballian, from the mere natural sympathy of their stupidity, will join and act together in spite of me." He accordingly begins with the Triballian by settling his dress for him ; and as soon as he has disposed of him and set him down as an unproduceable ruffian, he turns round to consult Hercules, who makes a stupid answer. Neptune, like a kind uncle, endeavours quietly and calmly to set him right. Up to this point everything appears promising ; but Neptune, alas ! is deficient in presence of mind ; he is encumbered with his dignity, and above all in the person of Peisthetairus, he is opposed to a politician infinitely his

[1] "fair indeed and tall,
Under a Platan."
Paradise Lost, Book iv. l. 477, 478.

superior in resources and address. They advance within sight of Peisthetairus, who affects not to notice them, and remains looking down among the dishes, apparently occupied with his sauces. Neptune, of course, advances no farther, but remains with a decided attitude and look of dignity, ready to meet his eye, as soon as it shall be raised to encounter his. Unfortunately, however, he is so much occupied with his own attitude, and with the look which seems to say, "Well, sir, now you're at leisure,"—that he omits to restrain Hercules, who more impatient and indignant, presses forward with an announcement of their arrival, calculated, as he thinks, to rouse and astonish Peisthetairus: failing in his attempt to make an impression, and feeling himself at a loss, he remains exposed to the influence of his natural instincts, which attract him towards the pans and dishes.—Hence a conversation is begun, a recognition takes place, the ice is broken, and the negotiation opened, while Neptune is left with his dignity in the back ground.

NEPTUNE, *the Triballian Envoy,* HERCULES.

Nep. There's Nephelococcugia, that's the town,
The point we're bound to, with our embassy.
(*Turning to the Triballian.*)
But you! What a figure have ye made yourself!
What a way to wear a mantle! slouching off
From the left shoulder! Hitch it round, I tell ye,
On the right side. For shame,—come,—so; that's better,
These folds too, bundled up. There, throw them round
Even and easy,—so. Why, you're a savage,
A natural born savage. Oh, democracy!
What will it bring us to? when such a ruffian
Is voted into an embassy!
Tri. (*to Neptune who is pulling his dress about*). Come, hands off!
Hands off!
Nep. Keep quiet, I tell ye, and hold your tongue,
For a very beast; in all my life in heaven,
I never saw such another. Hercules,
I say, what shall we do? What should you think?
Her. What would I do? What do I think? I've told you
Already—I think to throttle him—the fellow,
Whoever he is, that's keeping us blockaded.

Nep. Yes, my good friend ; but we were sent, you know,
To treat for a Peace. Our embassy is for peace.
Her. That makes no difference ; or if it does,
It makes me long to throttle him the more.
Peis. (*very busy, affecting not to see them*).
Give me the Silphium spice. Where's the cheese grater ?
Bring cheese here, somebody ! Mend the charcoal fire.
Her. Mortal, we greet you and hail you ! Three of us.
Three deities—
Peis. (*without looking up*). But I'm engaged at present ;
A little busy, you see, mixing my sauce.
Her. Why sure ! How can it be ? what dish is this ?
Birds seemingly !
Peis. (*without looking up*). Some individual birds,
Opposed to the popular democratic birds,
Render'd themselves obnoxious.
Her. So, you've pluck'd them,
And put them into sauce, provisionally ?
Peis. (*looking up*). Oh ! bless me, Hercules, I'm quite glad to see you !
What brings you here ?
Her. We're come upon an embassy
From Heaven, to put an end to this same war—
Serv. (*to Peisthetairus*). The cruet's empty, our oil is out.
Peis. No matter,
Fetch more, fetch plenty, I tell ye. We shall want it.
Her.. . . For, in fact it brings no benefit to us,
The continuance of the War prolonging it ;
And you yourselves, by being on good terms
Of harmony with the Gods—why, for the future,
You'd never need to know the want of rain,
For water in your tanks ; and we could serve ye
With reasonable, seasonable weather,
According as you wish'd it, wet or dry.
And this is our commission coming here,
As envoys, with authority to treat.
Peis. Well, the dispute, you know, from the beginning
Did not originate with us. The war
(If we could hope in any way to bring you
To reasonable terms) might be concluded.
Our wishes, I declare it, are for Peace.
If the same wish prevails upon your part ;

The arrangement in itself, is obvious.—
—A retrocession on the part of Jupiter.—
The Birds again to be reintegrated
In their estate of sovereignty.— This seems
The fair result; and if we can conclude,
I shall hope to see the ambassadors to supper.

Her. Well, this seems satisfactory; I consent.

Nep. (*to Hercules*). What's come to ye? What do ye mean? Are ye gone mad?
You Glutton! would you ruin your own father,
Depriving him of his ancient sovereignty?

Peis. (*to Neptune, with the civil, good-humoured sneer of a superior understanding*).
Indeed!—And would not it be a better method
For all you Deities, and confirm your power,
To leave the Birds to manage things below?
You sit there, muffled in your clouds above,
While all mankind are shifting, skulking, lurking,
And perjuring themselves here out of sight.
Whereas, if you would form a steady strict
Alliance with the Birds, when any man
(Using the common old familiar oath—
"By Jupiter and the crow") * forswore himself,
The Crow would pick his eyes out, for his pains.

* See p. 170 and note † to ine 579.

Nep. Well, that seems plausible—that's fairly put.

Her. I think so, too.

Peis. (*to the Triballian*). Well, what say you?

Trib. Say true.†

† It is singular that these two syllables are the last syllables of the word (or sentence) in his own language by which the Triballian expresses his consent.

Peis. (*very volubly,—quite at his ease*).
Yes. He consents, you see! But I'll explain now
The services and good offices we could do you.
Suppose a mortal made a vow, for instance,
To any o' You; then he delays and shuffles,
And says "The Gods are easy creditors."
In such a case, we could assist ye, I say,
To levy a fine.

Nep. (*open to conviction, but anxious to proceed on sure ground*).
How would you do it? Tell me.

Peis. Why, for example, when he's counting money,
Or sitting in the bath, we give the warrant
To a poursuivant of ours, a Kite or Magpie;

And they pounce down immediately, and distrain
Cash or apparel, money or money's worth,
To twice the amount of your demand upon him.

Her. Well, I'm for giving up the sovereignty,
For my part.

Nep. (*convinced, but wishing to avoid responsibility, by voting last*).
The Triballian, what says he?

Her. (*aside to the Triballian, shewing his fist*).
You, Sir; do you want to be well bang'd or not?
Mind, how you vote! Take care how you provoke me.

Trib. Yaw, yaw. Goot, goot.

Her. He's of the same opinion.

Nep. Then, since you're both agreed, I must agree.

Her. (*shouting to Peisthetairus, the negotiators having withdrawn to consult at the extremity of the stage*).
Well, you! We've settled this concern, you see,
About the sovereignty; we're all agreed.

Peis. O faith, there's one thing more, I recollect,
Before we part; a point that I must mention.
As for dame Juno, we'll not speak of her;
I've no pretensions, Jupiter may keep her;
But, for that other Queen, his manager,
The sovereign Goddess, her surrender to me
Is quite an article indispensable.

Nep. (*with gravity and dignity*). Your views, I find, are not disposed for peace:
We must turn homewards.

Peis. As you please, so be it.
Cook, mind what you're about there with the sauce;
Let's have it rich and savory, thicken it up!

Her. How now, man? Neptune! are you flying off?
Must we remain at war, here, for a woman?

Nep. But, what are we to do?

Her. Do? Why, make peace.

Nep. (*in great wrath, like a grave Uncle scolding a great fool of a Nephew*).
I pity you really! I feel quite ashamed
And sorry to see you; ruining yourself!
If anything should happen to your father,
After surrendering the sovereignty,
What's to become of you? When you yourself

Have voted away your whole inheritance:
At his decease, you must remain a beggar.
Peis. (*aside to Hercules*). Ah there! I thought so; he's coming over ye;
Step here, a moment! Let me speak to ye!
Your Uncle's chousing you, my poor dear friend,
You've not a farthing's worth of expectation,
From what your father leaves. Ye can't inherit
By law: ye're illegitimate, ye know.
Her. Heighday! Why, what do you mean?
Peis. I mean the Fact!
Your mother was a foreigner; Minerva
Is counted an heiress, every body knows;
How could that be, supposing her own father
To have had a lawful heir?
Her But, if my Father
Should choose to leave the property to me,
In his last Will.
Peis. The law would cancel it!
And Neptune, he that's using all his influence
To work upon ye, he'd be the very first
To oppose ye, and oust ye, as the testator's brother.
I'll tell ye what the law says, Solon's law:
"A foreign heir shall not succeed,[1]
Where there are children of the lawful breed:
But, if no native heir there be,
The kinsman nearest in degree
Shall enter on the property."
Her. Does nothing come to me then?—Nothing at all,
Of all my father leaves?
Peis. Nothing at all,
I should conceive. But you perhaps can tell me;
Did He, your Father, ever take ye with him,
To get ye enroll'd upon the register?
Her. No truly, I—thought it strange—he—never did.

---

[1] Memory must have been in the earliest times the sole repository of knowledge of every kind. Every means therefore of assistance to the memory was most carefully cultivated. Amongst other instances, in order to facilitate the requisite knowledge and recollection of them, the Laws themselves were composed and recorded in a metrical form. Hence the same word in Greek signifies both a *Song* and a *Law*.

Peis. Well, but don't think things strange. Don't stand there, stammering,
Puzzling and gaping. Trust yourself to me,
'Tis I must make your fortune after all!
If you'll reside and settle amongst us here,
I'll make you chief Commander among the Birds,
Captain, and Autocrat and every thing,
Here you shall domineer and rule the roast,
With splendour and opulence and pigeon's milk.

Her. (*in a more audible voice, and in a formal decided tone*).[1]
I agreed with you before: I think your argument
Unanswerable. I shall vote for the surrender.

Peis. (*to Neptune*). And what say you?

Nep. (*firmly and vehemently*). Decidedly, I dissent.

Peis. Then it depends upon our other friend,
It rests with the Triballian, what say you?

Tri. Me tell you; pretty girl, grand beautiful Queen,
Give him to Birds.

Her. Ay, give her up, you mean.

Nep. Mean! He knows nothing about it. He means nothing
But chattering like a Magpie.

Peis. Well, "The Magpies"
He means, the Magpies or the Birds in general.
The Republic of the Birds—their government—
That the surrender should be made to them.

Peisthetairus being sure of his point, amuses himself with arguing nonsensically to provoke Neptune.

Nep. (*in great wrath*). Well, settle it yourselves; amongst yourselves;
In your own style: I've nothing more to say.

Her. (*to Peisthetairus*). Come, we're agreed in fact to grant your terms;
But you must come, to accompany us to the sky;
To take back this same Queen, and the other matters.

Peis. (*very quietly*). It happens lucky enough, with this provision
For a marriage feast. It seems prepared on purpose.

---

[1] They had withdrawn apart, and their previous conversation was supposed not to have been audible to Neptune and the Triballian, whose bye-play might have consisted in Neptune's formal attempts to soothe and gain the Triballian, who would only shrug up his shoulders.

Her. Indeed, and it does. Suppose in the meanwhile,
I superintend the cookery, and turn the roast,
While you go back together.
Nep. (*with a start of surprise and disgust*). Turn the roast!
A pretty employment! Won't you go with us?
Her No, thank ye; I'm mighty comfortable here.
Peis. Come, give me a marriage robe; I must be going.

We have here another satyric song, of the same fanciful humour as the preceding, descriptive of imaginary wonders in an unknown world. In the last instance the Poet had exhibited a caricature of the Socratic school of Philosophy. The same vein of ridicule is now directed against another novelty, tending equally, in the opinion of the poet (more just in this than in the preceding instance) to produce an undesirable change in the general character of the nation.

Mercenary professors and teachers of rhetoric, for the most part foreigners (the Gorgias for instance here mentioned was a Sicilian), had of late been received and encouraged in Athens. Their public exhibitions, which were generally resorted to, had operated as an incentive to the natural propensity of the Athenian people, already more than enough disposed to divert their attention to the unproductive pursuits of litigation and speechifying. While at the same time their private lessons (the course of instruction by which they engaged to communicate the secrets of their art, and to form young practitioners) were purchased in some instances at an enormous price, by young men of wealth aspiring to political eminence and celebrity.

CHORUS.

Along the Sycophantic shore,
And where the savage tribes adore
The waters of the Clepsydra,*
There dwells a nation, stern and strong,
Armed with an enormous tongue,
Wherewith they smite and slay:†

With their tongues, they reap and sow,
And gather all the fruits ‡ that grow,
The vintage and the grain;

* The Clepsydra or Water Clock marked the time allotted to each Advocate. It was a prominent object in the Courts of Justice. The name also belonged to certain streams and springs.
† Dangerous as accusers.
‡ Their salaries and profits.

Gorgias is their Chief of pride,
And many more there be beside
  Of mickle might and main.

Good they never teach, nor shew
But how to work men harm and woe,
  Unrighteousness and wrong ;
And hence, the custom doth arise,
When beasts are slain in sacrifice,
  We sever out the tongue.*

* This sacrificial form was peculiar to the Athenians.

It has been already observed, that this play, in the success of which, as a sedative to the popular insanity, the higher orders of the community were essentially interested, was exhibited with a singular recklessness of expense.

The concluding scene seems to have been equal in magnificence to those of the most gorgeous tragedies ; and it is remarkable that in the passage immediately following, contrary to the invariable custom of the poet, there is no tinge of burlesque. The Poet has throughout, as a Poet, *imitated the style of Sophocles ; while under his direction* as the manager of a Comic Drama, *the actor who personated Peisthetairus must have been instructed to reduce the scene to the level of comedy, by his airs and gestures characteristic of unaccustomed dignity and authority. It must have been a very delicate and amusing piece of acting ! An elderly man, a sharp thorough going fellow—to see him*

Assume the God,
Affect to nod,
And seem to shake the spheres.

The Choral songs which follow are of a peculiar and by no means obvious character, which it is rather difficult to define, and not very easy to express in imitation. In the Comedy of the Peace *we have a Rustic Epithalamium, perfectly rustic, and probably not very different from the rustic extempore Poetry of the same race at the present day. But in this instance we have a Town Epithalamium, such as we may suppose to have been composed and perpetrated in honour of the nuptials of the more noble and wealthy families in Athens. The vulgar town Poet is anxious to exhibit his* education *by imitating and borrowing passages from the most approved lyrical poets, but at the same time reduces all their imagery and expressions to the natural level of his own dulness. Thus maintaining, in the verse itself, that balance of the ludicrous and sublime, which in the first part of the scene had resulted from the contrast of the Poetry and the action.*

Some parts of the Epithalamium of Catullus (See v. 100 *and the following stanzas) are evidently a humorous imitation of the vulgar Epithalamia at Rome. Under cover of this character, he amused himself at the expense of his newly married friends.*

HARBINGER *or* HERALD, *announcing the approach of Peisthetairus.*

O fortunate! O triumphant! O beyond
All power of speech or thought, supremely blest,
Prosperous happy Birds!—Behold your King,
Here in his glorious palace!—Mark his entrance,
Dazzling all eyes, resplendent as a Star;
Outshining all the golden lights, that beam,
From the rich roof, even as a summer Sun,
Or brighter than the Sun, blazing at Noon.
He comes; and at his side a female form
Of beauty ineffable; wielding on high,
In his right hand, the winged thunderbolt,
Jove's weapon. While the fumes of incense spread,
Circling around, and subtle odours steal
Upon the senses from the wreathed smoke,
Curling and rising in the tranquil air.
See there He stands! Now must the sacred Muse
Give with auspicious words her welcome due.

SEMICHORUS.

Stand aside and clear the ground,
Spreading in a circle round
With a worthy welcoming;
To salute our noble King
In his splendour and his pride,
Coming hither side by side,
With his happy lovely bride.

O the fair delightful face!
What a figure! What a grace!
What a presence! What a carriage!
What a noble worthy marriage!

Let the Birds rejoice and sing,
At the wedding of the King:
Happy to congratulate
Such a blessing to the state.
Hymen Hymen Hoh!

Jupiter, that God sublime,
When the Fates, in former time,
Match'd him with the Queen of Heaven,
At a solemn banquet given,
Such a feast was held above;
And the charming God of Love,
Being present in command,
As a Bridesman took his stand,
With the golden reins in hand.
Hymen Hymen Hoh!

Peis. I accept and approve the marks of your love,
Your music and verse I applaud and admire.
But rouse your invention, and raising it higher,
Describe me the terrible engine of Jove,
The thunder of Earth and the thunder above.

Peisthetairus puts an end to their nonsense with condescension and affability.

The reader may have already observed, that in more than one instance the Poet directs the attention of his audience to the lavish expenditure of the Choregus. This seems to have been the object of the following lines, introductory to a new display of theatrical thunder manufactured upon an improved principle.

CHORUS.

O dreaded Bolt of Heaven,
The Clouds with horror cleaving,
And ye terrestrial thunders deep and low
Closed in the subterranean caves * below,
That even at this instant growl and rage,
Shaking with awful sound this earthly stage;
Our King by you has gain'd his due;

* Caves of the Theatre.

By your assistance, yours alone,
Every thing is made his own,
Jove's dominion and his throne;
And his happiness and pride,
His delightful lovely bride.
Hymen Hymen Hoh!

PEISTHETAIRUS.

Birds of ocean and of air,
Hither in a troop repair,
To the royal ceremony,
Our triumphant matrimony!
Come for us to feast and feed ye!
Come to revel dance and sing!—
Lovely creature! Let me lead ye
Hand in hand, and wing to wing.

THE FROGS.

THE FROGS.

ACCHUS, the patron of the stage, in despair at the decline of the dramatic art (which had lately been deprived of its best tragic authors, Sophocles and Euripides), determines to descend the infernal regions with the intention of procuring the release of Euripides. He appears accordingly, equipped for the expedition, with the lion's skin and club (in imitation of Hercules, whose success in a similar adventure has encouraged him to the attempt); he still retains, however, his usual effeminate costume, which forms a contrast with these heroic attributes. Xanthias, his slave (like Silenus, the mythologic attendant of Bacchus), is mounted upon an ass; but, in conformity with the practice of other human slaves when attending their mortal masters upon an earthly journey, he carries a certain pole upon his shoulder, at the ends of which the various packages, necessary for his master's accommodation, are suspended in equilibrio. The first scene (which, if it had not been the first, might perhaps have been omitted) contains a censure of the gross taste of the audience (suitable to the character of Bacchus as patron of the stage) with allusions to some cotemporary rival authors, who submitted to court the applause of the vulgar by mere buffoonery.—The argument between Bacchus and Xanthias, at the end of this scene, probably contains some temporary allusion now unknown, but is obviously, and in the first place, a humorous exemplification of the philosophical, verbal sophisms, not, in all probability, new, even

then, but which were then, for the first time, introduced in Athens, and which may be traced from thence to the schoolmen of the middle ages. Xanthias carries the bundles passivè *et* formaliter, *the ass carries them* activè *et* materialiter.

THE FROGS.

BACCHUS. XANTHIAS.

Xanthias.

MASTER, shall I begin with the usual jokes
That the audience always laugh at?
B. If you please;
Any joke you please except "being overburthen'd."
—Don't use it yet—We've time enough before us.
X. Well, something else that's comical and clever?
B. I forbid being "overpress'd and overburthen'd."
X. Well, but the drollest joke of all—?
B. Remember
There's one thing I protest against—
X. What's that?
B. Why, shifting off your load to the other shoulder,
And fidgeting and complaining of the gripes.
X. What then do you mean to say, that I must not say
That I'm ready to befoul myself?
B. (*peremptorily*). By no means—
Except when I take an emetic.*
X. (*in a sullen, muttering tone, as if resentful of hard usage*).
What's the use, then,
Of my being burthen'd here with all these bundles,

* As a filthy joke might assist the operation of the medicine.

Xanthias considers these jokes as the lawful vails and perquisites of servants on such occasions.

If I'm to be deprived of the common jokes
That Phrynichus, and Lycis, and Ameipsias
Allow the servants always in their comedies,
Without exception, when they carry bundles?
B. Pray, leave them off—for those ingenious sallies
Have such an effect upon my health and spirits
That I feel grown old and dull when I get home.
X. (*as before, or with a sort of half mutinous whine*).
It's hard for me to suffer in my limbs,
To be overburthen'd and debarr'd from joking.
B. Well, this is monstrous, quite, and insupportable!
Such insolence in a servant! When your master
Is going afoot and has provided you
With a beast to carry ye.
X. What! do I carry nothing?
B. You're carried yourself.
X. But I carry bundles, don't I?
B. But the beast bears all the bundles that you carry.
X. Not those that I carry myself—'tis I that carry 'em.
B. You're carried yourself, I tell ye.
X. I can't explain it,
But I feel it in my shoulders plainly enough.
B. Well, if the beast don't help you, take and try;
Change places with the ass and carry him.
X. (*in a tone of mere disgust*).
Oh, dear! I wish I had gone for a volunteer,*
And left you to yourself. I wish I had.
B. Dismount, you rascal! Here, we're at the house
Where Hercules lives.—Holloh, there! who's within there
[*Bacchus kicks outrageously at the door.*

* Xanthias is wearied out by mere petulance and folly, not with hard usage.
Numbers of the slaves at that time had been enfranchised on condition of naval service.

HERCULES. BACCHUS. XANTHIAS.

H. Who's there? (He has bang'd at the door, whoever he is,
With the kick of a centaur.) † What's the matter, there?
B. (*aside*). Ha! Xanthias!
X. What?
B. (*aside*). Did ye mind how he was frighten'd?
X. I suppose he was afraid you were going mad.
H. (*aside*). By Jove! I shall laugh outright; I'm ready to burst.
I shall laugh, in spite of myself, upon my life.

† The expression is characteristic, the Centaur being a familiar beast to Hercules.

[*Hercules shifts about, and turns aside to disguise his laughter: this apparent shyness confirms Bacchus in the opinion of his own ascendancy, which he manifests accordingly.*

B. (*with a tone of protection*).
Come hither, friend.—What ails ye? Step this way;
I want to speak to ye.

H. (*with a good-humoured, but unsuccessful endeavour to suppress laughter, or to conceal it. Suppose him, for instance, speaking with his hand before his mouth.*)
But I can't help laughing,
To see the lion's skin with a saffron robe,
And the club with the women's sandals—altogether—
What's the meaning of it all? Have you been abroad?

B. I've been aboard—in the Fleet—with Cleisthenes.

H. (*sharply and ironically*). You fought—?

B. (*briskly and sillily*). Yes, that we did—we gain'd a victory;
And we sunk the enemies' ships—thirteen of 'em.

H. "So you woke at last and found it was a dream?"*

B. But aboard the fleet, as I pursued my studies,
I read the tragedy of Andromeda; †
And then such a vehement passion struck my heart,
You can't imagine.

H. A small one, I suppose,
My little fellow—a moderate little passion?

B. (*ironically: the irony of imbecility*).
It's just as small as Molon is—that's all—
Molon the wrestler, I mean—as small as he is—‡

H. Well, what was it like? what kind of a thing? what was it?

B. (*meaning to be very serious and interesting*).
No, friend, you must not laugh; it's past a joke;
It's quite a serious feeling—quite distressing;
I suffer from it—

H. (*bluntly*). Well, explain. What was it?

B. I can't declare it at once; but I'll explain it
Theatrically and enigmatically:
(*With a buffoonish assumption of tragic gesture and emphasis*)
Were you ever seized with a sudden passionate longing
For a mess of porridge?

* A proverbial sarcasm, by which the auditor of an improbable story affects to suppose that the narrator has been relating a dream.

† A play of Euripides.

‡ Molon was remarkable for his bulk and stature.

H. Often enough, if that's all.
B. Shall I state the matter to you plainly at once;
Or put it circumlocutorily?*
H. Not about the porridge. I understand your instance.
B. Such is the passion that possesses me
For poor Euripides, that's dead and gone;
And it's all in vain people trying to persuade me
From going after him.
H. What, to the shades below?
B. Yes, to the shades below, or the shades beneath 'em.
To the undermost shades of all. I'm quite determined.
H. But what's your object?
B. (*with a ridiculous imitation of tragical action and emphasis*). Why, my object is
That I want a clever poet—"for the good,
The gracious and the good, are dead and gone;
The worthless and the weak are left alive." †
H. Is not Iophon a good one?—He's alive, sure?
B. If he's a good one, he's our only good one;
But it's a question; I'm in doubt about him.‡
H. There's Sophocles; he's older than Euripides—
If you'd go so far for 'em, you'd best bring him.
B. No; first I'll try what Iophon § can do,
Without his father, Sophocles, to assist him.
—Besides, Euripides is a clever rascal;
A sharp, contriving rogue that will make a shift
To desert and steal away with me; the other
Is an easy-minded soul, and always was.
H. Where's Agathon? ‖
B. He's gone and left me too,
Regretted by his friends; a worthy poet—
H. Gone! Where, poor soul?
B. To the banquets of the blest!
H. But then you've Xenocles—¶
B. Yes! a plague upon him!
H. Pythangelus ** too—
X. But nobody thinks of me;
Standing all this while with the bundles on my shoulder.
H. But have not you other young ingenious youths
That are fit to out-talk Euripides ten times over;
To the amount of a thousand, at least, all writing tragedy—?
B. They're good for nothing—"Warblers of the Grove"—

* A ridicule of the circuitous preambles to confidential communications in tragedy.
† The quotation is from Euripides.
‡ Upon the subject of his own profession, Bacchus talks in a tone approaching very nearly to sense and consistency, and is treated by Hercules with more respect.
§ A tragic poet, the son of Sophocles, and supposed to have been assisted by him in the composition of his tragedies.
‖ A tragic poet, a young man of wealth and of refined habits, who had lately died at the Court of Archelaus, whither he had retired from Athens.
¶ One of the theatric family of Carcinus, the constant butts of Aristophanes' humour.
** An obscure writer of tragedies. The Scholiast notices the sarcastic effect of Xanthias's interruption.

—" Little, foolish, fluttering things "—poor puny wretches,
That dawdle and dangle about with the tragic muse ;
Incapable of any serious meaning—
—There's not one hearty poet amongst them all
That's fit to risk an adventurous valiant phrase.

H. How—" hearty ? " What do you mean by " valiant phrases ? "

B. (*the puzzle of a person who is called upon for a definition*).
I mean a...kind...of a...doubtful, bold expression
To talk about..." *The viewless foot of Time* "—
(*Tragic emphasis in the quotations*)
And..." *Jupiter's Secret Chamber in the Skies* "—
And about...*A person's soul...not being perjured
When...the tongue...forswears itself...in spite of the soul.

H. Do you like that kind of stuff?

B. I'm crazy after it.

H. Why, sure, it's trash and rubbish—Don't you think so?

B. " Men's fancies are their own—Let mine alone † "—

H. But, in fact, it seems to me quite bad—rank nonsense.

B. You'll tell me next what I ought to like for supper.

X. But nobody thinks of me here, with the bundles.

B. (*with a careless, easy, voluble, degagé style*).
—But now to the business that I came upon—
(*Upon a footing of equality.—The tone of a person who is dispatching business off-hand, with readiness and unconcern.*)
(With the apparel that you see—the same as yours)
To obtain a direction from you to your friends.
(To apply to them—in case of anything—
If anything should occur) the acquaintances
That received you there—(the time you went before
—For the business about Cerberus ‡)—if you'd give me
Their names and their directions, and communicate
Any information relative to the country,
The roads,—the streets,—the bridges, and the brothels,
The wharfs,—the public walks,—the public houses,
The fountains,—aqueducts,—and inns, and taverns,
And lodgings,—free from bugs and fleas, if possible,
If you know any such—

X. But nobody thinks of me.

H. What a notion! You! will you risk it? are ye mad?

* A confused, vulgarized recollection of Euripides. *The 1st citation is from Æschylus, the 2nd from Sophocles, the 3rd from Euripides.*

† Proverbial.

‡ Hercules was employed by Eurystheus to drag up Cerberus from the gates of Hell. This adventure furnishes several incidents in the course of this play.

B. (*meaning to be very serious and manly*).
I beseech you say no more—no more of that,
But inform me briefly and plainly about my journey:
The shortest road and the most convenient one.
H. (*with a tone of easy, indolent, deliberate banter*).
Well,—which shall I tell ye first, now?—Let me see now—
There's a good convenient road by the Rope and Noose;
The Hanging Road.
B. No; that's too close and stifling.
H. Then, there's an easy, fair, well-beaten track,
As you go by the Pestle and Mortar—
B. What, the Hemlock?
H. To be sure—
B. That's much too cold—it will never do.
They tell me it strikes a chill to the legs and feet.*
H. Should you like a speedy, rapid, downhill road?
B. Indeed I should, for I'm a sorry traveller.
H. Go to the Keramicus then.
B. What then?
H. Get up to the very top of the tower.
B. What then?
H. Stand there and watch when the Race of the Torch† begins;
And mind when you hear the people cry "*Start! start!*"
Then start at once with 'em.
B. Me? Start? Where from?
H. From the top of the tower to the bottom.
B. No, not I.
It's enough to dash my brains out! I'll not go
Such a road upon any account.
H. Well, which way then?
B. The way you went yourself.
H. But it's a long one,
For first you come to a monstrous bottomless lake.
B. And what must I do to pass?
H. You'll find a boat there;
A little tiny boat, as big as that,
And an old man that ferries you over in it,
Receiving twopence as the usual fee.
B. Ah! that same twopence‡ governs everything
Wherever it goes.—I wonder how it managed
To find its way there?

* The effects of the hemlock are thus described in Plato's account of the death of Socrates.

† A sacred race in honour of Minerva, Vulcan, and Prometheus. The runners carried a lighted torch.—A ludicrous description of it occurs further on towards the end of the 4th Act.

‡ Twopence, the salary of the poorer citizens who sat as jurymen, and who were in fact the arbiters of the lives and fortunes of their subjects and fellow-citizens.

H. Theseus introduced it.*
—Next you'll meet serpents, and wild beasts, and monsters,
(*Suddenly, and with a shout in Bacch us's ear*)
Horrific to behold!
B. (*starting a little*). Don't try to fright me;
You'll not succeed, I promise you.—I'm determined.
H. Then there's an abyss of mire and floating filth,
In which the damn'd lie wallowing and overwhelm'd;
The unjust, the cruel, and the inhospitable;
And the barbarous bilking Cullies that withhold
The price of intercourse with fraud and wrong;
The incestuous, and the parricides, and the robbers;
The perjurers, and assassins, and the wretches
That wilfully and presumptuously transcribe
Extracts and trash from Morsimus's plays.
B. And, by Jove! Cinesias with his Pyrrhic dancers
Ought to be there—they're worse, or quite as bad.
H. But after this your sense will be saluted
With a gentle breathing sound of flutes and voices,
And a beautiful spreading light like ours on earth,
And, myrtle glades and happy quires among,
Of women and men with rapid applause and mirth.†
B. And who are all those folks?
H. The initiated.
X. (*gives indications of restiveness, as if ready to throw down his bundles*).
I won't stand here like a mule in a procession
Any longer with these packages and bundles.
H. (*hastily, in a civil hurry, as when you shake a man by the hand, and shove him out of the room, and give him your best wishes and advice all at once*).
They'll tell you everything you want to know,
For they're establish'd close upon the road,
By the corner of Pluto's house—so fare you well;
Farewell, my little fellow. [*Exit.*
B. (*pettishly*). I wish you better.
(*to Xanthias*) You, sirrah, take your bundles up again.
X. What, before I put them down?
B. Yes! now this moment.
X. Nah! don't insist; there's plenty of people going
As corpses with the convenience of a carriage;
They'd take it for a trifle gladly enough.

* The Athenian hero, when his adventures led him to penetrate into the infernal regions, is supposed to have introduced the characteristic type of his native city.

† A description of the existence allotted to those who had been initiated in the mysteries of Ceres and Bacchus.

B. But if we meet with nobody?

X. Then I'll take 'em.

B. Come, come, that's fairly spoken, and in good time;
For there they're carrying a corpse out to be buried.

[*A funeral, with a corpse on an open bier, crosses the stage.*

—Holloh! you, there—you Deadman—can't you hear?
Would you take any bundles to hell with ye, my good fellow?

*Deadman.** What are they?

B. These.

D. Then I must have two drachmas.

B. I can't—you must take less.

D. (*peremptorily*). Bearers, move on.

B. No, stop! we shall settle between us—you're so hasty.

D. It's no use arguing; I must have two drachmas.

B. (*emphatically and significantly*). Ninepence!

D. I'd best be alive again at that rate. [*Exit.*

B. Fine airs the fellow gives himself—a rascal!
I'll have him punish'd, I vow, for overcharging.

X. Best give him a good beating: give me the bundles,
I'll carry 'em.

B. You're a good, true-hearted fellow;
And a willing servant.—Let's move on to the ferry.

* We collect from the Scholiast that the part of the Deadman was expressed with a tone of fastidious valetudinary languor.

The author has condescended to gratify the popular taste alluded to in the first scene, without intrenching upon the pure humour of his dialogue. Throughout the preceding scene, Xanthias acts a part in dumb show, exhibiting various attitudes and contortions of weariness and restlessness: his impatience breaks out in four interruptions, three of which are so managed as to produce a comic effect. In the first, Xanthias puts himself in a ridiculous juxtaposition with Pythangelus; the second terminates a discussion proverbially endless, and the last enables Hercules to put an end to a dialogue (which would otherwise have been too long) with an air of brevity and dispatch suited to his character. Hercules and Bacchus offer a contrast of the two extremes of manly and feeble character. Strength is represented in a state of calmness and playful repose, and feebleness in a paroxysm of occasional energy, conformably to the practice of ancient artists in their serious compositions.

The dialogue with the Deadman, besides its merit as an incomparable sample of humorous nonsense, has the advantage of introducing the spectators in imagination to the very suburbs of the infernal regions; for, if we look to the strict localities of the stage, nothing else intervenes between the dialogue at the door of Hercules's house (in Thebes, as the Scholiast supposes) and the passage of the Styx, which immediately follows.

CHARON. BACCHUS. XANTHIAS.

Ch. Hoy! Bear a hand, there—Heave ashore.
B. What's this?
X. The lake it is—the place he told us of.
By Jove! and there's the boat—and here's old Charon.
B. Well, Charon! — Welcome, Charon! — Welcome kindly!
Ch. Who wants the ferryman? Anybody waiting
To remove from the sorrows of life? A passage anybody?
To Lethe's wharf?—to Cerberus's Reach?
To Tartarus?—to Tænarus?—to Perdition?
B. Yes, I.
Ch. Get in then.
B. (*hesitatingly*). Tell me, where are you going?
To Perdition really—?
Ch. (*not sarcastically, but civilly, in the way of business*).
Yes, to oblige you, I will
With all my heart—Step in there.
B. Have a care!†
Take care, good Charon!—Charon, have a care!
(*Bacchus gets into the boat*).
Come, Xanthias, come!
Ch. I take no slaves aboard
Except they've volunteer'd for the naval victory.‡
X. I could not—I was suffering with sore eyes.
Ch. You must trudge away then, round by the end of the lake there.
X. And whereabouts shall I wait?
Ch. At the Stone of Repentance,
By the Slough of Despond beyond the Tribulations;
You understand me?

* Alluding to the change of scene which took place at this moment.

† See note.

‡ The victory of Arginusæ, where the slaves who were enlisted fought for the first time.

X. Yes, I understand you;
A lucky, promising direction, truly.

Ch. (*to Bac.*). Sit down at the oar—Come quick, if there's more coming!
(*To Bac. again*) Holloh! what's that you're doing?

(*Bacchus is seated in a buffoonish attitude on the side of the boat where the oar was fastened.*)

B. What you told me.
I'm sitting at the oar.

Ch. Sit *there*, I tell you,
You Fatguts; that's your place.

B. (*changes his place*). Well, so I do.

Ch. Now ply your hands and arms.

B. (*makes a silly motion with his arms*). Well, so I do.

Ch. You'd best leave off your fooling. Take to the oar,
And pull away.

B. But how shall I contrive?
I've never served on board—I'm only a landsman;
I'm quite unused to it—

Ch. We can manage it.
As soon as you begin you shall have some music
That will teach you to keep time.

B. What music's that?

Ch. A chorus of Frogs—uncommon musical Frogs.

B. Well, give me the word and the time.

Ch. Whooh up, up; whooh up, up.

Chorus of FROGS.

This Chorus, from the clutter of cognate consonants, g, k, and ch, which appears in some parts of it, should seem to have been intended by the author as a caricature of some cotemporary dramatical lyrics. With the assistance of the Northumbrian bur, some of the lines may be made to croak with very tolerable effect; others should seem intended as a contrast, and contain some pretty imagery.—The spelling of the words of the Chorus is accommodated to the actual pronunciation of the Frogs, which, it is presumed, has remained unaltered. The B in the Brekeke-kesh is very soft, and assimilates to the V. The e *in kesh is pronounced like* ei *in* leisure, *and the last syllable prolonged and accented with a higher tone. The word, as commonly pronounced by scholars, (with the ictus or English accent on the third syllable), bears no resemblance to the sound which it is meant to imitate; which has, on the contrary, a slight ictus on the first syllable.— The learned reader is requested to estimate the truth of this translation, not by direct collation with the text of the original, but by those impressions of its general spirit and effect which may remain in his memory, or (more fairly still) by a reference to the assignable or supposeable effects intended to be produced by the original.*

CHORUS.

Brekeke-kesh, koash, koash,
Shall the Choral Quiristers of the Marsh*
Be censured and rejected as hoarse and harsh;
  And their Chromatic essays
  Deprived of praise?
No, let us raise afresh
Our obstreperous Brekeke-kesh;
The customary croak and cry
  Of the creatures
  At the theatres,
In their yearly revelry.
Brekeke-kesh, koash, koash.

* The theatre of Bacchus in the marsh.— Anti-Lyrical caricature.

B. (*rowing in great misery*).
  How I'm maul'd,
  How I'm gall'd;
Worn and mangled to a mash—
There they go! "*Koash, koash!*"

Frogs. Brekeke-kesh, koash, koash.
B. Oh, beshrew,
  All your crew;
You don't consider how I smart.
Frogs. Now for a sample of the Art!
  Brekeke-kesh, koash, koash.
B. I wish you hang'd, with all my heart.
  —Have you nothing else to say?
  "*Brekeke-kesh, koash*" all day!
Frogs. We've a right,
  We've a right;
  And we croak at ye for spite.
  We've a right,
  We've a right;

Day and night,
Day and night;
Night and day,
Still to creak and croak away.
Phœbus and every Grace
Admire and approve of the croaking race;
And the egregious guttural notes
That are gargled and warbled in their lyrical throats.
In reproof
Of your scorn
Mighty Pan
Nods his horn;
Beating time
To the rhyme
With his hoof,
With his hoof.
Persisting in our plan,
We proceed as we began,
Breke-kesh,* Breke-kesh,
Kooash, kooash.

Anti-Lyrical caricature.

B. Oh, the Frogs, consume and rot 'em,
I've a blister on my bottom.
Hold your tongues, you tuneful creatures.

Frogs. Cease with your profane entreaties
All in vain for ever striving:
Silence is against our natures.
With the vernal heat reviving,
Our aquatic crew repair
From their periodic sleep,
In the dark and chilly deep,
To the cheerful upper air;
Then we frolic here and there
All amidst the meadows fair;
Shady plants of asphodel,
Are the lodges where we dwell;
Chaunting in the leafy bowers
All the livelong summer hours,
Till the sudden gusty showers
Send us headlong, helter skelter,
To the pool to seek for shelter;
Meagre, eager, leaping, lunging,
From the sedgy wharfage plunging

* The form of the chorus is here varied, to accommodate it to the rhythm of the preceding lines.

To the tranquil depth below,
There we muster all a-row;
Where, secure from toil and trouble,
With a tuneful hubble-bubble,
Our symphonious accents flow.
Brekeke-kesh, koash, koash.

B. I forbid you to proceed.

Frogs. That would be severe indeed;
Arbitrary, bold, and rash—
Brekeke-kesh, koash, koash.

B. I command you to desist—
—Oh, my back, there! oh, my wrist!
What a twist!
What a sprain!

Frogs. Once again—
We renew the tuneful strain.
Brekeke-kesh, koash, koash.

B. I disdain—(Hang the pain!)
All your nonsense, noise, and trash.
Oh, my blister! Oh, my sprain!

Frogs. Brekeke-kesh, koash, koash.
Friends and Frogs, we must display
All our powers of voice to-day;
Suffer not this stranger here,
With fastidious foreign ear,
To confound us and abash.
Brekeke-kesh, koash, koash.

B. Well, my spirit is not broke,
If it's only for the joke,
I'll outdo you with a croak.
Here it goes—(*very loud*) "Koash, koash."

Frogs. Now for a glorious croaking crash,
(*Still louder*).
Brekeke-kesh, koash, koash.

B. (*splashing with his oar*).
I'll disperse you with a splash.

Frogs. Brekeke-kesh, koash, koash.

B. I'll subdue
Your rebellious, noisy crew—
—Have amongst you there, slap-dash.
[*Strikes at them.*

Frogs. Brekeke-kesh, koash, koash.
We defy your oar and you.
Ch. Hold! We're ashore just—shift your oar. Get out.
—Now pay for your fare.
B. There—there it is—the twopence.

Charon returns. Bacchus, finding himself alone and in a strange place, begins to call out.

B. Hoh, Xanthias! Xanthias, I say! Where's Xanthias?
X. A-hoy!
B. Come here.
X. I'm glad to see you, master.
B. What's that before us there?
X. The mire and darkness.
B. Do you see the villains and the perjurers
That he * told us of?
X. Yes, plain enough, don't you?
B. Ah! now I see them, indeed, quite plain—and now too.† [*Turning to the audience.*
Well, what shall we do next?
X. We'd best move forward;
For here's the place that Hercules there inform'd us
Was haunted by these monsters.
B. Oh, confound him!
He vapour'd and talk'd at random to deter me
From venturing.—He's amazingly conceited
And jealous of other people, is Hercules;
He reckon'd I should rival him, and, in fact
(Since I've come here so far), I should rather like
To meet with an adventure in some shape.
X. By Jove! and I think I hear a kind of a noise.
B. Where? where?
X. There, just behind us.
B. Go behind, then.
X. There!—it's before us now.—There!
B. Go before, then.
X. Ah! now I see it—a monstrous beast indeed!
B. What kind?
X. A dreadful kind—all kinds at once.
It changes and transforms itself about

* Hercules v. 184.

† Similar compliments to the audience occur frequently in Aristophanes's plays.

To a mule and an ox,—and now to a beautiful creature;
A woman!

B. Where? where is she? Let me seize her.

X. But now she's turn'd to a mastiff all of a sudden.

B. It's the Weird hag! the Vampyre!*

X. (*collectedly*). Like enough.
She's all of a blaze of fire about the mouth.

B. (*with great trepidation*).
Has she got the brazen foot?

X. (*with cool despair*). Yes, there it is—
By Jove!—and the cloven hoof to the other leg,
Distinct enough—that's she!

B. But what shall I do?

X. And I, too?

[*Bacchus runs to the front of the stage, where there was a seat of honour appropriated to the priest of Bacchus.*

B. Save me, Priest, protect and save me,
That we may drink and be jolly together hereafter.

X. We're ruin'd, Master Hercules.

B. Don't call me so, I beg:
Don't mention my name, good friend, upon any account.†

X. Well, BACCHUS, then!

B. That's worse, ten thousand times.

[*Bacchus remains hiding his face before the seat of the priest—in the meantime affairs take a more favourable turn.*

X. (*cheerfully*). Come, master, move along — Come, come this way.

B. (*without looking round*).
What's happen'd?

X. Why, we're prosperous and victorious;
The storm of fear and danger has subsided,
And (as the actor said the other day)
"Has only left a gentle *qualm* behind."
The Vampyre's vanish'd.

B. Has she? upon your oath?

X. By Jove! she has.

B. No, swear again.

X. By Jove!

B. Is she, by Jupiter?

X. By Jupiter!

* The Empusa, a fabulous hag, known only in the mythology of the Athenian nursery.

† The Scholiast gives us no explanation of the motive which induced Aristophanes to play this trick upon the priest.

B. Oh dear! what a fright I was in with the very sight of her:
It turn'd me sick and pale—but see, the priest here!
He has colour'd up quite with the same alarm.*
—What has brought me to this pass?—It must be Jupiter
With his "*Chamber in the Skies*," and the "*Foot of Time*."†

[*A flute sounds. Bacchus remains absorbed and inattentive to the objects about him.*

X. Holloh, you!
B. What?
X. Why, did you not hear?
B. Why, what?
X. The sound of a flute.
B. (*recollecting himself*). Indeed! And there's a smell too;
A pretty mystical ceremonious smell
Of torches. We'll watch here, and keep quite quiet.

* An ancient Scholiast has ascertained that this was a personal allusion, and that the priest of Bacchus at that time was eminent for a red face.

† Vide v. 120.

The proper Chorus, consisting of the votaries of Bacchus, now appears upon the stage; or more properly speaking, on the orchestra; (a platform in front of the stage, but of inferior elevation) a circumstance which (as Schlegel has justly observed) has been wholly overlooked in all attempts to introduce a Chorus upon the modern stage, on which it is impossible for them to appear without embarrassing the actors and distracting the attention of the spectators. It is much to be regretted that the explanations which Mr. Schlegel has given of the local arrangement of the ancient stage (a subject on which he seems to have very clear ideas) have not been accompanied with graphic illustrations which would make them equally intelligible to his readers.

The following scene is a humorous representation of the concluding ceremony of the Eleusinian mysteries, on the last day of which the worship of Bacchus, under the invocation of Iacchus, was united with that of Ceres. Iacchus seems to have been the last Avatar of the worship of Bacchus, as Pan was the first. For an account of the character of this worship, and its extreme discrepancy from that of Ceres, with which it was united in this festival, see the learned and original work of Mr. Ouvaroff, which has been translated and illustrated by Mr. Christie. It is to be observed that though the votaries are celebrating the rites of Bacchus,

Bacchus being disguised and incognito, or not considering himself concerned in the invocation of Iacchus, does not take any notice of them as his *votaries or adherents.*

CHORUS OF VOTARIES. BACCHUS. XANTHIAS.

CHORUS. *Shouting and Singing.*

Iacchus! Iacchus! Ho!
Iacchus! Iacchus! Ho!

X. There, Master, there they are, the initiated;
All sporting about as he* told us we should find 'em.
They're singing in praise of Bacchus like Diagoras.†
B. Indeed, and so they are; but we'll keep quiet
Till we make them out a little more distinctly.

* Hercules.

† Ironically. Diagoras, a dithyrambic poet, and consequently a composer of hymns in praise of Bacchus; banished from Athens, and proscribed on a charge of Atheism.

CHORUS. *Song.*

Mighty Bacchus! Holy Power!
Hither at the wonted hour
Come away,
Come away,
With the wanton holiday,
Where the revel uproar leads
To the mystic holy meads,
Where the frolic votaries fly,
With a tipsy shout and cry;
Flourishing the Thyrsus high,
Flinging forth, alert and airy,
To the sacred old vagary,
The tumultuous dance and song,
Sacred from the vulgar throng;
Mystic orgies, that are known
To the votaries alone—
To the mystic chorus solely—
Secret—unreveal'd—and holy.

X. Oh glorious virgin, daughter of the goddess!
What a scent of roasted griskin reach'd my senses.
B. Keep quiet—and watch for a chance of a piece of th haslets.

CHORUS. *Song.*

Raise the fiery torches high!
Bacchus is approaching nigh,

Like the planet of the morn,
Breaking with the hoary dawn,
On the dark solemnity—
There they flash upon the sight;
All the plain is blazing bright,
Flush'd and overflown with light:
Age has cast his years away,
And the cares of many a day,
Sporting to the lively lay—
Mighty Bacchus! march and lead
(Torch in hand toward the mead)
Thy devoted humble Chorus,
Mighty Bacchus—move before us!

SEMICHORUS.

Keep silence—keep peace—and let all the profane
From our holy solemnity duly refrain;
Whose souls unenlighten'd by taste, are obscure;
Whose poetical notions are dark and impure;
Whose theatrical conscience
Is sullied by nonsense;
Who never were train'd by the mighty Cratinus*
In mystical orgies poetic and vinous;
Who delight in buffooning and jests out of season;
Who promote the designs of oppression and treason;
Who foster sedition, and strife, and debate;
All traitors, in short, to the stage and the state;
Who surrender a fort, or in private, export
To places and harbours of hostile resort,
Clandestine consignments of cables and pitch;
In the way that Thorycion† grew to be rich
From a scoundrelly dirty collector of tribute:
All such we reject and severely prohibit:
All statesmen retrenching the fees and the salaries
Of theatrical bards, in revenge for the railleries,
And jests, and lampoons, of this holy solemnity,
Profanely pursuing their personal enmity,
For having been flouted, and scoff'd, and scorn'd,
All such are admonish'd and heartily warn'd;
We warn them once,
We warn them twice,
We warn and admonish—we warn them thrice,

* Cratinus, doubly a votary of Bacchus, as a dramatic poet and a hard drinker.

† Neither the Scholiasts nor commentators give us any information respecting Thorycion, except that he had a command at Ægina.

To conform to the law,
To retire and withdraw;
While the Chorus again with the formal saw
(Fixt and assign'd to the festive day)
Move to the measure and march away.

SEMICHORUS.

March! march! lead forth,
Lead forth manfully,
March in order all;
Bustling, hustling, justling,
As it may befall;
Flocking, shouting, laughing,
Mocking, flouting, quaffing,
One and all;
All have had a belly-full
Of breakfast brave and plentiful;
Therefore
Evermore
With your voices and your bodies
Serve the goddess,
And raise
Songs of praise;
She shall save the country still,
And save it against the traitor's will;
So she says.

SEMICHORUS.

Now let us raise, in a different strain,
The praise of the goddess * the giver of grain;
Imploring her favour
With other behaviour,
In measures more sober, submissive, and graver.

* The author here marks the different character of the worship of Ceres, as compared with that of Bacchus.

SEMICHORUS.

Ceres, holy patroness,
Condescend to mark and bless,
With benevolent regard,
Both the Chorus and the Bard;
Grant them for the present day
Many things to sing and say,

Follies intermix'd with sense;
Folly, but without offence.
Grant them with the present play
To bear the prize of verse away.

SEMICHORUS.

Now call again, and with a different measure,
The power of mirth and pleasure,
The florid, active Bacchus, bright and gay,
To journey forth and join us on the way.

SEMICHORUS.

O Bacchus, attend! the customary patron
Of every lively lay;
Go forth without delay
Thy wonted annual way,
To meet the ceremonious holy matron:*
Her grave procession gracing,
Thine airy footsteps tracing
With unlaborious, light, celestial motion;
And here at thy devotion
Behold thy faithful quire
In pitiful attire;
All overworn and ragged,
This jerkin old and jagged,
These buskins torn and burst,
Though sufferers in the fray,
May serve us at the worst
To sport throughout the day;
And there within the shades
I spy some lovely maids;
With whom we romp'd and revell'd,
Dismantled and dishevell'd;
With their bosoms open,
With whom we might be coping.

X. Well, I was always hearty,
Disposed to mirth and ease,
I'm ready to join the party.

B. (*with a tone of imbecility, like Sir Andrew Aguecheek's "Yes, and I too"—"Ay or I either."*)
And I will, if you please.

* Ceres.

[*Some verses*[1] *follow, which are sung by the Chorus, and in which some of the characters of the State are lampooned; they are not capable of translation, but are introduced appropriately, as the Bacchic and Eleusinian processions, which are here represented, were accompanied by a great license of abuse and ribaldry.*]

Bacchus (to the Chorus).

Prithee, my good fellows,
Would you please to tell us
Which is Pluto's door,
I'm an utter stranger,
Never here before.

Chorus. Friend, you're out of danger,
You need not seek it far;
There it stands before ye,
Before ye, where you are.

B. Take up your bundles, Xanthias.

X. Hang all bundles;
A bundle has no end, and these have none.

[*Exeunt Bacchus and Xanthias.*

SEMICHORUS.

Now we go to dance and sing
In the consecrated shades;
Round the secret holy ring,
With the matrons and the maids.
Thither I must haste to bring
The mysterious early light;
Which must witness every rite
Of the joyous happy night.

SEMICHORUS.

Let us hasten—let us fly—
Where the lovely meadows lie;
Where the living waters flow;
Where the roses bloom and blow.
—Heirs of Immortality,

[1] Lines 417 to 431, ed. Bekk.

Segregated, safe and pure,
Easy, sorrowless, secure;
Since our earthly course is run,
We behold a brighter sun.
Holy lives—a holy vow—
Such rewards await them now.

Scene. The Gate of Pluto's Palace.

Enter BACCHUS *and* XANTHIAS.

* Compare this with Bacchus's behaviour at Hercules' door, where he knew he was quite safe.

B. (*going up to the door with considerable hesitation*).*
Well, how must I knock at the door now? Can't ye tell me?
How do the native inhabitants knock at doors?
X. Pah; don't stand fooling there; but smite it smartly,
With the very spirit and air of Hercules.
B. Holloh!
Æacus (*from within, with the voice of a royal and infernal porter*).
Who's there?
B. (*with a forced voice*). 'Tis I, the valiant Hercules!
Æ.[1] (*coming out*).
Thou brutal, abominable, detestable,
Vile, villanous, infamous, nefarious scoundrel!
—How durst thou, villain as thou wert, to seize
Our watch-dog, Cerberus, whom I kept and tended,
Hurrying him off, half-strangled in your grasp?
—But now, be sure we have you safe and fast,
Miscreant and villain!—Thee, the Stygian cliffs,
With stern adamantine durance, and the rocks
Of inaccessible Acheron, red with gore,
Environ and beleaguer; and the watch,
And swift pursuit of the hideous hounds of hell;

---

[1] The Scholiast informs us, that the horrific part of Æacus's speech is an imitation of an attempt at the sublime, in Euripides's tragedy of "Theseus," which is now lost; but which probably related to his descent to the infernal regions. The whole of the speech in the original is worth examining; it seems intended as a sportive display of poetical execution; passing, by short imperceptible gradations, through the whole *Scale of Style*, from the anger of comedy, to the loftiest and most exaggerated style of tragedy, till it is blown up into bombast, and finishes in burlesque.

And the horrible Hydra, with her hundred heads,
Whose furious ravening fangs shall rend and tear thee;
Wrenching thy vitals forth, with the heart and midriff;
While inexpressible Tartesian monsters,
And grim Tithrasian Gorgons, toss and scatter,
With clattering claws, thine intertwined intestines.
To them, with instant summons, I repair,
Moving in hasty march with steps of speed.

[*Æacus departs with a tremendous tragical exit, and Bacchus falls to the ground in a fright.*

X. Holloh, you! What's the matter there—?

B. Oh dear,
I've had an accident.

X. Poh! poh! jump up!
Come! you ridiculous simpleton! don't lie there,
The people will see you.

B. Indeed I'm sick at heart; lah!

(*Here a few lines are omitted.*)

X. Was there ever in heaven or earth such a coward?

B. Me?
A coward! Did not I shew my presence of mind—
And call for a sponge and water in a moment?
Would a coward have done that?

X. What else would he do?

B. He'd have lain there stinking like a nasty coward;
But I jump'd up at once, like a lusty wrestler,[1]
And look'd about, and wiped myself, withal.

X. Most manfully done!

B. By Jove, and I think it was;
But tell me, wer'n't you frighten'd with that speech?
—Such horrible expressions!

X. (*coolly, but with conscious and intentional coolness.*)
No, not I;
I took no notice—

B. Well, I'll tell you what,
Since you're such a valiant-spirited kind of fellow,
Do you be *Me*—with the club and the lion-skin,
Now you're in this courageous temper of mind;
And I'll go take my turn and carry the bundles.

---

[1] But whene'er at wrestling matches they were worsted in the fray,
Wiped their shoulders from the dust, denied the fall and fought away.
The Knights, v. 817.

X. Well—give us hold—I must humour you, forsooth;
Make haste, (*he changes his dress,*) and now behold the Xanthian Hercules,
And mind if I don't display more heart and spirit.

*B.** Indeed, and you look the character completely,
Like that heroic Melitensian hangdog—
Come, now for my bundles. I must mind my bundles.

* Bacchus, now his mind is at ease, begins to be humorous. Hercules had a temple at the village of Melite; but a sarcasm is implied against Callias, who was likewise of Melite, and used a lion-skin as his military dress.

Enter PROSERPINE'S SERVANT MAID (*a kind of Dame Quickly*), *who immediately addresses Xanthias.*

Dear Hercules. Well, you're come at last. Come in,
For the goddess, as soon as she heard of it, set to work
Baking peck loaves, and frying stacks of pancakes,
And making messes of furmety; there's an ox
Besides, she has roasted whole, with a relishing stuffing,
If you'll only just step in this way.

X. (*with dignity and reserve*). I thank you,
I'm equally obliged.

Serv. Maid. No, no, by Jupiter!
We must not let you off, indeed. There's wild fowl,
And sweetmeats for the dessert, and the best of wine;
Only walk in.

X. (*as before*). I thank you. You'll excuse me.

Serv. Maid. No, no, we can't excuse you, indeed we can't;
There are dancing and singing girls besides.

X. (*with dissembled emotion*). What! dancers?

Serv. Maid. Yes, that there are; the sweetest, charmingest things
That ever you saw—and there's the cook this moment
Is dishing up the dinner.

X. (*with an air of lofty condescension*). Go before then,
And tell the girls—those singing girls you mention'd—
To prepare for my approach in person presently.
(*To Bacchus.*) You, sirrah! follow behind me with the bundles.

B. Holloh, you! what, do you take the thing in earnest,
Because, for a joke, I drest you up like Hercules?

[*Xanthias continues to gesticulate as Hercules.*

Come, don't stand fooling, Xanthias. You'll provoke me.
There, carry the bundles, sirrah, when I bid you.

X. (*relapsing at once into his natural air*).
Why, sure, do you mean to take the things away
That you gave me yourself of your own accord this instant?
B. I never mean a thing; I do it at once.
Let go of the lion's skin directly, I tell you.
X. (*resigning his heroical insignia with a tragical air and tone*).
To you, just Gods, I make my last appeal,
Bear witness!
B. What! the Gods?—do you think they mind you?
How could you take it in your head, I wonder;
Such a foolish fancy for a fellow like you,
A mortal and a slave, to pass for Hercules?
X. There. Take them.—There—you may have them—but, please God,
You may come to want my help some time or other.

CHORUS.

Dexterous and wily wits
Find their own advantage ever;
For the wind where'er it sits,
Leaves a berth secure and clever
To the ready navigator;
That foresees and knows the nature
Of the wind and weather's drift;
And betimes can turn and shift
To the shelter'd easy side;
'Tis a practice proved and tried,
Not to wear a formal face;
Fixt in attitude and place,
Like an image on its base;
'Tis the custom of the seas,
Which, as all the world agrees,
Justifies Theramenes.*

* The political versatility of Theramenes is noticed in a subsequent passage, in the altercation between Æschylus and Euripides. The naval allusion may be supposed to refer to his conduct towards his colleagues in command, after the battle of Arginusæ.

BACCHUS.

How ridiculous and strange;
What a monstrous proposition,
That I should condescend to change
My dress, my name, and my condition,

To follow Xanthias, and behave
Like a mortal and a slave;
To be set to watch the door
While he wallow'd with his whore,
Tumbling on a purple bed;
  While I waited with submission,
To receive a broken head;
  Or be kick'd upon suspicion
Of impertinence and peeping
At the joys that he was reaping.

As Bacchus was before made answerable for the offence which Hercules had committed in seizing Cerberus, he is now accused of other misdemeanours which Hercules (agreeably to the character of voracity and violence which was attributed to him by the comic writers) might be supposed to have committed in the course of the same expedition.

Enter Two WOMEN, *Sutlers or Keepers of an Eating House.*

1 *Woman.* What, Platana! Goody Platana! there! that's he,
The fellow that robs and cheats poor victuallers;
That came to our house and eat those nineteen loaves.

2 *Woman.* Ay, sure enough that's he, the very man.

X. (*tauntingly to Bacchus.*) There's mischief in the wind for somebody!

1 *Woman.* —And a dozen and a half of cutlets and fried chops,
At a penny halfpenny a piece—

X. (*significantly.*) There are pains and penalties
Impending—

1 *Woman.* —And all the garlic: such a quantity
As he swallow'd—

B. (*delivers this speech with Herculean dignity, after his fashion; having hitherto remained silent upon the same principle*).
Woman, you're beside yourself;
You talk you know not what—

2 *Woman.* No, no! you reckon'd
I should not know you again with them there buskins.*

1 *Woman.* —Good lack! and there was all that fish besides.

* Buskins were peculiar to Bacchus: the woman mistaking him for Hercules, considers them as an attempt at disguise.

Indeed—with the pickle, and all—and the good green cheese
That he gorged at once, with the rind, and the rush-baskets;
And then, when I call'd for payment, he look'd fierce,
And stared at me in the face, and grinn'd, and roar'd—

X. Just like him! That's the way wherever he goes.

1 *Woman.* —And snatch'd his sword* out, and behaved like mad.

X. Poor souls! you suffer'd sadly!†

1 *Woman.* Yes, indeed;
And then we both ran off with the fright and terror,
And scrambled into the loft beneath the roof;
And he took up two rugs and stole them off.

X. Just like him again—but something must be done.
Go call me Cleon,‡ he's my advocate.

2 *Woman.* And Hyperbolus,‡ if you meet him send him here.
He's mine; and we'll demolish him, I warrant.

1 *Woman (going close up to Bacchus in the true termagant attitude of rage and defiance, with the arms akimbo, and a neck and chin thrust out).*
How I should like to strike those ugly teeth out
With a good big stone, you ravenous greedy villain!
You gormandizing villain! that I should—
Yes, that I should; your wicked ugly fangs
That have eaten up my substance, and devour'd me.

B. And I could toss you into the public pit
With the malefactors' carcases; that I could,
With pleasure and satisfaction; that I could.

1 *Woman.* And I should like to rip that gullet out
With a reaping hook that swallow'd all my tripe,
And liver and lights—but I'll fetch Cleon here,
And he shall summon him. He shall settle him,
And have it out of him this very day. [*Exeunt 1st and 2nd Woman.*

B. (in a pretended soliloquy).
I love poor Xanthias dearly, that I do;
I wish I might be hang'd else.

X. Yes, I know—
I know your meaning—No; no more of that,
I won't act Hercules—

B. Now pray, don't say so,
My little Xanthias.

X. How should I be Hercules?

* In allusion to Euripides's description of Hercules. Schol.

† X. inflames the women's wrath by judicious commiseration.

‡ Turbulent orators and public accusers (often mentioned by Aristophanes) lately dead.

*Alludes to what Bacchus had said, verse 692.

A mortal and a slave, a fellow like me ?—*
B. I know you're angry, and you've a right to be angry;
And if you beat me for it I'd not complain ;
But if ever I strip you again, from this time forward,
I wish I may be utterly confounded,
With my wife, my children, and my family,
And the blear-eyed Archedemus† into the bargain.
X. I agree then, on that oath, and those conditions.
[*Xanthias equips himself with the club and lion's skin, and Bacchus resumes his bundles.*

† Seems to have been a meddling foreigner ; his want of claim to the character of citizen is noticed by Aristophanes and in a fragment of Eupolis.

Chorus (*addressing Xanthias*).

Now that you revive and flourish
In your old attire again,
You must rouse afresh and nourish
Thoughts of an heroic strain ;
That exalt and raise the figure,
And assume a fire and vigour ;
And an attitude and air
Suited to the garb you wear ;
With a brow severely bent,
Like the god you represent.
But beware,
Have a care !
If you blunder or betray
Any weakness any way;
Weakness of the heart or brain,
We shall see you once again
Trudging in the former track,
With the bundles at your back.

Xanthias (*in reply to the Chorus*).

Friends, I thank you for your care ;
Your advice was good and fair ;
Corresponding in its tone
With reflections of my own.
—Though I clearly comprehend
All the upshot and the end,
(That if any good comes of it,
Any pleasure, any profit—

He, my master, will recede
From the terms that were agreed,)
You shall see me, notwithstanding,
Stern, intrepid, and commanding.
Now's the time! For there's a noise!
Now for figure, look, and voice!

ÆACUS *enters again as a vulgar executioner of the law, with suitable understrappers in attendance.*

Æacus is exhibited, in the following scene, as the ideal character of a perfect and accomplished bailiff and thief-taker, and is marked by traits which prove that the genus has remained unchanged in the 2,000 years between the times of Aristophanes and Fielding. The true hardness of mind is most strikingly apparent in those passages where he means to be civil and accommodating. Thus Foote has characterised his Miser by traits of miserly liberality. The unfeeling master is personated by a slave (as the unfeeling courtier is by Autolycus in the Winter's Tale); the scene is thus removed one degree further from reality, otherwise like the Tartuffe it would excite too strong a feeling of indignation, and outstep the true limits of Comedy.

Æ. Arrest me there that fellow that stole my dog.
There!—Pinion him!—Quick!
B. (*tauntingly to Xanthias*). There's somebody in a scrape.
X. (*in a menacing attitude*). Keep off, and be hang'd.
Æ. Oh, hoh! do you mean to fight for it?
Here! Pardokas,* and Skeblias, and the rest of ye,
Make up to the rogue, and settle him. Come, be quick.
[*A scuffle ensues, in which Xanthias succeeds in obliging Æacus's runners to keep their distance.*
B. (*mortified at Xanthias's prowess*).
Well, is not this quite monstrous and outrageous,
To steal the dog, and then to make an assault
In justification of it?
X. (*triumphantly and ironically*). Quite outrageous!
Æ. (*gravely, and dissembling his mortification*).
An aggravated case!
X. (*with candour and gallantry*). Well, now—by Jupiter,

* The persons employed in the forcible and personal execution of the law, as arrests, &c. &c. in Athens, were foreign slaves, Scythians purchased for that purpose by the state. These barbarous names are supposed to indicate persons of this description.

May I die, but I never saw this place before—
Nor ever stole the amount of a farthing from you:
Nor a hair of your dog's tail.—But you shall see now,
I'll settle all this business nobly and fairly.
—This slave of mine—you may take and torture him;
And if you make out any thing against me,
You may take and put me to death for aught I care.

Æ. (*in an obliging tone, softened into deference and civility by the liberality of Xanthias's proposal*).
But which way would you please to have him tortured?

X. (*with a gentlemanly spirit of accommodation*).*
In your own way—with . . . the lash—with . . . knots and screws,
With . . . the common usual customary tortures.
With the rack—with . . . the water-torture—any way—
With fire and vinegar—all sorts of ways.
(*After a very slight pause.*) There's only one thing I should warn you of:
I must not have him treated like a child,
To be whipt with fennel, or with lettuce leaves.

Æ. That's fair—and if so be . . . he's maim'd or crippled
In any respect—the valy† shall be paid you.

X. Oh no!—by no means! not to me!—by no means!
You must not mention it!—Take him to the torture.

Æ. It had better be here, and under your own eye.‡
(*To Bacchus.*) Come you—put down your bundles and make ready.
And mind—Let me hear no lies!

B. I'll tell you what:
I'd advise people not to torture me;
I give you notice—I'm a deity.
So mind now—you'll have nobody to blame
But your own self—

Æ. What's that you're saying there?

B. Why, that I'm Bacchus, Jupiter's own son:
That fellow there's a slave. [*Pointing to Xanthias.*

Æ. (*to Xanthias*). Do ye hear?

X. I hear him—
A reason the more to give him a good beating;
If he's immortal he need never mind it.

B. Why should not you be beat as well as I then,
If you're immortal, as you say you are?

* Xanthias is too much of a gentleman to enter into details; he wishes to do what is creditable, and handsome, and suitable to his rank and character.

† *Value*, the vulgar pronunciation is given.

‡ Æacus is represented as overpowered and won over by the profuse generosity with which Xanthias disposes of the joints and muscles of his slave.

X. Agreed—and him, the first that you see flinching,
Or seeming to mind it at all, you may set him down
For an impostor and no real deity.

Æ. (*to Xanthias with warmth and cordiality*).
Ah, you're a worthy gentleman, I'll be bound for't;
You're all for the truth and the proof. Come—Strip there both o' ye.

X. But how can ye put us to the question fairly,
Upon equal terms?

Æ. (*in the tone of a person proposing a convenient, agreeable arrangement*). Oh, easily enough,
Conveniently enough—a lash a piece,
Each in your turn: you can have 'em one by one.

X. That's right. (*Putting himself in an attitude to receive the blow.*)
Now mind if ye see me flinch or swerve.

Æ. (*strikes him, but without producing any expression of pain*).
I've struck.

X. . Not you!

Æ. Why it seems as if I had not.
I'll smite this other fellow. (*Strikes Bacchus.*)

B. (*pretending not to feel*). When will you do it?

Æacus perseveres and applies his discipline alternately to Bacchus and Xanthias, and extorts from them various involuntary exclamations of pain, which they immediately account for and justify in some ridiculous way. The passage cannot be translated literally, but an idea may be given of it. Suppose Bacchus to receive a blow, he exclaims—
Oh dear! (*and immediately subjoins*) Companions of my youthful years.

X. (*to Æacus*). Did ye hear? he made an outcry.

Æ. What was that?

B. A favourite passage from Archilochus.

(*Xanthias receives a blow, and exclaims*)
O Jupiter! (*and subjoins*) that on the Idean height;
and contends that he has been repeating the first line of a well-known hymn. Æacus (at length gives the matter up).
Well, after all my pains, I'm quite at a loss
To discover which is the true, real deity.
By the Holy Goddess—I'm completely puzzled;

I must take you before Proserpine and Pluto;
Being gods themselves they're likeliest to know.
B. Why, that's a lucky thought. I only wish
It had happen'd to occur before you beat us.

The changes of character between Bacchus and Xanthias in the preceding scenes have obviously no reference to the improvement or decline of the dramatic art, which is the main ostensible object of the comedy; but if we look to the critical and dangerous situation of the state, at the period when it was produced (viz. the 3rd year of the 93rd Olympiad) and attend to the unusually vehement and earnest political remonstrances in the address of the Chorus to the audience which follows, we shall see abundant reason to conclude that some part of the action of the stage must have been intended to be understood in a political sense.

The measure, which at that time was uppermost in the minds of everybody, but which nobody would venture openly to propose, was the recall of Alcibiades from his second banishment; a subject which is brought forward in the last scene but one, and upon which Æschylus and Euripides are made to deliver their opinions, the intention of the author being evidently in favour of Alcibiades, as he makes the favourable opinion proceed from the worthier and more manly character. It should appear that, in the preceding scenes in the infernal regions, Xanthias is the representative of Alcibiades, and Bacchus of the Athenian people, and that the changes of character represent the changes in their political relation to each other. The scene in which they are made to contend as to their ability to bear a beating without crying out, is merely a proverb dramatized and put into action like those of the French, who have made a part of the amusement to consist in guessing the proverb. The solution of the enigma in this case would be πότεροι κλαυσούμεθα μεῖζον, *which was applied to people who, to their mutual injury, persevered in refusing to be reconciled. Such was, at the time this play was produced, the relative situation of Alcibiades and of the Athenian people; he was living in exile upon his own estate in Thrace, while they were struggling with difficulties from which his genius and abilities might have relieved them; the blows of fortune fell equally upon them both, and the question as to which was the greater sufferer, might be deemed as difficult of decision* as it appeared to Æacus, who, after all the discipline impartially inflicted on the contending parties, was obliged to leave it undetermined.

The original and admirable speculation of Mr. Whiter upon the doctrine of the association of ideas considered as an instrument of criticism, is applicable to much higher purposes, but since it falls in our way, we may venture to employ it here. The recall of Alcibiades was considered as a measure which must place him at once at the head of the government, and be accompanied with a considerable retrenchment of the powers of the Democracy; on the other hand, it was expected by those who were favourable to the measure, that, under his conduct and management, the affairs of the Republic might be retrieved, and its ancient ascendency reasserted—that the result would be success abroad and a Government at home partly Democratic and partly Dictatorial. Now, if we were right in conjecturing that the proverb above-mentioned was alluded to in the foregoing scene, we shall see that it was connected in Aristophanes's mind with those very ideas of subsequent reconciliation, joint command, and external ascendency:

διακαυνιάσαι πότεροι κλαυσούμεθα μεῖζον,
'Εξὸν σπεισαμένοις κοινῇ τῆς 'Ελλάδος ἄρχειν.

I do not know whether it is worth while to mention some coincidences which may be casual. The pole with which Xanthias appears, and which seems to be the emblem of his situation, and which Bacchus calls ἀνάφορον, had another name, as we learn from the argument (viz. ἀλλακτὸν), which would make it a proper emblem of the representative of Alcibiades. Xanthias is, in the first instance, degraded in consequence of being invited to a banquet by Proserpine. Alcibiades's first exile was connected with a charge against him of having profaned the mysteries of Ceres and Proserpine at a banquet. The ludicrous song in which Bacchus justifies himself for having degraded Xanthias, is a fair burlesque representation of the mixture of envy and indignation which the undisguised ascendency and the insolent debauches of Alcibiades had excited in the minds of the Athenian people, and which contributed powerfully to produce his first banishment. The continuator of Brumoy seems to have been aware of the propriety of looking for some political inter-

pretation of these scenes; he supposes Xanthias to be a personification of the newly enfranchised slaves; but Aristophanes, as we see from the address of the chorus, approved of the measure, and certainly could not mean to hold out to the new citizens the possibility of their being again reduced to servitude. As Aristophanes's humour frequently carries double, this explanation might perhaps hold good as far as Xanthias's first investiture with the lion's skin, but is wholly inapplicable to the subsequent changes.

The passages which follow may be considered as a relic and sample of the primitive satyric comedy, which, as is well known, consisted solely of songs and recitations, unaccompanied by dramatic action or dialogue. We may venture to imagine that a gradual change in the form and conduct of comedy might have taken place, nearly in this manner.

Let it be supposed that, in process of time, some species of exhibition, in dumb show, was introduced to illustrate and relieve the continued series of singing and recitation which constituted the primitive satyric comedy—we may conceive, that these pantomimic actors would by degrees be emancipated from the obligation of silence: and we shall then see that, upon the ground of this emancipation, the Aristophanic, or ancient *comedy (as we may be allowed to call it, in contradistinction to the* primitive) *might have been originally founded.*

When once the pantomimic actors had, by dint of gradual and permitted encroachment, established themselves in the undisputed privilege of speech, *the ancient or Aristophanic comedy would in fact have received its existence, not as a declared innovation, but as an allowable improvement of the lawful primitive comedy such as it had existed in the preceding period, during which the satyric recital had been illustrated by interludes in dumb show. But as the change, though in fact a most essential one, was neither acknowledged nor avowed, it would not (in the first instance at least) occasion any alteration of the established forms of the primitive comedy, or the omission of any of the various kinds of recited compositions, which had formed the sum total of the original entertainment. It would seem even reasonable, a priori, to conclude that they would be retained and accommodated to the action, and to the dialogue then, for the first time, introduced. And that they were so retained, more strictly perhaps in the first instance, (and in the earliest attempts of each successive poet of the ancient comedy, before an established reputation enabled him to depart from the strict observation of theatric etiquette,) and, in process of time, less punctually, and with a greater degree of latitude, both by individuals, and by the whole school of ancient comedy, will, I think, appear probable to those whose recollection will furnish them with immediate instances from the comedies of Aristophanes, or who, with these and some farther suggestions presented to them, may think it worth while to examine them. The epirrema and antepirrema being, in almost every instance, totally unconnected with the action of the play, being addressed moreover to the audience, by the chorus remaining alone in possession of the stage during a suspension of the dramatic action, and frequently (as in the instance immediately following) conveying important political suggestions, or strong reflections upon the vices and abuses of the times, may, perhaps, upon a consideration of all these circumstances, be recognized without scruple, as a remnant of the recited satyric effusions of the primitive comedy. It is observable that the epirrema and antepirrema are occasionally repeated more than once in the same play, a circumstance which ought not to be overlooked, in any attempt which may be made to form an idea of the primitive satyric comedy, by reconstructing it from the vestiges which are discoverable in the Aristophanic comedy. The parabasis, which was likewise recited by the chorus alone and unaccompanied by the dramatic performers, will naturally be referred to the same origin. It seems to have been frequently omitted in Aristophanic comedy, and is generally introduced with some apology on the part of the chorus, for obtruding themselves on the attention of the audience, and for detaining them with (the common topic of a parabasis) an encomium or vindication of the author. In the present play it is omitted, unless the semi-chorus, p. 256, "Keep silence," &c., should be considered a very diminutive and imperfect specimen. We have then the parabasis, together with the epirrema and antepirrema, the two last (as was before observed) repeated more than once; and these (as we have seen) were recited by the chorus remaining in exclusive possession of the stage; these, therefore, as far as they go, may serve to give us an idea of the primitive comedy; but in order to furnish an entertainment of any tolerable length, it will be necessary to detect other portions of it, which, having been accommodated to, and incorporated with, the dramatic action, appear at present in a form which renders it less easy to recognize and reclaim them. Among these I should venture to place the ῥῆσις μακρὰ or long satyric narrative in iambics; considering, that narrative either real or fictitious is the most obvious of all the forms of satyric composition, I cannot but imagine that it must have existed even in the most early forms of satyric comedy, though not always retained in the plays of Aristophanes; it seems, whenever it was admitted, to have been considered as a regular feature of the play, and a subject for separate criticism or commendation. In the two earliest plays of Aristophanes (in which he may be supposed to have adhered most scrupulously to the established formalities of the theatre) the ῥῆσις, or narrative, occupies a very distinguished place, and is addressed to the chorus by a single actor who is (be it observed)* alone *in possession of the stage. All these circumstances, together with the existence of the long ῥῆσις, or narrative, in the tragic dramas, as a piece of composition much laboured and attended to, seem to point to the same conclusion, and to indicate, that the origin of these compositions is derived from the earliest institutions of tragedy and comedy, and from the primitive form of each of them, anterior to the introduction of dramatic dialogue: I say* dramatic *dialogue, for a form of dialogue not properly dramatic seems to have existed in the primitive comedy, and to have maintained its place in the ancient or Aristophanic comedy, in which it is still discernible. The two long argumentative dialogues, the one in tetrameter iambics, in which the advantage is given to the meaner character and the baser opinion, and the other in anapæsts, in which the superior character is represented as asserting a higher principle, these two dialogues occurring in almost all the plays of Aristophanes, are indeed usually connected with the dramatic action, but they do not tend in any degree to advance it; not at least in any degree proportionate to the space which they occupy, or to the attention which appears to have been bestowed upon them—they serve merely to exhibit a sharp encounter of wits upon a given controversial topic; and, if detached from the play, might be fairly considered a mere*

See, for instance, the two dialogues between Æschylus and Euripides, which follow, pp. 284 and 288.

In the present instance it is not unhappily connected with the action of the play—but it is in fact a mere controversy as to the comparative merits of the earlier and later school of tragic poetry.

satyric dialogue. If, therefore, we separate from the Aristophanic comedy, the two forms of satyric dialogue above mentioned, together with the ῥῆσις μακρὰ *(or long satyric narrative) the parabasis, (or address of the chorus to the audience on behalf of the author,) and finally the epirrema and antepirrema (repeated, as was before observed, sometimes more than once in the course of the same piece), and if we add to these a number of satyrical songs and lampoons, we shall be able to form to ourselves an idea, not wholly inadequate, of the form and nature of the primitive satyric comedy unaccompanied by dramatic action; if, again, we suppose (as was before suggested) that this series of songs and recitations and satyric dialogue and narrative was relieved at intervals by a pantomimic representation in dumb show, we shall have arrived upon the very confines of the Aristophanic comedy, where, in order to pass the boundary, nothing would be wanting but to remove the barrier which restrained the pantomimic actor from the privilege of speech.*

It may be worth while to point out a singular coincidence arising out of the suppositions before mentioned. The number of the actors by which each comedy was performed was by law and custom limited to three; this law or custom might have been occasionally transgressed, but the regulation which excluded a fourth actor was generally adhered to as conformable to authority and precedent, which, in matters of religious institution (for such these comedies were considered, being a portion of the ceremonies connected with the Bacchic worship), were not to be rashly or unnecessarily violated.

Now, if we suppose this precedent to have originated from the practice of the primitive comedy, and assume at the same time the suppositions respecting its form and substance, which have been before stated, we shall see that, in addition to the chorus, it admitted of three *actors who were entitled to the privilege of speech—namely, the reciter of the long* ῥῆσις, *or satyric narrative, and the two disputants in the controversial dialogues. As it would be difficult to account for this restriction from the general principles of dramatic art; we must, I apprehend, be content to attribute it to a precedent derived from the most ancient practice of the primitive comedy. It seems that the excessive number of actors had grown into what was considered to be an abuse; but when abuses are to be reformed, the regulations which restrain them are generally established upon the authority of the earliest examples, which, as we have seen, would not have admitted of more than three actors in addition to the chorus.*

We have, therefore, as remnants of the primitive satyric comedy, independent of dramatic or pantomimic action—

The parabasis,
The satyric songs and lampoons,
The epirrema and antepirrema,
The long narrative,
The dialogue in tetrameter iambics,
Another, on the same subject, in anapæsts,
The Epirrema and Antepirrema repeated,
Finally, a conclusion, probably not much unlike that of the Acharnians *or the* Peace, *the tone of which seems borrowed from a more primitive, jovial, rustic style.*

After the introduction of pantomime, a second narrative seems to have been introduced, explanatory and prefatory to the action which was to follow. This, too, appears to have preserved its place in the Aristophanic comedy, and is to be found in most of the plays, as Knights, *l.* 40, Wasps, *l.* 85, Peace, *l.* 50 (*ed. Bekk.*), *in all of which (it is to be observed) it is addressed by the speaker directly to the audience.*

The vehemence of the remonstrance conveyed in the following composition has been already noticed, *p.* 270. *For the state of things which gave rise to it, the reader must again be referred to a description of the critical and disgraceful condition of Athens at that period (the 3rd year of the 93rd Olympiad). Mr. Mitford has described it with his usual force and accuracy.*

It is observable that, in most of the plays of Aristophanes, there appears a sort of falling off in the antepirrema, as if the poet were, or affected to be, apprehensive of having ventured too far in the preceding epirrema. In this instance, the same warmth and energy is sustained throughout, but still with a slight distinction of character between the two. In the epirrema, the chorus begin gravely and authoritatively. In the antepirrema they resume the same subject, with a fanciful comparison.

The epirrema and antepirrema are (here, as elsewhere) preceded by a short personal lampoon, which has no obvious connexion with the action of the drama: a circumstance which, in addition to others already indicated, serves to mark the connexion between the primitive and the Aristophanic comedy.

CHORUS.

Muse, attend our solemn summons
And survey the assembled commons,
Congregated as they sit,
An enormous mass of wit,
—Full of genius, taste, and fire,
Jealous pride, and critic ire—
Cleophon among the rest
(Like the swallow from her nest,
A familiar foreign bird),
Chatters loud and will be heard,
(With the accent and the grace
Which he brought with him from Thrace);
But we fear the tuneful strain
Will be turn'd to grief and pain;
He must sing a dirge perforce
When his trial takes its course;
We shall hear him moan and wail,
Like the plaintive nightingale.

Cleophon, one of the chief demagogues in the then ruined and degraded democracy. His mother was a Thracian, and Plato (the comic writer) had introduced her speaking in a broken jargon. He was put to death in a popular tumult.

EPIREMMA.

Metre long trochaics, "As near Porto Bello."

It behoves the sacred Chorus, and of right to them belongs,
To suggest the best advice in their addresses and their songs.
In performance of our office, we present with all humility
A proposal for removing groundless fears and disability.
First that all that were inveigled into Phrynichus's treason,
Should be suffer'd and received by rules of evidence and reason
To clear their conduct—Secondly, that none of our Athenian race
Should live suspected and subjected to loss of franchise and disgrace,
Feeling it a grievous scandal when a single naval fight
Renders foreigners and slaves partakers of the city's right:
—Not that we condemn the measure; we conceived it wisely done,

Phrynichus. See Mitford, ch. 19, sect. 5 and 7.

See p. 247, l. 232, and note ‡.

As a just and timely measure, and the first and only one:
—But your kinsmen and your comrades, those with whom you fought and bore
Danger, hardship, and fatigue, or with their fathers long before,
Struggling on the land and ocean, labouring with the spear and oar
—These we think, as they profess repentance for their past behaviour,
Might, by your exalted wisdoms, be received to grace and favour.
Better it would be, believe us, casting off revenge and pride,
To receive as friends and kinsmen all that combat on our side
Into full and equal franchise: on the other hand we fear,
If your hearts are fill'd with fancies, haughty, captious, and severe;
While the shock of instant danger threatens shipwreck to the state,
Such resolves will be lamented and repented of too late.

Parody from a tragic chorus predicting the downfall of some reigning family. Cleigenes, one of the obscure demagogues of the time, not mentioned by the Scholiast.

If the Muse foresees at all
What in future will befall
Dirty Cleigenes the small—
He, the sovereign of the bath,
Will not long escape from scath;
But must perish by-and-by,
With his potash and his lye;
With his realm and dynasty,
His terraqueous scouring ball,
And his washes, one and all;
Therefore he can never cease
To declaim against a peace.

ANTEPIRREMA.

Often times have we reflected on a similar abuse,
In the choice of men for office, and of coins for common use;
For your old and standard pieces, valued, and approved, and tried,

In the exhaustion of their resources, the Athenians

Here among the Grecian nations, and in all the world beside;
Recognized in every realm for trusty stamp and pure assay,
Are rejected and abandon'd for the trash of yesterday;
For a vile, adulterate issue, drossy, counterfeit, and base,
Which the traffic of the city passes current in their place!
And the men that stood for office, noted for acknowledged worth,
And for manly deeds of honour, and for honourable birth;
Train'd in exercise and art, in sacred dances and in song,
All are ousted and supplanted by a base ignoble throng;
Paltry stamp and vulgar mettle raise them to command and place,
Brazen counterfeit pretenders, scoundrels of a scoundrel race;
Whom the state in former ages scarce would have allow'd to stand,
At the sacrifice of outcasts, as the scape-goats of the land.*
—Time it is—and long has been, renouncing all your follies past,
To recur to sterling merit and intrinsic worth at last.
—If we rise, we rise with honour; if we fall, it must be so!
—But there was an ancient saying, which we all have heard and know,
That the wise, in dangerous cases, have esteem'd it safe and good
To receive a slight chastisement from *a wand of noble wood.*[1]

had recourse to a debased currency—of course the good coin disappeared.

* The human scape-goat, the last unbloody remnant of human sacrifice.

Scene. XANTHIAS *and* ÆACUS.

When two persons, perfectly strangers, are thrown together in a situation which makes it advisable for them to commence an immediate intimacy, they commonly begin by discovering a marvellous coincidence of taste and judgment

---

[1] The original proverb says, "It is best to be hanged on a good tree." The English proverb says:—

"A bludgeon stands for death and blood,
But a wand of worthy wood
Chastises children for their good."

The measure suggested is the recall of Alcibiades, whose ascendancy would be less disgraceful than that of its existing ruler.

upon all current topics. This observation, which is not wholly superfluous here, appears to have been so far trite and hackneyed in the time of Aristophanes as to allow of its being exemplified in a piece of very brief burlesque. Xanthias and Æacus are the strangers; they discover immediately an uniformity of feeling and sentiment upon the topics most familiar to them as slaves, and conclude by a sudden pledge of friendship. It is to be observed that, in the dialogue which follows, Æacus never departs from the high ground of superiority in point of local information. *All his answers have a slight tinge of irony, as if he was saying*—"Yes—much you know about it!"

Æ. By Jupiter! but he's a gentleman,
That master of yours.
X. A gentleman! To be sure he is;
Why, he does nothing else but wench and drink.
Æ. His never striking you when you took his name—
Outfacing him and contradicting him!—
X. It might have been worse for him if he had.
Æ. Well, that's well spoken, like a true-bred slave.
It's just the sort of language I delight in.
X. You love excuses?
Æ. Yes; but I prefer
Cursing my master quietly in private.
X. Mischief you're fond of?
Æ. Very fond indeed.
X. What think ye of muttering as you leave the room
After a beating?
Æ. Why, that's pleasant too.
X. By Jove, is it! But listening at the door
To hear their secrets?
Æ. Oh, there's nothing like it.
X. And then the reporting them in the neighbourhood.
Æ. That's beyond everything.—That's quite ecstatic.
X. Well, give me your hand. And, there, take mine—and buss me.
And there again—and now for Jupiter's sake!—
(For he's the patron of our cuffs and beatings)
Do tell me what's that noise of people quarrelling
And abusing one another there within?
Æ. Æschylus and Euripides, only! *

* As if he said, It's what we're used to—you're a new comer.

X. Heh?—?—?

Æ. Why, there's a desperate business has broke out
Among these here dead people ;—quite a tumult.

X. As how?

Æ. First, there's a custom we have establish'd
In favour of professors of the arts.
When any one, the first in his own line,
Comes down amongst us here, he stands entitled
To privilege and precedence, with a seat *
At Pluto's royal board.

* A seat at the public table in the Prytaneum was the reward of superior merit and services in Athens.

X. I understand you.

Æ. So he maintains it, till there comes a better
Of the same sort, and then resigns it up.

X. But why should Æschylus be disturb'd at this?

Æ. He held the seat for tragedy, as the master
In that profession.

X. Well, and who's there now?

Æ. He kept it till Euripides appear'd ;
But he collected audiences about him,
And flourish'd, and exhibited, and harangued
Before the thieves, and housebreakers, and rogues,
Cut-purses, cheats, and vagabonds, and villains,
That make the mass of population here ; (*Pointing to the audience.*)
And they—being quite transported, and delighted
With his equivocations and evasions,
His subtleties and niceties and quibbles—
In short—they raised an uproar, and declared him
Archpoet, by a general acclamation.
And he with this grew proud and confident,
And laid a claim to the seat where Æschylus sat.

For a similar compliment to the audience, see p. 252, l. 372.

X. And did not he get pelted for his pains?

Æ. (*with the dry concise importance of superior local information*).
Why, no—The mob call'd out, and it was carried,
To have a public trial of skill between them.

X. You mean the mob of scoundrels that you mention'd?

Æ. Scoundrels indeed! Ay, scoundrels without number.

X. But Æschylus must have had good friends and hearty?

Æ. Yes ; but good men are scarce both here and elsewhere.

X. Well, what has Pluto settled to be done?

Æ. To have an examination and a trial
In public.

See p. 242, l. 101. Sophocles was noted for a mild, easy character.

X. But how comes it?—Sophocles?—
Why does not he put forth his claim amongst them?
Æ. No, no!—He's not the kind of man—not he!
I tell ye; the first moment that he came,
He went up to Æschylus and saluted him
And kiss'd his cheek and took his hand quite kindly;
And Æschylus edged a little from his seat
To give him room; so now the story goes,
(At least I had it from Cleidemides;)
He means to attend there as a stander-by,
Proposing to take up the conqueror;
If Æschylus gets the better, well and good,
He gives up his pretensions—but if not,
He'll stand a trial, he says, against Euripides.

Cleidemides, the favourite actor of Sophocles.

X. There'll be strange doings.
Æ. That there will—and shortly
—Here—in this place—strange things, I promise you;
A kind of thing that no man could have thought of;
Why, you'll see poetry weigh'd out and measured.
X. What, will they bring their tragedies to the steel-yards?*
Æ. Yes, will they—with their rules and compasses
They'll measure, and examine, and compare,
And bring their plummets, and their lines and levels,
To take the bearings—for Euripides
Says that he'll make a survey, word by word.
X. Æschylus takes the thing to heart, I doubt.
Æ. He bent his brows and pored upon the ground;
I saw him.
X. Well, but who decides the business?
Æ. Why, there the difficulty lies—for judges,
True learned judges, are grown scarce, and Æschylus
Objected to the Athenians absolutely.
X. Considering them as rogues and villains mostly.†
Æ. As being ignorant and empty generally;
And in their judgment of the stage particularly.
In fine, they've fix'd upon that master of yours,
As having had some practice in the business.
But we must wait within—for when our masters
Are warm and eager, stripes and blows ensue.

* In one of the latter scenes of this play, the two poets put single verses into the opposite scales of a balance.

† Consequently belonging to the faction before mentioned, l. 912.

CHORUS.

The full-mouth'd master of the tragic quire,
We shall behold him foam with rage and ire;
—Confronting in the list
His eager, shrewd, sharp-tooth'd antagonist.
Then will his visual orbs be wildly whirl'd
And huge invectives will be hurl'd.
  Superb and supercilious,
  Atrocious, atrabilious,
With furious gesture and with lips of foam,
And lion crest unconscious of the comb;
Erect with rage—his brow's impending gloom
O'ershadowing his dark eyes' terrific blaze.
  The opponent, dexterous and wary,
  Will fend and parry:
While masses of conglomerated phrase,
  Enormous, ponderous, and pedantic,
  With indignation frantic,
  And strength and force gigantic,
    Are desperately sped
    At his devoted head—
Then in different style
The touchstone and the file,
And subtleties of art
In turn will play their part;
Analysis and rule,
And every modern tool;
With critic scratch and scribble,
And nice invidious nibble;
Contending for the important choice,
A vast expenditure of human voice!

Scene. EURIPIDES, BACCHUS, ÆSCHYLUS.

Eu. Don't give me your advice, I claim the seat
As being a better and superior artist.
B. What, Æschylus, don't you speak? you hear his
language.
Eu. He's mustering up a grand commanding visage
—A silent attitude—the common trick
That he begins with in his tragedies.*

* See page 287. The instances of Niobe and Achilles.

B. Come, have a care, my friend — You'll say too much.

Eu. I know the man of old—I've scrutinized
And shewn him long ago for what he is,
A rude unbridled tongue, a haughty spirit;
Proud, arrogant, and insolently pompous;
Rough, clownish, boisterous, and overbearing.

Æs. Say'st thou me so?* Thou bastard of the earth,
With thy patch'd robes and rags of sentiment
Raked from the streets and stitch'd and tack'd together!
Thou mumping, whining, beggarly hypocrite!
But you shall pay for it.

B. (*in addressing Æschylus attempts to speak in more elevated style*). There now, Æschylus,
You grow too warm. Restrain your ireful mood.

Æs. Yes; but I'll seize that sturdy beggar first,
And search and strip him bare of his pretensions.

B. Quick! Quick! A sacrifice to the winds—Make ready;
The storm of rage is gathering. Bring a victim.†

Æs. —A wretch that has corrupted every thing;
Our music with his melodies from Crete;
Our morals with incestuous tragedies.‡

B. Dear, worthy Æschylus, contain yourself,
And as for you, Euripides, move off
This instant, if you're wise; I give you warning.
Or else, with one of his big thumping phrases,
You'll get your brains dash'd out, and all your notions
And sentiments and matter mash'd to pieces.
—And thee, most noble Æschylus (*as above*), I beseech
With mild demeanour calm and affable
To hear and answer.—For it ill beseems
Illustrious bards to scold like market-women.
But you roar out and bellow like a furnace.

Eu. (*in the tone of a town blackguard working himself up for a quarrel*).
I'm up to it.—I'm resolved, and here I stand
Ready and steady—take what course you will;
Let him be first to speak, or else let me.
I'll match my plots and characters against him;
My sentiments and language, and what not:
Ay! and my music too, my Meleager,
My Æolus and my Telephus and all.

* Æschylus was of a resolute, uncompromising character, proud of his ancient descent, of his own valour and that of his family. Euripides' mother was of a very low caste. See v. 1192.

† Bacchus does not call for a sacrifice. It is his buffoonish way of saying that Æschylus is going to be in a *stormy* passion.

‡ The stories of Phædra and Canace.

B. Well, Æschylus,—determine. What say you?

Æs. (*speaks in a tone of grave manly despondency*).
I wish the place of trial had been elsewhere,
I stand at disadvantage here.

B. As how?

Æs. Because my poems live on earth above,
And his died with him, and descended here,
And are at hand as ready witnesses;
But you decide the matter: I submit.

B. (*with official pertness and importance*).
Come—let them bring me fire and frankincense,
That I may offer vows and make oblations
For an ingenious critical conclusion
To this same elegant and clever trial—
(*To the Chorus.*)
And you too,—sing me a hymn there.—To the Muses.

CHORUS.

An attempt is here made to give some idea of the metre of the original, a mixture of the anapæst and hexameter.

To the Heavenly Nine we petition,
Ye, that on earth or in air are for ever kindly protecting
the vagaries of learned ambition,
And at your ease from above our sense and folly directing,
(or poetical contests inspecting,
Deign to behold for a while as a scene of amusing attention,
all the struggles of style and invention,)
Aid, and assist, and attend, and afford to the furious authors
your refined and enlighten'd suggestions;
Grant them ability—force and agility, quick recollections,
and address in their answers and questions,
Pithy replies, with a word to the wise, and pulling and hauling,
with inordinate uproar and bawling,
Driving and drawing, like carpenters sawing, their dramas asunder:
With suspended sense and wonder,
All are waiting and attending
On the conflict now depending!

B. Come, say your prayers, you two before the trial.
[*Æschylus offers incense.*

Æs. O Ceres, nourisher of my soul, maintain me
A worthy follower of thy mysteries.*
B. (*to Euripides*). There, you there, make your offering.
Eu. Well, I will;
But I direct myself to other deities.
B. Heh, what? Your own? some new ones?
Eu. Most assuredly!
B. Well! Pray away, then—to your own new deities.
[*Euripides offers incense.*
Eu. Thou foodful Air, the nurse of all my notions;
And ye, the organic powers of sense and speech,
And keen refined olfactory discernment,
Assist my present search for faults and errors.

* The first idea of tragedy was derived from the scenic exhibitions in the mysteries of *Ceres*, where they formed a part of the initiatory rites.

CHORUS.

Here beside you, here are we,
Eager all to hear and see
This abstruse and mighty battle
Of profound and learned prattle.
—But, as it appears to me,
Thus the course of it will be;
He, the junior and appellant,
Will advance as the assailant.
Aiming shrewd satyric darts
At his rival's noble parts;
And with sallies sharp and keen
Try to wound him in the spleen,
While the veteran rends and raises
Rifted, rough, uprooted phrases,
Wielded like a threshing staff
Scattering the dust and chaff.

The metre which follows is so essentially vulgar, that I am not able to recollect any line of it in English which is fit to be quoted.[1]

B. Come, now begin, dispute away, but first I give you notice

[1] See, however, *The Knights*, page 87, note after line 443.

That every phrase in your discourse must be refined, avoiding
Vulgar absurd comparisons, and awkward silly joking.

Eu. At the first outset, I forbear to state my own pretensions;
Hereafter I shall mention them, when his have been refuted;
After I shall have fairly shown, how he befool'd and cheated
The rustic audience that he found, which Phrynichus* bequeathed him.
He planted first upon the stage a figure veil'd and muffled,
An Achilles or a Niobe, that never show'd their faces;
But kept a tragic attitude, without a word to utter.

B. No more they did: 'tis very true.

Eu. —In the meanwhile the Chorus
Strung on ten strophes right-an-end, but they remain'd in silence.

B. I liked that silence well enough, as well, perhaps, or better
Than those new talking characters—

Eu. That's from your want of judgment,
Believe me.

B. Why, perhaps it is; but what was his intention?

Eu. Why, mere conceit and insolence; to keep the people waiting
Till Niobe should deign to speak, to drive his drama forward.

B. O what a rascal. Now I see the tricks he used to play me.

[*To Æschylus, who is showing signs of indignation by various contortions.*

—What makes you writhe and wince about?—

Eu. Because he feels my censures.
—Then having dragg'd and drawl'd along, half-way to the conclusion,
He foisted in a dozen words of noisy boisterous accent,
With lofty plumes and shaggy brows, mere bugbears of the language,
That no man ever heard before.—

Æs. Alas! alas!

B. (*to Æschylus*). Have done there

Eu. He never used a simple word.

* The earliest tragic poet whose dramas were in any degree esteemed among the ancients.

B. (*to Æschylus*). Don't grind your teeth so strangely.
Eu. But "Bulwarks and Scamanders" and "Hippogrifs and Gorgons."
"On burnish'd shields emboss'd in brass;" bloody, remorseless phrases
Which nobody could understand.
B. Well, I confess, for my part,
I used to keep awake at night, with guesses and conjectures
To think what kind of foreign bird he meant by griffin-horses.
Æs. A figure on the heads of ships; you goose, you must have seen them.
B. Well, from the likeness, I declare, I took it for Eruxis.*
Eu. So! Figures from the heads of ships are fit for tragic diction.
Æs. Well then—thou paltry wretch, explain What were your own devices?
Eu. Not stories about flying-stags, like yours, and griffin-horses;
Nor terms nor images derived from tapestry Persian hangings.
When I received the Muse from you I found her puff'd and pamper'd †
With pompous sentences and terms, a cumbrous huge virago.
My first attention was applied to make her look genteelly;
And bring her to a slighter shape by dint of lighter diet:
I fed her with plain household phrase, and cool familiar salad,
With water-gruel episode, with sentimental jelly,
With moral mincemeat; till at length I brought her into compass;
Cephisophon, who was my cook, contrived to make them relish.
I kept my plots distinct and clear, and, to prevent confusion,
My leading characters rehearsed their pedigrees for prologues.
Æs. 'Twas well, at least, that you forbore to quote your own extraction.
Eu. From the first opening of the scene, all persons were in action;

* The Scholiast informs us that he was eminent for ugliness.

† Euripides speaks in the style of the basest of all occupations; the speculator in female slaves—the leno of Terence.

The master spoke, the slave replied, the women, young and old ones,
All had their equal share of talk—

Æs. Come, then, stand forth and tell us,
What forfeit less than death is due for such an innovation?

Eu. I did it upon principle, from democratic motives.

**B.* Take care, my friend—upon that ground your footing is but ticklish.

Eu. I taught these youths to speechify.

Æs. I say so too.—Moreover
I say that—for the public good—you ought to have been hang'd first.

Eu. The rules and forms of rhetoric,—the laws of composition,
To prate—to state—and in debate to meet a question fairly:
At a dead lift to turn and shift—to make a nice distinction.

Æs. I grant it all—I make it all—my ground of accusation.

Eu. The whole in cases and concerns occurring and recurring
At every turn and every day domestic and familiar,
So that the audience, one and all, from personal experience,
Were competent to judge the piece, and form a fair opinion
Whether my scenes and sentiments agreed with truth and nature.
I never took them by surprise to storm their understandings,
With Memnons and Tydides's and idle rattle-trappings
Of battle-steeds and clattering shields to scare them from their senses;
But for a test (perhaps the best) our pupils and adherents
May be distinguish'd instantly by person and behaviour;
His are Phormisius the rough, Meganetes the gloomy,†
Hobgoblin-headed, trumpet-mouth'd, grim-visaged, ugly-bearded;
But mine are Cleitophon the smooth,—Theramenes the gentle.

B. Theramenes—a clever hand, a universal genius,
I never found him at a loss in all the turns of party
To change his watch-word at a word or at a moment's warning.

* The philosophic sect to which Euripides belonged, were known to be hostile to the democracy.

† Of these personages the Scholiast tells us that Phormisius wore a long beard, and affected to be formidable; and that Meganetes was a bold, rough soldier;—for Theramenes, see p. 263; for his past conduct, see Mr. Mitford, ch. 19, sect. 7, and ch. 20, sect. 3, and for his subsequent, sect. 5.

Eu. Thus it was that I began,
With a nicer, neater plan;
Teaching men to look about,
Both within doors and without;
To direct their own affairs,
And their house and household wares;
Marking every thing amiss—
"Where is that? and—What is this?
"This is broken—that is gone,"
'Tis the modern style and tone.*
B. Yes, by Jove—and at their homes
Nowadays each master comes,
Of a sudden bolting in
With an uproar and a din;
Rating all the servants round,
"If it's lost, it must be found.
Why was all the garlic wasted?
There, that honey has been tasted:
And these olives pilfer'd here.
Where's the pot we bought last year?
What's become of all the fish?
Which of you has broke the dish?"
Thus it is, but heretofore,
The moment that they cross'd the door,
They sat them down to doze and snore.

* General distress had produced a stricter economy, which is here humorously attributed to the precepts of Euripides.

Chorus.

"Noble Achilles! you see the disaster,
"The shame and affront, and an enemy nigh!" †
Oh! bethink thee, mighty master,
Think betimes of your reply;
Yet beware, lest anger force
Your hasty chariot from the course;
Grievous charges have been heard,
With many a sharp and bitter word,
Notwithstanding, mighty chief,
Let Prudence fold her cautious reef
In your anger's swelling sail;
By degrees you may prevail,
But beware of your behaviour
Till the wind is in your favour:

† From Æschylus's tragedy of "The Myrmidons," which opened with the death of Patroclus and the defeat of the Greeks.

Now for your answer, illustrious architect,
Founder of lofty theatrical lays!
Patron in chief of our tragical trumperies!
Open the floodgate of figure and phrase!

Æs. My spirit is kindled with anger and shame,
To so base a competitor forced to reply,
But I needs must retort, or the wretch will report
That he left me refuted and foil'd in debate;
Tell me then, What are the principal merits
Entitling a poet to praise and renown?
Eu. The improvement of morals, the progress of mind,
When a poet, by skill and invention,
Can render his audience virtuous and wise.
Æs. But if you, by neglect or intention,
Have done the reverse, and from brave honest spirits
Depraved, and have left them degraded and base,
Tell me, what punishment ought you to suffer?
B. Death, to be sure!—Take that answer from me.
Æs. Observe then, and mark, what our citizens were,
When first from my care they were trusted to you;
Not scoundrel informers, or paltry buffoons,
Evading the services due to the state;
But with hearts all on fire, for adventure and war,
Distinguish'd for hardiness, stature, and strength,
Breathing forth nothing but lances and darts,
Arms, and equipment, and battle array,
Bucklers, and shields, and habergeons, and hauberks,
Helmets, and plumes, and heroic attire.
B. There he goes, hammering on with his helmets,
He'll be the death of me one of these days.*
Eu. But how did you manage to make 'em so manly,
What was the method, the means that you took?
B. Speak, Æschylus, speak, and behave yourself better,
And don't in your rage stand so silent and stern.
Æs. A drama, brimful with heroical spirit.
Eu. What did you call it?
Æs. "The Chiefs against Thebes,"
That inspired each spectator with martial ambition,
Courage, and ardour, and prowess, and pride.
B. But you did very wrong to encourage the Thebans.

* The phrase of a person complaining of a noisy trade—an armourer's shop next door.

Indeed, you deserve to be punish'd, you do,
For the Thebans are grown to be capital soldiers,
You've done us a mischief by that very thing.
Æs. The fault was your own, if you took other courses;
The lesson I taught was directed to you:
Then I gave you the glorious theme of "the Persians,"
Replete with sublime patriotical strains,
The record and example of noble achievement,
The delight of the city, the pride of the stage.*
B. I rejoiced, I confess, when the tidings were carried
To old King Darius, so long dead and buried,
And the chorus in concert kept wringing their hands,
Weeping and wailing, and crying, Alas!
Æs. Such is the duty, the task of a poet,
Fulfilling in honour his office and trust.
Look to traditional history—look
To antiquity, primitive, early, remote:
See there, what a blessing illustrious poets
Conferr'd on mankind, in the centuries past,
Orpheus instructed mankind in religion,
Reclaim'd them from bloodshed and barbarous rites:
Musæus deliver'd the doctrine of medicine,
And warnings prophetic for ages to come:
Next came old Hesiod, teaching us husbandry,
Ploughing, and sowing, and rural affairs,
Rural economy, rural astronomy,
Homely morality, labour, and thrift:
Homer himself, our adorable Homer,
What was his title to praise and renown?
What, but the worth of the lessons he taught us,
Discipline, arms, and equipment of war?
B. Yes, but Pantacles† was never the wiser;
For in the procession he ought to have led,
When his helmet was tied, he kept puzzling, and tried
To fasten the crest on the crown of his head.
Æs. But other brave warriors and noble commanders
Were train'd in his lessons to valour and skill;
Such was the noble heroical Lamachus;‡
Others besides were instructed by him;
And I, from his fragments ordaining a banquet,
Furnish'd and deck'd with majestical phrase,
Brought forward the models of ancient achievement,

* In this play the ancient Persian councillors evoke the ghost of Darius, and relate to him the calamitous result of his son's expedition against Greece.

† Of Pantacles nothing is known but that he was laughed at for his awkwardness by the comic poets; probably an *absent man*, not a usual character among the Athenians.

‡ Lamachus,

Teucer, Patroclus, and chiefs of antiquity;
Raising and rousing Athenian hearts,
When the signal of onset was blown in their ear,
With a similar ardour to dare and to do;
But I never allow'd of your lewd Sthenobœas,
Or filthy, detestable Phædras—not I—
Indeed, I should doubt if my drama throughout
Exhibit an instance of woman in love.

Eu. No, you were too stern for an amorous turn,
For Venus and Cupid too stern and too stupid.

Æs. May they leave me at rest, and with peace in my breast,
And infest and pursue your kindred and you,
With the very same blow that despatch'd you below.*

B. That was well enough said; with the life that he led,
He himself in the end got a wound from a friend.

Eu. But what, after all, is the horrible mischief?
My poor Sthenobœas, what harm have they done?

Æs. The example is follow'd, the practice has gain'd,
And women of family, fortune, and worth,
Bewilder'd with shame in a passionate fury,
Have poison'd themselves for Bellerophon's sake.†

Eu. But at least you'll allow that I never invented it,
Phædra's affair was a matter of fact.

Æs. A fact, with a vengeance! but horrible facts
Should be buried in silence, not bruited abroad,
Nor brought forth on the stage, nor emblazon'd in poetry.
Children and boys have a teacher assign'd them—
The bard is a master for manhood and youth,
Bound to instruct them in virtue and truth,
Beholden and bound.

Eu. But is virtue a sound?
Can any mysterious virtue be found
In bombastical, huge, hyperbolical phrase?

Æs. Thou dirty, calamitous wretch, recollect
That exalted ideas of fancy require
To be clothed in a suitable vesture of phrase;
And that heroes and gods may be fairly supposed
Discoursing in words of a mightier import,
More lofty by far than the children of man;
As the pomp of apparel assign'd to their persons,
Produced on the stage and presented to view,

killed at Syracuse—in the "Ach." p. 28, as a promoter of the war he is ridiculed, but without contempt; spoken of in the "Thesm." with respect; and in the "Peace" with an evidently kind intention.

* Euripides's death is said to have been hastened by his wife's misconduct.

† In a tragedy of Euripides, now lost, Sthenobœa poisons herself for love of Bellerophon. Probably in some cases of female suicide, this tragedy of Euripides had held the same place that the "Phædon" of Plato does in the story of the death of Cato.

Surpasses in dignity, splendour, and lustre
Our popular garb and domestic attire,
A practice which nature and reason allow,
But which you disannull'd and rejected.

Eu. As how?

Æs. When you brought forth your kings, in a villanous fashion,
In patches and rags, as a claim for compassion.

Eu. And this is a grave misdemeanour, forsooth!

Æs. It has taught an example of sordid untruth;
For the rich of the city, that ought to equip,
And to serve with, a ship, are appealing to pity,
Pretending distress—with an overworn dress.

B. By Jove, so they do; with a waistcoat brand new,
Worn closely within, warm and new for the skin;
And if they escape in this beggarly shape,
You'll meet 'em at market, I warrant 'em all,
Buying the best at the fishmonger's stall.

Æs. He has taught every soul to sophisticate truth;
And debauch'd all the bodies and minds of the youth;
Leaving them morbid, and pallid, and spare;
And the places of exercise vacant and bare:—
The disorder has spread to the fleet and the crew;
The service is ruin'd, and ruin'd by you—
With prate and debate in a mutinous state;
Whereas, in my day, 'twas a different way;
Nothing they said, nor knew nothing to say,
But to call for their porridge, and cry, "Pull away."

B. Yes—yes, they knew this,
How to f . . . in the teeth
Of the rower beneath;
And befoul their own comrades,
And pillage ashore;
But now they forget the command of the oar:—
Prating and splashing,
Discussing and dashing,
They steer here and there,
With their eyes in the air,
Hither and thither,
Nobody knows whither.

Æs. Can the reprobate mark in the course he has run,
One crime unattempted, a mischief undone?

With his horrible passions, of sisters and brothers,*
And sons-in-law, tempted by villanous mothers,
And temples defiled with a bastardly birth,
And women, divested of honour or worth,
That talk about life "as a death upon earth;"
And sophistical frauds and rhetorical bawds;
Till now the whole state is infested with tribes
Of scriveners and scribblers, and rascally scribes—
All practice of masculine vigour and pride,
Our wrestling and running, are all laid aside,
And we see that the city can hardly provide
For the Feast of the Founder, a racer of force †
To carry the torch and accomplish a course.

* See note ‡, p. 284.

† See note †, p. 244.

B. Well, I laugh'd till I cried
The last festival tide,
At the fellow that ran,—
'Twas a heavy fat man,
And he panted and hobbled,
And stumbled and wabbled,
And the pottery people about the gate,
Seeing him hurried, and tired, and late,
Stood to receive him in open rank,
Helping him on with a hearty spank
Over the shoulder and over the flank,
The flank, the loin, the back, the shoulders,
With shouts of applause from all beholders;
While he ran on with a filthy fright,
Puffing his link to keep it alight.

If the table of contents assigned to the primitive comedy in page 276 should be thought too scanty, we may venture to add to it all those regular debates, which are managed by two disputants acting alternately as opponent and respondent, in which the chorus appears as the moderator and generally (though in the present instance that office is assigned to Bacchus) as the judge of the controversy, the arguments on both sides, the attack, and the reply, being regularly preceded by a short exhortation from the chorus. Formal disputation of this kind would be wholly out of place in comedy (such as we generally conceive it, namely, a comedy consisting of dramatic action); accordingly, no instance of the kind is to be found, I believe, in modern comedy or in what was called the new *comedy of the Greeks, the remains of which have been preserved to us in the translations of Plautus and Terence. It should seem therefore that the frequent recurrence of this sort of disputations in the comedies of Aristophanes can hardly be accounted for in any way more probably, than by supposing them to have existed in the* primitive *comedy, that undramatic form, from which the* ancient *(as it is called) or Aristophanic form was immediately derived.*

We may venture therefore to enumerate, among the constituent parts of the primitive undramatic comedy, controversies upon debated points or upon a comparison of their own respective merits, in which two disputants were engaged with the chorus presiding as judge and moderator.

If this inference is not strictly logical, it may at least be allowed to be geological. The primary stratum of primitive comedy is lost—but a conjecture may be formed as to its composition by observing those substances, which, though they abound in the strata of transition, are no longer discoverable in those of more recent formation. We conclude that such substances must have formed a component part of that elder stratum which has disappeared. In the case now before us the stratum of transition is the ancient *or Aristophanic comedy, forming a connecting link between the* primitive undramatic *comedy and the* new *comedy, of the Greeks (the comedy of Menander and Terence), the character of which is exclusively dramatic and in no respect different from that of modern comedy. In this view of the subject the* middle *comedy (as it was called by the critics of antiquity) is not taken into account; it was, in fact, merely a mutilated form of the Aristophanic comedy stripped of its chorus, of its personalities, and of its privileges of political satire—it is identified with the ancient or Aristophanic comedy by its main characteristic, the utter impossibility of the story; and upon this ground stands (equally with the ancient comedy) in direct contrast with the new comedy, in which (as in modern comedy) an adherence to the probabilities of real life is an essential requisite. The ancient comedy, amidst its infinite variety of supernatural and incredible subjects, admitted burlesque representations of mythological and heroic traditions, and among the titles of his comedies that are lost, the Dædalus, the Danaids, the Lemnian Women, (or the story of Jason and Hypsipyle) prove that Aristophanes, even before the sup-*

pression of the genuine ancient comedy, did not neglect subjects of this kind. Cratinus too, who died long before that period, among the scanty fragments that remain of him, has still left in existence a single line from a comedy representing Ulysses in the cave of the Cyclops. But subjects of this kind formed the main resource of the writers of the middle comedy, and their productions of this description were much more numerous. Therefore, as the result of this digression, it may be allowable to observe, if nobody should have observed it before, that (in addition to the Plutus of Aristophanes) the Amphitryon of Plautus (undoubtedly translated from Greek) may be regarded as a specimen of the middle comedy of the Greeks; and this result, however interesting, being not much to the purpose of the present translation, we will proceed forthwith to the lines in which the Chorus perform their part in animating and encouraging the disputants.

CHORUS.

Ere the prize is lost and won
Mighty doings will be done.
Now then—(though to judge aright
Is difficult, when force and might
Are opposed with ready slight,
When the Champion that is cast
Tumbles uppermost at last)*
—Since you meet in equal match,
Argue, contradict and scratch,
Scuffle, and abuse and bite,
Tear and fight,
With all your wits and all your might.
—Fear not for a want of sense
Or judgment in your audience,
That defect has been removed; †
They're prodigiously improved,
Disciplined, alert and smart,
Drill'd and exercised in art:
Each has got a little book,
In the which they read and look,
Doing all their best endeavour
To be critical and clever;

* An allusion to the combats of the Pancratium, in which all means of attack and defence were employed, as they are by the rival poets in the scenes which follow.

† Here is a little coaxing to the audience, but also a little irony. I suspect that Aristophanes was no great friend to reading and writing as compared with the ancient system of memory and recitation.

Thus their own ingenious natures,
  Aided and improved by learning,
Will provide you with spectators
  Shrewd, attentive, and discerning.

The altercation which follows, turning upon a question of verbal criticism, is incapable of an exact translation. The attack with its answer occupies about 45 lines in the original; Euripides begins it, saying that his opponent is incorrect in his use of words, and offers to prove it from those parts of his tragedies which were usually the most carefully composed (the opening speeches, or prologues as they were called).—He then calls upon Æschylus to repeat the first lines from the tragedy of Orestes; in this tragedy Orestes is represented as having returned secretly to Argos, standing at the tomb of his father, and invoking Mercury, (not the vulgar patron of thieves and pedlars and spies,) but that more awful deity, the terrestrial Hermes, the guardian of the dead, and inspector general of the infernal regions, the care of which had been delegated to him by the paternal authority of Jupiter.

The obscurity and ambiguity of the original may be represented by the following lines,

Terrestrial Hermes with supreme espial,
Inspector of that old paternal realm,
Aid and assist me now, your suppliant,
Revisiting and returning to my country!

This is variously misinterpreted. The espial *is supposed to refer to the treason practised against Agamemnon,—the* paternal realm *to be that of Argos; and the last line is objected to as containing a tautology;—Æschylus defends himself by the explanation of his meaning, which has been already given, and in answer to the last objection contends that for an exile to* revisit *his country and to* return *to it is not the same thing: to which Euripides replies:*

It is not justly express'd, since he return'd
Clandestinely without authority.

B. That's well remark'd; but I don't comprehend it.

Eu. (*tauntingly and coolly*).
Proceed—Continue!

B. (*jealous of his authority*). Yes, you must continue, Æschylus, I command you to continue.

(*To Euripides.*)
And you, keep a look-out and mark his blunders.
Æs. "From his sepulchral mound I call my father
"To listen and hear"—
Eu. There's a tautology!
"To listen and hear"—
B. Why, don't you see, you ruffian!
It's a dead man he's calling to—Three times*
We call to 'em, but they can't be made to hear.
Æs. And you: your prologues, of what kind were they?
Eu. I'll show ye; and if you'll point out a tautology,
Or a single word clapt in to botch a verse—
That's all!—I'll give you leave to spit upon me.
B. (*with an absurd air of patience and resignation*).
Well, I can't help myself; I'm bound to attend.
Begin then with these same fine-spoken prologues.
Eu. "Œdipus was at first a happy man." . .
Æs. Not he, by Jove!—but born to misery;
Predicted and predestined by an oracle
Before his birth to murder his own father!
—Could he have been "at first a happy man?"
Eu. . . . "But afterwards became a wretched mortal."
Æs. By no means! he continued to be wretched,
—Born wretched, and exposed as soon as born
Upon a potsherd in a winter's night;
Brought up a foundling with disabled feet;
Then married—a young-man to an aged woman,
That proved to be his mother—whereupon
He tore his eyes out.
B. To complete his happiness,
He ought to have served at sea with Erasinides.*

* The custom at funerals of invoking the dead by name three times.

* Erasinides was condemned to death with five of his colleagues in command, immediately after having obtained the naval victory at Arginusæ. See Mitford, ch. 20, sec. 2 and 3.

Æschylus then attacks Euripides for the monotony of his metre, and the continued recurrence of a pause on the fifth syllable, which he ridicules by a burlesque addition subjoined to all the verses in which this cadence is detected. The point and humour of this supplementary phrase is not explained to us by the ancient Scholiasts, nor has the industry of modern commentators enabled them to detect it. Euripides repeats the first lines of several of his tragedies, but falls perpetually upon the same pause, and is met at every turn with the absurd supplement, till Bacchus calls out to him—

There !—that's enough—now come to music, can't ye?
Eu. I mean it; I shall now proceed to expose him
As a bad composer, awkward, uninventive,
Repeating the same strain perpetually.—

CHORUS.

I stand in wonder and perplext
To think of what will follow next.
Will he dare to criticize
The noble bard, that did devise
Our oldest, boldest harmonies,
Whose mighty music we revere?
Much I marvel, much I fear.—
Eu. Mighty fine music, truly! I'll give ye a sample;
It's every inch cut out to the same pattern.

Of the part of the entertainment which followed, however amusing it might have been to the musical critics of Athens, it is impossible for a modern to form any satisfactory notion. It consisted of a musical burlesque, in which each of the rival candidates (Euripides and Æschylus) is represented as exhibiting a caricature of the style of his opponent. This caricature seems to have consisted of a series of musical phrases selected from their works, but (as the music was the only object, while the words served only to indicate the music which was attached to them), the words which now remain alone (the music having shared the common fate of all the other music of the ancients) presents little more than a jumble of sentences incapable of being connected by any continuous meaning. We have seen that Æschylus is accused of repeating the same strain perpetually—this, it should seem, was exemplified by bringing together passages from the choruses of different plays, which were marked by the recurrence of the same musical phrase. *The scholiasts point out passages from the choruses of four plays, which are thus brought into juxtaposition; but the main subject of burlesque appears to have been a chorus from the tragedy of the* Myrmidons *(the soldiers of Achilles) in which they were represented as addressing their chief after the death of Patroclus and the discomfiture of the Greeks. We may easily suppose that the peculiarities of Æschylus's style would be most strongly exemplified in a chorus composed of such characters.*

It might have been deemed allowable, and perhaps advisable (after the explanation already given) to relinquish any attempt at representing what is so little capable of being represented; but as nature in general, and the nature of translation more particularly, abhors a vacuum, a few lines are put together in an Æschylean metre, which may serve as a substitute to fill up the chasm, and to represent the chorus (that of the Myrmidons) *which was the chief subject of this burlesque criticism. It must be left to the musical reader, if the reader should happen to be musical, to imagine to himself a noisy, boisterous accompaniment on a wind instrument. Though perhaps his imagination might be more amusingly employed in conceiving a similar scene of contest between the great musical favourites of the last and the present century, between Gluck or Handel, for instance, and Rossini.*

B. I'll mark—I've pick'd these pebbles up for counters.
Eu. Noble Achilles! Forth to the rescue!
Forth to the rescue with ready support!
Hasten and go,
There is havoc and woe,
Hasty defeat,
And a bloody retreat,
Confusion and rout,
And the terrible shout
Of a conquering foe,
Tribulation and woe!
B. Whoh hoh there! we've had woes enough, I reckon;
Therefore I'll go to wash away my woe
In a warm bath.
Eu. No, do pray wait an instant,
And let me give you first another strain,
Transferr'd to the stage from music to the lyre.*
B. Proceed then—only give us no more woes.
Eu. The supremacy sceptre and haughty command
Of the Grecian land—with a flatto-flatto-flatto-thrat—
And the ravenous sphinx, with her horrible brood,
Thirsting for blood—with a flatto-flatto-flatto-thrat,
And armies equipt for a vengeful assault,
For Paris's fault—with a flatto-flatto-flatto-thrat.

* Is Æschylus censured for adapting music composed for the lyre to the accompaniment of wind instruments, which is indicated by nonsensical imitative sounds?

B. What herb is that same flatto-thrat? some simple,
I guess, you met with in the field of Marathon:
—But such a tune as this! you must have learnt it
From fellows hauling buckets at the well.*

Æs. Such were the strains I purified and brought
To just perfection—taught by Phrynichus,
Not copying him, but culling other flowers
From those fair meadows which the Muses love—
—But he filches and begs, adapts and borrows
Snatches of tunes from minstrels in the street,
Strumpets and vagabonds—the lullabys
Of nurses and old women—jigs and ballads—
I'll give ye a proof—Bring me a lyre here, somebody.
What signifies a lyre? the castanets
Will suit him better—Bring the castanets,
With Euripides's Muse to snap her fingers
In cadence to her master's compositions.

B. This Muse, I take it, is a Lesbian Muse.†

Æs. Gentle halcyons, ye that lave
Your snowy plume,
Sporting on the summer wave;
Ye too that around the room,
On the rafters of the roof
Strain aloft your airy woof;
Ye spiders, spiders ever spinning,
Never ending, still beginning—
Where the dolphin loves to follow,
Weltering in the surge's hollow,
Dear to Neptune and Apollo;
By the seamen understood
Ominous of harm or good;
In capricious, eager sallies,
Chacing, racing round the galleys.

What follows is not very intelligible; it should seem that Æschylus beats the measure of the music which he ridicules. He says, Do you see this foot? *or (as the Scholiast explains it)* this rhythm? *to which Bacchus answers,* I see it—

Æs. Well now. Do you see this? *B.* I see it—

After which Æschylus turns to his antagonist:

* Music is apt to be vulgarized by continued popularity. In Goldsmith's time the minuet in "Ariadne" had become a tune for a dancing bear. The shabby old Juryman in the "Wasps" sings Phrynichus's music. Yet Phrynichus is classed with Anacreon and Alcæus as a great improver and master in music. Thesm. 164.

† The Lesbian women were of very bad fame.

Such is your music. I shall now proceed
To give a specimen of your monodies*—

The Burlesque which follows admits of a tolerably close translation.

O dreary shades of night!
What phantoms of affright
Have scared my troubled sense
With saucer eyes immense;
And huge horrific paws
With bloody claws!
Ye maidens haste, and bring
From the fair spring
A bucket of fresh water; whose clear stream
May purify me from this dreadful dream:
But oh! my dream is out!
Ye maidens search about!
O mighty powers of mercy, can it be;
That Glyke, Glyke, she,
(My friend and civil neighbour heretofore,)
Has robb'd my henroost of its feather'd store?
With the dawn I was beginning,
Spinning, spinning, spinning, spinning,
Unconscious of the meditated crime;
Meaning to sell my yarn at market-time.
Now tears alone are left me,
My neighbour hath bereft me,
Of all—of all—of all—all but a tear!
Since he, my faithful trusty chanticleer
Is flown—is flown!—Is gone—is gone!
—But, O ye nymphs of sacred Ida,† bring
Torches and bows, with arrows on the string;
And search around
All the suspected ground:
And thou, fair huntress of the sky;
Deign to attend, descending from on high—
—While Hecate, with her tremendous torch,
Even from the topmost garret to the porch
Explores the premises with search exact,
To find the thief and ascertain the fact—

B. Come, no more songs!

Æs. I've had enough of 'em;

* Monodies—verses sung by a single actor unaccompanied by the chorus. The burlesque turns upon the faults of Euripides's style, the false sublime—the vulgar pathetic; and impertinent supplications for divine assistance.

† There is a similar invocation in the "Lysistrata," where the dawdling Chorus, instead of going to put out the fire, stand with buckets of water in their hands, praying to Minerva to bring more water.

For my part, I shall bring him to the balance,
As a true test of our poetic merit,
To prove the weight of our respective verses.
B. Well then, so be it—if it must be so,
That I'm to stand here like a cheesemonger
Retailing poetry with a pair of scales.
[*A huge pair of scales are here discovered on the stage.*

CHORUS.

Curious eager wits pursue
Strange devices quaint and new,
Like the scene you witness here,
Unaccountable and queer;
I myself, if merely told it,
If I did not here behold it,
Should have deem'd it utter folly,
Craziness and nonsense wholly.

B. Move up; stand close to the balance!
Eu. Here are we—
B. Take hold now, and each of you repeat a verse,
And don't leave go before I call to you!
Eu. We're ready.
B. Now, then, each repeat a verse.
Eu. "I wish that Argo with her woven wings."*
Æs. "O streams of Sperchius, and ye pastured plains."†
B. Let go!—See now—this scale outweighs that other
Very considerably—
Eu. How did it happen?
B. He slipp'd a river in, like the wool-jobbers,
To moisten his metre—but your line was light,
A thing with wings—ready to fly away.
Eu. Let him try once again then, and take hold.
B. Take hold once more.
Eu. We're ready.
B. Now repeat.
Eu. "Speech is the temple and altar of persuasion."‡
Æs. "Death is a God that loves no sacrifice."§
B. Let go!—See there again! This scale sinks down;
No wonder that it should, with Death put into it,
The heaviest of all calamities.
Eu. But I put in persuasion finely express'd
In the best terms.

* The first line of the "Medea," still existing.

† From the "Philoctetes," now lost.

‡ From the "Antigone," now lost.

§ From the "Niobe," now lost.

B. Perhaps so; but persuasion
Is soft and light and silly—Think of something
That's heavy and huge, to outweigh him, something solid.
Eu. Let's see—Where have I got it? Something solid?
B. "Achilles has thrown twice—Twice a deuce ace!"*
Come now, one trial more; this is the last.
Eu. "He grasp'd a mighty mace of massy weight."†
Æs. "Cars upon cars, and corpses heap'd pell mell."‡
B. He has nick'd you again—
Eu. Why so? What has he done?
B. He has heap'd ye up cars and corpses, such a load
As twenty Egyptian labourers could not carry—§
Æs. Come, no more single lines—let him bring all,
His wife, his children, his Cephisophon,
His books‖ and every thing, himself to boot—
I'll counterpoise them with a couple of lines.
B. Well, they're both friends of mine—I shan't decide
To get myself ill-will from either party;
One of them seems extraordinary clever,
And the other suits my taste particularly.
Pluto. Won't you decide then, and conclude the business?
B. Suppose then I decide; what then?
P. Then take him
Away with you, whichever you prefer,
As a present for your pains in coming down here.
B. Heaven bless ye—Well—let's see now—Can't ye advise me?
This is the case—I'm come in search of a poet—
P. With what design?
B. With this design; to see
The City again restored to peace and wealth,
Exhibiting tragedies in a proper style.
—Therefore whichever gives the best advice
On public matters I shall take him with me.
—First then of Alcibiades, what think ye?¶
The City is in hard labour with the question.
Eu. What are her sentiments towards him?
B. What?
"She loves and she detests and longs to have him."**
But tell me, both of you, your own opinions.
Eu. (*Euripides and Æschylus speak each in his own tragical style.*) I hate the man, that in his country's service

* That is, Euripides (for Achilles)—has failed twice.—In the "Telephus" Euripides had represented Achilles playing at dice. This line was ridiculed by Eupolis.

† From the "Meleager," now lost.

‡ From a play called "Glaucus Potniensis," of which the subject, I believe, is not known.

§ The reconquest of Egypt by the Persians had driven the natives to seek subsistence with their allies at Athens. They are mentioned in "The Birds" as masons and artificers, p. 200.

‖ Euripides was a collector of books. Cephisophon was the chief actor in Euripides's tragedies, and partly, it was said, the author of some of them.

¶ See p. 270.

** From a verse of one of the tragedies of Ion of Chios.

Is slow, but ready and quick to work her harm ;
Unserviceable except to serve himself.
B. Well said, by Jove !—Now you—Give us a sentence.
Æs. 'Tis rash and idle policy to foster
A lion's whelp within the city walls,
But when he's rear'd and grown you must indulge him.
B. By Jove then I'm quite puzzled ; one of them
Has answer'd clearly, and the other sensibly :
But give us both of ye one more opinion ;
—What means are left of safety for the state ?
Eu. To tack Cinesias* like a pair of wings
To Cleocritus's shoulders, and dispatch them
From a precipice to sail across the seas.
B. It seems a joke ; but there's some sense in it.
Eu. . . . Then being both equipp'd with little cruets
They might co-operate in a naval action,
By sprinkling vinegar in the enemies' eyes.
—But I can tell you and will.
B. Speak, and explain then—
Eu. If we mistrust where present trust is placed,
Trusting in what was heretofore mistrusted—†
B. How ! What ? I'm at a loss—Speak it again
Not quite so learnedly—more plainly and simply.
Eu. If we withdraw the confidence we placed
In these our present statesmen, and transfer it
To those whom we mistrusted heretofore,
This seems I think our fairest chance for safety :
If with our present counsellors we fail,
Then with their opposites we might succeed.
B. That's capitally said, my Palamedes !‡
My politician ! was it all your own ?
Your own invention ?
Eu. All except the cruets ;
That was a notion of Cephisophon's.§
B. (*to Æsch.*) Now you—What say you ?
Æs. Inform me about the city—
What kind of persons has she placed in office ?
Does she promote the worthiest ?
B. No, not she,‖
She can't abide 'em.
Æs. Rogues then she prefers ?
B. Not altogether, she makes use of 'em

* See above, v. 186. He was a ridiculously slim figure, a dithyrambic poet and musician. Cleocritus appears afterwards as joined with Thrasybulus in the short civil war of the Piræus. He is ridiculed in "The Birds," p. 186.

† Under cover of ridiculing Euripides's style, harsh and obscure where it aspires to be sententious, and prosaic where it is meant to be familiar, Aristophanes contrives to impress and to repeat twice the same sentiment (his own, see p. 279). In the "Acharnians," a caricature of Euripides' harangues serves as a cover for very bold opinions.

‡ Euripides had written a tragedy on the death of Palamedes, describing him as a most wise and virtuous politician.

§ See note ‖ in p. 305.

‖ See p. 278, the "Antepirrema."

Perforce as it were.
Æs. Then who can hope to save
A state so wayward and perverse, that finds
No sort of habit fitted for her wear?
Drugget or superfine, nothing will suit her!
B. Do think a little how she can be saved.
Æs. Not here; when I return there, I shall speak.
B. No, do pray send some good advice before you.
Æs. When they regard their lands as enemy's ground,
Their enemy's possessions as their own,
Their seamen and the fleet their only safeguard,
Their sole resource hardship and poverty,
And resolute endurance in distress—
B. That's well,—but juries eat up every thing,
And we shall lose our supper if we stay.*
P. Decide then—
B. You'll decide for your own selves,†
I'll make a choice according to my fancy.
Eu. Remember, then, your oath to your poor friend;
And, as you swore and promised, rescue me.
B. "It was my tongue that swore"‡—I fix on Æschylus.
Eu. O wretch! what have you done?
B. Me? done? What should I?
Voted for Æschylus to be sure—Why not?
Eu. And after such a villanous act, you dare
To view me face to face—Art not ashamed?
B. Why shame, in point of fact, is nothing real:
Shame is the apprehension of a vision
Reflected from the surface of opinion—
—The opinion of the public—They must judge.
Eu. O cruel!—Will you abandon me to death?
B. Why perhaps death is life, and life is death,
And victuals and drink an illusion of the senses;
For what is Death but an eternal sleep?
And does not Life consist in sleeping and eating?
P. Now, Bacchus, you'll come here with us within.
B. (*a little startled and alarmed*).
What for?§
P. To be received and entertain'd
With a feast before you go.
B. That's well imagined,
With all my heart—I've not the least objection.

* A double allusion to the pay of the juries which drained the treasury, and to the hurry of the comedians, poets, actors, and *judges*, to go to the supper which concluded the business of the day. See "Eccl." v. 1178.

† Addressed by the actor to the judges of the prize.

‡ A line in the "Hippolytus" which had given great offence, see p. 243, v. 123.—Here and in what follows, Bacchus pays Euripides in his own philosophic coin vulgarized after his own (Bacchus's) fashion. The intention of the author has been made clearer by a little amplification.

§ See Peisthetairus in "The Birds" when he is invited to the mansion of the Hoopoe p. 175.

Chorus.

Happy is the man possessing
The superior holy blessing
Of a judgement and a taste
Accurate, refined and chaste;*
As it plainly doth appear
In the scene presented here;
Where the noble worthy Bard
Meets with a deserved reward,
Suffer'd to depart in peace
Freely with a full release,
To revisit once again
His kindred and his countrymen—
Hence moreover
You discover,
That to sit with Socrates,
In a dream of learned ease;†
Quibbling, counter-quibbling, prating,
Argufying and debating
With the metaphysic sect,
Daily sinking in neglect,
Growing careless, incorrect,
While the practice and the rules
Of the true poetic Schools
Are renounced or slighted wholly,
Is a madness and a folly.

Pluto.

Go forth with good wishes and hearty good-will,
And salute the good people on Pallas's hill;
Let them hear and admire father Æschylus still
In his office of old which again he must fill:
—You must guide and direct them,
Instruct and correct them,
With a lesson in verse,
For you'll find them much worse;
Greater fools than before, and their folly much more,
And more numerous far than the blockheads of yore—
—And give Cleophon‡ this,
And bid him not miss,

* The style of the original seems to be taken from that of the moral and instructive verse intended for the improvement of children and young persons.

† It is curious to see Aristophanes' opinion as to the cause of the defects which he so frequently notices in Euripides; namely, that they arose from an indolent philosophic curiosity, and the want of a true zeal for the perfection of his art.

‡ See note, p. 277, other names of obscure demagogues occur in the original.

But be sure to attend
To the summons I send:
To Nicomachus* too,
And the rest of the crew
That devise and invent
  New taxes and tribute,
Are summonses sent,
  Which you'll mind to distribute.
Bid them come to their graves,
Or, like runaway slaves,
If they linger and fail,
We shall drag them to jail;
Down here in the dark
With a brand and a mark.
  Æs. I shall do as you say;
But the while I'm away,
Let the seat that I held
Be by Sophocles fill'd,
As deservedly reckon'd
My pupil and second
In learning and merit
And tragical spirit—
—And take special care;
Keep that reprobate there
Far aloof from the Chair;
Let him never sit in it
An hour or a minute,
By chance or design
To profane what was mine.

P. Bring forward the torches!—The Chorus shall wait
And attend on the Poet in triumph and state
With a thundering chaunt of majestical tone
To wish him farewell, with a tune of his own.

* Nicomachus, see Mitford's History, ch. 22, sec. 1.

[Hexameters.]

In order to give English Hexameters a fair chance, it should be recollected that they are essentially a very slow and solemn measure, each line consisting of six bars, and each bar either of two crotchets, or of a crotchet and two quavers —whereas, the English Heroic verse contains only two bars and a half, and in those instances in which the half bar is placed at the end, may be regarded as a truncated form of the scazon Iambic: the regular metrical Hexameter may consequently be considered as somewhat longer, or slower at least in enunciation, than an entire Heroic couplet.

*The reader may perhaps observe an irregularity in the second line, (what the grammarians call an Anacrousis—*i. e. *unaccented syllables prefixed to the first ictus;) this would be inadmissible in the regular Classical Hexameter, but the irregularity is so little offensive to the ear, that the writer in other attempts to construct English Hexameter has found himself in more than one instance unconsciously falling into it. He has therefore preferred to leave it as it stands, an instance of the liberty which may be deemed allowable in adapting to the English language this difficult, but by no means impracticable metre.*

CHORUS.

Now may the powers of the earth give a safe and speedy departure
To the Bard at his second birth, with a prosperous happy revival;
And may the city, fatigued with wars and long revolution,
At length be brought to return to just and wise resolutions;
Long in peace to remain—Let restless Cleophon hasten
Far from amongst us here—since wars are his only diversion,
Thrace, his native land, will afford him wars in abundance.

THE PEACE.

A TRANSLATION OF PARTS OF THAT PLAY.

The proofs of this play from "We're cheated," p. 314, to "realize our hopes," p. 317 (line 218 to 300, ed. Bekk.), were corrected by Mr. Frere himself. The other parts were prepared by him for printing, except the last twenty lines, which were taken down from his dictation, but never submitted to him for correction.

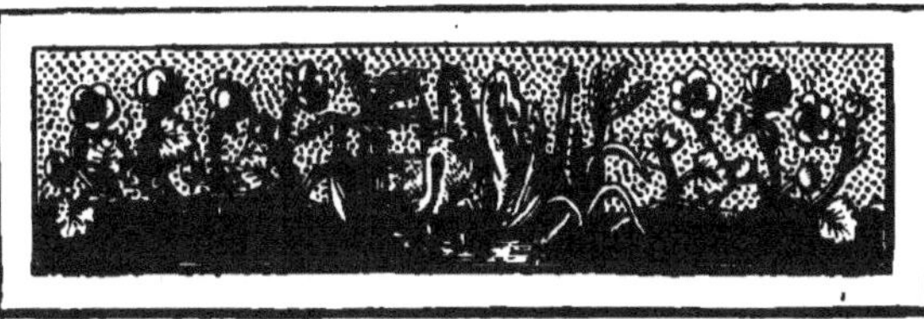

THE PEACE.

SCENE. *The entrance of Heaven, where* TRYGÆUS *appears, alights from his flying Beetle, and calls about him.*

ΕΡΜΗΣ. Πόθεν βροτοῦ με προσέβαλ'; l. 180.

Mercury.

WHAT'S that? the sound of a human voice? Oh,
Hercules,
What the plague have we got here?

Trygæus (with a foolish air of triumph).
My flying Beetle.

Mer. (assuming a degree of fury suited to the occasion).
Thou villanous, vile, audacious, desperate,
Atrocious, infamous, nefarious villain!
Who are you? What's your name? Speak out.

Try. Nefarious—

Mer. —And what was your father? Who was he?

Try. Nefarious—

Mer. Tell me your rascally name, whatever it is,
Or by all the powers of earth, thou dog, thou diest.

Try. My name's Trygæus: I'm a vine-dresser,
A peaceable neighbour and handy workman,
Not given to mischief-making nor informing.

Mer. And what's your errand here?

Try. This bit of meat,
That I brought you for a present.

Mer. Ah! poor creature
Poor soul! but how did you come?

Try. Ah! there! see there, now!
I'm not such a rascal. Go call Jupiter here;
I want to speak to him.
Mer. Speak to Jupiter?
You'll never get to the speech of the gods, I promise you;
They're all pack'd off on a journey yesterday.
Try. Whither? why where upon earth?
Mer. Upon earth!
Try. Why, where then?
Mer. To the furthermost uttermost corner of the heavens.
Try. And how came you left here behind?
Mer. I stay'd
To look to the household stuff—the pots and pans,
The tressels and the tables, and so forth.
Try. And what was the reason why they went away?
Mer. Quite tired of the Greeks. So here in their own residence
They've left the Demon of War with his establishment,
And left you at his discretion to dispose of;
And settled themselves at a distance out of the way
That they might not see you fighting constantly,
Nor hear you saying your prayers against each other.
Try. But why should they treat us in that way? Do tell me.
Mer. Because you were always wilfully bent on war
In spite of them, when they were giving you means
To have made a peace. If the Spartans had the advantage
They bit their lips and mutter'd amongst themselves,
"Ah! now, my little Athenian, you shall pay for it."
And if the little Athenians got the better,
Ever so little (when the Spartans came
To treat for peace), they scream'd and made an uproar.
"It's all a trick—by Jove!—By the holy goddess
We're cheated, we're betray'd!—No, never trust them,
Keep Pylos.[1]—They'll come back here fast enough."
Try. That was the style of the thing, to be sure, exactly.
Mer. So I doubt if you're ever likely to see Peace
As long as you live.—
Try. Why what's become of her?

---

[1] A fortified insular point on the Lacedæmonian coast, occupied by the Athenians.

Mer. The Demon of War has plunged her into a pit.
Try. A pit?
Mer. Yes, here below—look here—what a heap
Of stones he has whelm'd upon her to keep her down.
Try. And what does he mean to do with us?—What will he do?
Mer. I don't know much about it—only I saw him
Bringing in a mortar when he came last night,
A monstrous, oversized, uncommon mortar.
Try. What's that for?—What is it meant for, do you think?
Mer. To pound the cities of Greece in, I suppose—
But I'll move off—for he'll be here, I reckon,
He's bustling and banging about him there within.
Try. And I'll run off too—There—I'm sure I heard him,
And the warlike sound of that tremendous mortar.

[*A change of Scene.*—WAR *appears on one side with his mortar*—TRYGÆUS *on the other is watching his proceedings.—It is to be remarked that in the ancient Theatres the back of the stage was divided by a projection which made scenes of this kind less inconsistent with probability than the* "asides" *of the modern stage.*

War. O mortal men!—disastrous, dismal mortals!
How miserably must you be mash'd and mangled!
Try (*aside*). Oh, bless me, what a monster of a mortar!
And what a monster he is, and what a countenance!
That's he, to be sure, that people run away from,
Grim-visaged War, that frightens every body.
War. Thrice wretched Prasians, thrice and three times thrice,
Your doleful doom is destined for to-day.
Try. That's no concern of ours—we need not mind it—
The Lacedæmonians may look to that—
War. O Megara, Megara, how must thou be minced
With pickle and sauce, and pounded and confounded.
Try. Why, what a vengeance has he vow'd against them!
War. O Sicily, Sicily, Sicily must be sliced
With other sundry cities.—Stop a minute,
I must mix some Athenian honey with the mess.

Try. No! not the Athenian honey—let me advise you,
Don't use the Athenian—save it, it's so dear.
War (*not perceiving Trygæus*).
Holloh there, Skirmish!

Enter SKIRMISH.

Skir. Here, sir!
War. You'll get beat, boy,
You're loitering there.—Do you know this Fist of mine;
Is it strong, do you think? [*Holding his fist close to his face.*
Skir. Yes, sure—quite strong of garlic.
War. Will you bring me the pestle this instant?
Skir. La! why surely
We've never a one; we came but yesterday.
War. Will you get me one from Athens, sirrah—this instant?
Skir. Ay, that's what I must, or I shall howl for it.
Try. (*to the Chorus*). Alas! what shall we do? what shall we do?
(O miserable mankind!) if he gets the pestle,
We perish utterly, for there he'll sit
And pound the Cities with it at his ease.
Oh, blessed Bacchus, break the bearer's neck
Before he brings that cursed pestle back.
War. Holloh there.
Skir. Here.
War. Have you brought it?
Skir. Truly, indeed,
The Athenian pestle is lost—the tanner* I mean
That pounded and confounded Greece—he has perish'd.
Try. Well! heavenly Goddess! he has done right at last.
He could not have perish'd at a better moment,
Nor more conveniently nor seasonably,
Than at the present most alarming crisis,
When we were ready to be soused in sauce.
War. What ails you—can't you get me one from Sparta?
Make haste—
Skir. I will, sir.
War. And come back directly.
Try. What will become of us? our time draws near:
But if any amongst you here have been initiated

* Cleon.

In Samothrace, let them say their prayers immediately
For a mischief to overtake the messenger.

Skir. Good lack! good lack! oh dear! oh dear! oh dear!

War. Who's there? What, have not you brought it?

Skir. No forsooth,
The Spartans have lost that villanous pestle of theirs.* * Brasidas.

War. How's that, you scoundrel?

Skir. Sending it to Thrace
They lent it out from home, and so they lost it—

Try. That's well! Well done, ye twins of Jupiter![1]
There's some hope left. Ye mortal men, take courage!

War. There, clear away the things, and take them in,
And I'll go make a pestle for the purpose.

[*Exeunt* War *and* Skirmish; *manent* Trygæus *and Chorus.*

Try. Now we may sing the song that Datis made
To that rascally tune of his, "*Rejoice, rejoice,*
Be joyful and rejoice"—now, noble Grecians,
This is the time to have done with wars and tumults;
(To deliver Peace, and drag her up to daylight,
That's the friend and benefactor of us all,)
Before any other pestle interposes.

Come all! Come yeomen! merchants! artisans!
And denizens and resident foreigners!
And islanders, and all, come all in a body;
Bring your poles, your planks and levers, and your pulleys and your ropes,
Fortune favours our endeavours, we shall realize our hopes.—

Some Scenes follow of considerable humour, and which must have presented a striking theatrical effect when combined with the music, ballet, action, and machinery of the original representation. War is supposed to fall asleep; but the Chorus, instead of assisting in the rescue of Peace, persevere in their old habits of singing and dancing. Trygæus remonstrates; they negociate and compromise for permission to cut a few more capers, after which the different states of Greece unite in the labour of dragging up Peace

[1] Castor and Pollux, the patron deities of Sparta.

from the bottom of the well, with various observations from Trygæus as to the different degrees of backwardness or alacrity with which they contribute to the work; till she is at last drawn up by the exertions of the agricultural part of the community.

[MERCURY *brings forward* PEACE, *who had been rescued from her subterraneous confinement, and presents her to the Chorus of Rustics.*

ΕΡΜ. Ὦ σοφώτατοι γεωργοί. l. 586.

Wise and worthy country-people! Listen to the words I say,
If you wish to hear of Peace, or why she was removed away:
Phidias—was the first beginning; his indictment, and undoing,
First alarm'd his friend and patron for his own approaching ruin.
Pericles—incensed with terror (to bewilder, and distract
Your malignant dangerous humours) risking an outrageous act,
Singly set the town on fire, and blew the blaze from sea to sea,
Kindled from the petty spark of that Megarian decree;
Overshadowing all the land with smoky clouds and smouldering reek,
Darkening all our cheerful days, and drawing tears from every cheek;
Till the figs, the vines, and olives, and the very jugs and jars,
Bounced about and broke each other, as associates in the wars.

Try. Well, I never heard of this—nor I never understood
Phidias was her connexion,—nor a kinsman of her blood.

Cho. No,—nor I, before you told us—but her comely look betrays
Her relation to the artist—"Live and learn" the proverb says.

Mer. (*in continuation*). Then the cities of your empire—when the rival states were seen,
Snarling in each other's faces,—full of bitterness and spleen;
Dreading arbitrary taxes, form'd apart their private leagues,
And prevail'd upon the Spartans by their presents and intrigues;

They (according to their natures), avaricious, bold, and base,
Repudiating Peace espoused War's vixen furies in her place;
But their land and tillage suffer'd, when our galleys, in return,
Retaliating their aggression, sail'd to plunder, waste, and burn,
Ruining their helpless peasants, and the harmless corn and wine.

Try. Yes! and they were rightly served for cutting down those figs of mine!

Cho. Rightly served—I had a jar, an earthen vessel of my own,
Held half a dozen comb of corn, the tyrants smash'd it with a stone.

Mer. (*in continuation*). Then the country people flocking like the victims to a fold,
Found themselves within the city fairly sacrificed and sold;
Pining for their old refreshments, cooling juices, early fruit;
Gazing at the Rhetoricians, hungry, destitute, and mute,
They perceiving their advantage (with a people poor and tame,
Broken-hearted and dependent) drove her off whene'er she came;
Often turning and returning with her offers in her hand,
Praying to be re-admitted to this fair and lovely land;
But the speakers all combined with pitchforks of collusive lies,
Thrust her headlong from the ramparts and began to tyrannize
(With their treasonable charges) over all the first and best,
And the richest of our subjects—and to ransack every chest:—
Made a mess of confiscations which they dealt to you for food,
And with hasty condemnations train'd you to the taste of blood;
For the City pale and sickly,—lonely, lurid, and forlorn—
Sat in stench and darkness waiting for the victims to be torn,
And whene'er the jails were open'd, with devouring fury pounced

On the wealthy carrion paunches cast before her and denounced.
Lashes, stripes, and groans were sounding, and the States that heard the crash
Stopt the mouths of our accusers with a plug of present cash,
Thus they rose to wealth and greatness, Greece declined to want and ruin,
Such were all your faults and errors, this was all the *Tanner's* doing.

Trygæus.

Gentle Hermes! prithee cease—
Let the man remain in peace—
Press no farther—Let him go—
Leave him—where he lies—below.
Leave him—if he was by nature
Avaricious—and ambitious;
A seditious,—and pernicious
Noisy sycophant, and prater—
A corrupt calumniator—
And a tyrant, and a traitor
To the state and her allies:
Let us leave him where he lies.

Mer. (*to the Chorus, supporting Peace, who remains silent and angry*). Ho! she won't speak to you; she has been insulted
And injured and offended, and she feels it.—

Try. Perhaps she would speak her mind to you in private.

Mer. (*with a tone of coaxing kindness*). Come, dearest, let me hear it—in a whisper—
All your complaints against them: you detest
Those nasty straps of theirs—I know you do;
Yes, and their buckles—beyond any woman.

[*Here Peace appears to be whispering to Mercury.*

Ay, there, I hear you—that's the thing—I thought so.

[*To Trygæus and the Chorus in a different tone.*

Hear you there, the complaint she makes against you.
She came (she says) after the affair of Pylos,
Of her own accord, with a trunk brimful of treaties,
And was outvoted and expell'd repeatedly.

Try. Ah, that was very wrong—But you'll forgive us;
Our souls were in the tan-pits[1] all that time.
Mer. (*after attending to a whisper from Peace*).
Hear now this question which she ask'd this instant:
"Which of you all is her worst enemy?
And who are her good friends that abhor bloodshed?"
Try. Her greatest friend of all? Cleonymus.
Mer. What kind of a soldier is Cleonymus?
Try. A noble warrior, only that he is subject
To fits of absence in the warmth of action,
And so sometimes mislays his shield and loses it.
Mer. Hear now this other question that she asks me:
"Who is your chief commander in the assembly?"
Try. Hyperbolus is the governor there at present.
—But what's the matter? why do you turn aside?
—What makes her make those faces?
Mer. Merely loathing,—
Disgust at the people for so poor a choice.
Try. Well then, we'll leave him off. The case is this:
The state being taken suddenly by surprise,
Forlorn and naked, just from decency
Has slipt him on in a hurry for the moment.
Mer. How can this turn to good? she bids me ask you.
Try. Somehow; we shall do better in some measure.
It happens he's a lampmaker—Now before
We groped out matters in the dark at random,
But now by lamplight we shall see things plainly.
Mer. (*after listening to another whisper*). Hah! hah! hah!
What a set of questions has she bid me ask!
Try. Why what?
Mer. All kind—things out of date, from the time she left us.
She asks you what's become of Sophocles?
Try. He's well, but something strange has happen'd.
Mer. What?
Try. From being Sophocles he's turn'd Simonides.
Mer. How so?
Try. He's grown penurious and greedy
In his old age; impatient after gain.
Mer. And the famous Poet, old Cratinus?

[1] Alluding to the administration of Cleon.

Try. Died
At the time of the invasion.
Mer. How did it happen?
Try. Quite struck to the heart—He fainted and fell ill
At seeing a favourite jar of wine demolish'd;
And other horrors that occurr'd at that time—
—Therefore, sweet Peace, we'll keep and cherish you,
And never part with you from this time forward.
Mer. Agreed. Then take this lusty damsel here,
Vintage by name, and keep her for your wife.
Return to the farm, and live in joy together,
Begetting generations of young grapes.
Try. Come here, my charmer—kiss me. Mercury!
I say now—Mercury! might I venture, think you,
To fall to work like a good husbandman?
Mer. You had best refresh and rest yourself a little.
—This other virgin, fair Negotiation,
Must be presented instantly to the senate.
Try. Oh, happy senate! how I envy you
That fair Negotiation![1] three days' rations
Of soup, and flesh, and fish, and boil'd, and roast!
(*To Mercury, with an air of joyous familiarity.*)
Dear Mercury, fare you well!
Mer. (*with gravity*). The same to thee.
O, mortal, fare thee well—Remember me.
Try. Hoy there! my jolly Beetle! we must be going.
Mer. He's gone away, friend.
Try. Where? which way? what for?
Mer. Promoted to the rank of Thunder-bearer
In Jupiter's chariot.
Try. Well then—What must I do?
Which way must I get back, pray?
Mer. Well enough.
The Goddess here will take you—never fear.
Try. Come here, dear damsels. There's a multitude
Erect with expectation waiting for you.

---

[1] Alluding to the public entertainments on such occasions. See "The Acharnians," p. 46.

Parabasis.

(The address of the Chorus to the audience on behalf of the Author.)

When a comical poet so far misbehaves
As to bring his own chorus, to praise him before us,
We think that the Wardens, with wands and with staves,
Should perforce interpose, and disperse them with blows;
But, heavenly goddess, there never was known
Such a glorious Author, as this of our own,
That deserved such a crown of immortal renown.
—'Tis fit you should know it—This eminent poet,
Whose rivals are crush'd and reduced to the dust,
Has scouted and routed their paltry conceits ;
And expell'd and exposed them as beggarly cheats ;
With their jests ten times told against hunger and cold,
And a merry device about vermin and lice,
That made Hercules hungry, impatient and angry :
And then for a feat made him raven and eat,
And growl over his meat; or brought slaves to be beat,
And all for the sake of this noble conceit,
That when they're in tears some comrade appears
With his jibes and his jeers and this notable jest,
(Which is just like the rest, and as good as the best:)
" Your shoulders, I doubt, have been put to the rout,
Some sudden attack has invaded your back
With a cudgel or lash." This detestable trash,
This contemptible style, so degrading and vile—
His efforts have banish'd—at length it has vanish'd,
And since in its place he has built from the base
A palace of verse, polish'd and terse,
Rear'd with rapidity, framed with solidity,
In majestical style, a magnificent pile.
—His slaves are enfranchised and free from the whip:
He has scorn'd from the first to descend and to dip,
Peddling and meddling in private affairs:
To detect and collect every petty defect
Of husband and wife, and domestical life ;
But intrepid and bold, like Alcides of old,
When the rest stood aloof, put himself to the proof
In his country's behoof, essaying his might

In a perilous fight: descending downright
On a dismal adventure, daring to enter
The terrible Tanpits,[1] where Stygian stenches
Astounded the senses: and sights on all sides
Of the horns and the hides: and a horrible din
(With a howl and a grin) from the monster within,
And flashes that came, from his eyeballs like flame,
His locks all alive with a poisonous list
Of sycophant serpents that twisted and hiss'd;
—This horrid Hobgoblin our hero beheld,
But disdain'd at the sight to be daunted or quell'd,
And stood like a rampire, defying the Vampire,
Defending your empire, risking his blood
For the general good; besides and moreover,
When this was all over, his general behaviour
Was such as entitles him justly to favour.
On former occasions he never made use
Of the credit he gain'd to corrupt or seduce;
But pack'd up his awls, after gaining the day,
Contented and joyous, and so went away:
Never molesting,
In earnest or jesting;
Never at rest,
But doing his best;
In each obligation
Befitting his station;
Therefore we make bold
To request young and old,
And good boys and good men,
To befriend him again.
And those that are bald
Are especially call'd
To favour his cause
With the warmest applause:
For all men will say,
When we're feasting away,
At the close of the play—
" Bring forward the best
For our bald-pated guest!

---

[1] Alluding to his attack on the administration of Cleon.

Let nothing be spared
For the bald-pated bard."
And in all other places,
In similar cases,
Such honours as these shall all people bestow
On his partners in baldness wherever they go,
For his noble intention
And glorious invention
And the boldness and baldness and breadth of his brow.

Οὐ γὰρ ἔσθ' ἥδιον.—l. 1105.

How sweet it is to see the new-sown corn-field fresh and even,
With blades just springing from the soil that only ask a shower from Heaven.
There, while kindly rains are falling, indolently to rejoice,
Till some worthy neighbour calling, cheers you with his hearty voice.
"Well, with weather such as this, let us hear, Trygæus, tell us
What should you and I be doing? You're the king of us good fellows."
Since it pleases Heaven to prosper your endeavours, friend, and mine,
Let us have a merry meeting, with some friendly talk and wine.
In the vineyard there's your lout, hoeing in the slop and mud—
Send the wench and call him out, this weather he can do no good.
Dame, take down two pints of meal, and do some fritters in your way;
Boil some grain and stir it in, and let us have those figs, I say.
Send a servant to my house—any one that you can spare,
* * * * * pie of hare,[1]
There should be four of them in all, if the cat has left them right;
We heard her racketing and tearing round the larder all last night.

---

[1] The Translator had forgotten all but the hare-pies.

Boy, bring three of them to us—take the other to my father:
Cut some myrtle for our garlands, sprigs in flower, or blossoms rather.
Give a shout upon the way to Charinades our neighbour,
To join our drinking bout to-day, since Heaven is pleased to bless our labour.

THEOGNIS RESTITUTUS.

THE PERSONAL HISTORY OF THE POET

THEOGNIS

REDUCED FROM AN ANALYSIS OF HIS EXISTING FRAGMENTS.

A hundred of these Fragments translated or paraphrased in English Metre are arranged in their proper biographical order with an accompanying commentary—with a Preface in which the suggestion of Mr. Clinton, as to the true date of the Poet's birth (viz. in Olymp. 59), is confirmed by internal evidence.

THEOGNIS RESTITUTUS.

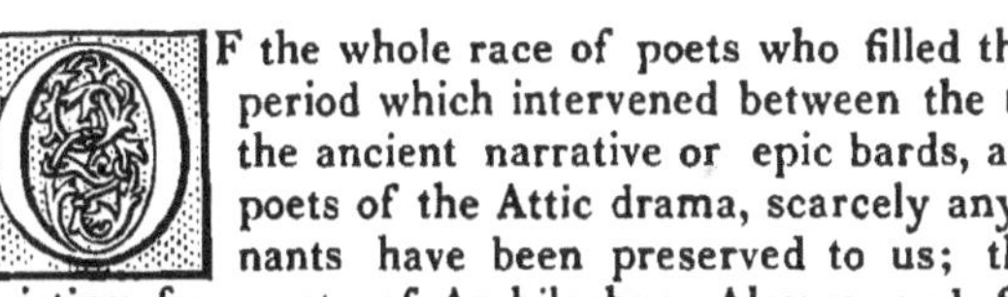

OF the whole race of poets who filled the long period which intervened between the time of the ancient narrative or epic bards, and the poets of the Attic drama, scarcely any remnants have been preserved to us; the few existing fragments of Archilochus, Alcæus and Sappho excite the regret of the scholar by the beauty of the versification and language; but the loss of their entire works is also to be regretted on another account:—They and the class to which they belong, were decidedly and peculiarly the poets of active life, differing in this respect from their epic predecessors and from the dramatic tribe which succeeded them.—Their lives were not passed in wandering from town to town with occasional entertainment at the public charge, as tradition (applying to the individual, what was characteristic of a class) has recorded of Homer; nor were they menial minstrels, such as Homer himself has described; established, like Phemius or Demodocus, in the mansion of a petty Sovereign; neither were they occupied like the dramatists, in contests for a theatrical prize, engaged in schooling their actors and uniting in their vocation the several offices of manager, ballet-master and director of the band.

With the poets above mentioned, verse was the vehicle of their feelings and passions, excited as they were by the tumult of an agitated existence; feuds, factions, expatriation to distant colonies, sudden usurpations, revolution and exile were the elements by which they were surrounded, and of whose influence they partook ; and they themselves appear sometimes to have been among the leading spirits of these tempests ; the faculty of composing animated and popular poetry giving to the person who applied it to party purposes, a power of producing impressions, less forcible indeed in the first instance, but more durable and diffusive than the effect of oratory.

Hence their poetry, turning wholly upon the feelings and passions produced by the events and characters with which they were surrounded, contained, what we should call, the materials for an *Autobiography;* and we see in fact, that the ancients, who were in possession of their writings, were enabled to form a clear idea of the *Life and Times* of Alcæus and Archilochus. The loss therefore of their works is not only to be lamented by the admirers of ancient Poetry, but must be regretted, as depriving us of a view of civil and political society at a period antecedent to what is considered as the full development of Grecian civilization ; though it might be considered, perhaps more justly, in a point of view not less interesting, as an equally perfect form of the same civilization, though in some respects differently characterized ; being modified in the countries of Asia Minor and the Islands (to which the most eminent of this class of poets belong) by the circumstances of a more fertile and extended territory, by more advantageous situations for commercial enterprise, and above all, by their Colonial origin, which removing them from the influence of a locality, connected with ancient institutions, left them free to proceed to development and decay, by a more rapid progress, than the old hidebound states, from which they had been severed.—But, it is useless to speculate upon the value of the treasures which we have lost ; or to diminish by comparison, the worth of the single remnant of this school, which has been preserved to us.

Theognis belongs undoubtedly to the class of poets above described ; a native of Megara in Greece, he was nearly the last in point of time, and far from being the first in point of poetical merit ; yet there is an air of truth and reality in his verses, accompanied by a general terseness of expression, which gains upon the attention of the reader, and which is apt to engage him to frequent reperusals and reflections. The style is in fact, what according to modern notions of poetic language, would be characterized as prosaic; consisting as it does, of the expressions and phrases of ordinary speech, never in any respect vulgar, but wholly without ornament or the affectation of ornament; it has no pretension to beauty, nor attempts at the sublime; it is the language of actual feeling arising out of real circumstances; and its title to the name of poetry must perhaps be rested on the correctness of its metre; nevertheless, this very simplicity gives to it in some respects a greater interest, as an authentic, unadorned document, illustrative of the state of social existence and domestic politics in Greece, at a period anterior to the Persian war. It should seem therefore, that an useful and agreeable addition to our knowledge of antiquity might be obtained, if the confused mass of fragments, which constitute the present text, could be reduced to a rational order, exhibiting in a regular series, the various events of the poet's life which are indicated by them, and the successive changes of circumstance and situation under which they were composed.

A task of a similar description, and of nearly equal difficulty, was accomplished several years ago, by the ingenious Mr. Stevenson of Norwich. Being a great lover of antiquities, and particularly and more especially, a most passionate admirer and collector of painted glass, he had availed himself of the treaty of Amiens, to make a tour in the Netherlands; and succeeded in purchasing many fine windows, the spoils of the monasteries, which had passed into private hands; he then returned, having agreed with the vendor that the glass should be sent after him; and so it was; but on its arrival, Mr. Stevenson was appalled by the discovery, that the lead, not having been specially included in the purchase, had been stript off; and that the treasure which he expected, was reduced to a chaos of painted glass, of all shapes, sizes, and colours. He was not however discouraged, but finally by continued patience and attention, at the end of two or three years, succeeded in recomposing the whole.

The state in which the remains of Theognis have been transmitted to us, resembles that in which Mr. Stevenson received his purchase of painted glass; but with this additional difficulty, that they are not the misarranged parts of any complete compositions, but detached pieces, the fragments of occasional poems, composed at very different times, and under very different circumstances.

Such is the confusion of the present text that, in the same page, the poet is to be found speaking of himself as rich and poor, old and young, an exile and a citizen; and so on promiscuously, without the slightest appearance of order or coherence from the beginning to the end.—Out of this confusion, an attempt is made to construct a sort of autobiography by arranging the fragments in the order of the incidents to which they refer; a task of no small difficulty; considering that the testimony of ancient authors is contradictory upon two such important points as those of the place and time of his birth. If however, renouncing all dependence upon these conflicting authorities, we recur to the evidence of the text itself, we find that the city to which he belonged was founded by Alcathous; and since all authorities are agreed, and his own testimony proves, that the name of his native city was Megara, this circumstance, as Mr. Brunck has shown, is decisive in favour of the more ancient Megara, the Megara of Greece proper. Again, the same Megara is described by the poet as exposed to imminent danger from the expected invasion of the Persians: lastly, the only other Megara, the Megara in Sicily (to which it may be added that the last mentioned circumstance would not apply) is moreover positively excluded by his mention of Sicily, as one among the number of foreign countries which he had visited.

A satisfactory conclusion with respect to the time of his birth may in like manner be deduced from internal evidence, though by a process somewhat more circuitous. At the time when he was practically philosophizing upon the subject of hard drinking, we must conclude him to have been a very young man; and this paroxysm of experimental conviviality cannot be supposed to have been of very long duration; but it appears, that during its continuance, verses illustrative of his theory and practice (Frag. VI., VII., VIII.) were addressed to two of his poetic and toping companions, Simonides and Onomacritus. Now the only time in which it is at all probable that these two persons could have been associated as joint compotators with Theognis, must have been that period of Hipparchus' reign, subsequent to the arrival of Simonides, and anterior to the exile of Onomacritus: now this first arrival of Simonides is fixed by Mr. Clinton (the highest authority on such questions) in the year 525 B.C. With respect to the age of Simonides at the time of his arrival at Athens, there is no difficulty, his birth being fixed, by the most undoubted testimony (that of his own verses) in the year 556. With respect to Theognis, the case is different; chronologers are agreed in assigning to him the 59th Olympiad 544 B.C. but whether as the date of his birth, or the period at which he became famous and celebrated, is a point which their opposite and ambiguous testimony has left undetermined; but the internal evidence is wholly in favour of the conclusion which Mr. Clinton has suggested; namely, that "*Theognis might be supposed to have been born, rather than to have flourished in Olympiad* 59." Upon this supposition, he must have been twelve years younger than Simonides, and their respective ages at the time of Simonides' arrival would have been nineteen and thirty-one; he might then at the age of three-and-twenty have illustrated his philosophic theory of inebriety, in verses addressed to Simonides and Onomacritus, after which there would remain the latter half of Hipparchus' reign, six or seven years, in any one of which, the exile of Onomacritus might have taken place. The tone of his verses to Simonides in three different instances, shews them to have been addressed to a person older than himself, and is utterly irreconcilable with the supposition of his having been a man of fame and celebrity nineteen years before the time when he could have had an opportunity of forming that very free and familiar acquaintance, which seems, at one time, to have subsisted between them. This is particularly manifest in a fragment, which is not translated, but of which the original will be found in the portion of his poetry lately discovered. He is apologizing for his debaucheries, in verses addressed to Simonides, and justifying them by an appeal to poetical mythology!! Supposing the writer to have been in his senses, such verses could not possibly have been composed by a man of mature age, and addressed to a person many years younger, with whom he had only become lately acquainted.—On the other hand, if we suppose him to have

See Fasti Hellenici, vol. ii. p. 7.

been the younger man, and that his acquaintance with Simonides had taken place when he was at the age of nineteen or twenty; the whole becomes perfectly natural and probable. A young man of wealth and (as far as it appears) entirely his own master, careless at that time of money, but eager for knowledge, and passionately addicted to the joint arts of music and poetry, would hardly have failed to avail himself of the advantages for improvement and instruction, which were afforded him by the establishment of so celebrated a man of letters in his immediate vicinity; and Simonides, who had been attracted and fixed at the court of Hipparchus by "great gifts and pensions," would not, it may be presumed, have avoided the society of a young poet of rank and wealth, who manifested a wish for instruction, and a willingness to pay for it. Upon this footing an intimacy might have been formed very rapidly; his literary instructor might very properly under these circumstances, have assumed the character of a mentor; and his moral remonstrance might have been met with a bantering reply (for such it is), an argumentum ad hominem, an appeal to his own authentic precedents and examples, attested by fable and poetry! "How could Simonides, a mythologist and a poet, venture to disapprove of the conduct of Jupiter!" These then are evidently the bantering verses of a young man replying to the admonition of a senior. Again, the verses in which he represents Simonides, as presiding at a convivial meeting, and not knowing how to conduct himself, are suitable enough to the petulant vivacity of a young man, who with a sincere respect and regard for his senior, cannot forbear to notice his defects in manner and behaviour. Criticisms of this kind, which if they proceeded from a person of more advanced age, would be felt as seriously offensive, are frequently received from a younger companion with perfect good humour; and for a very good reason—they do not imply contempt. The same difference of age is marked equally, though in a very different manner, at a later period, when Theognis must have been seriously disgusted—when he declines Simonides' invitation, and anticipates that the lines in which he conveys his refusal (Frag. LXIII.), will be communicated to his enemies; notwithstanding all this, and the irritation and agitation of his own mind, there is in this fragment an evident tone of forbearance and reserve, betokening the remains of habitual respect; such as he might be supposed to retain for his senior, and the instructor of his youth. From all these considerations, we should infer, that it is impossible to suppose the 59th Olympiad to have been the period of his celebrity—such a supposition (even allowing him to have attained to celebrity at the earliest age possible) would place him more in advance of Simonides in point of years, than, from what has been said above, it should seem that Simonides must have been with respect to him. We must therefore incline to that chronology which marks this Olympiad as the time of his birth—upon this supposition, he would have been thirty years of age at the time of the murder of Hipparchus, which seems to have given occasion to some lines in which he discussed the question of tyrannicide (Frag. XXIII.) and to others in which he speaks slightingly of the solemnities of a royal funeral (Frag. XXIV. and XXV.).

These lines are such as no man living in exile would have ventured to write, the friends of the deceased ruler (as appears from the magnificence with which the funeral is celebrated) being evidently still in power. The poet therefore, at the time when they were composed, must have been a citizen of Megara; the funeral, moreover, must have taken place in some state immediately adjoining to that town, at so short a distance, as to make his non-attendance a marked act, which he thought it necessary to justify and explain.

The reform of Cleisthenes at Athens, and the revolution in Megara, of which the materials had been long in preparation, appear to have been events nearly contemporary, and probably had a reciprocal influence on each other.— Upon this supposition, it would have taken place in the 35th year of the poet's age. Three years after, we find him an exile, a witness of the devastation of the Lelantian plain, and cursing the Corinthians, by whose example and intrigues the confederate army under Cleomenes had been broken up, leaving the Thebans and Eubœans exposed to defeat and invasion.

We then find him at Thebes, living (as he says himself) as an exile, and exposed to the mortifications incident to a life of exile.—Thebes seems to have been the scene of those hopes of a triumphant restoration, which he and his brother emigrants at one time entertained; (see Frag. LXXVIII.) and all mention of it is accordingly omitted, in the verses composed long afterwards, when by the indulgence of the ruling party, he had been permitted to return. Thebes had been the *Coblentz* of the party; a place of which the name was not to be pronounced by a returned emigrant. Some disagreements, some disappointments, which are discoverable by the glimmer of inference and allusion, (but of which as they are foreign to the question of chronology, it may be sufficient to say that they might have been comprised in a short space of time,) combined with the pressure of utter poverty, had the effect of inducing the poet to separate from his companions, and to seek his fortune for himself. Sicily was the great mart for destitute men of talent, and to Sicily he repaired, being then, it may be supposed, in his 40th or 41st year.—Then follows the period to which we may refer all those fragments in which he complains of poverty and degrading occupation, in which he vindicates himself against imputations of meanness and parsimony, and in which he exults in the gradual acquisition of property.

Nothing is more remarkable in a view of private life among the Greeks, than the rapid transition from wealth to poverty, and again from poverty to wealth; and Theognis was destined to exhibit an example of both; for he appears to have accumulated rapidly what, considering it probably in a Megarian point of view, he regarded as a respectable amount of property; for wealth at Syracuse was proverbially tenfold the amount of what would have constituted wealth in any other Grecian state.

The only historical fact connected with his sojourn in Sicily is the siege of Syracuse by Gelo, acting at that time as lieutenant to Hippocrates (as related by Herodotus in his brief summary of the steps by which Gelo had risen to power, Book VII.) This siege was terminated by the joint intervention of the Corinthians and Corcyreans, under whose mediation a treaty was concluded. We learn from the testimony of Suidas, that Theognis composed a long poem, (*εἰς τοὺς σωθέντας τῶν Συρακουσίων ἐν τῇ πολιορκίᾳ*) verses " addressed during the siege to the survivors of the

Syracusan army;" for the siege, as Herodotus states, had been preceded by the entire overthrow of their army on the banks of the Elorus; and when we consider that the flight of their routed forces must have followed the same track which was afterwards traversed by the Athenians in their retreat from Syracuse, and that Gelo, as the general of cavalry, must have been in pursuit of them, the defeat (as indeed we may infer from its being followed by the immediate siege of Syracuse itself) must have been little short of extermination; and those of the army, who, effecting their escape, formed afterwards the most efficient part of the garrison, might well have been addressed as *τοὺς σωθέντας*, the survivors.

Four verses are still to be found, which may be supposed to belong to this poem (Frag. C.); the description of the *ἄχρηστοι* being applied to the expelled Gamori as contrasted with the party who defended the city.

In the chronological table annexed by Professor Müller to his admirable work on the Dorians, the first year of the 72nd Olympiad B.C. 492 is assigned as an approximate date to the battle of Elorus; considering the events which must have intervened, the siege of Syracuse and the death of Hippocrates, followed by the usurpation of Gelo, who in the year 492 B.C. (see "Fasti Hellenici," ii. p. 24) made himself master of Gela, this seems to be the latest date that can be assigned to it; but either this date or a year earlier might afford sufficient time for a man of talents and activity, (living in a wealthy and liberal community, earning as much as he could, and spending as little as possible) to acquire considerable wealth. Adventurers to India and Mexico (even without extraordinary economy, such as Theognis seems to have practised) have sometimes realized good fortunes in a shorter time; and to come to a nearer and more apposite instance, Gorgias and Hippias must have made money much faster and probably spent it more liberally than Theognis appears to have done, at least if we may judge from his verses to Timagoras and Damocles (Frag. XCIII. and XCVIII.). This difficulty, if indeed it be such, might have been eluded; for there is nothing but the date (which, in contradiction to all moral probability, would make Theognis an older man than Simonides) which should prevent us from assigning the verses, in which, after his return to Megara, he alludes to the impending invasion of Persia, to a later period than the battle of Marathon; for it is most certain that the alarms of invasion were not terminated by that battle. Corsini, as quoted by Professor Müller, assigns the poem noticed by Suidas to the last year of the 73rd Olympiad, which would have allowed two additional Olympiads, during which Theognis might have been growing rich; and the deprecation of the approach of old age might not appear quite absurd, in verses composed two years afterwards, at the age of sixty-one. In the chronological table of Professor Müller, Theognis is said to be still composing poetry in the 2nd year of the 74th Olympiad, the year immediately preceding the march of Xerxes.

As the grounds upon which this determination is founded are not stated, we are at a loss to guess whether Professor Müller refers to the verses now in existence, in which the apprehensions of a Persian invasion are expressed, or whether his extensive and acute researches have furnished him with other evidence in proof that Theognis was composing poetry at the time which he states. At this period he would have been, according to the proposed date, sixty-one years of age; according to that which has been commonly received, eighty-five; a time of life at which no man who retained his faculties would seriously deprecate, as he does, the approach of old age! If, therefore, the verses now in existence are those which Professor Müller had in view, we must suppose him (and the rather, as he has not noted in his tables any time for the poet's birth) to have rejected tacitly the earlier date for that event; being, as it is, inconsistent with the latest of his existing compositions. Any difficulty, therefore, which there might appear in supposing Theognis to have accumulated at Syracuse, in the space of twelve years, what to a Megarian would have appeared considerable wealth, might have been eluded by adopting the determination of Corsini, and prolonging his residence in Sicily to the end of the 73rd or the 1st year of the 74th Olympiad.

But the writer of these pages would not consent to avail himself of this evasion, or dissemble the strong conviction impressed on his mind, that the Corinthian negotiator who, in conjunction with the Corcyrean, had acted as mediator between Gelo and the besieged Syracusans, was also the mediator between the poet and his fellow-citizens of Megara. It should seem that, having secured the good offices of his Corinthian friend (whose dexterity and powers of persuasion are alluded to in the enigmatic mention of Sisyphus the Corinthian), he removed to the Peloponnese, to await the result. It was at this time that he presented himself at Sparta, and had the good fortune to be well received, a circumstance which he probably considered as of some importance in giving him additional consideration in the eyes of his fellow-citizens; for it is observable that, in the accounts which remain to us of the most eminent persons of Greece, any mark of esteem or respect which might have been shown them by the community of Sparta is always recorded as an authoritative testimony in their favour.

To this residence in Lacedæmon we may assign those verses (Frag. CII.) in which Theotimus is mentioned; the melancholy images which they exhibit are not apt to beset the fancy at a much earlier age. While we are ascending the hill of life, the acclivity before us screens the future from our sight; but when we have reached the summit, and are preparing to descend, it bursts suddenly upon us, and remains before us as a fixed and constant prospect.[1] These lines therefore cannot, it should seem, with any probability be referred to a period anterior to his long residence in Sicily, but would be perfectly suitable to the period of life (54 or 55) at which he obtained his recall from banishment; an event of which, at the time when they (Frag. CIII.) were written, he must have been in immediate expectation. There are also other verses written in Lacedæmon, alluding to the trust which he reposed in his friend; for it should seem that money must have been an ingredient among the other considerations under which his recall was effected. The verses in which the apprehension of a Persian invasion is alluded to (Frag. CV. and CVI.), have all the character of

[1] Swift says, writing to Lord Bolingbroke, "I was forty-seven years old when I began to think of Death; and the reflections upon it now begin when I wake in the morning, and end when I am going to sleep."

an emigrant very lately returned, and must have been composed about the time of the battle of Marathon; but there seems no absolute necessity for supposing that they were composed before that event. For this disappointment of Darius' expedition was followed by preparations infinitely more formidable and extensive; during which the whole Eastern world was agitated (as Herodotus describes) with musters and levies, which could not, as before, be supposed to be directed against the Athenians or Eretrians alone, but were evidently made in contemplation of the entire subjugation of Greece; there is therefore no absolute necessity for limiting the composition of these lines to a date anterior to the battle of Marathon. That they could not have been written long after, seems probable from what was before observed; that they mark the character of an emigrant very lately returned, and from the probability that a negotiation, so simple in its nature as that upon which his return depended, was not likely to have remained long in suspense.

Most of the points here mentioned will be found illustrated more at large in the running commentary which accompanies a series of translated fragments, arranged in the order here proposed. Such a work, it was thought, might afford some amusement and information to the general reader, and to young persons not far advanced in classical studies, affording, at the same time, a groundwork for the formation of a very useful schoolbook; for it so happens that, in the whole mass of Greek literature which has remained to us, nothing is to be found in a poetic form, which presents such an easy introduction to the knowledge of the language; nothing which, to the school-boy who began his Latin with Phædrus and Ovid, presents similar facilities of easy construction, short sentences, and a metre of quick recurrence, serving to fix in the memory the words and phrases which are gradually acquired. The scanty remnants of Tyrtæus, the short fragments of Solon, and some extracts from Anacreon form at present the only resources available for rudimental instruction. To this stock, it should seem, that nearly the whole of Theognis (with the exception of passages corrupt or otherwise objectionable) might be added; for it will be found, that all the other fragments may be distributed in the order here proposed.—One point, however, must be mentioned which has been omitted, and from a very humble motive. It appears that the poet, at some time previous to his emigration, describes the duties and qualifications of a Theorus (the legate charged to consult and report the responses of the oracle at Delphi) in a manner which seems to imply, that he was either aspiring to that office, or already in the exercise of it; and it appears from another fragment that he was, during the same period of his life, engaged in certain judicial functions connected with public worship. These are points which, as the writer has reason to suppose that they may have been already elucidated in works which (from an ignorance of the language in which they are written) are to him inaccessible, he has judged it more expedient to pass over.[1]

The motives which induce him to produce such a work, and to give it somewhat of a more popular form, have been already explained; in the mean time, a just deference to the judgment of more learned and accurate scholars has dictated this essay,—in which the main chronological conclusions, the result of much time and reflection bestowed upon the subject, are briefly, and, to the best of his ability, as far as the obscurity of the subject will permit, distinctly stated.

SYNOPSIS OF HISTORICAL DATES.

THE following table may perhaps be convenient to the reader, as presenting at one view the series of dates which is here assumed.

Olympiad 59. B. C. 544. Theognis born in this Olympiad, and probably in the beginning of it; for thirty-nine years after, we find him and his friend Kurnus both in exile: Kurnus, who was the younger of the two,

[1] It appears from "the Knights" (p. 137) that this office of Theorus was a convenient one for "distressed gentlemen:" a probable date might therefore be assigned to these lines, after the ruin of the poet's fortunes and before his emigration.

having been a short time before that event placed in high office and authority.

B. C. 525. Theognis in his twentieth year; Simonides and Anacreon arrive at Athens, invited by Hipparchus, whose society presented a singular combination of men of genius, including Onomacritus and Lasus, the instructor of Pindar. Theognis cultivates the acquaintance of Simonides and Onomacritus. Verses of a very juvenile character, and implying very familiar intercourse, are addressed to them both. He appears to have been celebrated at a very early age for poetry of a light and licentious character, for in his first serious verses addressed to Kurnus, he speaks of his poetical reputation as being already very extensively diffused. These serious verses are communicated to his friend under a strict injunction of secrecy; and if we suppose, as is otherwise probable, that they were composed in the last years of Hipparchus' reign, and remained undivulged at the period of his death, the supposition will serve to account for what would otherwise appear extraordinary. The assassination of Hipparchus occurred in the third year of the 66th Olympiad B. C. 514, in the thirty-first year of Theognis' age; and it is singular, considering the apparent congeniality of their characters, and the sympathy implied in their joint partiality to the same individual (Simonides), that Theognis speaks so slightingly of the ceremonies of his funeral; which he even refuses to attend, and expresses his persuasion that the deceased entertained little or no regard for him; such a feeling, however, upon the supposition before stated, might have been perfectly natural. His serious and moral poetry had remained a secret communicated only to his most intimate friend, while his reputation for poetry of a different character was widely extended; but such a reputation, though it might attract notice, would not have recommended him to the esteem and friendship of a person like Hipparchus, who cultivated and encouraged poetry as an instrument of moral improvement, and a means of practical benefit to society. We are apt (and this appears to have been the case with Theognis) to feel resentment mixed with our mortification at a disparaging estimate; and our irritation is not much diminished by the consideration, that the person by whom this unfavourable estimate is formed, has in fact formed it fairly in reference to our apparent merits and character: we still regard it as a kind of injustice to be deprived of that consideration which, though the title has never been produced, we nevertheless feel to be our due. Of the two next events which are recorded in history, and which were likely to have produced a strong impression in the adjoining state of Megara, the expulsion of Hippias took place[1] B.C. 510, in the thirty-fifth year of Theognis' age.

The reform of Cleisthenes, including a total overthrow of the ancient aristocratic government of Athens, must have been effected, as may be inferred from the tables of Prof. Müller, in the following year B.C. 509, in the thirty-sixth of Theognis.

No allusion to either of these events is to be found in the scanty remains of his poetry which have been preserved to us. It seems certain, however, that about this time, and probably in some degree from the influence of foreign example, that revolution must have taken place in Megara, which the poet, judging only from the necessary operation of internal causes, had, some years before, in his first moral and serious verses, pronounced to be inevitable. This revolution does not appear to have been a hasty insurrectionary movement, but to have proceeded gradually and regularly to a crisis which obliged the poet and his friend Kurnus suddenly to leave the country.

The third expedition of Cleomenes took place, according to Professor Müller, in the year B.C. 506, in the thirty-ninth year of Theognis. He was at this time an exile, living in Eubœa, and an eye witness of the devastation of the Lelantian plain, which took place in consequence of the defeat of the Thebans and Chalcidians, immediately subsequent to the failure of Cleomenes' expedition. We then find him at Thebes, living as an exile, indulging for a while the hopes of a triumphant restoration; finally disgusted with his associates; endeavouring, and failing in his endeavour, to conciliate the faction by which he had been expelled; and ultimately determining to seek his fortune for himself.

The next historical date places him at Syracuse, at the

[1] See "Fasti Hellenici," vol. ii. p. 16.

time of the siege, an event which Herodotus, who enumerates Syracuse among the cities besieged by Gelo, mentions as having been preceded by the overthrow of the Syracusan army on the banks of the Elorus.

The first year of the 72nd Olympiad is assigned by Professor Müller as an approximate date to this battle; we may perhaps assume the same date for the siege by which it was immediately followed, viz. B. C. 492, the fifty-third year of Theognis' age.

Here, then, we have from the last known date, B. C. 506 (the time when he was driven from Eubœa), an interval of fourteen years, of which, if we allot two to his residence at Thebes, which is a large admission, considering that his stock of money when he emigrated was little or nothing, and his stock of patience apparently not very ample, there would then remain twelve years, during which, renouncing all incumbrances of rank and birth, he devoted himself earnestly, after the manner of his old instructor Simonides, to the acquisition of money, spending in the mean time as little as possible, and rejoicing in the increasing amount of his accumulations. His return appears evidently to have been a peculiar act of indulgence and exception obtained in his favour from the ruling party in Megara, the same by which he had been expelled fourteen years before. That such a favour should have been granted to a single individual, living in a situation so remote as that of Syracuse, implies the agency of some very able and influential person; and some fortunate concurrence of circumstances, affording him, in the first instance, an opportunity of securing the services and good offices of a person of this description. Such an opportunity appears to have presented itself in the arrival of the Corinthian deputy, who in conjunction with the Corcyreans, succeeded in persuading Gelo to raise the siege of Syracuse, and to rest satisfied with the cession of Camarina.

That some citizen of Corinth of distinguished political ability and address was in some way connected with the poet's return, and exerting himself to effect it, seems to be the fact which lies at the bottom of the otherwise inexplicable episode of the story of Sisyphus (Frag. CI.). Whatever difficulty there may appear in supposing him, at this time, to have amassed a satisfactory amount of property, will appear much less than that which is involved in the opposite alternative, which would suppose a similar advantageous opportunity to have occurred a second time, and to have been accompanied with the same circumstance of an able and influential citizen of Corinth undertaking, on the poet's behalf (like the fabulous old politician, his own countryman), to conciliate Persephone, the Persephone of Megara, the power from which a grant of amnesty was to be obtained.

His actual return was preceded by a short residence in the Peloponnese and a visit to Sparta, during which time the negotiation for his readmission to Megara was brought to a conclusion by the assistance of his friend and the sacrifice of a little money. If we suppose him to have returned at the eve of the battle of Marathon, B.C. 490, he would have been in his fifty-fifth year, and in this supposition there is little difficulty. The fears of a Persian invasion indeed were not terminated by that battle, but the manner in which old age is spoken of in the same lines (Frag. CV.) does not appear suitable to a more advanced period of life.

With the exception of some lines belonging to a later and undeterminate time, when he was occupied in arranging, reciting, and publishing his collected stock of poetry, there are no existing verses of Theognis which can be assigned to a later date than that of the period immediately subsequent to his return. The verses marking his ungracious reception by his own family must have been composed when the impression was recent.

THEOGNIS.

HE verses of Theognis, which, in a regular arrangement of his Fragments, appear entitled to stand as the first of the series, are those which represent him as a prosperous young heir just entering into life, and looking forward to the enjoyment of pleasure and happiness. His vows are addressed to Jupiter as the sovereign deity, and to his own immediate patron, Apollo, the founder and protector of Megara. We shall see, that at a later period, (in anticipation of the Persian invasion,) his vows are addressed separately to the same two Deities.

I.

[1] (*Gaisford*, line 1115-1118.)

Guided and aided by their holy will,
Jove and Apollo, may they guard me still,
My course of youth in safety to fulfil;
Free from all evil, happy with my wealth,
In joyous easy years of peace and health.

His amusements and accomplishments at this time, his fondness for the pipe, which he delighted to *accompany* (for it was not allowable for a gentleman to *play* upon so ungainly an instrument) and the pleasure which he took in playing on that graver and more decorous instrument the lyre, are expressed in another fragment.

II.

(*Gaisford*, 531-534.)

My heart exults the lively call obeying,
When the shrill merry pipes are sweetly playing:
With these to chaunt aloud, or to recite,
To carol and carouse, is my delight:
Or in a steadfast tone, bolder and higher,
To temper with a touch the manly lyre.

It will be seen hereafter that these lines were in all probability composed at a later period; but the very argument by which that probability is supported will show, that the cultivation of this talent must have been the pursuit of his early youth, and that he had attained to great perfection in it.

Other verses evidently composed in his early years (but

---

[1] References to the corresponding lines in Gaisford's editions of Theognis are prefixed to each section or fragment for the convenience of scholars. § LXIX. and XCVII. have not been identified, and the correspondence of § XXXV. XXXIX. and XLI. seems open to question.—ED.

of which the first lines are untranslatable) terminate in professing his fondness for this kind of music.

III.

(*Gaisford*, 1061-1064.)

To revel with the pipe, to chaunt and sing,
This likewise is a most delightful thing:
Give me but ease and pleasure! What care I
For reputation or for property?

It will be curious, if the reader should attain to the end of these pages, to look back upon this passage; and to see Theognis, in his graver and more parsimonious years, repeating this last sentiment, as that of the silly spendthrift whom he is there describing; the very sort of character he had before exhibited in his own person.

It will be seen elsewhere that his passion for this kind of music betrayed him on the one hand into some absurdities; and again, after his misfortunes, was among the means by which he contrived to maintain himself, and to reacquire a competence. But we are now considering him in the period of his youth and prosperity. His eagerness in the pursuit of knowledge is strongly marked in a passage which (in whatever period it may have been produced) serves to indicate a feeling, which is always strongest in early youth.

IV.

(*Gaisford*, 1153-1156.)

Learning and wealth, the wise and wealthy find
Inadequate to satisfy the mind;
A craving eagerness remains behind;
Something is left, for which we cannot rest;
And the last something always seems the best,
Something unknown, or something unpossess'd.

Young Mr. Theognis, as it should seem, from his own poetical statement, had succeeded in seducing a woman; unfortunately, however, after a time, his delicacy was alarmed, by the discovery of a rival or rivals; hereupon he resolves either to transfer the same virtuous attachment elsewhere, or to diffuse it liberally and promiscuously. These circumstances and this resolution, so singularly calculated to attract approbation and sympathy, are here recorded by the author both as a credit to himself and an example to posterity, according to the worthy practice of what are called amatory poets.

V.

(*Gaisford*, 953-956.)

My thirst was sated at a secret source,
I found it clear and limpid; but its course
Is alter'd now; polluted and impure!
I leave it; and where other springs allure,
Shall wander forth; or freely quaff my fill
From the loose current of the flowing rill.

We may now proceed to the congenial and equally edifying subject of hard drinking.

It is observable, however, that even here, Theognis exhibits traces of a peculiar mind, in a tendency to general remark and fixed method. "I sought in my heart to give myself unto wine (yet acquainting my heart with wisdom) and to lay hold on folly, till I might see what was that good for the sons of men, that they should do under heaven all the days of their life."—Such is the account which the Hebrew writer of proverbs is supposed to give of himself, and perhaps it would have applied equally to the Grecian; but, in Theognis, we see the actual course of experiment, arising from a spirit of systematic curiosity; whereas in the book of Ecclesiastes, assumed to have been written upon a retrospect, we have the motives and the result.

VI.

(*Gaisford*, 499-502.)

To prove our gold or silver coarse or fine,
Fire is the test; for man the proof is wine:
Wine can unravel secrets, and detect
And bring to shame the proudest intellect,
Hurried and overborne with its effect.

The following lines are curious, as affording a chronological approximation. Onomacritus, to whom they are addressed (but whose name could not easily be brought into an English verse), was a favourite of Hipparchus, but afterwards banished by him for a sacrilegious forgery; being at the time the curator of a collection of oracles in the possession of the two brothers[1] he had been detected in a wilful interpolation. If we take the middle of the fourteen years of Hipparchus' reign, as the probable date of these lines, they would have been composed by Theognis at the age of twenty-three or twenty-four, which, considering the nature of the subject, seems probable enough.

VII.

(*Gaisford*, 503-508.)

My brain grows dizzy, whirl'd and overthrown
With wine; my senses are no more my own;
The ceiling and the walls are wheeling round.
But, let me try!—perhaps my limbs are sound:
Let me retire with my remaining sense,
For fear of idle language and offence.

The next fragment is addressed to Simonides. Simonides had been invited to Athens by Hipparchus, and attached to his service and society by liberal payments and presents. Onomacritus and he were probably joint visitors at Megara, or Theognis might have joined their society at Athens. The lines seem to have been written about the same time, and during the same paroxysm of experimental conviviality as the preceding. Theognis, who in his own opinion is not more drunk than a man ought to be, remonstrates with Simonides, who, being president of the meeting and further advanced in liquor, had become overbearing and absurd. Theognis, as in the former fragment, takes his leave, being apprehensive of exceeding the precise bounds of inebriety which he had prescribed to himself. These lines shew great previous familiarity, and the petulance of a young man who takes upon himself to give a lecture to his friend and instructor on the principles of the sublime art of *savoir-vivre*. Such a lecture, coming from

---

[1] Hippias and Hipparchus, the sons of Peisistratus, joint rulers of Athens.

a senior, would have been felt seriously as an offensive reprimand.

VIII.

(*Gaisford*, 467-496.)

Never oblige your company to stay!
Never detain a man; nor send away!
Nor rouse from his repose the weary guest,
That sinks upon the couch with wine oppress'd!
These formal rules, enforced against the will,
Are found offensive. Let the bearer fill
Just as we please—freely to drink away;
Such merry meetings come not every day.
For me—since for to-night my stint is finish'd,
Before my common-sense is more diminish'd,
I shall retire—(the rule, I think, is right)
Not absolutely drunk nor sober quite.
For he that drinks beyond the proper point
Puts his own sense and judgment out of joint,
Talking outrageous, idle, empty stuff;
(The mere effect of wine more than enough)—
Telling a thousand things, that, on the morrow,
He recollects with sober shame and sorrow:
At other times, and in his proper nature,
An easy, quiet, amiable creature.
  Now you, Simonides, mind what I say!
You chatter in your cups and prate away,
Like a poor slave, drunk on a holiday.
You never can resolve to leave your liquor;
The faster it comes round, you drink the quicker—
There's some excuse—"The slave has fill'd the cup,
"A challenge or a pledge"—you drink it up!
"'Tis a libation"—and you're so devout,
You can't refuse it! Manly brains and stout
Might stand the trial, drinking hard and fast,
And keep their sense and judgment to the last.
  Farewell! be merry! may your hours be spent—
Without a quarrel or an argument—
In inoffensive, easy merriment;
Like a good concert keeping time and measure,
Such entertainments give the truest pleasure.

These verses are not very elegant nor very dignified;

and if they were, they would not be a just representation of the original: we may, however, consent to read them, as we do others of no greater merit in our own language, in illustration of the tone and manners of the time to which they belong. In both we have natural unelevated prose conveyed in the form of metre. This seems to be the proper style of Theognis, when not raised above himself by passion or feeling, or by the higher character of his subject.

We now proceed to his moral and political verses which (as mankind are usually more ashamed of wisdom than of folly, or, from prudential reasons, more cautious in concealing it) seem to have been suppressed for a time, and to have been communicated to his most intimate friend under an injunction of secrecy.

IX.

(*Gaisford*, 19-26.)

Kurnus, these lines of mine, let them remain
Conceal'd and secret—verse of such a strain
Betrays its author—all the world would know it!
"This is Theognis, the Megarian poet,
So celebrated and renown'd in Greece!"
Yet some there are, forsooth, I cannot please;
Nor ever could contrive, with all my skill,
To gain the common liking and good will
Of these my fellow citizens.—No wonder!
Not even he, the God that wields the thunder
(The Sovereign all-wise almighty Jove)
Can please them with his government above:
Some call for rainy weather, some for dry,
A discontented and discordant cry
Fills all the earth, and reaches to the sky.

In a passage preserved to us by Stobæus, Xenophon, after quoting from the preceding fragment the fourth line of the translation, proceeds to connect it with the fragment which follows, explaining it in his own manner: "*These are the verses of Theognis of Megara.*"—"The subject which the poet seems to me to have had in view, appears to have been simply a treatise on the good and bad qualities of mankind. He treats of man in the same manner as a writer would do of any other animal (of horses, for instance,) his exordium seems to me a perfectly proper one, for he begins with the subject of breed; considering that neither men nor any other animals are likely to prove good for anything, unless they are produced from a good stock. He illustrates his principle by a reference to those animals in which breed is strictly attended to; these lines, therefore, are not merely an invective against the mercenary spirit of his countrymen (as the generality of readers imagine), they seem to me to be directed against the negligence and ignorance of mankind in the management and economy of their own species." Such was the judgment of Xenophon upon this passage; different, as it should seem, from that of his countrymen and contemporaries.

But we must recollect that the maintenance of a physical and personal superiority was considered as a point of paramount importance by all the aristocracies of Doric race. The Spartans, the most perfect type of such an aristocracy, reared no infants who appeared likely to prove defective in form; and condemned their King Archidamus to a fine, for having married a diminutive wife. Xenophon himself speaks of it elsewhere as a well known fact, that the Spartans were eminently superior in strength and comeliness of person. As a result of this principle, we can account for what would otherwise appear a very singular circumstance; that the most eminent of the Olympic champions upon record, Diagoras and Milo, were both of the most distinguished families in their native Doric states, Rhodes and Crotona. Xenophon, therefore, who considered Theognis as belonging to a Doric aristocracy, and who was himself a Dorian in his habits and partialities, interprets him more in a physical, than in a moral sense; and considers misalliances as a cause, rather than a consequence, of the debasement of the higher orders.

X.

(*Gaisford*, 183-192.)

With kine and horses, Kurnus! we proceed
By reasonable rules, and choose a breed
For profit and increase, at any price;
Of a sound stock, without defect or vice.

But, in the daily matches that we make,
The price is every thing: for money's sake,
Men marry: women are in marriage given;
The churl or ruffian, that in wealth has thriven,
May match his offspring with the proudest race:
Thus every thing is mix'd, noble and base!
  If then in outward manner, form and mind,
You find us a degraded, motley kind,
Wonder no more, my friend! the cause is plain,
And to lament the consequence is vain.

From birth, we proceed to education. Here we find Theognis taking the same side with Pindar and Euripides, in a question which seems to have been long agitated in the heathen world: "*Whether virtue and vice were innate?*" concluding, like them, for the affirmative. This fragment is separated from the preceding; yet, according to the opinions of those times, there was a connexion between them, and the process of thought is continuous. The existence of the evil had been stated, and the poet proceeds to argue, that it is not capable of being remedied by human contrivance. After which, in two succeeding fragments, we shall see him following the cause into its consequences, as exemplified in the degradation of the higher orders and the comparative elevation of their former inferiors.

XI.

(*Gaisford*, 429-438.)

To rear a child is easy, but to teach
Morals and manners, is beyond our reach;
To make the foolish wise, the wicked good;
That science never yet was understood.
  The sons of Æsculapius, if their art
Could remedy a perverse and wicked heart,
Might earn enormous wages! But, in fact,
The mind is not compounded and compact
Of precept and example; human art
In human nature has no share or part:
Hatred of vice, the fear of shame and sin
Are things of native growth, not grafted in:
Else wise and worthy parents might correct
In children's hearts each error and defect;

Whereas, we see them disappointed still—
No scheme nor artifice of human skill
Can rectify the passions or the will.

We now come to those fragments, which must have occasioned the injunctions of secrecy, and which mark the peculiarity of the Author's mind. He distinctly prognosticates an approaching revolution originating in the misrule of the party to which he himself naturally belonged, and of which his friend Kurnus was, if not the actual, the anticipated chief, for we shall see him driven from his country at an early age, after having been for some time at the head of the state; he warns him of the rising intelligence and spirit of the lower orders; the feebleness, selfishness and falsehood of the higher; and the discontent which their mode of government was exciting.

XII.

(*Gaisford*, 53-68.)

Our commonwealth preserves its former frame,
Our common people are no more the same.
They, that in skins and hides were rudely dress'd,
Nor dreamt of law, nor sought to be redress'd
By rules of right, but in the days of old
Flock'd to the town, like cattle to the fold,
Are now the brave and wise. And we, the rest,
(Their betters nominally, once the best)
Degenerate, debased, timid, and mean!
Who can endure to witness such a scene?
Their easy courtesies, the ready smile,
Prompt to deride, to flatter and beguile!
Their utter disregard of right or wrong,
Of truth or honour! Out of such a throng
(For any difficulties, any need,
For any bold design or manly deed)
Never imagine you can choose a just
Or steady friend, or faithful in his trust.
But change your habits! let them go their way!
Be condescending, affable, and gay!
Adopt with every man the style and tone
Most courteous and congenial with his own!

But in your secret counsels keep aloof
From feeble paltry souls that at the proof
Of danger or distress are sure to fail;
For whose salvation, nothing can avail!

In the sixth line of the foregoing fragment the writer does not profess to have given an exact version of the original, which, to say the truth, he does not quite understand, but it is evident that the poet is speaking of the former condition of the commonalty as that of a class of inferior animals.

XIII.

(*Gaisford*, 39-52.)

Our state is pregnant; shortly to produce
A rude avenger of prolong'd abuse.
The commons hitherto seem sober-minded,
But their superiors are corrupt and blinded.
The rule of noble spirits, brave and high,
Never endanger'd peace and harmony.
The supercilious, arrogant pretence
Of feeble minds, weakness and insolence,
Justice and truth and law wrested aside
By crafty shifts of avarice and pride;
These are our ruin, Kurnus!—never dream,
(Tranquil and undisturb'd as it may seem)
Of future peace or safety to the state;
Bloodshed and strife will follow soon or late.
Never imagine that a ruin'd land
Will trust her destiny to your command,
To be remodell'd by a single hand.

The meaning and intention of the writer (such as I conceive it) is not so clearly expressed, either in the original or in the translation as not to require a commentary. If expanded into its full dimensions, it would stand thus: "The governments by an aristocracy of caste, such as ours, have never been overthrown while they have been directed by men of generous character and resolute magnanimous spirits; the danger does not arise till they are succeeded by a poor-spirited selfish generation, exercising the same arbitrary authority with mean and mercenary views."

In the concluding triplet, an enigmatic allusion to the views and expectations of his friend is expanded into an intelligible form. In the preceding generation,[1] the instances had not been unfrequent of able men being invested with discretionary power to re-organize a distracted commonwealth; but this confidence had been in many instances abused—the plenary power committed to them for a time, having been converted into a permanent

---

[1] Solon had been ridiculed and censured for having missed the opportunity, which was thus placed in his hands, of establishing himself as a despotic ruler in Athens. He himself describes, in some admirable trochaïc lines, the kind of language that was held by his aspiring, unscrupulous, scoundrelly contemporaries.

"Solon, as a politician, shew'd a weak and empty mind,
Destitute of resolution, when the Destinies design'd
To reward and elevate him: when the mighty net was cast,
And the prey securely compass'd, undecided and aghast,
He refrain'd and hesitated; till the noble, wealthy prize
In an instant burst the tackle, and escaped before his eyes.
I despise him for the failure,—for myself I fairly say,
'Only let me rule in Athens, for a year, a month, a day!
Then depose, assassinate—exterminate my name and kin!
Murder and demolish all! Flay me alive and tan my skin!'"

Vide suprà, p. 51, *note*.

To which he answers:—

"Truth it is, that I declined the bloody desperate career
Of tyrannical command, to rule alone and domineer,
In my native happy land, with arbitrary force and fear:
Neither have I since repented; unreproach'd, without a crime;
Placed alone, unparallel'd, among the statesmen of the time."

Fragments, 25 and 27.

Flay me alive and tan my skin! The original, for which this phrase is given, does not, I imagine, appear quite intelligible to the generality of readers. The writer, who had long admired these lines, had never been able to account for the epithet ὑστερον, as applied to a *wine skin*, till the difficulty was accidentally solved by a sight of the thing signified. It is a wine skin in which the maker has chosen to exhibit his skill, by including *the extremities.* It was a kind of proverbial pledge, expressive of a readiness to submit to extreme suffering and hardship,—*I will submit to be flayed and made into a wine skin!* But a phrase, which had become trite and trivial, was not suited to the earnestness with which Solon's politician is made to express himself. He is represented as giving a new form and vivacity to the common phrase by specifying the particular sort of wine skin (the one already described) into which he would consent to be transformed.

despotism. The poet, therefore, is warning his friend that the citizens of Megara are too wary to have recourse to such an expedient, and that his expectations of being invested with supreme authority were not likely to be fulfilled.

Upon this subject it is curious to observe, how frequently republics have felt the necessity of submitting to an uncontrolled irresponsible power. Even in Athens, towards the end of the Peloponnesian war, the question seems to have been mooted in favour of Alcibiades.[1] The Italian republics had recourse to foreigners; sometimes to a person of high rank, sometimes to a learned lawyer from Bologna, but always to a foreigner. The precaution adopted by the Roman republic was different, and proved a decided failure. They appointed a board of commissioners—the Decemvirs!

The following examples and warnings are adduced from traditional fable and later history.

XIV.

(*Gaisford*, 541, 542.)

My friend, I fear it! pride, which overthrew
The mighty Centaurs and their hardy crew—
Our pride will ruin us, your friends, and you.

XV.

(*Gaisford*, 1099, 1100.)

Pride and oppressive rule destroy'd the state
Of the Magnesians—such was Smyrna's fate—
Smyrna the rich, and Colophon the great!
And ours, my friend, will follow soon or late.

Of the history of those governments we know nothing; they were known to Theognis, probably by the poems of authors like himself: one of whom (in a fragment accidentally preserved) speaks of his fellow citizens of Colophon as "overbearing and oppressive from the time of their first settlement."[2] But the example of the Mag-

[1] See "the Frogs," the last lines of the Antepirrema, p. 279, and p. 306, l. 1701.

[2] *Mimnermus*, ix. 3.

nesians (whatever it may have been) seems to have presented to Theognis a most apposite parallel to the state of Megara; accordingly, as an anxious and earnest adviser, regardless of repetition, he recurs to the conduct and fate of the Magnesian government, with a preface, too, almost in the same words as in Frag. XIII.

XVI.

(*Gaisford*, 39, 40; 603, 604.)

Kurnus, our state is pregnant to produce
The avenger of oppression and abuse!
The birth (believe me) will not tarry long;
For the same course of outrage and of wrong,
Which ruin'd the Magnesian state of old,—
That very same, we witness and behold.

In this state of things the line of conduct which the poet prescribed to himself is explained in the following lines.

XVII.

(*Gaisford*, 939-942.)

I walk by rule and measure, and incline
To neither side, but take an even line;
Fix'd in a single purpose and design.
With learning's happy gifts to celebrate,
To civilize and dignify the State;
Not leaguing with the discontented crew,
Nor with the proud and arbitrary few.

By an unavoidable consequence of his neutrality, he was (as it appears) blamed and abused on all sides, consoling himself, in the meantime, with the consciousness of his intellectual superiority.

XVIII.

(*Gaisford*, 367-370.)

That happy man, my friend, was never seen
Nor born into the world, whom saucy spleen
Forbore to scandalize! I know not, I!
What they would have? but whether I comply

To join with others in pursuit of ill,
Or keep myself aloof, they blame me still.
Such is my fortune; never understood,
But censured by the wicked or the good!
My consolation still remains the same;
Fools cannot imitate the man they blame.

In poetry which is evidently in every instance suggested by circumstances, and which in its style approaches to the language of conversation, we must not be surprised, any more than we should be in actual conversation, to find the same person, at different times, repeating occasionally the same thoughts and expressions. The following fragment is almost entirely a repetition from Fragments IX. and XVIII.

XIX.

(*Gaisford*, 799-802.)

That happy man, my friend! that has through life
Pass'd unobnoxious to reproach or strife . . . .
. . . . Never existed yet; nor ever will!
A task there is which Jove could not fulfil,—
Infinite power and wisdom, both combined,
Would not avail to satisfy mankind.

This sensibility to public opinion appears again strongly marked in the following fragment.

XX.

(*Gaisford*, 795-798.)

The generous and the brave, in common fame,
From time to time encounter praise or blame:
The vulgar pass unheeded; none escape
Scandal or insult in some form or shape.
Most fortunate are those, alive or dead,
Of whom the least is thought—the least is said.

The apparent contradiction which is to be found in this passage exists also in the original. That his understanding was undervalued by the practical busy persons of the time may be inferred from the following lines.

XXI.

(*Gaisford*, 221-226.)

The worldly-minded and the worldly wise,
In ignorance and arrogance, despise
All talents and attainments but their own;
Wisdom is their's, they think—and their's alone.
But no! the lessons of deceit and wrong,
In point of fact, are neither hard nor long:
And many know them; but a better will,
Prohibits some from practising their skill;—
Some have a taste for good, and some for ill.

Of himself, in the mean time, as a practical politician, he speaks in substance rather disqualifyingly.

XXII.

(*Gaisford*, 419, 420.)

Many true counsels in this breast of mine
Lie buried: many a just and fair design,
But inefficient, indolent and weak;
I know my nature, and forbear to speak.

The period of comparative happiness and tranquillity was now drawing to a close: and the poet, whose mind had hitherto been only occasionally saddened by the prospect of approaching evils, was doomed to witness a revolution, to be stript of his property, and some time after, forced to abandon his native city in company with his friend, and to commence a long course of exile and poverty.

The elements of a revolution, as appears from the preceding fragments, were already in existence; but they were called into activity by the example of the powerful neighbouring state of Athens, where the murder of Hipparchus had been followed, at the end of three years, by the expulsion of Hippias, upon which the ancient form of Athenian government had been again established for a short time; after which, the weaker faction of the nobility, joining themselves with the people, effected an entire abolition of the aristocracy of caste:—the very same species of aristocracy which was in existence in Megara; but whose existence was threatened (as has been seen in the preceding fragments) by its own misrule, and by the growing discontent of a more intelligent commonalty. A revolution therefore at Megara was unavoidable, and we shall see that it took place accordingly.

As a preface to the fragments which belong to this turbulent period, the following lines, referring to the assassination of Hipparchus and the splendour of his funeral, may properly find their place.

The question of obedience or resistance to a sovereign *de facto*, as it was viewed in Greece, by a man of speculative and original mind, upwards of two thousand three hundred years ago, may be considered as a matter of curiosity.

XXIII.

(*Gaisford*, 821, 822; 1183, 1184.)

Court not a tyrant's favour, nor combine
To further his iniquitous design!
But, if your faith is pledged, though late and loth,
If covenants have pass'd between you both,
Never assassinate him! keep your oath!
But should he still misuse his lawless power,
To trample on the people, and devour;
Depose or overturn him—any how!
Your oath permits it, and the gods allow.

The two following fragments are also found separate; but though relating to the same subject of a royal funeral, and appearing to be extracts from the same poem, they have not the same mark of continuity as the two preceding, and are therefore put separately.

XXIV.

(*Gaisford*, 1203-1206.)

I shall not join the funeral train, to go
An idle follower in the pomp of woe:
For why—no duty binds me? nor would he,
Their arbitrary chief, have mourn'd for me.

XXV.

(*Gaisford*, 1191-1194.)

I envy not these sumptuous obsequies,
The stately car, the purple canopies;

Much better pleased am I, remaining here,
With cheaper equipage and better cheer.
A couch of thorns, or an embroider'd bed,
Are matters of indifference to the dead.

Two fragments are found (singularly enough) in immediate juxtaposition with each other, and with one of the preceding. The first of the two appears to be descriptive of the character of Hipparchus; and the second, to have been suggested by the sudden catastrophe which befell him.

XXVI.

(*Gaisford*, 1185, 1186.)

Easy discourse with steady sense combined
Are rare endowments in a single mind.

XXVII.

(*Gaisford*, 1187-1190.)

No costly sacrifice nor offerings given
Can change the purpose of the powers of heaven:
Whatever fate ordains, danger or hurt
Or death predestined, nothing can avert.

In the following fragment, the phrase ὁ εἷς[1] is evidently used in the same sense as its corresponding term, "*The single person*," which was so frequently employed in England, during the ten years from 1650 to 1660, to signify an individual exercising the functions of royalty.

XXVIII.

(*Gaisford*, 641, 642.)

The sovereign single person—what cares he
For love or hate, for friend or enemy?
His single purpose is—utility.

Some remarks on the probable causes of this coldness of feeling towards Hipparchus will be found stated in the

[1] "It should, perhaps, be mentioned that the true reading is κ' εἰδείης (for κήδει ὁ εἷς). The meaning is that you cannot discern whether a man is really your friend or not until you try him in some serious matter." *G. C. Lewis.*

short chronological abstract, and may serve to illustrate this last fragment.

The exact order of time and events, in the short and confused period between the commencement of the changes which took place at Megara, and the emigration or escape of Theognis and his friend, cannot be satisfactorily deduced from the fragments which exist. It appears, however, that Theognis, by some means or other, was, at a very early period, deprived of the greater part of his property: since two events are mentioned subsequent to his ruin and anterior to his flight from Megara. The first is the arrival of his friend Clearistus (Frag. LIX.), and of his old friend and instructor Simonides (Frag. LXIII.); moreover, two seasons of the year are mentioned—ploughing and harvest (Frags. LX. and LXI.). That the loss of his property was, in some way or other, the work of the opposite faction is clear, from the circumstance of his looking to the triumph of his own friends, as the means of recovering it, and avenging himself upon those who had despoiled him of it,—as he says, "With violence and outrage"—but by what process or under what pretence this spoliation was effected, it is by no means easy to conjecture.

Kurnus in the mean time had held the first authority in the State; for his deposition from the highest office will be found distinctly alluded to in the verses (Frag. LXIII.) occasioned by the visit of Simonides above-mentioned. The same verses show that the state of things had become in consequence more desperate; and it appears from another passage that, under these circumstances, Theognis himself had become the advocate of bold and violent measures, which up to that time he had deprecated.

Finally, the flight of the two friends from Megara was determined by the approach of an auxiliary force, despatched (probably from Corinth) as a reinforcement to their opponents. These events must have succeeded to each other within a short period of time, for when the Athenians invaded Eubœa, Theognis was already an exile (Frags. LXX., LXXI., LXXII.).

Having now brought together the few fragments which serve to illustrate the political condition of the community to which he belonged, and the situation and sentiments of the poet himse.f, during the period anterior to the commencement of civil commotion, it may be convenient to place under a single point of view other passages referable to the same time, and illustrative of the character of the friend to whom these and other poems were addressed; and to whose person and fortunes (in spite of some occasional intervals of aversion and offence) he appears to have been most sincerely attached. They consist of advice, strictly personal; those which relate to the general aspect of affairs having been given already. There are also remonstrances relative to misconduct and defect of character. It being impossible to determine the order in which they succeeded, they have been assembled promiscuously. Those of anger and reproach are classed apart. The conduct which Theognis recommends to his friend, in the first instance, is similar to that which he had prescribed to himself,—namely, to remain indifferent between the two contending factions.

XXIX.

(*Gaisford*, 219, 220.)

If popular distrust and hate prevail,
If saucy mutineers insult and rail,
Fret not your eager spirit! take a line
Just, sober, and discreet,—the same as mine!

But such advice was not likely to be followed. Kurnus appears to have been the spoiled child of his friends and his fellow-citizens,—the man on whom his party had placed their hopes; possessing all the advantages of person, wealth, birth, and abilities, accompanied with the defects by which those advantages are so frequently counterbalanced, and which, in a similar but more celebrated instance (that of Alcibiades), proved ruinous to their possessor. He seems to have been at no pains to conceal his natural arrogance, or to dissemble his feelings of antipathy or contempt, and to have been (at one time at least) incapable of bending his mind to the performance of necessary disagreeable duties. This last defect is noted in the following lines, in which the sense of the original has been adhered to, though the expression has been unavoidably amplified.

XXX.

(*Gaisford*, 1079-1082.)

My friend, the feeling you can not correct
Will work at last a ruinous effect
To disappoint your hopes. You cannot learn
To bear unpleasant things with unconcern;
Nor work without repugnance or disgust
In tasks that ought to be perform'd, and must.

In the choice of his associates and adherents, the conduct of Kurnus seems to have been in contradiction with the advice of his friend. We have seen in Frag. XII. that he warns him against placing any reliance on a particular class of persons, whom he there describes. Admonitions to the same effect are repeated in other instances.

The kind of qualities which Theognis required in a friend may serve to give a notion of the violent character of the times, and of the critical condition of the party to which he belonged.

XXXI.

(*Gaisford*, 973-976.)

I care not for a friend that at my board
Talks pleasantly: the friend that will afford
Faithful assistance with his purse and sword
In need or danger, let that friend be mine!
Fit for a bold and resolute design;
Not for a conversation over wine!

The two following fragments are nearly to the same effect.

XXXII.

(*Gaisford*, 101-112.)

Let no persuasive art tempt you to place
Your confidence in crafty minds and base!
How can it answer? Will their help avail
When danger presses, and your foes assail?
The blessing which the gods in bounty send,
Will they consent to share it with a friend?

No! To bestrew the waves with scatter'd grain,
To cultivate the surface of the main,
Is not a task more absolutely vain,
Than cultivating such allies as these,
Fickle and unproductive as the seas!
Such are all baser minds; never at rest,
With new demands importunately press'd—
A new pretension or a new request;
Till, foil'd with a refusal of the last,
They disavow their obligations past.
But brave and gallant hearts are cheaply gain'd—
Faithful adherents, easily retain'd;
Men that will never disavow the debt
Of gratitude, or cancel or forget.

XXXIII.

(*Gaisford*, 93-100.)

The civil person (he that to your face
Professing friendship, in another place
Talks in an alter'd tone) is not the man
For a determined, hearty partisan.
Give me the comrade eager to defend,
And, in his absence, vindicate a friend!
Whose strong attachment will abide the brunt
Of bitter altercation, and confront
Calumnious outrage with a fierce reproof,
Like brethren bred beneath a father's roof:
Friends such as these may serve for your behoof.
None others.—Mark my words! and let them be
Fix'd as a token in your memory
For aftertimes,—to make you think of me!

That nothing may be omitted, a fourth fragment on the same subject is subjoined.

XXXIV.

(*Gaisford*, 113-128.)

Never engage with a paltroon or craven,—
Avoid him, Kurnus, as a treacherous haven!

These friends and hearty comrades, as you think,
(Ready to join you, when you feast and drink,)
These easy friends from difficulty shrink.
For a shrewd intellect, the best employ
Is to detect a soul of base alloy;
No task is harder nor imports so much;
Silver or gold, you prove it by the touch;
You separate the pure, discard the dross,
And disregard the labour and the loss:
But a friend's heart, base and adulterate,—
A friendly surface with a core of hate!
Of all the frauds with which the Fates have cursed
Our simple easy nature—is the worst:
Beyond the rest ruinous in effect;
And of all others hardest to detect:
For men's and women's hearts you cannot try
Beforehand, like the cattle that you buy.
Nor human wit nor reason, when you treat
For such a purpose, can escape deceit;
Fancy betrays us, and assists the cheat.

If these fragments were considered separately, we might imagine that Theognis was exciting his friend to some violent measure, and exhorting him to surround himself with adherents capable of putting it in execution. We shall see, however, elsewhere, that this was not the case, and that he is only warning him (as we have already seen in the last lines of Frag. XII.) against placing a false confidence in inefficient associates, and encumbering himself with the sort of burdensome and unprofitable dependency described in Frag. XXXII. The Athenian, Alcibiades, had been considered the hope and future support of the party of the nobility to which he naturally belonged; till an impatience of the superiority of older men, whose talents and services had placed them at the head of that party, led him to connect himself with the popular faction. Kurnus, either not meeting with the same obstacles to ascendancy in his own party, or from whatever other reason, seems to have adhered to the cause of the aristocracy of Megara with perfect tenacity; upholding and partaking in their worst abuses; as may be inferred from the remonstrances of his friend.

XXXV.

(*Gaisford*, 461, 462?)

Waste not your efforts, struggle not, my friend,
Idle and old abuses to defend!
Take heed! the very measures that you press,
May bring repentance with their own success.

We have seen in Frag. XIII. that iniquitous and partial decisions formed one of the main grievances which endangered the public tranquillity; and the following fragment expresses, though less distinctly than in the original, that Kurnus himself was a principal in iniquities of this kind.

XXXVI.

(*Gaisford*, 331, 332.)

Kurnus, proceed like me! Walk not awry!
Nor trample on the bounds of property!

The commission of some other offence (an offence against the gods) probably something in the nature of sacrilege or perjury, is obscurely, as if unwillingly, intimated, and attributed to the bad associates with whom he was engaged.

XXXVII.

(*Gaisford*, 1171, 1172.)

"Bad company breeds mischief." Kurnus, you
Can prove that ancient proverb to be true
In your own instance; you yourself were driven
To an unrighteous act, offending Heaven!

Of the prudential and practical defects in Kurnus's character, we have seen an instance in Frag. XXX. The following is probably of a much earlier date; it seems to be the sort of advice suited to a young man just entering the world, but marks a degree of rashness and irritability in the character to which such admonitions were addressed. The original is miserably mangled, two lines being evidently wanting between 203 and 204;[1] since, in

---

[1] The edition of Theognis from which these translations were made is of Leipsic, 1817, edited by Brunck.

this last, there is a pronoun without an antecedent, and a verb also (for δόκει, I apprehend, cannot be here in the imperative mood) without its nominative case. It should seem that a person spoken of in an injurious manner is the antecedent to the pronoun, and the person so speaking (and who flatters himself that the absent person whom he has been abusing will never hear of it) is the nominative case to the verb. The sense and intention of the original, though not literally interpreted, is at least intelligibly given in the following lines.

XXXVIII.

(*Gaisford*, 309-312.)

At entertainments show yourself discreet:
Remember that, amongst the guests you meet,
The absent have their friends, and may be told
Of rash or idle language which you hold.
  Learn to endure a jest—you may display
Your courage elsewhere, in a better way.

The last line of the original is left untranslated; it has no connexion with the preceding, and seems to mark another chasm, which it would not be easy to supply. The above has the appearance of being part of a series of maxims; but a propensity to anger and intemperate language seems to be indicated in another fragment, apparently of later date than the former; but they are both probably earlier than any of the admonitory ones.

XXXIX.

(*Gaisford*, 631, 632?)

Rash, angry words, and spoken out of season,
When passion has usurp'd the throne of reason,
Have ruin'd many. Passion is unjust,
And for an idle transitory gust
Of gratified revenge dooms us to pay
With long repentance at a later day.

A sort of Coriolanus-like insolence and contempt of the commonalty is marked in the following.

XL.

(*Gaisford*, 151-158.)

The gods send Insolence, to lead astray
The man whom Fortune and the Fates betray,
Predestined to precipitate decay.
Wealth nurses Insolence, and wealth, we find,
When coupled with a poor and paltry mind,
Is evermore with Insolence combined.
Never in anger with the meaner sort
Be moved to a contemptuous, harsh retort,
Deriding their distresses ; nor despise,
In hasty speech, their wants and miseries.
Jove holds the balance, and the gods dispense
For all mankind, riches and indigence.

Among the defects of Kurnus's character, one, not uncommonly incident to men of genius, but peculiarly unfortunate in a public man, seems to have been a morbid fastidiousness, producing a sort of premature misanthropy ; such at least is the inference deducible from the following lines. Observe, too, that the last lines of Frag. X. refer to Kurnus's contemptuous estimate of his contemporaries.

XLI.

(*Gaisford*, 893-898 ?)

Learn, Kurnus, learn, to bear an easy mind ;
Accommodate your humour to mankind
And human nature—take it as you find !
A mixture of ingredients, good or bad,
Such are we all, the best that can be had.
The best are found defective, and the rest,
For common use, are equal to the best.
Suppose it had been otherwise decreed—
How could the business of the world proceed ?
Fairly examined, truly understood,
No man is wholly bad, nor wholly good,
Nor uniformly wise. In every case,
Habit and accident, and time, and place
Affect us :—'tis the nature of the race !

Theognis's admonitions and suggestions, in counteraction of this defect, are not very magnanimous; they resemble the concluding lines of Frag. XII.

XLII.

(*Gaisford*, 213-218.)

Join with the world! adopt, with every man,
His party views, his temper, and his plan!
Strive to avoid offence! study to please!
Like the sagacious inmate of the seas,
That an accommodating colour brings,
Conforming to the rock to which he clings,
With every change of place changing his hue—
The model for a statesman, such as you!

The bickerings and quarrels between Kurnus and his friend, since no precise order can be assigned to them, must be necessarily classed together; though it is probable they belong to very different periods, from the time of their first entrance into the world to the date of their expatriation. That these quarrels took place in more instances than one seems evident from the different position in which Theognis is placed. In one he intimates that he has been deceived, and his confidence abused; in another, he deprecates unrelenting resentment for a slight offence; in another, he speaks as a person unjustly calumniated. Another fragment, which seems to have arisen out of the same circumstances, I should be inclined to assign to the time when Kurnus was at the head of affairs, and when Theognis's fortunes were ruined; the others were probably anterior, but at what time, or in what order, it is not easy to conjecture.

In the absence of all other motives of choice, a fragment is placed here, similar in its tone to the last of the preceding series. There can be little doubt that the friend alluded to is Theognis himself.

XLIII.

(*Gaisford*, 323-328.)

Let not a base calumnious pretence,
Exaggerating a minute offence,

Move you to wrong a friend! If every time
Faults in a friend were treated as a crime,
Here upon earth, no friendship could have place.
But we, the creatures of a faulty race,
Amongst ourselves offend and are forgiven:—
Vengeance is the prerogative of Heaven.

The following must have arisen out of some other ground of difference; though indirectly expressed, it is evidently intended to bear a personal application.

XLIV.

(*Gaisford*, 1219, 1220.)

A rival or antagonist is hard
To be deceived, they stand upon their guard:
But an old friend, Kurnus, is unprepared!

In the following, a feeling of coldness and distrust is marked on the part of the poet; he is rejecting some proposal made to him by his friend, as tending to engage and compromise him.

XLV.

(*Gaisford*, 539, 540; 371, 372.)

That smith, dear Kurnus, shows but little wit,
Who forges fetters his own feet to fit.
Excuse me, Kurnus; I cannot comply
Thus to be yoked in harness;—never try
To bind me strictly, with too close a tie.

With respect to the next fragment there can be no doubt; it is sufficiently decided and angry enough.

XLVI.

(*Gaisford*, 87-92.)

No more with empty phrase and speeches fine
Seek to delude me—let your heart be mine!
Your friendship or your enmity declare
In a decided form, open and fair,
An enemy disguised, a friend in show!—
I like him better, Kurnus, as a foe!

The next expresses a consciousness of innocence and a defiance of unjust calumny. It is observable that we find here the same singular association of ideas (water and gold) as in the first lines of Pindar. In Pindar they are probably meant to be significant, and to mark his initiation in the mysteries, in which the successive degrees were connected with these symbols; and he, the most scrupulous and devout of all heathen poets, begins his book with them upon the same principle as a Catholic (in some countries at least) begins his letters with the sign of the cross. In Theognis, the association may have been, perhaps, an involuntary result.

XLVII.

(*Gaisford*, 447-452.)

Yes!—Drench me with invective! not a stain
From all that angry deluge will remain!
Fair harmless water, dripping from my skin,
Will mark no foulness or defect within.
As the pure standard gold of ruddy hue,
Proved by the touchstone, unalloy'd and true,
Unstain'd by rust, untarnish'd to the sight;
Such will you find me—solid, pure and bright.

This image of the trial of gold seems, from some reason or other, to have been peculiarly familiar to the poet's mind. It occurs in Frag. VI. and XXXIV., and will be found again in verses composed during his exile, Frag. LXXX. See the extraordinary work of Mr. Whiter on the association of ideas, considered as an instrument of criticism, and his application of it to the peculiar turns of transition observable in Shakespeare.

The two next relate apparently to minor differences; in the first, the poet is out of humour at being in his turn advised and admonished.

XLVIII.

(*Gaisford*, 576, 577.)

Change for the worse is sooner understood,
And sooner practised, than from bad to good.
Do not advise and school me! good my friend!
I'm past the time to learn. I cannot mend.

The next treats of that useless and interminable question, "Whose fault it was?"

XLIX.

(*Gaisford*, 407, 408.)

You blame me for an error not my own:
Dear friend! the fault was yours, and yours alone.

The two following look more like a decided rupture than any of the foregoing; they seem both to belong to the same time, and the tone is similar; the services mentioned in the first are insisted upon more at length in the second; (which seems to show that the obligation consisted in the celebrity conferred upon his friend, by the poetry in which his name was recorded.) A conjecture as to the time of their composition has been already hazarded.

L.

(*Gaisford*, 1087-1092.)

My mind is in a strange distracted state;
Love you I cannot!—and I cannot hate!
'Tis hard to change habitual good-will,
Hard to renounce our better thoughts for ill,—
To love without return is harder still.
But mark my resolution and protest!
Those services, for which you once profess'd
A sense of obligation due to me,
On my part were gratuitous and free;
No task had I, no duty to fulfil,
No motive, but a kind and friendly will.
  Now like a liberated bird I fly,
That having snapt the noose ranges on high,
Proud of his flight, and viewing in disdain
The broken fetter and the baffled swain,
And his old haunt, the lowly marshy plain!
  For you! the secret interested end
Of him, your new pretended party friend,
Whose instigation moved you to forego
Your former friendship, time will shortly shew;
Time will unravel all the close design,
And mark his merits, as compared with mine.

The second of these fragments has been injudiciously subdivided by Mr. Brunck, a gentleman, to whose memory the cause of literature is deeply indebted, for the zeal with which he attached himself to its service, with great acuteness, and an energy truly admirable; but whose edition of Theognis, though it has the merit of being the first in which any attempt was made to mark the beginnings and ends of the separate fragments (which had been fused into one uniform dense and unintelligible mass), bears, nevertheless, evident marks of the haste and eagerness which enabled him to accomplish so many great works in so short a space of time. The fragment in question, whether perfect or not, is evidently one and indivisible; the argument throughout being continuous. The expostulation is a full development of the allusion to former services and obligations expressed in the preceding (really a separate) fragment. It may be observed, that the similes in both are parallel and to the same effect, expressing a renunciation of friendship, under the image of an escape from bondage.

The argument of the second fragment, if coarsely stated, would stand thus, "I have conferred upon you a celebrity similar to that which would have resulted to you from a victory at the Olympic Games"—(the great object of personal ambition among the most eminent individuals and sovereigns of the Grecian race, and requiring for the chance of its attainment, a most profuse expenditure). "Moreover, the celebrity which I have thus gratuitously conferred upon you is much more lasting, more brilliant, and more extensive; but instead of any suitable return for such a service, you are so destitute of those first blessings, common sense and common justice, that you treat me with neglect; and when, like every body else, I have an object which I am anxious to obtain, you disregard my application to you. I am like one of those horses at the Olympic Games, which has acquired a celebrity for his master, but being ill treated, longs to escape." Such would have been the remonstrance, if stated by a resolute, hard, bitter claimant. In the poet's hands, it assumes a more poetical and delicate form; expatiating on the more graceful parts, and suppressing the undignified, he still leaves the solid logical substance distinctly discernible, under the texture with which he has invested it.

LI.

(*Gaisford*, 237-260; 131, 132.)

You soar aloft, and over land and wave
Are borne triumphant on the wings I gave,
The swift and mighty wings, music and verse;
Your name in easy numbers smooth and terse,
Is wafted o'er the world; and heard among
At banquetings and feasts, chaunted and sung,
Heard and admired: the modulated air
Of flutes and voices of the young and fair
Recite it, and to future times shall tell;
When closed within the dark sepulchral cell
Your form shall moulder, and your empty ghost
Wander along the dreary Stygian coast,
Yet shall your memory flourish, fresh and young,
Recorded and revived on every tongue,
In continents and islands, every place
That owns the language of the Grecian race!
No purchased prowess of a racing steed,
But the triumphant muse, with airy speed,
Shall bear it wide and far, o'er land and main,
A glorious and imperishable strain;
A mighty prize, gratuitously won,
Fix'd as the earth, immortal as the sun!
But for all this—no kindness in return!
No token of attention or concern!
Baffled and scorn'd, you treat me like a child,
From day to day, with empty words beguiled.
Remember! common justice, common sense
Are the best blessings which the Gods dispense:
And each man has his object; all aspire
To something which they covet and desire.
Like a fair courser, conqueror in the race,
Bound to a charioteer sordid and base,
I feel it with disdain; and many a day
Have long'd to break the curb and burst away.

To be celebrated by an eminent poet, or to obtain the victory at the Olympic Games, were the only two means by which an individual belonging to one of the numberless petty States and Colonies of Greece (not being himself a poet) could aspire to that universal celebrity among his countrymen, which was the common object of ambition among all the more gifted individuals of the race. Hence arose a singular, and to modern imaginations, an unaccountable association of ideas: Muses and Horses! we have seen it in the preceding fragment, and it is to be met with in Pindar; among other instances, in that fragment preserved by the humorous quotation of Aristophanes, where the begging poet comes with a ready made inaugural ode, which he pretends to have composed expressly on the occasion of the foundation of the famous city of Nephelococcugia. Peisthetairus, the projector and acting manager of the concern, expresses his surprise and doubt:—

"*Peis.* That's strange! when I'm just sacrificing here,
For the first time; to give the town a name."

To which the bard replies, in the phrase of Pindar:—

"Intimations, swift as air,
To the Muse's ear are carried,
Swifter than the speed and force
Of the fiery-footed horse,
Hence the tidings never tarried."[1]

We shall see in another fragment (XCVIII.) that as Theognis, in this instance, (where he speaks of the celebrity conferred by poetry) has tacitly so contrasted it with an Olympic victory; so he will be found, stating his own claim to indulgence and consideration from his fellow citizens, under cover of the parallel case of a conqueror at the games. In either case, the success of the victorious competitor, or the applauded poet, would have reflected honour on his native state; and we shall see, that what the poet will affirm of the one, he will leave to be inferred of the other; namely that neither of them, without a sacrifice of money, would have been able to obtain that indulgence which, according to the feelings and opinions of the time, ought in such cases to have been extended to them honourably and gratuitously.

We now come to the period of the poet's misfortunes, beginning with the loss of his property; indeed, the two last fragments are in all probability subsequent to it.

---

[1] The *Birds*, p. 188, v. 1120.

Respecting the cause of this disaster, it is not easy to form a conjecture, founded upon assumptions deducible from one passage, which is not liable to be overset by comparing it with others. A very unintelligible line, which (probably from the omission of an intervening couplet) has little relation to the preceding verse, seems to mark his misfortunes as somehow connected with a sea voyage; yet, notwithstanding the known propensity of the Greeks to trade and navigation, it seems difficult to conceive Theognis in the character of a merchant adventurer. Allowing, however, that what was true of Solon (a poet also, and a politician), might be equally true of Theognis, we find, on the other hand, that he speaks of his ruin, not as the result of any casual mischance, but as the work of enemies, upon whom he hopes and prays to be revenged. But, does not this sea voyage allude to his emigration by sea, after which his property would have been confiscated? No! According to all appearances, he escaped by land; and his first place of refuge seems to have been Eubœa, separate only from the main land by a very narrow channel: and it will be seen from the fragments which follow, that he must have remained at Megara some time after being reduced to comparative poverty. We might have no difficulty in supposing, that in times of violent faction the party opposed to Kurnus, if they forbore to make a direct attack upon him, might (like the party opposed to Pericles in their attacks upon Aspasia, Anaxagoras and Phidias) seek to discredit him, by ruining a person known to be attached to him; but there are no indications of this in the passages where we should expect to find them.

If, from any other source, we could obtain a knowledge of Theognis' life and history, we might be able to account for some singularities: one of which (his familiarity with the language of the assay office) has been already pointed out in the note to Fragment XLVII.; but there is another, not a little remarkable, namely, his strong objections and remonstrance against the rule of Providence, by which the sins of the father were visited upon his descendants! Can we suppose that he is remonstrating with respect to his own case? that, as we have seen in Frag. XII., that judicial iniquity was the most crying grievance of the state, so (as was the case in Rome, after the death of Sylla) it might have been among the first remedied, and in a similar manner, namely, by transferring the judicature, to another order of citizens: a measure which might give rise to a course of equal partiality in an opposite direction. Such a supposition would afford the best explanation of the state of alarm and confusion, short of actual violence, which filled the period antecedent to the poet's emigration. Can we suppose, that while things were in this state, an old family law suit, arising out of commercial matters, and unjustly decided in favour of his father or ancestor, had been revived under this new tribunal; and that the sentence, so ruinous to his fortune, was at the same time so arbitrary and excessive, as to excite the resentment and eagerness for revenge, which he expresses elsewhere?

Fragment LII. might seem to relate to some confidential deposit; which, perhaps, in expectation of an unfavourable decision, he would have set apart as a contingent resource, but which was either treacherously detained or surrendered to his adversary.

Since writing the above, the following lines, which had not been noticed before, have appeared to bear a meaning referable to the suppositions above stated.

Where on the father's and the mother's side
Justice is found, no treasure you can hide,
Is a resource more certain to abide.

They certainly have the appearance of a general maxim, assumed for the sake of a particular application, and are such as might well have been written by a person who conceived himself suffering under a retribution for the injustice of his predecessors; and whose mind was occupied, at the same time, with the notion of providing some concealed resource as a security against misfortune. The association of ideas is so singular, that some such supposition seems necessary to account for it.

The result of his precaution appears as follows:—

LII.

(*Gaisford*, 829-834.)

Bad faith hath ruin'd me; distrust alone
Has saved a remnant; all the rest is gone

To ruin and the dogs! [*] The powers divine,
I murmur not against them, nor repine:
Mere human violence, rapine and stealth
Have brought me down to poverty from wealth.

* Sic in Orig. —ἐν κοράκεσσι καὶ ἐν φθορᾷ.

The following is a soliloquy, in which he is endeavouring to bring his mind into a more composed state.

LIII.

(*Gaisford*, 1023-1030.)

Learn patience, O my soul! though rack'd and torn
With deep distress—bear it!—it must be borne!
Your unavailing hopes and vain regret
Forget them, or endeavour to forget:
Those womanish repinings unrepress'd,
Which gratify your foes, serve to molest
Your sympathising friends. Learn to endure!
And bear calamities you cannot cure;
Nor hope to change the laws of destiny
By mortal efforts! Vainly would you fly
To the remòtest margin of the sky,
Where ocean meets the firmament; in vain
Would you descend beneath, and dive amain,
Down to the dreary subterraneous reign.

The following lines, in a more composed and manly strain, seem to belong to the same period.

LIV.

(*Gaisford*, 441-446.)

Entire and perfect happiness is never
Vouchsafed to man; but nobler minds endeavour
To keep their inward sorrows unreveal'd.
With meaner spirits nothing is conceal'd:
Weak, and unable to conform to fortune,
With rude rejoicing or complaint importune,
They vent their exultation or distress.
Whate'er betides us—grief or happiness—
The brave and wise will bear with steady mind,
Th' allotment, unforeseen and undefined,
Of good or evil, which the gods bestow,
Promiscuously dealt to man below.

What has been said, a little while ago, of Theognis' remonstrances against the rules of Providence, requires to be illustrated; and the illustration may not improperly be placed here, as it is by no means improbable that the verses might have been composed about this time.

LV.

(*Gaisford*, 729-750.)

O mighty Jove! I wish the powers of heaven
Would change their method!—that a rule were given
Henceforward, for the wicked and profane
To check their high presumption, and restrain
Their insolences and their cruelties:
Who mock your ordinances, and despise
Justice and right;—henceforth should every man,
In his own instance, justify the plan
Of Providence: and suffer for his crime
During his life: or at the very time,
With punishment inflicted on the spot;
For now, so long retarded or forgot,
The retribution ultimately falls
Wide of the mark—the vilest criminals
Escape uninjured; and the sad decree
Affects their innocent posterity,
(As oftentimes it happens) worthy men,
Blameless and inoffensive:—here again
The case is hard! where a good citizen,
A person of an honourable mind,
Religiously devout, faithful and kind,
Is doom'd to pay the lamentable score
Of guilt accumulated long before—
Some wicked ancestor's unholy deed.
I wish that it were otherwise decreed!
For now we witness wealth and power enjoy'd
By wicked doers; and the good destroy'd
Quite undeservedly, doom'd to atone
In other times, for actions not their own.

The same notion of a posthumous hereditary retribution overtaking the descendants of wicked men, appears in another fragment, but without that tone of querulous expostulation which marks the preceding and other fragments.

LVI.

(*Gaisford*, 197-208.)

Lawful and honest gain, the gift of heaven,
Is lasting, and abides where it is given:
But where a man, by perjury or by wrong,
Rises in riches, though secure and strong
In common estimation, though he deem
Himself a happy man, (and so may seem)
Yet the just sentence on his wicked gains
Already stands recorded, and remains
For execution. Hence, we judge amiss;
And the true cause of our mistake is this:
  The punishment ordain'd by heaven's decree
Attaches to the sin, but, as we see
In many cases, leaves the sinner free.
Death follows, and is faster in his rate:
While vengeance travels slowly, speedy fate
Arrests the offender at a shorter date.

The same tone of querulousness which was before noticed, and the same singular style of respectful, but confident and familiar expostulation with the Deity, which the reader will have observed in a preceding fragment, is marked in another, which is placed here; though in the order of time, it should seem to be contemporary with Frags. LXXVIII. and LXXIX.

LVII.

(*Gaisford*, 373-396.)

Blessed, almighty Jove! with deep amaze
I view the world; and marvel at thy ways!
All our devices, every subtle plan,
Each secret act, and all the thoughts of man,
Your boundless intellect can comprehend!
On your award our destinies depend.
  How can you reconcile it to your sense
Of right and wrong, thus loosely to dispense
Your bounties on the wicked and the good?
How can your laws be known or understood?
When we behold a man faithful and just,
Humbly devout, true to his word and trust,

Dejected and oppress'd; whilst the profane,
And wicked, and unjust, in glory reign,
Proudly triumphant, flush'd with power and gain;
What inference can human reason draw?
How can we guess the secret of thy law,
Or choose the path approved by power divine?
We take, alas, perforce the crooked line,
And act unwillingly the baser part,
Though loving truth and justice at our heart;
For very need reluctantly compell'd
To falsify the principles we held;
With party factions basely to comply;
To flatter, and dissemble, and to lie!
Yet He, the truly brave, tried by the test
Of sharp misfortune, is approved the best;
While the soul-searching power of indigence
Confounds the weak, and banishes pretence.
Fix'd in an honourable purpose still,
The brave preserve the same unconquer'd will,
Indifferent to fortune, good or ill.

The misery of the heathen world is singularly manifest in the preceding lines; they were unable to find, in their national belief, any sanction, even for those imperfect notions of right and wrong which natural reason suggested to them; and the concluding passage shews, that the better and nobler minds among them framed to themselves a rule of conduct, more elevated than that which their religion authorized. Their mode of piety, consisting in patient submission to the dispensations of an irresistible and inexplicable destiny, is exemplified in the lines which follow.

LVIII.

(*Gaisford*, 133-142.)

Kurnus, believe it! Fortune, good or ill,
No mortal effort, intellect, or skill,
Determine it; but heaven's superior will
We struggle onward, ignorant and blind,
For a result unknown and undesign'd;
Avoiding seeming ills, misunderstood,
Embracing evil as a seeming good;
In our own plans unable to detect

Their final, unavoidable effect:
Tormented with unsatisfied desire,
The fortunate to further aims aspire
Beyond the bounds of mortal happiness;
Restless and wretched in their own success!
We strive like children, and the almighty plan
Controls the froward children of weak man!

We may now return, from his metaphysical and moral speculations, to a view of the poet's personal situation. It is described in a few lines of welcome to a friend, connected with him by those relations of hospitality which were most carefully maintained by the first families of Greece, as a resource against utter destitution, in the event of any of those sudden reverses of fortune, to which, from the unsettled condition of their governments, they were so frequently exposed. Clearistus, being ruined or distressed at home, comes by sea to Megara, probably on a trading voyage; but reckoning, at the same time, on the hospitality of the poet as his hereditary ally.

LIX.

(*Gaisford*, 511-522.)

In a frail bark across the seas you come,
Poor Clearistus, to my poorer home!
Yet shall your needy vessel be supplied
With what the Gods in clemency provide:
And if a friend be with you, bring him here!
With a fair welcome to my simple cheer.
I am not yet a niggard, nor by stealth
Dissemble the poor remnant of my wealth:
Still shall you find a hospitable board,
And share in common what my means afford.
Then, should inquirers ask my present state,
You may reply,—my ruin has been great:
Yet, with my means reduced, a ruin'd man,
I live contented on a humbler plan:
Unable now to welcome every guest—
But greeting glad and freely, though distress'd,
Hereditary friends—of all the best.

A natural incident brings back to his mind the recollection of his misfortunes—this fragment concludes with the obscure line before mentioned, relative to a sea voyage.

LX.

(*Gaisford*, 1197-1202.)

The yearly summons of the creaking crane,
That warns the ploughman to his task again,
Strikes to my heart a melancholy strain—
When all is lost, and my paternal lands
Are till'd for other lords, with other hands,
Since that disastrous wretched voyage brought
Riches and lands and every thing to nought.

The following is an incident relative to another season of the year. Theognis' passion for singing to the music of the pipe has been already noticed (Frag. II.). The scene of this fragment is in the market-place of Megara; and the lines represent the poet's sudden exclamation, at a sight which puts an end to the amusement in which he was indulging. The text is apparently mutilated, and (to the translator at least) hardly intelligible; he has endeavoured, however, to restore the original picture from the traces which are still distinguishable.

LXI.

(*Gaisford*, 823-828.)

How could I bear it? In the public place
To chaunt and revel, when, before my face,
Seen in the distance, I discern the train
Of harvest-triumph, and the loaded wain
And happy labourers with garlands crown'd,
Returning from the hereditary ground,
No more my own! My faithful Scythian slave!
Break off this strain of idle mirth, and shave
Your flowing locks, and breathe another tone
Of sorrow for my fair possessions gone!

Independent of the unbecoming contrast between the levity of his amusements, and the serious nature of his misfortunes, the reflection could not but occur to the mind of the poet, that he was now arrived at a time of life when the privileges and pretensions of early youth could no longer be pleaded in justification of similar frolics. In minds of a poetic temperament, the spirit of childhood and early youth remains commonly unabated to a much longer period than among the generality of mankind; and those successive gradations of gravity, which maturer years require (and which their co-evals assume naturally and unconsciously) are often felt as oppressive restraints by minds so constituted. Hence, in such cases, we see the same individuals censured for untimely levity in their latter years, as they had been before for premature seriousness. Theognis, in this respect at least, appears to have been eminently a poet. His feelings of melancholy foresight were contemporary with the composition of his licentious poetry; and, among other considerations, this probably may have been one which induced him to suppress, for the time, those verses which a more serious spirit had inspired. He was unwilling to betray to the world such incongruities of thought and feeling subsisting at the same time in the same mind. The same incongruity is visible in a comparison between the last fragments, and those already given, Nos. LIII., LIV., and LV.

Omitting these considerations, however, and considering him merely as a man of wit and pleasure about town—the town of Megara—the period of life to which he had arrived was a melancholy one—already on the wrong side of five and thirty, and having immediately before him the prospect of lapsing into the deplorable and irretrievable condition of a decayed dandy or *ci-devant jeune homme!* This is the first shock which we receive from the hand of time. The second will be found differently characterized, in verses composed at the age of fifty-four. It was then no longer the departure of youth, and prospect of age, but the slow and distant approach of death, which was become, for the first time, a torment to his imagination. It will appear singular, that in verses composed probably not many months after those last mentioned, he will still be found speaking of old age as a future evil, of which he deprecates the approach[1]—but so it is;

"Ask, where's the north? In York, 'tis at the Tweed;

[1] Compare Frag. CII. with CV.

In Scotland, at the Orcades ; and there,
At Zembla, Greenland, and the Lord knows where."

In like manner, old age is always a relative period, a little in advance of that to which we have already arrived. The fragment here given, and the somewhat tedious argument with which it is accompanied, might have been omitted if the writer had not thought it his duty, for the satisfaction of others, to give a solution of the apparent contradictions by which his own research had been at one time perplexed.

LXII.

(*Gaisford*, 1125-1128.)

Elate with wine, my losses I despise,
And rude attacks of railing enemies.
But youth departing, and remember'd years
Of early mirth and joy, move me to tears ;
While, in the dreary future, I behold
The dark approach of age, cheerless and cold.

It is evident that these lines must have been written in the period which immediately preceded his banishment, when the ruin of his affairs was a recent event, and his adversaries animated against him. He was not yet in exile ; for the ἄνδρες ἐχθροὶ *his railing enemies* must have been his fellow citizens of the opposite faction, not strangers among whom he was casually resident. Moreover, to lament the departure of his youth would have been absurd and impertinent in an exile subject to so many evils of a much more serious nature. An older poet, Tyrtæus,[1] had said:—"A wanderer of this kind neither enjoys the favour and popularity (ὥρη) which accompanies youth, nor the respect and reverence (αἰδὼς) which is attendant upon old age." It is equally impossible to assign them to the period after his return, for which he was indebted to the indulgence of the faction, to which those very ἐχθροὶ, who were now abusing him, belonged; and when he himself was devoted to a passive literary existence.

The melancholy thoughts which, in the spirit of a true

---

[1] I. 11.

Greek, he was endeavouring to dissipate (as has been seen in the two last fragments) with wine and music, but which were apt to return upon him thus suddenly and unawares, seem to have been revived by the arrival of Simonides. I say revived, for the lines addressed to him are put (I think properly) the last in the order of the series: the political complaints and forebodings contained in them indicating that the revolution was very far advanced—Kurnus's administration being already at an end, and every thing in the utmost confusion. These lines, therefore, may be reckoned as among the very last which were written at Megara, before his expatriation. His feelings upon Simonides' arrival might be supposed to have been aggravated by the comparative change which had taken place in their circumstances; for, at the time to which we are now arrived, Theognis was ruined, and Simonides (whose attachment to the main chance was proverbial) was probably by this time a rich man, for he appears to be giving an entertainment to which Theognis was invited.

It is not unlikely that this visit of Simonides (to Athens probably in the first place, but, as in former instances, extended to Megara) may be the same which is mentioned as having left a singular mark of meanness upon his character, when revisiting Athens, after the expulsion of Hippias, he engaged to compose a panegyrical poem, in honour of the assassins of his old friend and benefactor Hipparchus. Arriving at Megara, the same man would undoubtedly pay his court to the faction then in power in that city; but he could not omit sending an invitation to Theognis. And what sort of invitation would such a man, under such circumstances, have contrived to send? something, it may be supposed, to this effect:—"*The company and conversation to be wholly literary,*" *&c. &c.*; "*persons of distinguished talents, all anxious for an opportunity,*" *&c. &c.*; "*a person so eminent for his genius and acquirements.*" Now the lines of Theognis are (as we shall see) an answer, distinctly replying to and declining an invitation of this description. "The sense of his own misfortunes, and the distracted state of public affairs, had rendered him unfit for company, and incapable of joining in any literary conversation." It may remind us of Swift, after the fall of his friends, replying in bitterness to the flummery literary letter of Pope, whom he suspected of being upon too good terms with the Whigs.

The last line serves to show, that among the "literati," whose company he had been expected to join, and to whom his poetical excuses would be communicated, he would have had a chance of meeting persons disagreeable to him (*κακοὶ* in political language)—persons of the opposite party.

What has been observed above may serve to show that the tone of extreme dejection and prostration of spirit, which is exhibited in the following lines, might at the time have appeared genuine and unaffected; yet we shall see that there is good reason to suppose that it must have been either assumed altogether or intentionally exaggerated. We shall find that the poet must have been, at this very period, engaged in some enterprise of a very dangerous nature; such a description of himself, therefore, if communicated to his opponents (as he calculated that it would be), would excite no suspicion, and might serve perhaps to counteract any which already existed.

The answer to Simonides' "very obliging invitation" is as follows:—

LXIII.

(*Gaisford*, 667-682.)

Simonides! if with my learning's store
I still retain'd my riches as before,
I should not shrink from joining as a guest
In converse with the wisest and the best.
But now, with idle shame oppress'd and weak,
I sit dejected, and forbear to speak;
Feeble, forgetful, melancholy, slow,
My former pride of learning I forego,
My former knowledge I no longer know.
Such is our state! in a tempestuous sea,
With all the crew raging in mutiny!
No duty follow'd, none to reef a sail,
To work the vessel, or to pump or bale;
All is abandon'd, and, without a check,
The mighty sea comes sweeping o'er the deck;
Our steersman,* hitherto so bold and steady,

* Kurnus.

Active and able, is deposed already:
No discipline, no sense of order felt,
The daily messes are unduly dealt;
The goods are plunder'd; those that ought to keep
Strict watch are idly skulking or asleep;
All that is left of order or command
Committed wholly to the basest hand.
In such a case, my friend, I needs must think
It were no marvel though the vessel sink.
This riddle to my worthy friends I tell,
But a shrewd knave will understand it well.

This long simile of a ship is not original in Theognis; it was to be found in an ode of Alcæus, an older poet, from whom Horace has copied it. Theognis probably made use of figurative language in order to avoid giving the *κακοὶ* of the company an opportunity of quoting expressions which, if more intelligible and direct, would have been more likely to compromise him as a disaffected person. We shall see the same apprehension expressed elsewhere in Fragment LXIX.

The last fragment has already anticipated the greater part of what can be learnt from the few remaining fragments relative to the revolution, the deposition of Kurnus, the low character of his successor, and the general confusion and disorder of the community.

No lines can be found of which it can be decidedly said that they relate to Kurnus's appointment to the highest authority of the state. The following will probably be thought (as they appear) too feeble, and not sufficiently pointed for such an occasion, if addressed to Kurnus at all (for his name does not occur in the original); they may have related to some earlier and inferior object of ambition.

LXIV.

(*Gaisford*, 401-406.)

Schemes unadvisable and out of reason
Are best adjourn'd—wait for a proper season!
Time and a fair conjuncture govern all.
Hasty ambition hurries to a fall,
A fall predestined and ordain'd by heaven:

By a judicial blindness madly driven,
Mistaking and confounding good and evil,
Men lose their senses, as they leave their level.

If the conjecture was right, which assigned the two fragments, L. and LI., to the period of Kurnus's elevation, they would account sufficiently for the non-appearance of any admonitory or political lines directly referring to it. If again (as is probable) a reconciliation took place after his deposition, the next lines may have been intended to obviate the influence of rash or treacherous advisers upon a proud spirit recently mortified by the loss of power.

LXV.

(*Gaisford*, 283-292.)

Stir not a step! risk nothing! but believe
That vows and oaths are snares, meant to deceive!
Jove is no warrant for a promise given,—
Not Jove himself, nor all the gods in heaven.
Nothing is safe, no character secure,
Nor conduct, the most innocent and pure:
All are corrupt, the commons and the great,
Alike incapable to save the state.
The ruin of the noblest and the best
Serves for an idle ballad or a jest.
Shame is abolish'd, and in high command
Rage, impudence, and rapine rule the land.

It should seem that Kurnus was now disposed to follow the advice which his friend had before given him respecting the choice of followers and adherents; see Frag. XXXII., III., IV. Theognis thinks such a party could not be formed of assured fidelity and in sufficient force for the purposes which were in contemplation.

LXVI.

(*Gaisford*, 77-86.)

A trusty partisan, faithful and bold,
Is worth his weight in silver or in gold
For times of trouble; but the race is rare,—
Steady, determined men, ready to share
Good or ill fortune! Such, if such there are,

Could you survey the world, and search it round,
And bring together all that could be found,
The largest company you could enrol,
A single vessel would embark the whole!
So few there are! the noble, manly minds,
Faithful and firm, the men that honour binds,
Impregnable to danger and to pain
And low seduction in the shape of gain.

The next fragment serves to mark more distinctly that Kurnus was no longer in office; it is an ironical exhortation to his successor, the chief of the opposite party, who, it should seem, was ruling away with a vengeance!

LXVII.

(*Gaisford*, 845-848.)

Lash your obedient rabble! lash and load
The burden on their backs! spurn them and goad!
They'll bear it all; by practice and by birth
The most submissive humble slaves on earth!

Another fragment seems to have been addressed to some person possessed at one time of influence, which he had misemployed, and whom the progress of the revolution had reduced to insignificance.

LXVIII.

(*Gaisford*, 453-456.)

Friend! if your sense and judgment had been wholly,
Or nearly, equal to your pride and folly,
You might have seen yourself approved and prized
As much precisely as you're now despised.

But the time was come when it was no longer safe to speak so openly—the time, probably, of the visit of Simonides; see the concluding note subjoined to the verses addressed to him, Frag. LXIII.

LXIX.

Scarce can I venture plainly to declare
Our present state, or what the dangers are.
Let the worst happen! I shall bear, I trust,

Whatever fate determines—bear we must!
Inextricable difficulties rise,
And death and danger are before our eyes.

We now find Theognis no longer averse to the desperate measures suited to a desperate situation—but still, as before, distrustful of the firmness and fidelity of the majority of the persons upon whom his friend relied.

LXX.

(*Gaisford*, 73-76.)

From many a friend you must withhold your plans!
No man is safe with many partisans,
No secret! With a party sure, but small,
Of bold adherents, trusty men withal,
You may succeed; else ruin must ensue,
Inevitable, for your friends and you.

This advice seems to have been followed: for we now come to a passage of singular interest—the speech of Theognis, at a secret meeting of Kurnus's party friends. The exordium and the conclusion of this speech are found in separate fragments, but the character of each is clearly marked. The exordium addresses Kurnus, in the presence of his assembled partisans, on the necessity of efficacious remedies for the maladies of the state. It is evidently the prelude to a speech addressed to a council of conspirators, and the conclusion is marked by a conspirator's oath (a very curious and remarkable one) by which he binds himself to the assistance of his comrades, and to the execution of utter vengeance upon his enemies. Some other fragments, which are found separate, and which are not likely to have been composed at any other time, by a man who had hitherto been averse to all violent and hazardous measures, are arranged in the only order which can be assigned to them.

LXXI.

(*Gaisford*, 1129, 1130; 355-358; 867-870.)

Kurnus! since here we meet friends and allies,
We must consult in common, to devise
A speedy remedy with brief debate,

To meet the new disorders of the state.
More practice is required, and deeper skill,
To cure a patient than to make him ill.
The wise in easy times will gladly rest;
When things are at the worst a change is best.

* * * * *

Kurnus! in power and honour, heretofore,
Your former fortunes you discreetly bore.
Fortune has alter'd! bear it calmly still,
Endeavouring, with a firm and steady will,
With other changes, our affairs to mend,
With a bold effort, and with heaven to friend.

* * * * *

If, Kurnus, our support has been displaced,
Our main defence dismantled and defaced,
Must we, like cowards, of all hope forsaken,
Lament and howl, as if the town were taken?
Though now reduced, no more a numerous host,
Courage, and sense, and honour are our boast.

* * * * *

Danger and hope are over-ruling powers
Of equal influence, and both are ours!
Where counsel and deliberation fail,
Action and strenuous effort may prevail.

* * * * *

My spirit they shall never bend nor check,
Though mountain-heaps were loaded on my neck:
Let feeble coward souls crouch with affright,
The brave are ever firm—firm and upright.

* * * * *

Then let the brazen fiery vault of heaven
Crush me with instant ruin, rent and riven!
(The fear and horror of a former age)
If, from the friends and comrades that engage
In common enterprise, I shrink or spare
Myself or any soul! If I forbear
Full vengeance and requital on my foes!
All our antagonists! all that oppose!

Whether this conspiracy succeeded to the extent of obtaining a temporary superiority within the town, or whether it was baffled by their opponents, or abandoned in despair by the party who projected it, we have no means of forming any conjecture; in any one of these cases the incident which appears next in order might equally have taken place.

The march of an armed force from some neighbouring state (whose politics were opposed to those of the party of Kurnus and Theognis) is indicated by a fire signal, and determines them to abandon their country and escape without delay.

LXXII.

(*Gaisford*, 549-560.)

A speechless messenger, the beacon's light,
Announces danger from the mountain's height!
Bridle your horses and prepare to fly:
The final crisis of our fate is nigh!
A momentary pause, a narrow space
Detains them, but the foes approach apace!
We must abide what fortune has decreed,
And hope that heaven will help us at our need.
Make your resolve! at home your means are great;
Abroad you will retain a poor estate,
Unostentatious, indigent, and scant,
Yet live secure, at least from utter want.

In addition to the local and other relations between Corinth and Megara, whoever examines the political character of Corinth at this time, and remarks the evident bias of that government in favour of the democratic party at Athens, will feel no hesitation in concluding that they must have been equally disposed to protect a party of similar principles in their own immediate neighbourhood; and that the armed force above mentioned must have been dispatched from Corinth. This conclusion will be confirmed by the next fragment. Of the other two powerful neighbouring states, Thebes was of opposite politics, hostile in the extreme to the Athenian revolution, and (as we shall see afterwards) became a place of refuge for the Megarian exiles. Athens, an Ionian state, would not at that period have presumed to interpose in the internal disputes of a Doric city; and, least of all, at that particular crisis when, with the whole weight of the Doric confederacy opposed to her, under the ascendancy of Sparta, and directed by the ability and inveteracy of Cleomenes, she was reduced to the then unheard of expedient of soliciting assistance from the King of Persia; and, her envoys arriving at Sardis (though blamed for it afterwards when the danger was over, yet at the time upon deliberate consultation), consented to perform the required homage by presenting earth and water to the great king. Placed in such a precarious situation, it would have been an act of madness on the part of the Athenians to have risked an offensive proceeding, which could have added nothing to their military security; which would have disgusted Corinth, and which, at any rate, would have prevented the success of those intrigues by which the Corinthians (themselves nominally and formally members of the confederacy) succeeded in disbanding the combined army, at a time when it was already advanced into the plain of Eleusis, and on the eve of a battle, likely to have been the most bloodily decided of any that ever occurred in the internal wars of Greece. Availing themselves of the dissolution of the main army, the Athenians lost no time in advancing against the Thebans and Chalcidians, who, in the meanwhile, had been making inroads upon the points bordering upon their own territory; encountering them severally in rapid succession, they overthrew the Thebans, and immediately (the historian says on the same day), passing over into Eubœa, attacked and defeated the Chalcidians, seizing upon the territory and expelling the proprietors.

It should seem that Theognis, in escaping from Megara, had taken up his residence in Eubœa, where the politics of the leading party were congenial to his own. Upon this occasion then, he was a witness of the calamity which overwhelmed his friends and hospitable partisans. The following lines are descriptive of what occurred. Chalcis would have been very unlike any other city or state of Greece if it had not contained a depressed party (in this instance the democratic party) eager to enjoy the exercise of power upon any conditions, and to consider the public distresses as an opportunity for party triumph. From what has been observed, it will be seen how justly the poet's malediction in the concluding line is bestowed upon the Corinthians.

LXXIII.

(*Gaisford*, 887-890.)

Alas, for our disgrace! Cerinthus lost!
The fair Lelantian plain! a plundering host
Invade it—all the brave banish'd or fled!
Within the town, lewd ruffians in their stead
Rule it at random.—Such is our disgrace!
May Jove confound the Cypselizing race!

The term of the "Cypselizing race" could not possibly apply to any other people than the Corinthians; but it may be a question, upon what grounds, and with what particular intention the term is applied to them in this instance. Cypselus was entirely out of date; his son Periander, who succeeded him as Tyrant of Corinth, had died, after a long reign, in the last year of the 48th Olympiad (see *Fasti Hellenici*), having in his old age, and as one of his last acts of sovereignty, sent three hundred boys of the best families in Corcyra, as a present to Alyattes, the father of Crœsus, to be manufactured into eunuchs. Why then should Cypselus be mentioned? the memory of his tyranny being in point of time obsolete, and in point of atrocity effaced by that of his son, after whose death a free government had been established, which had continued, as it appears, without interruption from that time. But Cypselus was the first underminer and destroyer of the Dorian aristocracy; having supplanted the oligarchy of the Bacchiadæ, he had continued banishing and destroying, without intermission, during the whole of his life; and his son (after the usual interval of milder government in a new reign) had resumed his father's policy, and pushed it indiscriminately to a more severe extreme.

But the system had originated with Cypselus. He began as a democratic leader, attacking and overturning an exclusive oligarchy, and afterwards individually destroying and extinguishing them. This, we may suppose, he had pretty well accomplished during the course of his reign; and that the momentary pause of tyranny, at the succession of his son, must have been connected with the consideration that the old opponents of the father's party had been annihilated, and a consequent notion in his mind that it might not be impossible for him to maintain himself in the sovereignty, with a mild administration, as the chief of the triumphant party, like a kind of Lorenzo de Medici.

This scheme of policy, entertained at the outset by Periander, and finally abandoned for one directly opposite, seems to be the point which lies at the bottom of the story of the advice required from his more ancient and experienced fellow-tyrant Thrasybulus, and of the enigmatic speechless answer which he received, in consequence of which he determined to destroy everything which had *grown* above the common *level*—the adherents of his father or their representatives, the opponents of the former exclusive caste and unconnected with it, but who could boast of illustrious descent in another line, derived perhaps, like his own, from the race of the Lapithæ,—everything, in short, which by birth, abilities, wealth, or distinction of any kind, was capable of giving umbrage. But the effect of such a tyranny, when exercised for such a length of time, would be manifest in a continuance of the same policy surviving the overthrow of the government in which it had originated; for the chief persons of Corinth, at the time when it was released from this long course of oppression, must have belonged to families who, from their very obscurity and insignificance, had escaped destruction. Such persons, therefore, and their successors, administering the affairs of the state, would not, in their external relations, be disposed to favour an aristocracy of caste; indeed, their own traditions were very unfavourable to it—the memory of the government of the Doric Aristocracy of the Bacchiadæ having remained little less odious than that of Periander himself.

The policy, therefore, of Corinth, at this time baffling the designs of Sparta, which were directed to the maintenance of the established aristocracies, might not be improperly called the policy of Cypselus, the drift of his tyranny having been carried on, as the champion of the subject classes, in opposition to the Doric aristocracy; while that of Periander was indiscriminate and unsparing, wholly selfish and unsupported by any pretence of party motive. Cypselus, at least as compared with his son, might be considered as a "glorious deliverer;" and a good, steady partisan might have contended that his measures were justifiable upon principle, allowing, at the same time, that "they had been carried a little too far" like those of the "glorious Henry VIII.," whose memory, it is to be observed, remained popular for a length of time after his death. As to his usurpation, that is a point which no true partisan is ever found fastidious enough to impute as a delinquency to the leader of his own party. Sosicles the Corinthian indeed, in a speech delivered at Sparta, in presence of a general convention of the Doric States, describes Cypselus as a bloody tyrant, though greatly surpassed in tyranny by his son; but it must be remembered that Sosicles is arguing generally against arbitrary power in the hands of a single individual, in opposition to the proposal brought forward by the Spartans; who, on discovering that, in deposing Hippias, they had been the dupes of a suborned oracle, were determined to retrace their steps, and to reinstate him in the sovereignty from which they had ejected him. Pleading, therefore, in opposition to this project, it was the object of the Corinthian envoy to place the memory of Cypselus in the most odious light, wholly without modification, and omitting all mention of any favourable recollection which in the minds of the Corinthians themselves might be attached to it. It might be very true that, in the estimation of his own countrymen, Cypselus might have the merit of having destroyed an aristocracy of caste, similar in its origin and principles to that which the Spartans exercised over the subject cities of Laconia; but such a statement would have been highly offensive, and in no way conducive to the success of his argument. The Bacchiadæ, whom Cypselus had destroyed, had in fact been regarded by the Spartans as a kindred clan; but if, considering the occasion which called for it, and the presence in which it was delivered, it is impossible to draw from the speech of Sosicles any clear conclusion with regard to the real feelings of the Corinthians towards the memory of their great revolutionist, there are, on the other hand, circumstances apparently trivial, but which serve to indicate that a favourable feeling must have predominated. That the oracle delivered to him, predicting the future fortunes of his family, and those by which his birth had been in two instances announced, as the predestined destroyer of the Bacchiadæ and the "founder of equal law," should have been repeated and recorded, and that the very chest, in which when a child he was said to have been concealed from the pursuit of the Bacchiadæ, should have been kept as a relic and memorial till it became ultimately interesting as an object of antiquity, are circumstances sufficiently indicative of a long surviving partiality for his memory. But surely this argument must seem superfluous to any man who merely reads the newspapers; the degrading articles from Paris,[1] which daily meet our eyes, may serve as a sufficient proof that the most prodigal waste of human life, a most utter disregard of the sufferings of mankind—finally, a spirit and conduct, exhibiting the most perfect type of the tyrannic character, are in no respect disqualifications for posthumous popularity.

Cypselus was a tyrant and an usurper, but the system of which he was the personification was persevered in after his death. The principle upon which his usurpation had been founded (a hatred of the hereditary oligarchies) still continued to influence the policy of Corinth, and manifested itself in their support of the democratic revolution of Athens and Megara. This was the point which Theognis (doubly a sufferer from the effects of this policy) meant to mark; and if this view of the subject is admissible, his intention in characterizing the Corinthians as a *Cypselizing race* may be capable of explanation. It is to be feared that no authority is likely to be found for any shorter and more decided mode of interpreting the passage.

After so long a digression, it is fortunate, that we have to change the scene and the subject. Expelled from Eubœa, Theognis seems to have retired to Thebes, a state whose politics were congenial to his own; fellow sufferers also, like his friends in Eubœa, from the unexpected vigour of the Athenians, who up to that time, when they became animated (as Herodotus observes) by the new excitement of liberty, had never been accounted very formidable antagonists; while the Thebans, considering themselves, as they were, a superior race of men, distinguished by a peculiar system of tactics, and singular personal prowess

---

[1] The details of the *Translation* of the *Corpo Santo* of Buonaparte.

in the field, upon which the success of their tactical system depended, were wholly unable to digest the disgrace of a defeat. It should seem, both from local situation, and the temper and spirit of the people, that Thebes must have been the scene of those projects and hopes which Theognis and his friends at one time entertained, of recovering possession of their native city either by force or stratagem, and executing a severe vengeance upon their opponents.

But we must first exhibit him in a familiar scene, a stranger among strangers; affording an instance of the unpleasant results arising from that social defect which Shakespeare characterizes as

> "Some humour, which too much o'erleavens
> The form of plausive manners."

The story for the present must be taken upon trust, the proofs and vouchers, being postponed, as they would be too tedious at the outset. The Thebans, we may suppose, did not depart from their usual character of hospitality in the instance of the Megarian exiles; and it so happened, that in the house of a Theban nobleman, a favourite facetious female slave, Arguris by name, was admitted to enliven the party. The music of the pipes was introduced after dinner. This was a temptation which Theognis could not resist, and which overset all the σεμνότης (grave good breeding) befitting his condition as an exiled noble. He offered to accompany the music, and performed so well, as to excite general admiration and applause, and probably, at the same time, to lower himself to a certain degree, in the estimation of the company; which Arguris perceiving (like a sarcastic little wretch as she was) joined in the general expression of admiration. "It was very extraordinary—very extraordinary indeed;—the gentleman must have had a great deal of practice—he must have practised very young,—perhaps his mother might have been a flute-player"—to which we may suppose the poet to have answered "No! that his acquirements were not so limited; that like all other persons of tolerable education in Megara, he had also learned to accompany himself upon the lyre:" thereupon, the lyre being handed to him, he sung to it some extempore verses, acknowledging that passion for accompanying the music of the pipe, which had subjected him to so severe an insinuation; replying to it at the same time by an assertion of the nobility of his birth, and a severe retaliation upon the condition and origin of the person who had offended him. These lines, originally produced extempore, formed a short poem, of which the lines already given in illustration of his early pursuits (and which are here repeated in what appears to be their proper place) would have been the conclusion, at least as far as regarded the affront received, and the person who had offered it.

LXXIV.

(*Gaisford*, 531-534; 535-538; 1209-1216; 529, 530.)

My heart exults, the lively call obeying,
When the shrill merry pipes are sweetly playing;
With these, to chaunt aloud or to recite,
To carol and carouse, is my delight:
Or in a stedfast tone, bolder and higher,
To temper with a touch, the manly lyre.

* * * * *

The slavish visage never is erect;
But looks oblique and language indirect
Betray their origin—no lovely rose,
Or hyacinth, from the rude bramble grows;
Nor from a slavish and degraded breed,
Can gentle words or courteous acts proceed.

* * * * *

From noble Æthon my descent I trace,
Thebes grants me refuge and a resting place;
Forbear then, Arguris, with empty mirth,
Yourself a slave, to scandalize my birth:
Woman! I tell thee, wandering and forlorn,
In exile and distress, much have I borne,
Sorrows and wrongs and evils manifold;
But, to be purchased as a slave and sold
Has never been my fate, nor ever will;
And I retain a town and country still,
Along the banks of the Lethæan river,
In a fair land, where I shall live for ever;
For a firm friend, a steady partisan,
A faithful and an honourable man,

Disdaining every sordid act and mean,
No slave am I, nor slavish have I been.

We must now proceed to justify the probability of the incident which has been above related. It is evident, from the original, that the poet is provoked to assert the nobility of his birth, in reply to some disparaging insinuation. But how does he characterize this insinuation? Not according to the usual forms of the language, which in such case would have described it as injurious to his family or his forefathers—*γένος καὶ πατέρας*; instead of either of these, the phrase which he actually makes use of, is *τοκῆας, my parents*, a term quite unusual in discussing any question of descent. It seems difficult to account for this particular phrase; but one solution presents itself—namely, that as (without naming her) it evidently includes the poet's mother, it might have been meant to refer to some sarcasm particularly directed against her; but here again, what could there have been in the manner and behaviour of Theognis, a well educated man, a stranger and a guest at the table of her master, which could suggest even to the most impertinent upper-servant, the idea of any insinuation against the gentleman's mother? Theognis's proficiency in accompanying the music of the pipe, and his passion for exhibiting it (of which we have already seen an instance), would furnish an answer to this difficulty. The pipe was commonly played by a female musician, and the occupation was by no means a reputable one.

Another circumstance may be mentioned as giving strength to this conjecture; the existing text of Theognis is so strange a jumble, so evidently compiled without sense or order, that no stress can be laid upon the juxtaposition of passages as inferring any connexion between them (at least in the intention of the transcriber) but the consideration, that he might have been led mechanically to make various extracts, at the same time, from the same portion of the original, which lay open before him, is not entirely to be overlooked. We have already seen an example of this, in the fragment which alludes to the fate of Hipparchus, and the others descriptive of his character, which are found in juxtaposition with lines evidently relating to his funeral. In like manner it will be found, that three of these fragments, given above, stand in juxtaposition in the present text; and that the fourth is connected by its sense with two of the others, as they all three relate to some altercation with a slave, an incident which, though it might have occurred to him again, was not likely to be made on any other occasion a theme for poetry.

At no great distance from two of the preceding, a fragment is found separated into two, in Brunck's edition; but which, though two or more intermediate lines may possibly be wanting, appear connected by the particle δὲ and by the infinitive form of the verb, which runs through both. These lines belong clearly to the same period as the preceding, when he was hospitably entertained at Thebes, and while he still cherished hopes of a triumphant return to Megara. Now, if we figure to ourselves the preceding scene, and do not suppose Theognis to be utterly destitute of civility and common sense, we may fairly take it for granted that the extempore effusion, in which he retaliated the offence given by the slave, would not have terminated without some marked expression of respect and deference to the master of the house, who was wholly guiltless of the offence which had been given him. In the translation which follows, the fragment last mentioned is understood and interpreted in this sense.

LXXV.

(*Gaisford*, 561-566.)

To seize my lost possessions, and bestow,
Among my friends, the spoils of many a foe,—
Such is my trust and hope; meanwhile I rest
Content and cheerful, an admitted guest
Conversing with a wise and worthy mind
Profound in learning, and in taste refined:
Watching his words and thoughts, to bear away
Improvement and instruction day by day.

If we consider the word *χρεὼν* in its relation to *σοφίην πᾶσαν*, we see that the apparent maxim is only one of those forms of speech arising out of, and implying, an instance actually present. "You ought always to take a glass of good Burton ale with your cheese" is a maxim which, whatever may be its value, is never heard except in cases where ale of that description is actually at hand. Thus when Theognis says—"One *ought* to be invited to a feast, and to sit in company with an excellent person possessed of *universal* knowledge," he is to be understood as saying—"I think it a good thing to be as I am at present, invited, and sitting at table in company with an excellent person of universal knowledge."

The hopes and projects of an exile, briefly alluded to in the preceding fragment, are more distinctly marked in a passage alluding to the story of Ulysses. He anticipates, like him, a safe return from hell (in his own case, the hell of banishment), and a similar triumphant re-establishment in his native country; with an equally full revenge upon his antagonists, and a joyful meeting with his Penelope and his Telemachus, his wife and son, whom, it should seem, that he had left behind. The same allusion to his state of banishment as a kind of hell will be found in another passage, (composed long after, under the influence of very different views and expectations), where the example, which he takes as a parallel to his own, is that of Sisyphus.

LXXVI.

(*Gaisford*, 1119-1124.)

Talk not of evils past! Ulysses bore
Severer hardships than my own, and more;
Doom'd to descend to Pluto's dreary reign,
Yet he return'd, and view'd his home again,
And wreak'd his vengeance on the plundering crew,
The factious haughty suitors, whom he slew:
Whilst all the while, with steady faith unfeign'd,
The prudent, chaste Penelope remain'd,
With her fair son, waiting a future hour,
For his arrival and return to power.

The above allusion to the good conduct of his wife is confirmed by lines addressed to Kurnus, who, it should seem, was equally fortunate.

LXXVII.

(*Gaisford*, 1223, 1224.)

Kurnus, of all good things in human life,
Nothing can equal goodness in a wife.
In our own case, we prove the proverb true ;—
You vouch for me, my friend, and I for you.

A mixture of hope and despondency accompanied by a vehement passion for revenge are marked in the following lines. Singular as they may appear, they are, to the best of the translator's ability, a faithful representation of the style, tone, and *phraseognomy* which mark the original; such, in short, as the author would have written in English, if we could suppose the English language to have been employed in directing such strange addresses to the Supreme Being. It must be observed, however, that in the concluding lines a proverb, contracted from a simile, is expanded into the simile from which it originated, no equivalent proverb being to be found in the English language.

The word *χαράδρα* in the original may perhaps have been intended to convey a local meaning; it signified a gully, the bed of a wintry torrent. A ravine of this kind, called the Charadra, was one of the boundaries of the Megarian territory. Theognis, therefore, may have meant to allude to the direction in which he had passed the frontier.

LXXVIII.

(*Gaisford*, 337-350.)

May Jove assist me to discharge the debt
Of kindness to my friends ; and grant me yet
A further boon—revenge upon my foes !
With these accomplish'd, I could gladly close
My term of life—a fair requital made ;
My friends rewarded, and my wrongs repaid.
Gratitude and revenge, before I die,
Might make me deem'd almost a Deity !
Yet hear, O mighty Jove, and grant my prayer !
Relieve me from affliction and despair !
O take my life, or grant me some redress,
Some foretaste of returning happiness !

Such is my state—I cannot yet descry
A chance of vengeance on mine enemy,
The rude despoilers of my property.
Whilst I, like to a scared and hunted hound,
That scarce escaping, trembling and half drown'd,
Crosses a gulley swell'd with wintry rain,
Have crept ashore in feebleness and pain.
Yet my full wish—to drink their very blood—
Some power divine, that watches for my good,
May yet accomplish—soon may he fulfil
My righteous hope—my just and hearty will.

The pleasures of hope (the proverbial consolation of a banished man) are the subject of the next fragment.

LXXIX.

(*Gaisford*, 1131-1146.)

For human nature Hope remains alone
Of all the deities—the rest are flown.
Faith is departed, Truth and Honour dead,
And all the Graces, too, my friends, are fled.
The scanty specimens of living worth,
Dwindled to nothing and extinct on earth.
Yet whilst I live, and view the light of heaven,
(Since Hope remains, and never has been driven
From the distracted world), the single scope
Of my devotion is to worship Hope:
When hecatombs are slain and altars burn
With all the deities adored in turn,
Let Hope be present, and with Hope, my friend,
Let every sacrifice commence and end.
Yes! insolence, injustice, every crime,
Rapine and wrong, may prosper for a time;
Yet shall they travel on to swift decay,
That tread the crooked path and hollow way.

The fourth line is characteristic; the victim of a popular revolution lamenting that democracy had destroyed the Graces: like the Commander in that admirable proverb of Mons. Le Clercq's—"Le Souper."

With an expatriated party the disappointment of their hopes is usually fatal to that spirit of cordiality which had originated in a feeling of common interests. It is then that each individual, as the object of their union appears unattainable, begins to confine his views to his own personal interests; and a tone of selfishness and querulous recrimination succeeds to that spirit of good humour and good fellowship, which, as long as they are not wholly destitute of hope, is frequently characteristic of a defeated party.

It should seem that the hopes entertained by the poet, and the emigrant party to which he belonged, were never realized; and that (as was naturally to be expected) a spirit of impatience and discontent must have begun to be prevalent amongst them. The following lines seem to belong to this period, and to be descriptive of the altered temper of his associates in misfortune.

LXXX.

(*Gaisford*, 415-418.)

I search among my friends—none can I find,
No sterling unadulterated mind;
None that abides the crucible like mine,
Rising above the standard—superfine!

In these lines the sense which is assigned to the word ὑπερτερίη (above the standard) is assumed from the context: the lexicons do not give it; nor is it to be expected that lexicographers should find in ancient authors the technical terms of the assay office; but we have seen already, (Frag. VI., XXXIV.) that it was an object familiar to the mind of the poet.

Theognis, it should seem, must have been among the poorest of the party, having escaped from Megara πάντ' ἀποσεισάμενος, "stript of everything"—a circumstance necessarily omitted in the translation of Frag. LXXVIII. as it would have appeared somewhat absurd if combined with the simile of the dog. The following lines seem to have been occasioned by the illiberality of some of his companions, who were less destitute than himself.

LXXXI.

(*Gaisford*, 209, 210.)

An exile has no friends! no partisan

Is firm or faithful to the banish'd man;
A disappointment and a punishment,
Harder to bear and worse than banishment!

The reader is here requested to turn back to the fragment marked LVII. beginning "Blessed, Almighty Jove," which, from the singularity of its tone, had been placed in juxtaposition with others of a like character. He will probably be of opinion that in chronological order it ought to stand here, as it marks a time when the notion of abandoning his party and endeavouring to conciliate the victorious faction, though not admitted or approved, has distinctly presented itself to his mind.

The next fragment marks his resolution upon this subject as already taken. In consequence of the neglect of his associates, he declares his intention of negotiating for himself, and endeavouring to conciliate the faction by which he had been expelled.

LXXXII.

(*Gaisford,* 809-812.)

The last and worst of ills, save death alone,
The worst of human miseries is my own!
Those friends of mine have cast me off—and I
Must seek perforce a last resource, to try
To treat and tamper with the enemy.

The English reader is desired to interpret the words "cast me off" as an expression indirectly implying a refusal of pecuniary assistance. The word in the original (προὔδωκαν) is used in this sense in another passage of the poet (not here translated), in which a poor courtezan is describing her own condition, v. 841.[1]

The same tone of complete despondency, the same complaint of abandonment on the part of his friends, and the consequent necessity of endeavouring to conciliate his enemies, are apparent in the following fragment.

---

[1] v. 859 *ed.* Gaisford.

LXXXIII.

(*Gaisford*, 1007-1010.)

Happy the man, with worldly wealth and ease,
Who, dying in good time, departs in peace:
Not yet reduced to wander as a stranger,
In exile and distress, and daily danger;
To fawn upon his foes, to risk the trial
Of a friend's faith, and suffer a denial!

A short fragment is to be found, of little merit in itself, but which (as it evidently marks a particular turn in the views and feelings of the poet) cannot, according to the strict rules of criticism, be overlooked in any attempt to ascertain and arrange the incidents of his life. The original of this singular and perplexing passage, if expanded into the dimension which is necessary to render its intention and meaning discernible to an English reader, might stand thus:

LXXXIV.

(*Gaisford*, 1077, 1078.)

No mean or coward heart will I commend
In an old comrade or a party friend;
Nor with ungenerous hasty zeal decry
A noble-minded gallant enemy.

The original couplet (for it is a couplet in the original) appears, like others of the detached couplets which are found in our present copies, to have been the exordium of a separate poem; a poem of which, as of many others, only the initial lines have been preserved. In this poem, then (as is apparent from the supposed introductory lines) the poet's intention must have been to pass in review the characters of his own partisans, and also those of his adversaries, with professed impartiality, but with a *candid* bias in favour of his opponents.

With respect, then, to a poem of this description, or to any other poem of which the lines in question could consistently have formed a part, a difficulty would arise as to the period of the poet's life (if such a period could be found) to which it might with any probability be assigned. We have already seen that his fear and hatred of the opposite party had been progressively becoming more and more intense up to the very moment of his expatriation; it is impossible, therefore, to assign this fragment (or any poem to which it could have belonged) to the period preceding that event. Again, the tone of it, (from which it is evident that the poet still considered himself as a personage whose estimate of individuals might be deemed a matter of importance,) is totally at variance with the character which, many years after, when he succeeded in obtaining permission to return to Megara, he found himself obliged to assume. An utter and entire abjuration of all party feelings and reminiscences seems to have been the implied condition of his recall—a condition to which he adhered with an excess of caution.

The reader, if he arrives in safety to the concluding pages of this essay, will see that the tone of this fragment, implying a critical estimate of the characters of the poet's friends and opponents, would have been wholly unsuited to the situation in which he was placed at this latter period.

The length of this discussion may seem perhaps disproportionate to the very moderate merit of the passage to which it relates. If it had been the intention of the writer to compose a mere romance, illustrative of early Grecian manners, and diversified with occasional scraps of something in the shape of poetry, making use of the text of the author merely as a canvas for the exercise of invention: in such a case, undoubtedly, it might have been advisable to have avoided all notice of any passage apparently inconsistent with the assumed narrative, but of which the incongruity would not be manifest, except to the accurate and diligent inquirer, who, noticing the passage in the first instance, might follow it out into the primary inferences which it legitimately suggests, and in so doing might be conducted to a conclusion irreconcilable with the series of deductions founded upon the coherent and concurrent testimony of other fragments. But it has been the wish and endeavour of the writer to trace a series of real events more rationally interesting, in his judgment, than any work of fiction which he could have ventured to attempt. He is therefore anxious to remove those impediments which had obstructed his own investigation, and which might equally impede the researches of any other person whose attention might happen to be directed to the same author. This passage had long appeared a decided stumbling block; and it is some satisfaction to have been able to convert it into a stepping-stone. It had, in fact, been taken for granted, naturally enough, that the poem to which this passage belonged must have been composed at Megara. Upon this supposition it had appeared utterly unaccountable, and wholly at variance with the inferences deducible from other fragments; but it sometimes happens that a very simple reflection may serve for the solution of what had been long considered as a serious difficulty. It is clear from Frags. LXXXIII. and LXXXIV. that Theognis must have been in negotiation, or at least attempting to negotiate, with the party in possession of the city, the party by whom he had been expelled. With a view then to conciliate his adversaries, and to prepare the way for his own recall, what method would be most likely to be employed by a man who was in the habit of employing poetry upon all occasions: who replies in verse to the impertinence of a female slave: and whom we have seen composing in metre the speech which he delivered at a party meeting, assembled at a critical time, and deliberating upon the adoption of the most dangerous measures? There should seem to be little difficulty in supposing that the habitual and natural language of the poet must have been employed upon this occasion: that verse would have been the vehicle of his first overtures: and that a poem of affected candour, in which, as he says himself, his friends (the bad ones at least) were not to be praised, and his enemies (the good ones at least) were not to be blamed, must have been the first overture to the treaty which he was endeavouring to open with the victorious party.

The failure of this negotiation will, in the meanwhile, serve to account for the tone of utter dejection and despondency which is marked in the next fragment.

LXXXV.

(*Gaisford*, 425-428.)

Not to be born—never to see the sun!
No worldly blessing is a greater one!
And the next best is speedily to die—
And lapt beneath a load of earth to lie!

We are now approaching to a very different period of the poet's existence—his long residence in Sicily. That island and the country of Magna Græcia, as it was called (the maritime portion of the continental territory of Naples), stood at that time in the same relation to the older states of Greece, as the coasts of Asia-Minor had done at an early period; nearly the same as that of the States of America with respect to the present European world. The western colonies of the little world of Greece were the common refuge of unemployed talent. Abounding in wealth to a degree that was become proverbial, and profuse in their encouragement of all the arts by which their customary forms of life could be polished or adorned, they afforded an asylum and the means of employment and maintenance to talents and ingenuity of every kind.

Among the many persons who sought refuge in this new world, there could have been hardly any one who was determined to such a measure, by circumstances of more complete destitution than those in which Theognis must have found himself. Forced into exile—as he described himself, "stript of everything:" disappointed in his hopes of a victorious return and triumphant retaliation upon his enemies; disgusted with his associates, and neglected by them; and failing of success in the conciliatory overture from which he had hoped to obtain a remission of his exile, his situation was one which, if it did not terminate in irretrievable despair, must have suggested some decided and extraordinary resolution. This resolution is announced in the following lines; the last, as it should seem, in which the name of Kurnus occurs. In the original there is a point of character and feeling which is imperfectly represented in the translation. In taking leave of his friend he repeats his name several times.

LXXXVI.

(*Gaisford*, 173-182.)

For noble minds the worst of miseries,
Worse than old age or wearisome disease,
Is poverty—from poverty to flee,
From some tall precipice prone to the sea
It were a fair escape to leap below!
In poverty, dear Kurnus, we forego

Freedom in word and deed, body and mind :
Action and thought, are fetter'd and confined.
Let me then fly, dear Kurnus, once again !
Wide as the limits of the land and main,
From these entanglements ; with these in view
Death is the lighter evil of the two.

We now come to the period of his long residence in Sicily, where the following lines were composed under the pressure of distress and difficulty, probably soon after his arrival, and while the impressions of a sea-voyage were uppermost in his mind.

LXXXVII.

(*Gaisford*, 619, 620.)

Wearied and sick at heart, in seas of trouble,
I work against the wind, and strive to double
The dark disastrous cape of poverty.

The following lines seem to have been composed about the same time, and under the same circumstances. It is curious that the habit of generalization should follow him, even when reflecting upon his own situation. His mind expands itself naturally into a comprehensive observation.

LXXXVIII.

(*Gaisford*, 623, 624.)

All kinds of shabby shifts are understood,
All kinds of arts are practised, bad and good ;
All kinds of ways to gain a livelihood.

His personal talents and acquirements seem at this time to have been his sole resource ; and amongst them, the most obvious and the most marketable was the proficiency which he had attained to as a vocal performer, accompanying the music of the pipe.

In this character we find him assisting at a musical festival, and apologising for his voice, which is likely, he says, to be affected by "having accompanied a party of revellers and serenaders the night before ; moreover, the other performer, who ought to have borne a part with him, has failed in his engagement. But he has no objection to the piper whom they have provided, and will proceed with his engagement."*

LXXXIX.

(*Gaisford*, 933-938.)

I cannot warble like a nightingale; †
This voice of mine, I fear, is like to fail,
With rambling on a revel late at night. ‡
  I shall not make a poor excuse, to slight
Your piper's art and practice; but the friend,
That ought to bear his part here and attend,
In fact is absent—I must do my best,
And put my talent fairly to the test.
So, praying to the gods for help and grace,
Close to the piper's side I take my place.

In the original there is an ambiguity which could not be represented in English; δεξιὸς in one sense implies his skill as a musician, in the other it describes his position at the side of the piper.

Exhibition such as this must have been felt as mortifying by a man of birth, and who had been originally a person of rank and consequence in his native city. Accordingly, we find feelings, such as might be expected from him, expressed in the following fragment, written probably about the same time.

XC.

(*Gaisford*, 649-652.)

O poverty! how sorely do you press,
Debasing soul and body with distress:
To such degrading offices you bind
A manly form, an elevated mind,
Once elegantly fashion'd and refined.

It is but too natural to suppose that the attempts of a poor gentleman to obtain a living by the exercise of talents which had formerly served for his amusement, would be exposed to the censure of professional performers: one of them, it should seem, (Academus by name), had spoken of him as not being a *thoroughbred* musician, but a kind of *mule* between an artist and amateur. To this taunt he replies in the first of the two following fragments; the

* Sic in orig.

† ὥσπερ ἀηδών.

‡ Where he had been hired to attend.

second, though separated in the present text, seems to belong to it, as an easy conciliatory conclusion to the previous reprimand.

XCI.

(*Gaisford*, 987-990; 1051-1054.)

I wish that a fair trial were prepared,
Friend Academus! with the prize declared,
A comely slave, the conqueror's reward;
For a full proof, betwixt myself and you,
Which is the better minstrel of the two.
Then would I show you that a *Mule* surpasses,
In his performance, all the breed of *Asses*.

* * * * *

Enough of such discourse. Now let us try
To join our best endeavours, you and I,
With voice and music, since the muse has bless'd
Us both with her endowments; and possess'd
With the fair science of harmonious sound
The neighbouring people and the cities round.

The last lines mark his position as a foreign artist,—he is complimenting the natives.

We now find that he was beginning to get together a little money, and the next fragment will shew that he was become very careful of it.

XCII.

(*Gaisford*, 1111, 1112.)

You boast of wealth, and scornfully deplore
My poverty—something I have in store;
And with God's blessing I shall make it more.

Being now under the necessity of vindicating himself from a charge of meanness and parsimony, his defence is made in the same spirit of generalization which has been already noticed as a peculiar feature of his mind.

XCIII.

(*Gaisford*, 1055-1059.)

Though gifted with a shrewd and subtle ken,
Timagoras!—the secret hearts of men

(You'll find it) are a point hard to be guess'd ;
For poor and shabby souls, in riches dress'd,
Make a fair show ; while indigence and care
Give to the noble mind a meaner air.

Theognis might have been enabled to maintain himself at first, and possibly to make a little money in the way above described, and perhaps by teaching music and poetry ; but his most important occupation (like that of his instructor Simonides), and that from which the chief source of his gains would have arisen, was the direction of the choral entertainments which were exhibited in competition by the different tribes, at the expense of the wealthiest citizens of each. The person charged with this burdensome office was called the Choregus, a word signifying properly, the *Leader of the Chorus ;* though afterwards, owing to this circumstance, it was employed to signify the person who was chargeable with the expenses of any undertaking, or who voluntarily engaged to defray them. The Choregus then, not being, it may be supposed, usually capable of directing an entertainment consisting of music, poetry and dancing, was under the necessity of employing another person, under the designation of Chorodidascalus, or *teacher of the chorus*, a professed artist, a poet, musician and ballet-master, characters which were anciently united in the same person. The Chorodidascalus, charged to prepare and direct the details of the entertainment, did not lead an easy life. He had to compose the poetry and the music : to discipline and superintend the evolutions of the chorus of dancers : it was necessary that he should be perfect in the system of choral tactics, capable of inventing new manœuvres, and of directing their execution. He had, moreover, to manage the vocal and instrumental performers, and to negotiate with the machinist and the makers of dresses, masks, &c. ; but a most mortifying circumstance would arise, when the Choregus, from the mere paltry consideration of additional expense, had the bad taste to refuse his consent to some manifest improvement in the exhibition. Theognis, on one occasion, seems to have met with a Choregus who was insensible to the advantages of some proposed improvement ; and he is led to the conclusion expressed in the following verses, that the rarity of the union of wealth and good taste in the same individual is highly unfavourable to the progress of the fine arts!

XCIV.

(*Gaisford*, 683-686.)

Dunces are often rich, while indigence
Thwarts the designs of elegance and sense;
Nor wealth alone, nor judgment can avail:
In either case, art and improvement fail.

Finding himself become an active person, the reflection seems to have occurred to him that he had formerly been equally active in pursuits of a very different kind. This reflection, according to his usual habit, is generalized in the following lines:

XCV.

(*Gaisford*, 1227, 1228.)

The passions and the wants of nature breed
Winged desires, that with an airy speed
Hurry abroad, for pleasure or for need,
On various errands, various as their hue—
A fluttering, eager, ever busy crew.

As his circumstances improved, his spirits seem to have risen, and he rejoices in the success of his exertions, though conscious of their derogatory character.

XCVI.

(*Gaisford*, 1113, 1114.)

Plutus, of all the Gods the first and best!
My wrongs with your assistance are redress'd;
Now reinstated in respectability,
In spite of all my baseness and humility.

Though now relieved from poverty, he was unable, or did not deem it advisable, to indulge his wishes and fancies, as he had been in the habit of doing formerly. This change seemed to require an apology, which he addressed to them, as follows.

XCVII.

My old companions, Fancy and Desire!
To treat you both, as each of you require,
My means are insufficient—never mind!
Ours is the common case of human-kind.

At length he finds himself in a situation in which he is led to consider the question of greater indulgence and a larger expenditure. This question, after viewing it on both sides, he seems disposed to determine in favour of continued economy.

The perplexity, of which Theognis complains, is one which in our times would be easily solved by sinking a portion of capital, or the whole of it, in a life-annuity; but he was fearful of infringing upon his capital, apprehending that (as is said to have been the case with Pope's father) he might live more than long enough to consume the whole.

XCVIII.

(*Gaisford*, 899-932.)

Current expenditure—to bring it all
Within the compass of our capital,
Is a wise plan, but difficult withal.
Could we beforehand ascertain the date
Of our existence, we might fix a rate
For our expense, and make it more or less;
But, as it is, we must proceed by guess.
The road divides! which path am I to choose?
Perplex'd with opposite diverging views.
Say, shall I struggle on, to save and spare,
Or lead an easy life, and banish care?
Some have I seen, with competence of wealth,
Indifferent to friendship, pleasure, health,
Struggling and saving; till the final call,
Death sends his summons, and confiscates all!
Allotting to the thankless heedless heir,
The produce of his economic care!
Yet others have I seen reckless of pelf—
"I take my pastime, and I please myself—"
Such was the jolly phrase: the same gallant

Have I beheld an utter mendicant;
In sad dependence, at his latter end,
Watching and importuning every friend.
  Our wiser course then, Damocles I deem,
Is that which steers aloof from each extreme:
Not to consume my life with care and pain,
Economizing for another's gain;
And least of all, to risk the future fears
Of indigence in my declining years.
With this reflection, therefore, I incline
To lean a little to the saving line;
For something should be left, when life is fled,
To purchase decent duty to the dead;
Those easy tears, the customary debt
Of kindly recollection and regret.
Besides, the saving of superfluous cost
Is a sure profit, never wholly lost;
Not altogether lost, though left behind,
Bequeathed in kindness to a friendly mind.
  And for the present, can a lot be found
Fairer and happier than a name renown'd,
And easy competence, with honour crown'd;
The just approval of the good and wise,
Public applauses, friendly courtesies;
Where all combine a single name to grace
With honour and pre-eminence of place,
Coevals, elders, and the rising race!

This last passage is separated from the preceding, in Brunck's edition. It is possible that some intermediate lines may have been lost; but the train of thought seems to have been continuous: he feels that the estimation which he has acquired in society is such as to supersede any temptation to increase it, by living at an increased expense.

It is difficult to assign a place to the following fragment: that it was written in exile is evident.

Whether this picture has a reference to the battle of Elorus, or to some petty unrecorded hostilities which might have taken place while he was resident in Thebes, it is not easy to determine. The address to companions, who like himself had no interest in the cause, seems to indicate a time when he had not separated himself from his fellow emigrants; and the passage altogether, has more of a tone of freedom and alacrity than would seem to belong to the later period of his residence in Syracuse. It is therefore placed here rather for the sake of marking the time of the battle of Elorus, than in any confidence that it actually related to it. The tone of carelessness and indifference in which he speaks of going to battle, as upon a mere point of honour, forbids us to assign this fragment to the time of the action between the Chalcidians and Athenians; in which he must have felt a strong interest.

XCIX.

(*Gaisford*, 881-886.)

Peace is my wish,—may peace and plenty crown
This happy land, the people and the town!
May peàce remain! and may we never miss
Good cheer and merry meetings such as this!
Whether at home or here, all wars I hate,
All battle I detest and execrate.
Then never hurry forward! for we fight
Not for ourselves nor for our country's right.
But with the bawling herald, loud and clear,
Shouting a noisy summons in my ear,
And with my own good horse, for very shame,
We must engage and join the bloody game.

The battle of Elorus, in which the Syracusans were totally defeated, was followed by the siege of Syracuse; which appears to have been long protracted, since it afforded time for a singular combination—that of the Corinthians and Corcyreans, habitually enemies, but each of them interested in behalf of the Syracusans as a kindred race. The joint assistance and interposition of these two states effected the deliverance of the Syracusans, under a compromise, by which they surrendered to Gelo the sovereignty of Camarina. Suidas says, that during the siege, Theognis wrote a poem to "those who had escaped," meaning probably, those who, having escaped from the battle, were afterwards the defenders of the besieged town. Of this poem a small fragment may be traced in the confused medley which at present exists. It seems to reflect on the unwarlike character of the exiled nobility: a defect which notoriously belonged to them. The poem itself would have been interesting and curious, but the remaining lines are of little value.

C.

(*Gaisford*, 863-866.)

The Gods have granted mighty stores of pelf
To many a sluggard, useless to himself
And his own partisans: but high renown
Awaits the warrior who defends the town.

The events above mentioned seem to have led to Theognis' return from his long exile. The state of Corinth was at that time strongly influenced by democratic policy. The Corinthians had promoted the revolution at Megara, and favoured that of Athens; they were "the Cypselizing race" whom Theognis had execrated as the authors of his misfortunes and disappointments. The Corinthian deputies and commanders, however, on their arrival at Syracuse, must have found their old aristocratic victim, transformed by circumstances into a very passable democrat, engaged in the defence of the city against a besieging force, commanded by the patron of the exiled aristocracy. Theognis having, no doubt, introduced himself to the acquaintance of the Corinthian commander (an influential person in a state which possessed a great ascendancy over Megara), conscious moreover of a literary reputation which would do honour to his country, and sufficiently provided with certificates of civism, seems to have thought that nothing more was wanting to procure his erasure from the "List of Emigrants:" his Corinthian friend, however, whose political sagacity seems to have suggested the story of Sisyphus and Proserpine, was unable to extricate him from the "Hell of Banishment," upon the simple consideration of his late political conduct. An amnesty for his old political offences on the part of the government, accompanied on his side by a practical renunciation of his former principles and attachments, seems to have been the basis of the treaty; but there was also another indispensable article, the consideration of which brings us back to the extracts immediately preceding the last, which refers to the private finances of the poet. Drachmas, it should seem, he had accumulated: and a certain sacrifice of drachmas was necessary to the success of the negotiation. Under these circumstances the following characteristic lines were produced. They express the poet's satisfaction at the acquisition and possession of wealth, mixed with a strong feeling of mortification at being obliged to purchase as a favour what he might have expected to have received honourably and gratuitously as a tribute to his reputation and talents. The long history of Sisyphus and Proserpine is an allegory. Proserpine is the power, whose connivance or indulgence can enable him to return from the infernal regions of exile; not as he had expected to return before, after a visit to the same dismal abodes, like Ulysses, with a bloody vengeance on his enemies (Frag. LXXVI.), but upon condition of a mutual oblivion of the past, which he describes as "a grant of oblivion accompanied by a sacrifice of his judgment and understanding;"—the precise condition of the emigrant who obtains his return from the indulgence of a hostile party, and who binds himself, at the same time, to an inoffensive behaviour in word and deed. On these conditions he enjoys the benefit of *oblivion* on the one hand; while, on the other, his judgment of men and things is suppressed and practically annihilated.

The story of Sisyphus and Proserpine appears, at first sight, not only foreign to the main subject and purpose (an expression of devout gratitude to the God of wealth), but is, moreover, unaccountably tedious. This very tediousness, however, is an artifice of the poet, by which he directs the attention of the reader to a meaning which he could not venture more distinctly to express. We are at first offended, and exclaim,—"*What can be the meaning of all this stuff?*" till, after a little reflection, the meaning presents itself.

Though much mortified, it should seem, at the pecuniary sacrifice required of him, Theognis does not suffer his indignation to get the better of his modesty and self-respect; he disdains to state his own case, but exemplifies it by a similar one. "If a man," says he, "possessed the speed of the Harpies or the sons of Boreas (that is to say, if he could obtain the greatest honour, for so it was considered, for himself and his native city, by gaining a victory at the Olympic games) it would be of no avail to him; he would still have to learn that the only effectual influence is that of gold." We here again trace the association of ideas, before noticed, between successful poetry and success at the Olympic games. In the present case, what is affirmed of the one is implied of the other;—both would be useless.

CI.

(*Gaisford*, 523-526; 697-718.)

O Plutus! justly to your gifts and you
Mankind attribute praise and honour due.
With your assistance, we securely face
Defeat and disappointment and disgrace.
Thus to reward the virtuous, and to slight
Wicked and dirty knaves, is surely right;
For with the world at large, no merit tells,
But Plutus and his bounty,—nothing else!
No! not the sense of Rhadamanthus old,
Nor all the shrewd devices manifold
Which Sisyphus, the keen Corinthian, knew;
That wily chief, that, if old tales are true,
Made a most strange escape, so poets tell,—
By dint of rhetoric, he return'd from hell!
For she (that kind oblivion can dispense,
But takes away the judgment and the sense)
The Goddess Proserpine, by strong persuasion,
Consented to connive at his evasion—
A thing unheard of, and unknown before;
That, having pass'd the dark infernal door,
And visited those dreary realms below,
From that disastrous prison-house of woe,
A man by policy should work his way,
Emerging into light and upper day!
  Sisyphus gain'd a point which none beside
(Of all that ever lived or ever died)
Could have achieved—yet Sisyphus would fail:
Nor would Ulysses with his arts prevail:
Nor aged Nestor with his eloquence—
No merit would avail you, no pretence,
Though you possess'd the vigour and the speed

Of the swift Harpies, or the winged breed
Of Boreas—in the proud Olympic game
A conqueror! your native place and name
Recorded and announced with loud acclaim;
Still, would you find the common saying hold,
"Fame is a jest: favour is bought and sold:
No power on earth is like the power of gold."

Whether the preceding lines were composed at Syracuse, or afterwards in Greece (Lacedæmon), where, it should seem, he waited the result of his negotiation, cannot be determined. They are placed here, as forming a natural sequel to the fragments referable to Syracuse, and as an introduction to those which, from their internal marks, must be assigned to Lacedæmon. The first of these bears a strong indication of having been composed at the time when the poet had passed the meridian of life. The "black fear of death which saddens all" is strongly marked in the first lines. He endeavours to escape from the ghastly images which it presents to him, by running into a long digression about Theotimus, and the history of his vineyard; and finally attempts to give a fillip to his spirits by a forced joke on the double sense of the word *θωρηχθείς*. The same word is punned upon elsewhere—all this seems characteristic of a mature age; while the mention of persons and things indicates reminiscences which imply that he must have already visited the same country at an earlier period of his life.

CII.

(*Gaisford*, 1067, 1068; 875-880.)

Enjoy your time, my soul! another race
Will shortly fill the world, and take your place,
With their own hopes and fears, sorrow and mirth:
I shall be dust the while, and crumbled earth.
But think not of it! Drink the racy wine
Of rich Taÿgetus, pressed from the vine
Which Theotimus in the sunny glen,
(Old Theotimus, loved by Gods and men)
Planted, and water'd from a plenteous source,
Teaching the wayward stream a better course—

Drink it, and cheer your heart, and banish care—
A *load* of wine will *lighten* our despair.

I should be inclined to think that Theognis must have been connected by the ties of hospitality with some Spartan or Laconian families; that of Theotimus, for instance, here mentioned, or that Clearistus (before mentioned, as so connected with him) may have been a Laconian.

The following lines appear also to have been written in Lacedæmon, and evidently relate to some matter of important trust; probably to the friendly and confidential agency through which he was enabled to purchase a remission of his exile.

CIII.

(*Gaisford*, 1083-1086.)

Ye twins of Jove! an undivided twain,
That on Eurotas' shore and happy plain
In endless harmony preside and reign,
Punish our guilt! If ever by design,
I wrong my friend, let all the loss be mine:
But, if the fault is his, double the fine!

The next lines, though referable to Lacedæmon, may have been composed there at an earlier period of the poet's life. Though in both instances the conclusion points to hard drinking, they seem much too juvenile for the author of Fragment CII. The four concluding verses have been subjoined as a natural sequel. In the original they are separated, and stand as a distinct fragment in Brunck's edition.

CIV.

(*Gaisford*, 991-996; 1065, 1066.)

Now that in mid career, checking his course,
The bright sun pauses in his pride and force,
Let us prepare to dine, and eat and drink
The best of every thing that heart can think;
And let the shapely Spartan damsel fair
Bring, with a rounded arm and graceful air,
Water to wash, and garlands for our hair.

In spite of all the systems and the rules
Invented and observed by sickly fools,
Let us be brave, and resolutely drink,
Not minding if the dog-star rise or sink.

The two first lines of the original are hardly intelligible. It seems probable that two lines may have been lost between the first and the second.

The next fragments bring us back to Megara, and represent Theognis as a returned emigrant, studiously and anxiously patriotic and popular, ready to sympathize equally with the grave apprehensions or the mirthful entertainments which occupied the attention of his fellow citizens; and giving an indirect pledge in the first fragment, and a more decided one in the second, of his resolution to abstain from party politics, and to confine himself to the cultivation of poetry, and of the sister arts with which it was immediately connected, music and the management of the chorus.

The last lines of the first fragment serve to confirm Mr. Clinton's suggestion, that he was born in the 59th Olympiad; in which, according to some accounts, he is said to have flourished;—but, as Mr. Clinton justly observes, these computations would suppose Theognis to have been near eighty in 490 B.C.—the time of the battle of Marathon. The concluding lines certainly give a decided negative to such a supposition. The character of mature age (as has been already observed) is marked in a preceding fragment (the last but two). The same association of ideas is also observable in this, which must have been written a very short time after: in both of them, the pleasures of conviviality are connected with the fear of death (the evil with its remedy); but in extreme age, such remedies are not resorted to: moreover, old age itself is here spoken of as a distant evil.

CV.

(*Gaisford*, 755-766.)

May Jove, the Almighty, with his own right hand
Guard and uphold this happy town and land!
With all the glorious blessed Gods above!
And may the bright Apollo guide and move

My voice and fancy, cunningly to carp
In songs accordant to the pipe and harp!
When, after solemn rites of sacrifice,
At feasts and banquets freely we devise
Of mirth and pastime, banishing afar
All fears of Persia and her threaten'd war;
With joyous airy songs of merry verse,
Quaffing and chanting—"May we ne'er be worse,"
But better, if a better thing can be,
Than thus to live at ease, cheerful and free;
While far remote, no fears our thoughts engage
Of death approaching, or disastrous age.

The phrase ὧδ' εἶναι καὶ ἄμεινον is evidently what we should call a toast or sentiment, equivalent to the Scotch—"May there ne'er be worse among us!" or the sailor's—"Here's better luck still!"

The next fragment is of the same time, as appears not only from the tone and character, but from the same mention of an apprehended invasion from Persia. It may be considered as a kind of sequel to the preceding; the invocation to the inferior protecting Deity of the town naturally following the preceding address to the supreme ruler of the world. This fragment is of considerable importance, as Mr. Brunck, by comparing the lines in which Alcathous is mentioned, with an inscription discovered at Megara, has shown that Theognis must have been a native of Megara in Greece, and not, as Plato (undoubtedly from a mere supercilious affectation of ignorance) had asserted, a Sicilian. Moreover, it appears, that Sicily is mentioned as one of the foreign countries visited by him during his long absence from his native land.

The line in which Sicily is mentioned has not been characteristically translated; in the original, there is a tone of hesitation and sneaking, as if he had said in English—"And truly, indeed! at one time I went to Sicily." This the translator was quite unable to account for, and was inclined to imagine, that it might be an unfounded fancy of his own; not having at the time any suspicion that the poet's departure for Sicily had been immediately preceded by an unsuccessful address to the adverse party. As it is, however, pretty clear that this must have been the case, the poverty and meanness of such a style would be easily accounted for, as not unsuited to the subject; recalling, as it must have done to his own mind and that of others; the recollection of an act of humiliation gratuitous in its commencement, and unprofitable in its result: his voyage to Sicily (as has been seen already) having been determined upon in consequence of the rejection of the submissive overtures indicated in Frags. LXXXII., LXXXIII., and LXXXIV.

It has been already remarked, that the poet avoids all mention of Thebes, the Coblentz of the emigrant party, the head-quarters of their meditated hostilities.

CVI.

(*Gaisford*, 771-790; 939-942.)

You, great Apollo, with its walls and towers
Fenced and adorn'd of old this town of ours!
Such favour in thy sight Alcathous won,
Of Pelops old the fair and manly son.
Now therefore in thy clemency divine,
Protect these very walls, our own and thine!
Guide and assist us, turn aside the boast
Of the destroying, haughty Persian host!
So shall thy people each returning spring
Slay fatted hecatombs; and gladly bring
Fair gifts, with chaunted hymns, and lively song,
Dances and feasts, and happy shouts among;
Before thy altar, glorifying Thee,
In peace and health and wealth, cheerful and free.
  Yet much I fear the faction and the strife,
Throughout our Grecian cities raging rife,
And their wild councils. But, do thou defend
This town of ours, our founder and our friend
  Wide have I wander'd, far beyond the sea,
Even to the distant shores of Sicily;
To broad Eubœa's plentiful domain,
With the rich vineyards, in its planted plain;
And to the sunny wave and winding edge
Of fair Eurotas with its reedy sedge—
Where Sparta stands in simple majesty:
Among her manly rulers, there was I!

Greeted and welcomed (there and every where)
With courteous entertainment—kind and fair;
Yet still my weary spirit would repine,
Longing again to view this land of mine.
Henceforward no design nor interest
Shall ever move me but the first and best,
With learning's happy gift to celebrate,
Adorn and dignify my native State.
The song, the dance, music and verse agreeing,
Will occupy my life, and fill my being:
Pursuits of elegance and learned skill
(With good repute and kindness and good will,
Among the wiser sort) will pass my time
Without an enemy, without a crime;
Harmless and just with every rank of men,
Both the free native and the denizen.

The lines "Henceforward no design nor interest" are intended to mark a point of character, not immediately obvious in the original; *νεώτερον πρᾶγμα* was an habitual phrase for an attempt to change the government. Theognis, meaning to imply that he is resolved to abstain from all factious schemes, varies the established phrase, and substitutes *μελέδημα νεώτερον*, *Thought* for *Action*, as a more modest form of expressing the same assurance.

It may be observed that *νέον* would be a much better supplement than *κακὸν* for the verse of *Tyrtæus*,[1] in which he is describing the duties and obligations of the Spartan commonalty.

We cannot imagine that the oracle, or the poet in the name of the oracle, could have cautioned the Spartans against betraying their country: a warning against innovation might be proper enough.

The reader, if this note has led him to consult the original, will see that the next couplet is an amplification not to be found in this fragment; but if he will again refer to line 925 he will find the authority for it. It is true, that these lines (923 to 926) appear to have been written before

---

[1] See note (*r*) Müller's Dorians, vol. ii. p. 15, Tufnell and Lewis' translation.

his exile; but in his character of a poet, at least, there was no occasion why Theognis should speak of himself less confidently than before.

The following lines show that his return was embittered by the undutiful behaviour of his family, who had grown up in his absence.

CVII.

(*Gaisford*, 271-278.)

The Gods in just allotment have assign'd
Youth and old age, the portion of mankind,
Alike for all; impartially we share
Youth's early pleasures; equally we bear
The latter ills of life, sickness and care.
One single evil, more severe and rude
Than age or sickness or decrepitude,
Is dealt unequally; for him that rears
A thankless offspring, in his latter years
Ungratefully requited for his pains,
A parsimonious life, and thrifty gains
With toil and care acquired for their behoof,
And no return but insolent reproof,
Such as might scare a beggar from the gate,
A wretch unknown, poor and importunate!
To be reviled, avoided, hated, cursed;
This is the last of evils, and the worst!

Theognis had left his wife, and at least one son, behind him when he quitted Megara:—some verses written in the early part of his banishment serve to show that she was behaving well in his absence. There are no further notices to be found respecting her; but a family of children, growing up under the tuition and protection of the ruling party, would probably become connected with them; and would be liable to be extremely disgusted and annoyed at the return of so near a connection, who, abjuring rank and pretensions of every kind, had subsisted for many years as a mere artist, and who now reappeared with a fixed determination to confine himself scrupulously to those pursuits by which he had before obtained a livelihood; all the money which he had made in Sicily would not compensate for such a mortification.

The following lines appear evidently to belong to the

period subsequent to his return from exile; they are perfectly in harmony with the unobnoxious line of conduct which he had chalked out for himself; they represent him as communicating his acquirements from a natural feeling of public duty and public spirit, obviously to the exclusion of any mercenary inducement; they cannot therefore be assigned to the period of his lucrative professional practice in Sicily;—again, they would be wholly out of place in the earlier years of his exile (at Thebes or Eubœa) or in the tumultuous times which immediately preceded; and if we go back to a still earlier period, we find that the system of secresy and reserve which he then practised (see Frag. IX.) is that which (in allusion perhaps to his former habit) he now condemns.

CVIII.

(*Gaisford*, 767–770.)

The servant of the Muse, gifted and graced
With high pre-eminence of art and taste,
Has an allotted duty to fulfil;
Bound to dispense the treasure of his skill,
Without a selfish or invidious view;
Bound to recite, and to compose anew;
Not to reserve his talent for himself,
In secret, like a miser with his pelf.

POSTSCRIPT.

HE modern reader, to whom the original is inaccessible, will probably close this volume with a feeling of suspense—and a doubt in his own mind, "whether these things are so?" Whether the picture which has been presented to him is a correct one, exhibiting the true representation of a human mind at a period so remote, and formed under circumstances so different from those of modern times, or whether the original has served merely as a canvas upon which the translator has been endeavouring to trace a fanciful picture for his own amusement and that of his readers. To this question a satisfactory answer can be given, at least as far as regards the design of the work and the degree of attention which has been bestowed upon it. Its merit, if it has any, consists in a constant endeavour to convey to the English reader an exact and complete notion of the intention of the original, and a clear impression of the temper, character, and style which it exhibits ; but it is safer to speak of negative than of positive merits. The writer then ventures to say that nothing has been heightened by embellishment, nor modified in conformity to modern ideas or modern taste ; nor aggravated, on the other hand, in order to produce an effect in those passages which exhibited the strongest contrast with the feelings and opinions of the present time. Those, for example, in which the poet discusses the subject of the order of Providence in an address to Jupiter, stating his objections and debating the question in a tone of respectful familiarity ; or in which he expresses a wish "to drink the blood of his enemies," accompanied by the hope that some benignant deity will assist him in the accomplishment of that desirable purpose. In these and similar passages the English reader may be assured that it has been the endeavour of the translator to express, to the best of his ability, the true *phraseognomy* of the original without in any degree heightening it; though, for the sake of making it more palpable, it may in some instances have been expanded and exhibited more at length. This defect of expansion is in fact unavoidable, or avoidable only by sacrificing the very object which, to an intelligent modern reader, is the only one which makes the translation of an ancient author, such as Theognis, in any degree interesting. It might not be difficult to crowd into a given number of lines or words an exact verbal interpretation ; but this verbal interpretation would convey almost in every instance either an imperfect meaning or a false character ; the relative and collateral ideas, and the associations which served as stepping-stones to transitions apparently incongruous and abrupt would still be wanting; and the author, whose elliptical familiar phraseology was a mere transcript of the language of daily life, would have the appearance of a pedantic composer studiously obscure and enigmatic.

With respect to the smaller fragments, something must be assumed upon probability or taken upon trust; much time and attention have been bestowed in assigning to them the order in which they are here placed, and in conjecture as to the circumstances which gave rise to them (or to the poems of which they formed a part) as well as to their real meaning and intention. To justify those inferences in every instance would have required a separate dissertation for each fragment; but of writing dissertations there is no end, nor is there any task more difficult, or in its results more unsatisfactory, than that of attempting to accommodate a demonstration to the various apprehensions of different readers. With the generality of readers he is apprehensive that he may appear to have erred in the prolixity of his commentary, encumbering and retarding the progress of a narrative otherwise interesting and amusing.

To the learned, who may be disposed to follow the same train of investigation, the consideration of an analogous case is respectfully submitted.

It is recorded of persons who have been long confined in situations of apparently total darkness, that they have by degrees acquired the power of distinguishing objects, and that ultimately time and habit have enabled them to enjoy the faculty of vision in a medium so obscure as to present no distinguishable object to a stranger newly introduced into the same abode. The author of this essay has subjected himself to voluntary confinement in one of the darkest cells in the whole dungeon of literature, being persuaded that, by time and patience, he might adapt his vision to the obscurity in which he was placed, and that some object of interest and curiosity would be finally discoverable. At his first entrance everything was obscure; by degrees, however, many points became dimly discernible, and finally distinctly manifest. But he cannot expect that the same objects, even when they are pointed out and described, should be at once recognized by a stranger, however acute his natural power of vision may be, who passes at once from the broad glare of daylight and transfers himself suddenly into the situation in which the writer has been so long secluded.

To the consideration, therefore, of such persons (much

his superiors, for the most part, in learning and critical knowledge) he would wish to suggest, in the first place, the apparent truth and probability of the whole narrative, coupled with the fact that, of the remaining fragments of the poet, there is not one to which a place may not be assigned in one or other of the periods into which his life is divided. Where the flowing line of a probable and easy narrative passes like a catenary curve through a long series of incidents and allusions, without deviation or interruption, we are led to an inference like that of the mathematical axiom, *Ut pendet continuum flexile ita stabit continuum rectum.* We conclude that the narrative which complies with these conditions must be the true one, and that it may be admitted to stand as an independent construction, without the aid of external props, supporting itself by the mutual bearing and pressure of the parts. The only external props in the present instance consist of the few historical data, which may be considered as the piers and abutments upon which the separate arches of conjecture have been constructed. But phrases of this magnitude, applied to so minute a subject, serve to remind the writer who has made use of them that he is in danger of falling into the common error of estimating any trifling advance in knowledge, not according to its real value, but in proportion to the time and labour which have been bestowed upon it.

THE END.

CHISWICK PRESS:—PRINTED BY WHITTINGHAM AND WILKINS, TOOKS COURT, CHANCERY LANE.

www.ingramcontent.com/pod-product-compliance
Lightning Source LLC
Chambersburg PA
CBHW032259280326
41932CB00009B/631

* 9 7 8 3 7 4 4 6 8 8 3 3 8 *